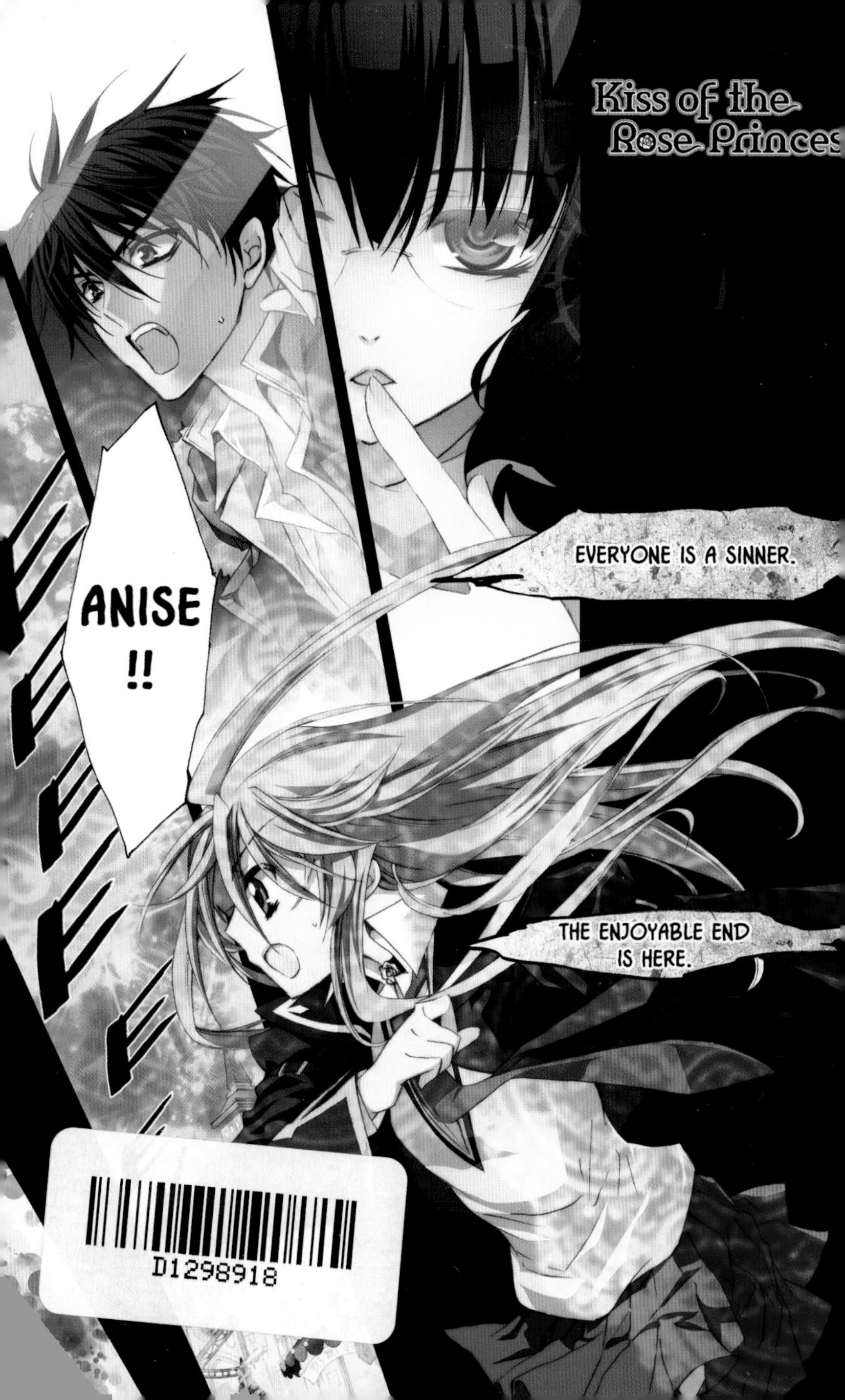

Kiss of the Rose Princess
EVERYONE IS A SINNER.
ANISE !!
THE ENJOYABLE END IS HERE.

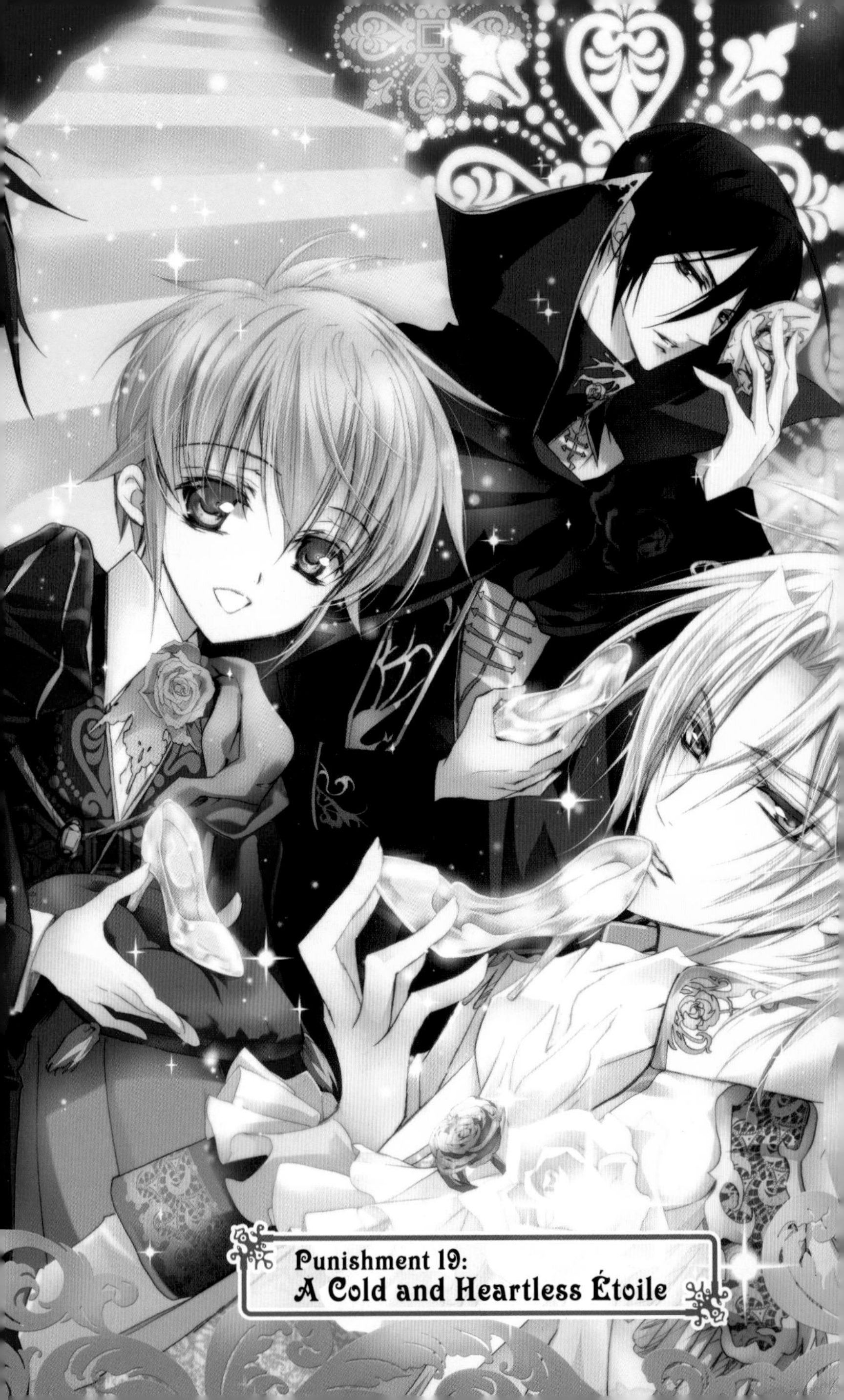
Punishment 19:
A Cold and Heartless Étoile

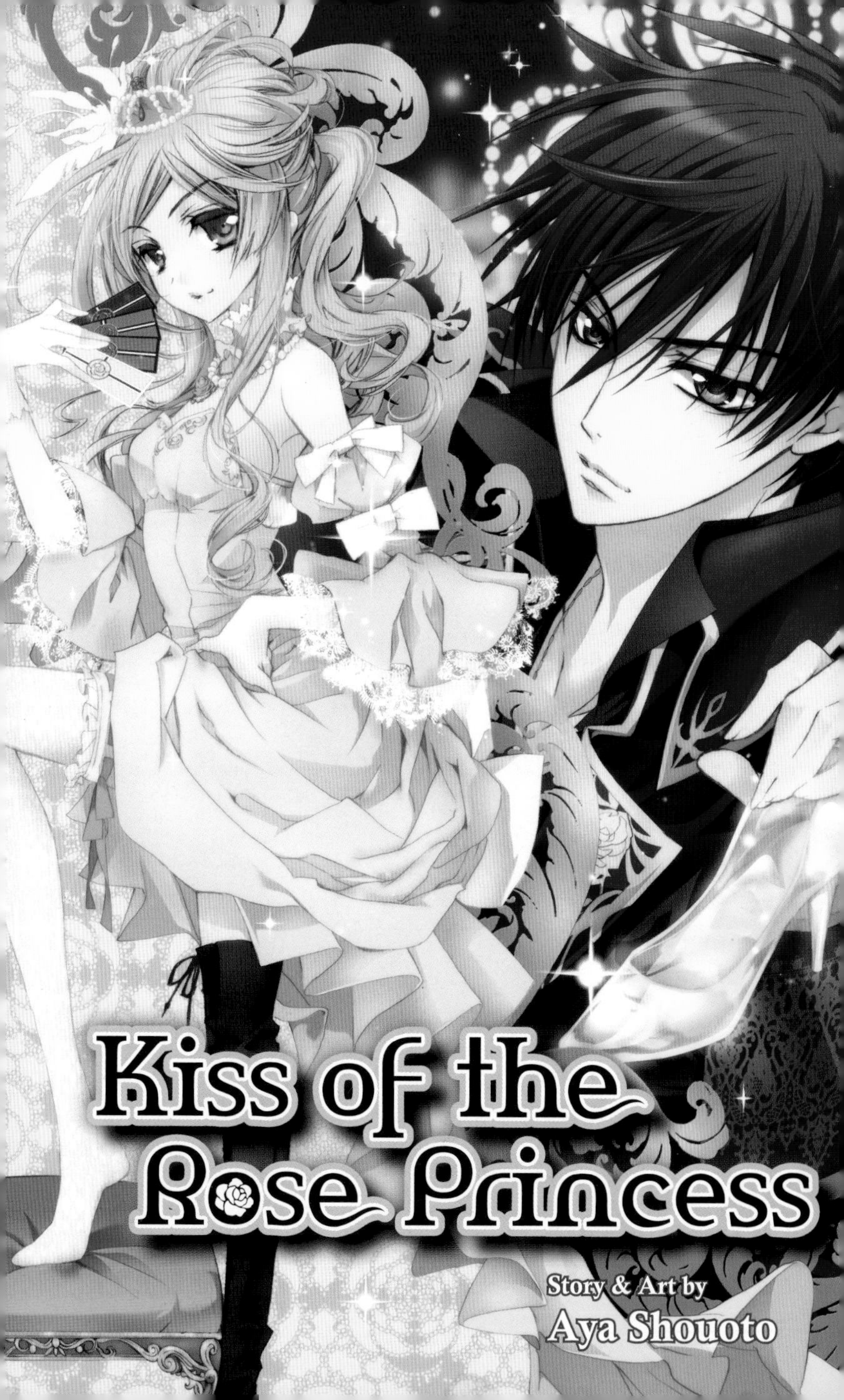
Kiss of the Rose Princess
Story & Art by
Aya Shouoto

Kiss of the Rose Princess

Contents

Characters

Anise Yamamoto

First-year at Shobi Academy. She was an ordinary girl who became the Rose Princess after her choker was removed from her neck.

Rose Knights

Kaede Higa
(Red Rose)

Anise's classmate. He's an excellent athlete who often teases Anise.
Specialty: Offence

Mitsuru Tenjo
(White Rose)

Third-year and Student Council President. He is revered by both male and female students. Super-rich.
Specialty: Healing, Defense

Seiran Asagi
(Blue Rose)

First-year. This boy is cuter than any girl at school, and he doesn't know he's the school idol. He's well-versed in a wide range of topics.
Specialty: Alchemy, Science

Mutsuki Kurama
(Black Rose)

Second-year. There are many frightening rumors about this mysterious student. Apparently he lives in the basement of Tenjo's house.
Specialty: Discovery, Capture

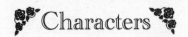

Characters

Itsushi Narumi
(Classics Teacher)

He is the most knowledge-able about the "Sovereign," her "Rose Knights," and the "Rose Contract" that binds them...

Ninufa (Guardian)

The guardian who has been protecting the cards since ancient times.

Schwarz Yamamoto

Anise's father. It seems he had a motive in putting the rose choker on Anise.

Kiss of the Rose Princess

Story Thus Far

Anise Yamamoto has become the "Rose Princess" who has control over the four most popular boys at school. Anise and the Rose Knights take part in an idol audition to win an Arcana Card that is needed to help repair the seal placed on the Demon Lord. But things take a sharp turn when the idol group Rhodecia suddenly appears! Later, Anise sets up Kaede and Mikage on a date at an amusement park, but she comes face-to-face with the "Fake Rose Princess" and her "Fake Rose Knight"...

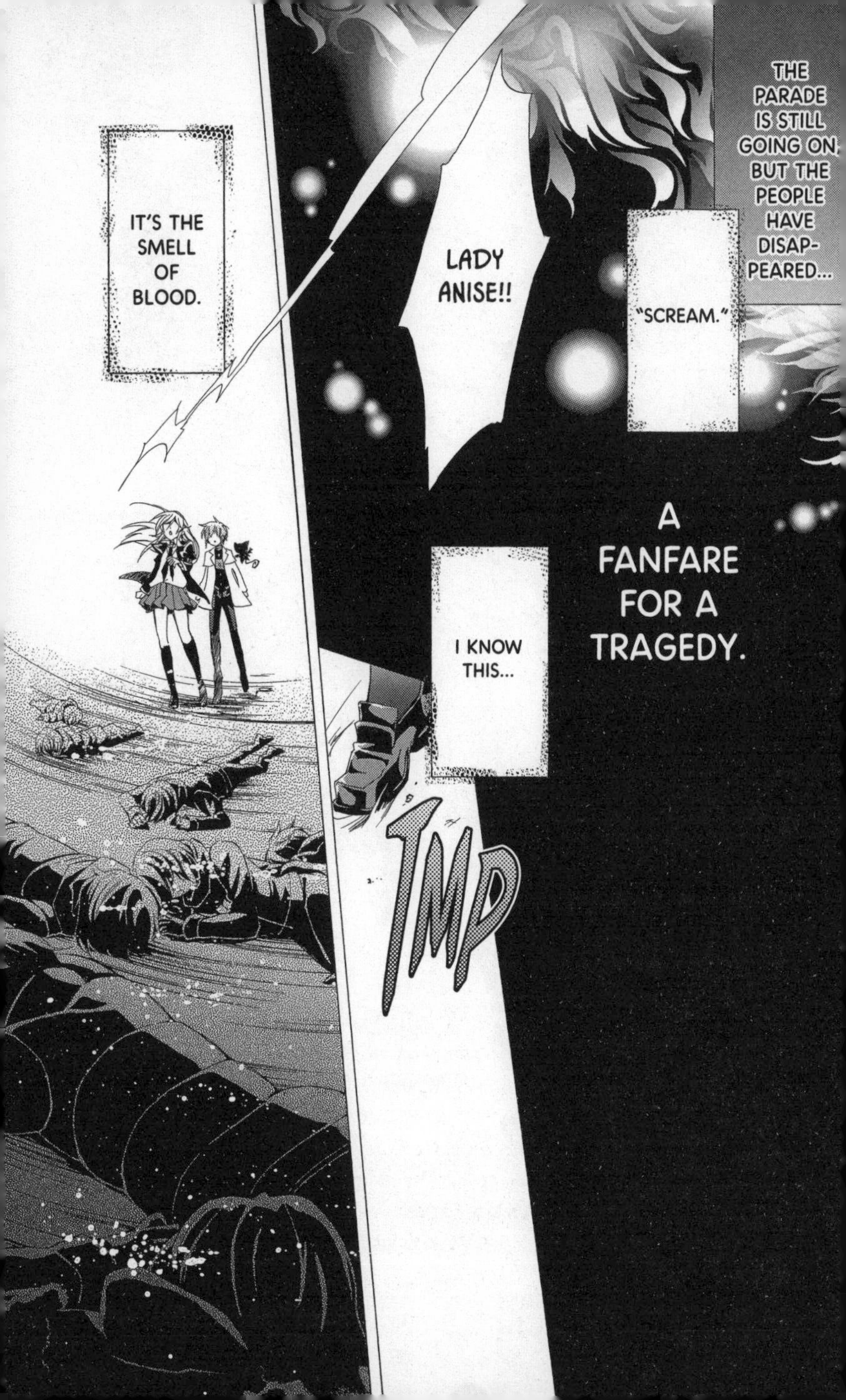
THE PARADE IS STILL GOING ON, BUT THE PEOPLE HAVE DISAPPEARED...
"SCREAM."
A FANFARE FOR A TRAGEDY.
I KNOW THIS...
LADY ANISE!!
TMP
IT'S THE SMELL OF BLOOD.

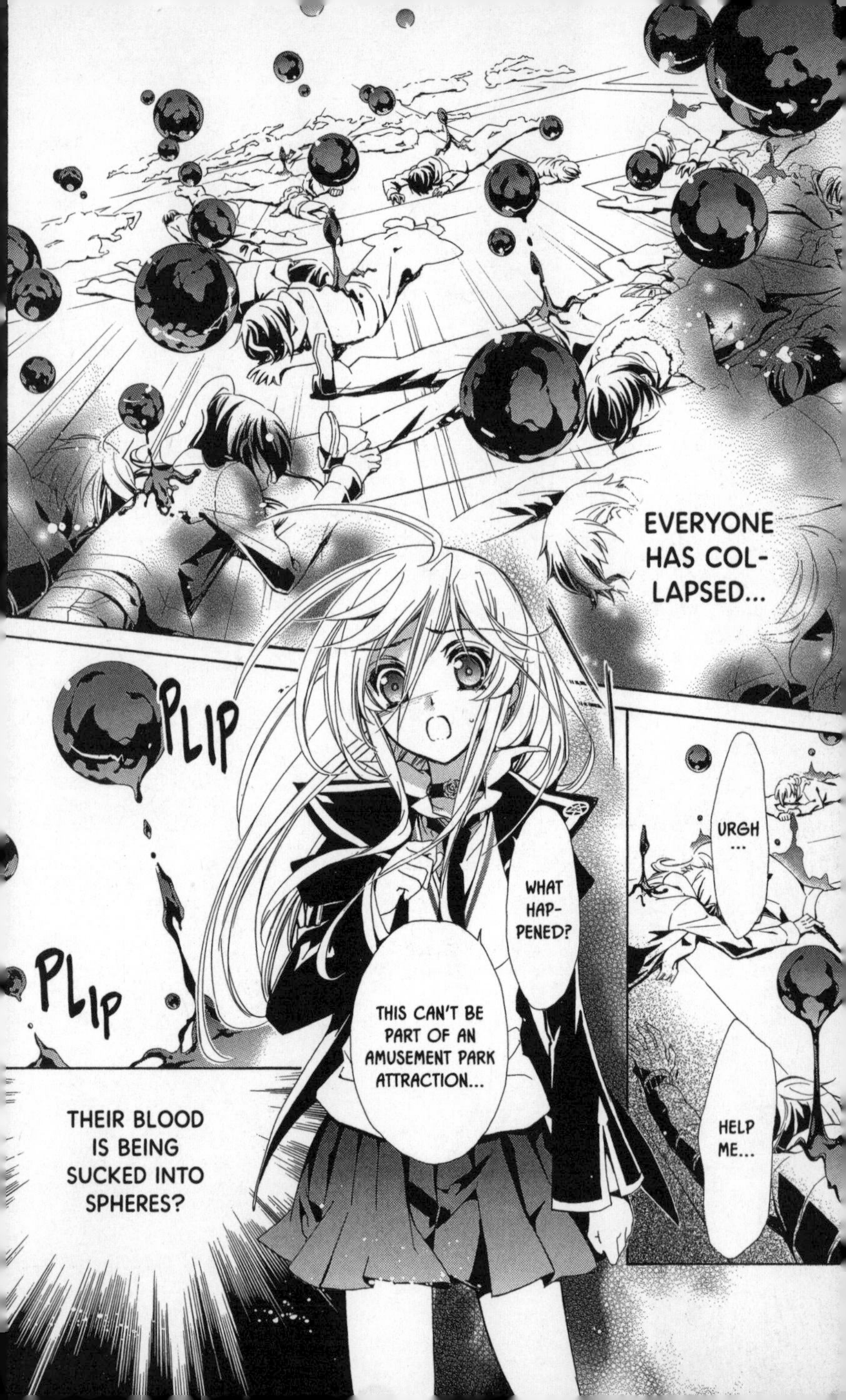
EVERYONE HAS COL-LAPSED...
URGH ...
HELP ME...
WHAT HAP-PENED?
THIS CAN'T BE PART OF AN AMUSEMENT PARK ATTRACTION...
PLIP
PLIP
THEIR BLOOD IS BEING SUCKED INTO SPHERES?

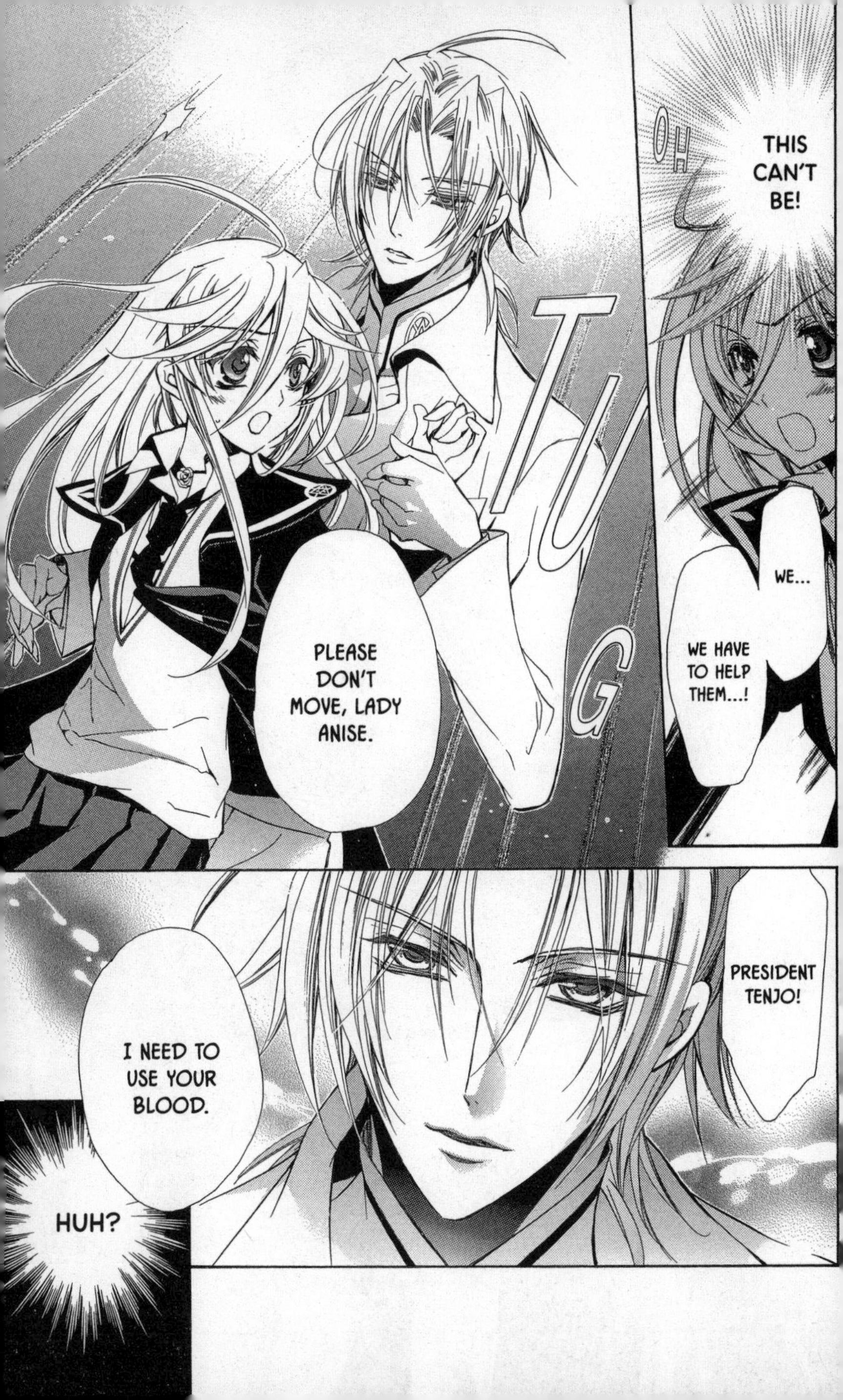
OH
THIS CAN'T BE!
WE...
WE HAVE TO HELP THEM...!
TUG
PLEASE DON'T MOVE, LADY ANISE.
PRESIDENT TENJO!
I NEED TO USE YOUR BLOOD.
HUH?

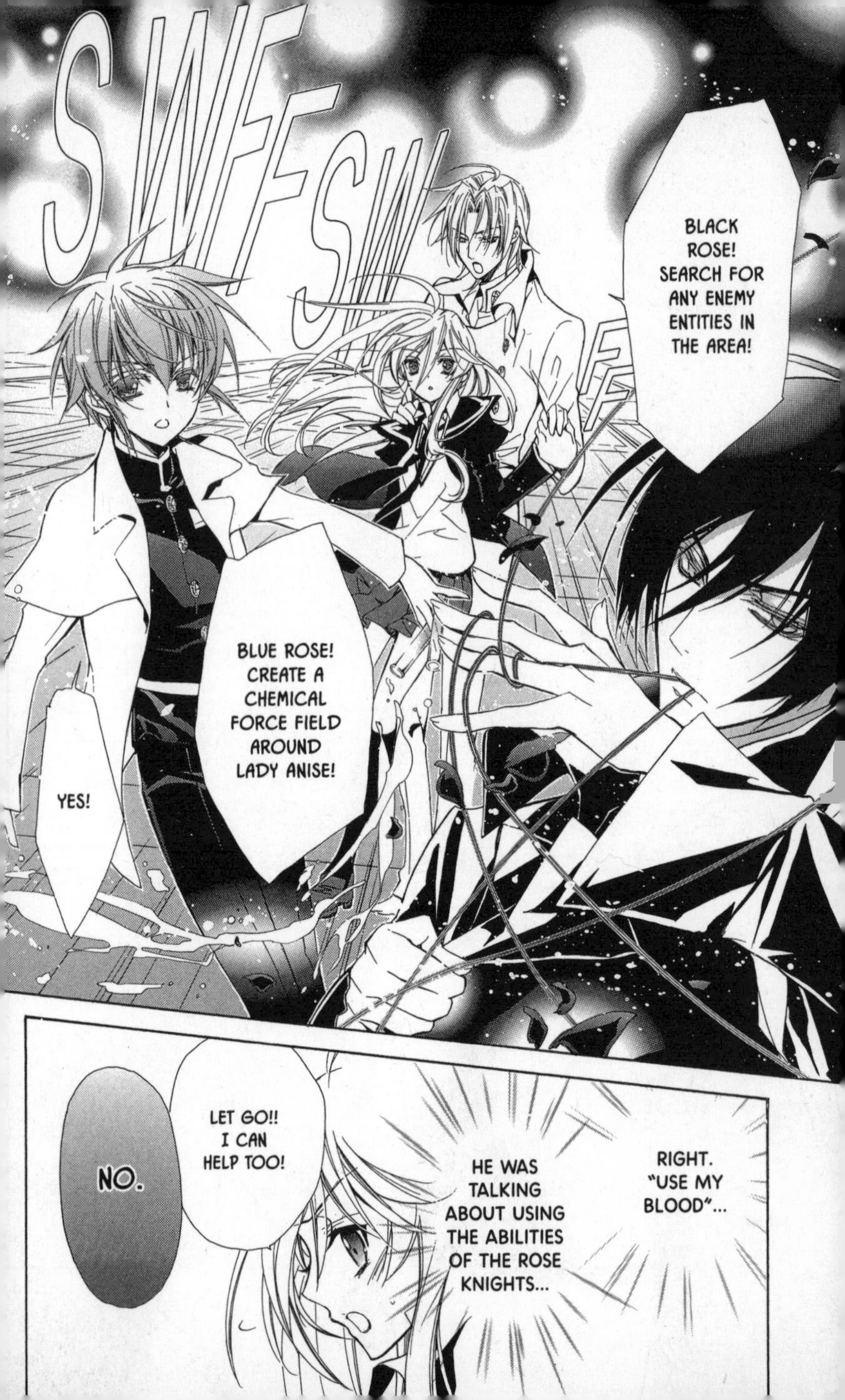
SWFF SWFF
BLACK ROSE! SEARCH FOR ANY ENEMY ENTITIES IN THE AREA!
BLUE ROSE! CREATE A CHEMICAL FORCE FIELD AROUND LADY ANISE!
YES!
RIGHT. "USE MY BLOOD"...
HE WAS TALKING ABOUT USING THE ABILITIES OF THE ROSE KNIGHTS...
LET GO!! I CAN HELP TOO!
NO.

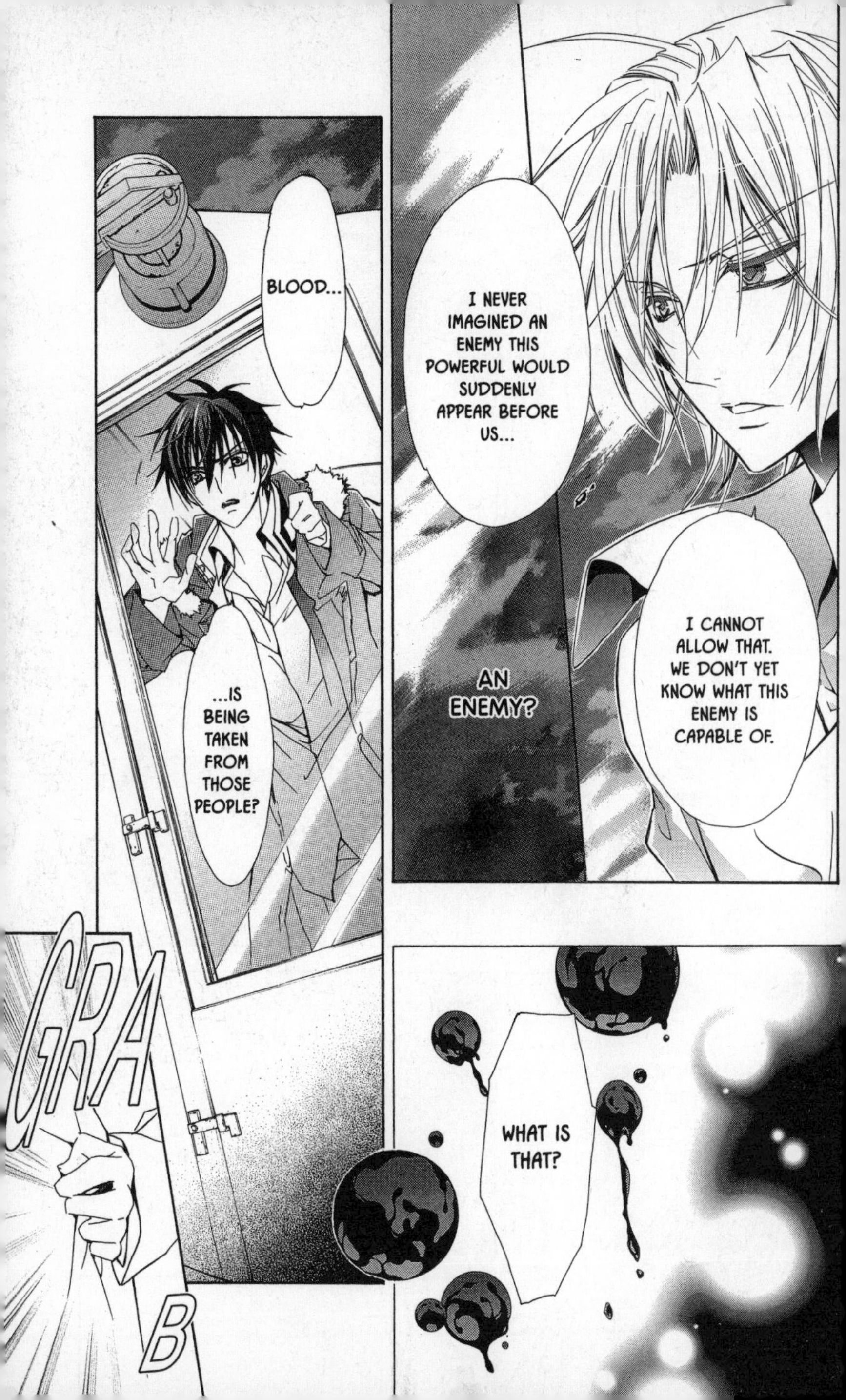
I NEVER IMAGINED AN ENEMY THIS POWERFUL WOULD SUDDENLY APPEAR BEFORE US...
AN ENEMY?
I CANNOT ALLOW THAT. WE DON'T YET KNOW WHAT THIS ENEMY IS CAPABLE OF.
BLOOD...
...IS BEING TAKEN FROM THOSE PEOPLE?
WHAT IS THAT?
GRAB

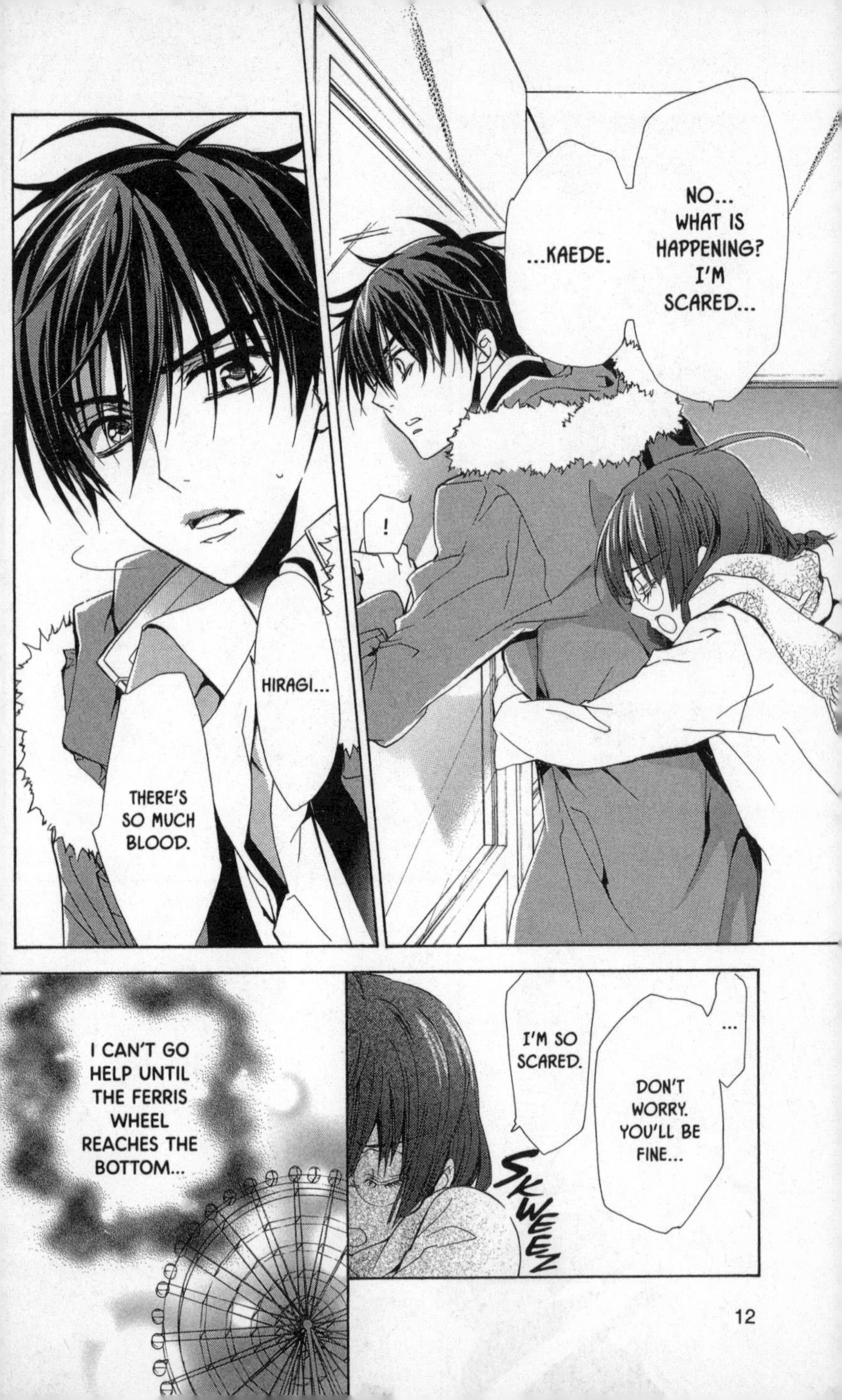
NO... WHAT IS HAPPENING? I'M SCARED...
...KAEDE.
!
HIRAGI...
THERE'S SO MUCH BLOOD.
...
DON'T WORRY. YOU'LL BE FINE...
I'M SO SCARED.
SKWEEZ
I CAN'T GO HELP UNTIL THE FERRIS WHEEL REACHES THE BOTTOM...

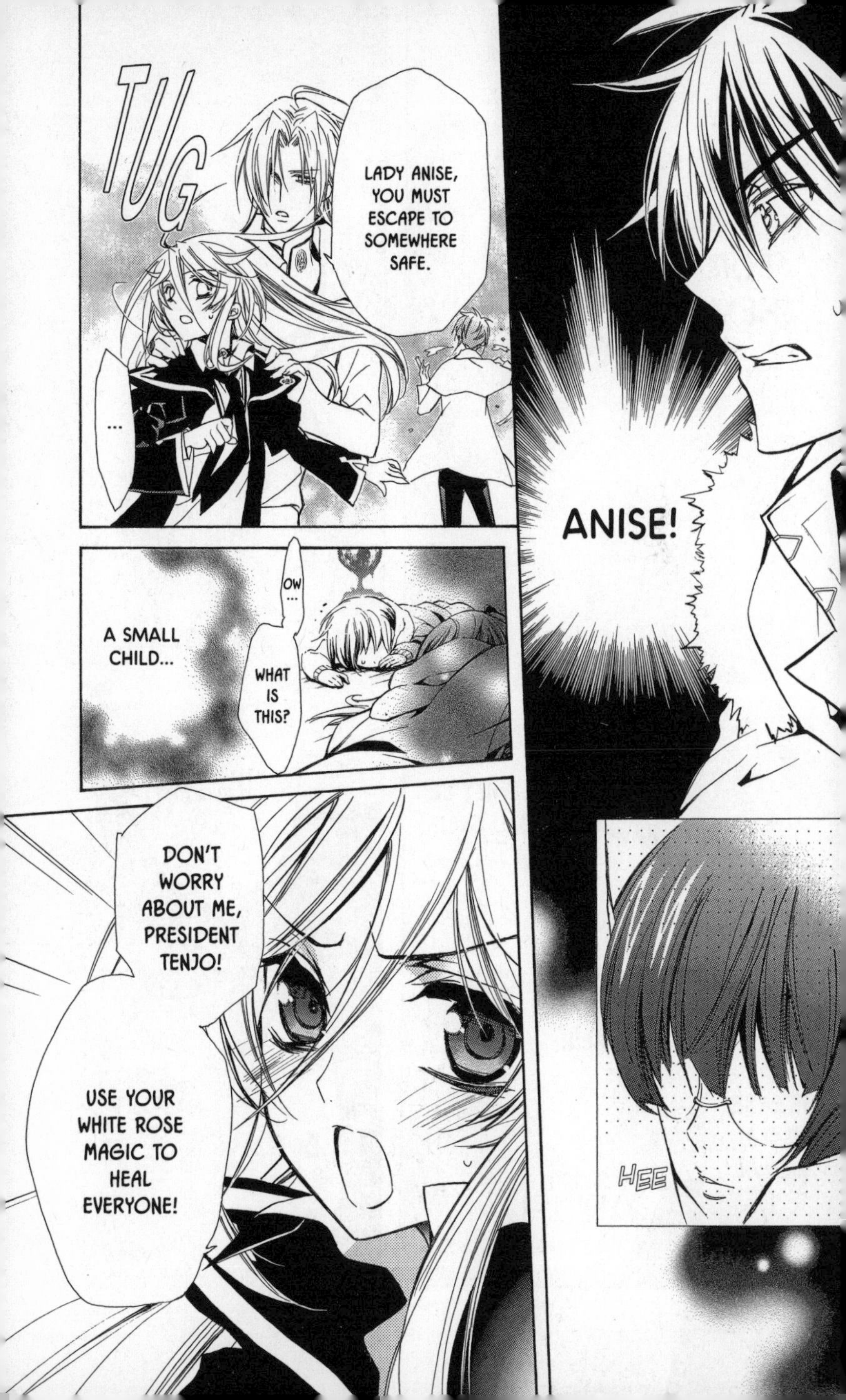
ANISE!
LADY ANISE, YOU MUST ESCAPE TO SOMEWHERE SAFE.
TUG
...
OW...
WHAT IS THIS?
A SMALL CHILD...
HEE
DON'T WORRY ABOUT ME, PRESIDENT TENJO!
USE YOUR WHITE ROSE MAGIC TO HEAL EVERYONE!

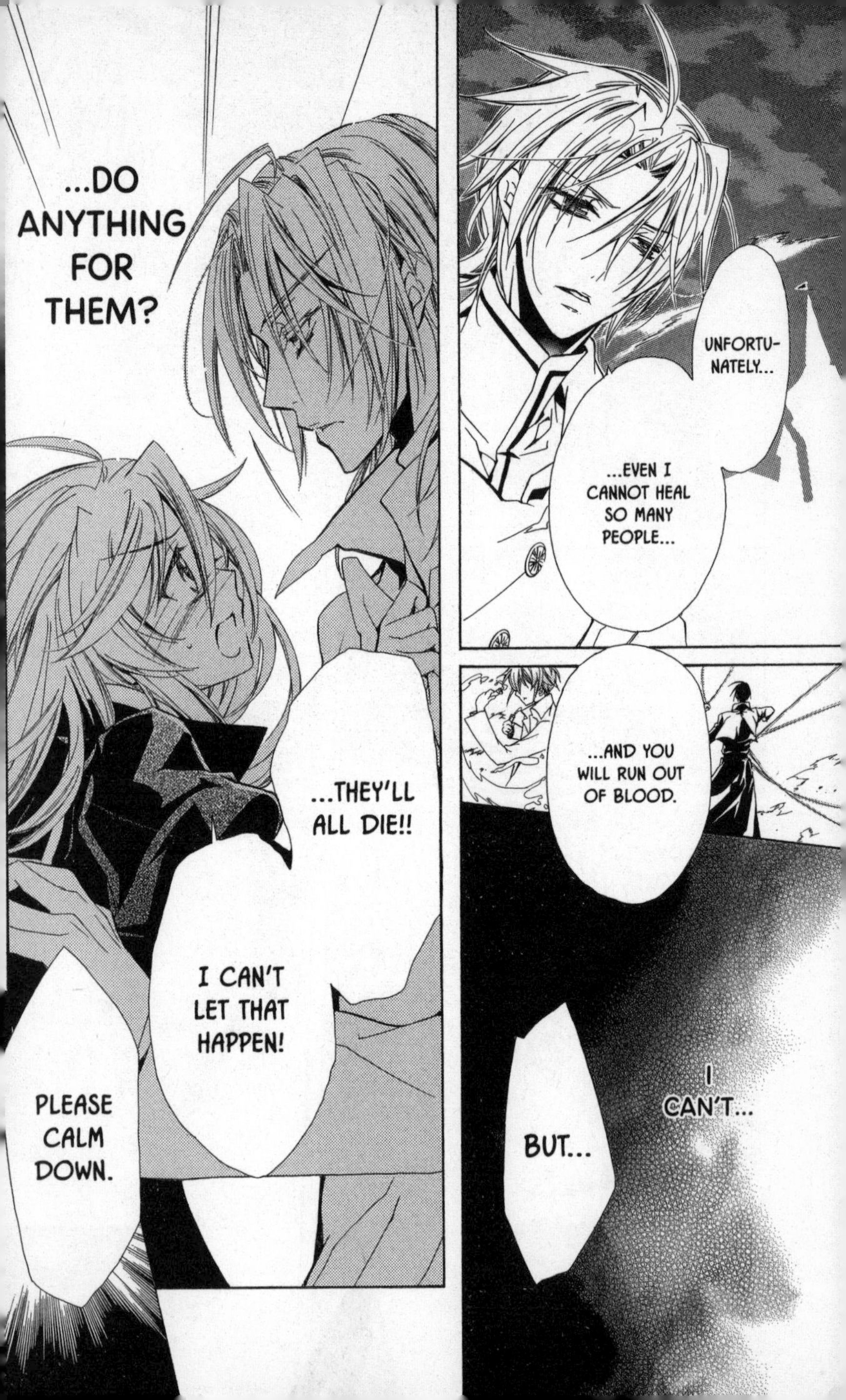
UNFORTUNATELY...
...EVEN I CANNOT HEAL SO MANY PEOPLE...
...AND YOU WILL RUN OUT OF BLOOD.
I CAN'T...
BUT...
...DO ANYTHING FOR THEM?
...THEY'LL ALL DIE!!
I CAN'T LET THAT HAPPEN!
PLEASE CALM DOWN.

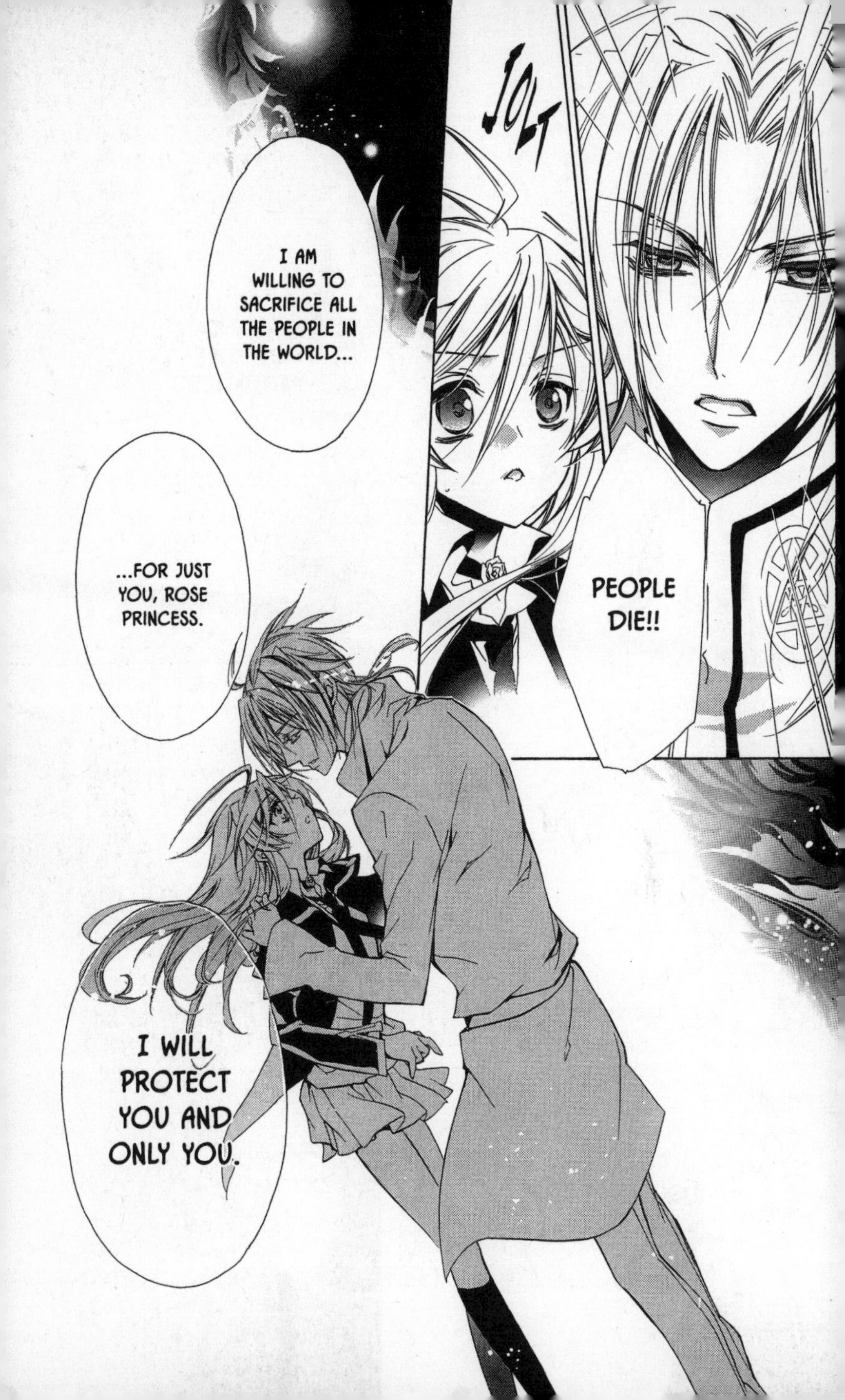
JOLT
PEOPLE DIE!!
I AM WILLING TO SACRIFICE ALL THE PEOPLE IN THE WORLD...
...FOR JUST YOU, ROSE PRINCESS.
I WILL PROTECT YOU AND ONLY YOU.

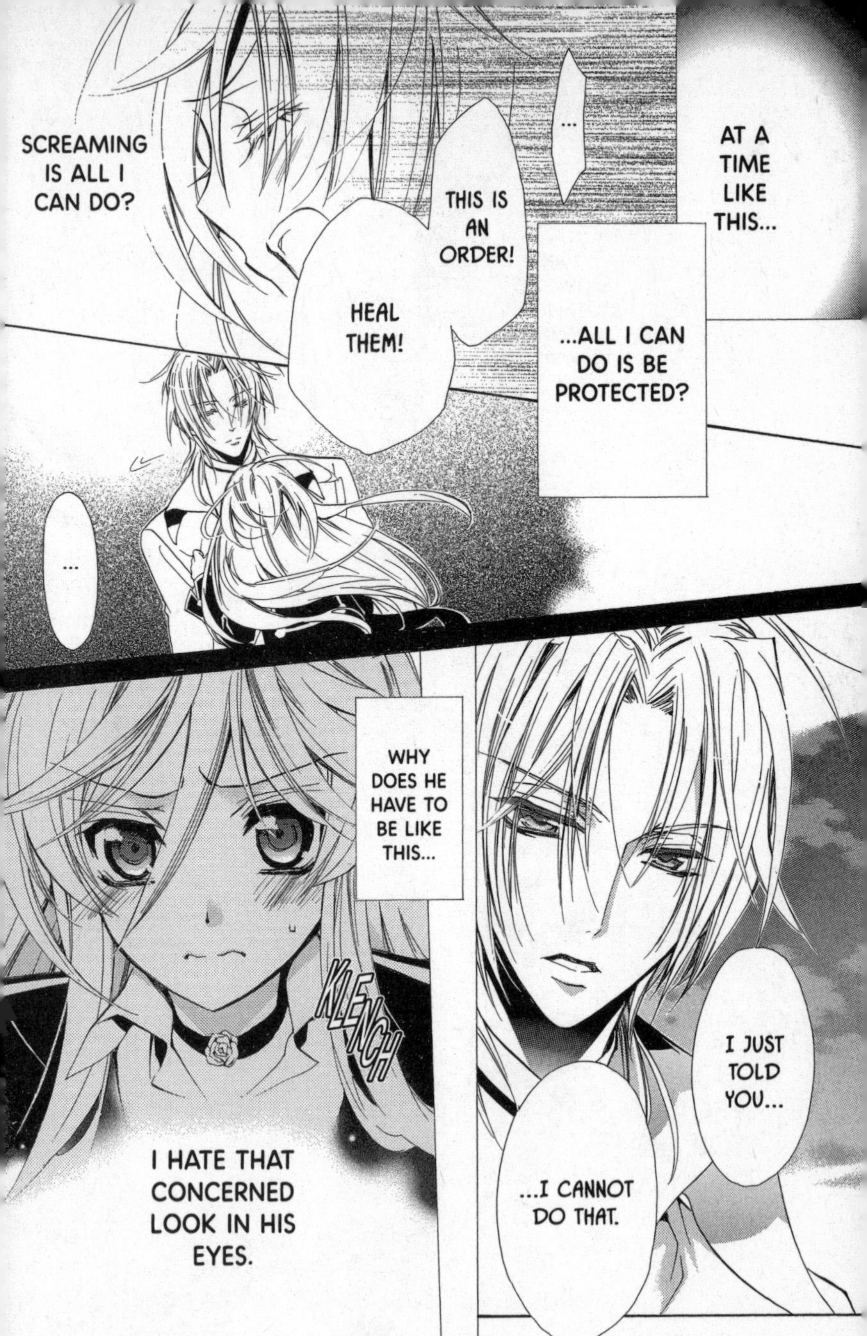
AT A TIME LIKE THIS...
...
THIS IS AN ORDER!
HEAL THEM!
...ALL I CAN DO IS BE PROTECTED?
SCREAMING IS ALL I CAN DO?
...
I JUST TOLD YOU...
...I CANNOT DO THAT.
WHY DOES HE HAVE TO BE LIKE THIS...
KLENCH
I HATE THAT CONCERNED LOOK IN HIS EYES.

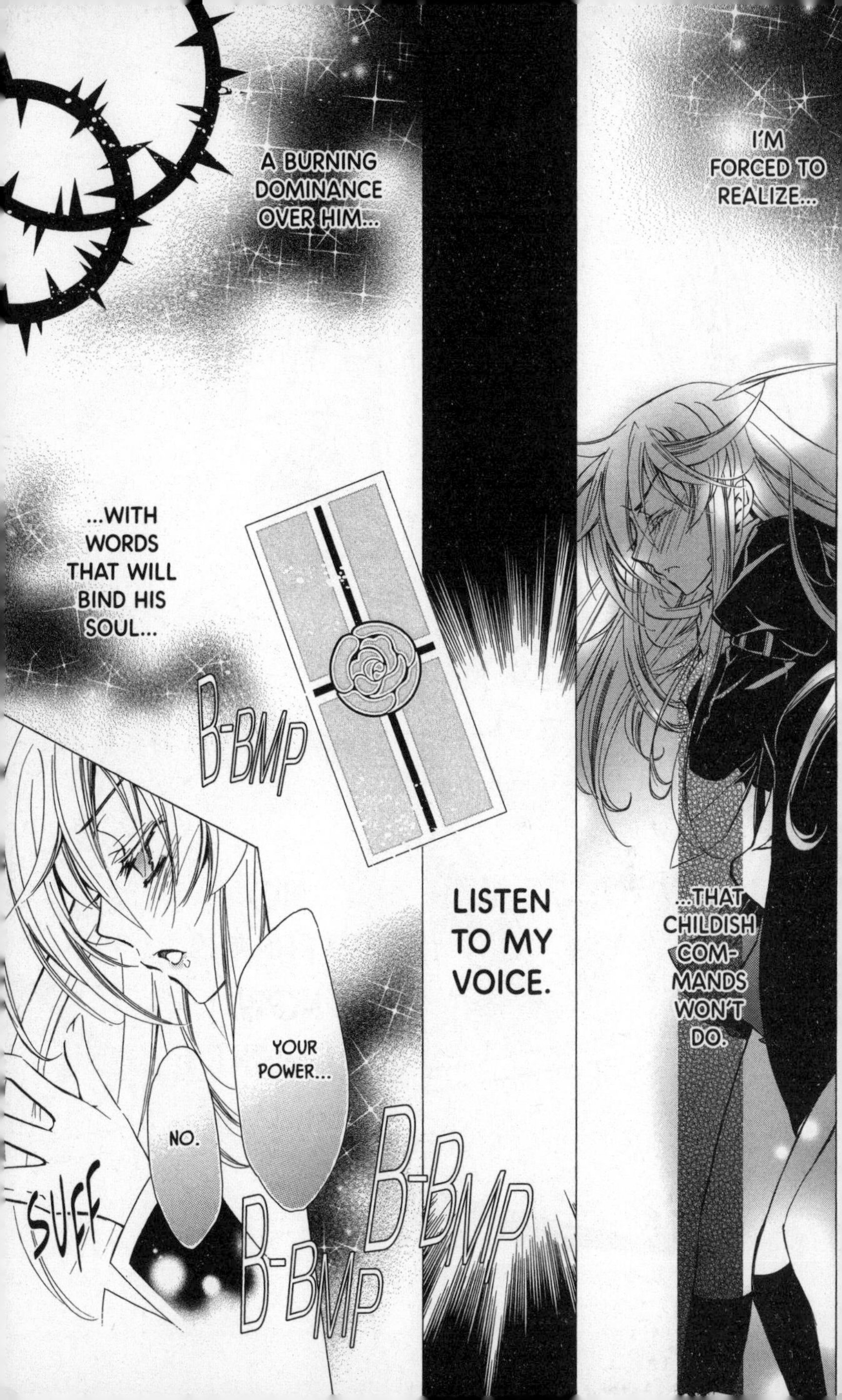
I'M FORCED TO REALIZE...
...THAT CHILDISH COM-MANDS WON'T DO.
LISTEN TO MY VOICE.
A BURNING DOMINANCE OVER HIM...
...WITH WORDS THAT WILL BIND HIS SOUL...
B-BMP
YOUR POWER...
NO.
B-BMP
B-BMP
SUFF

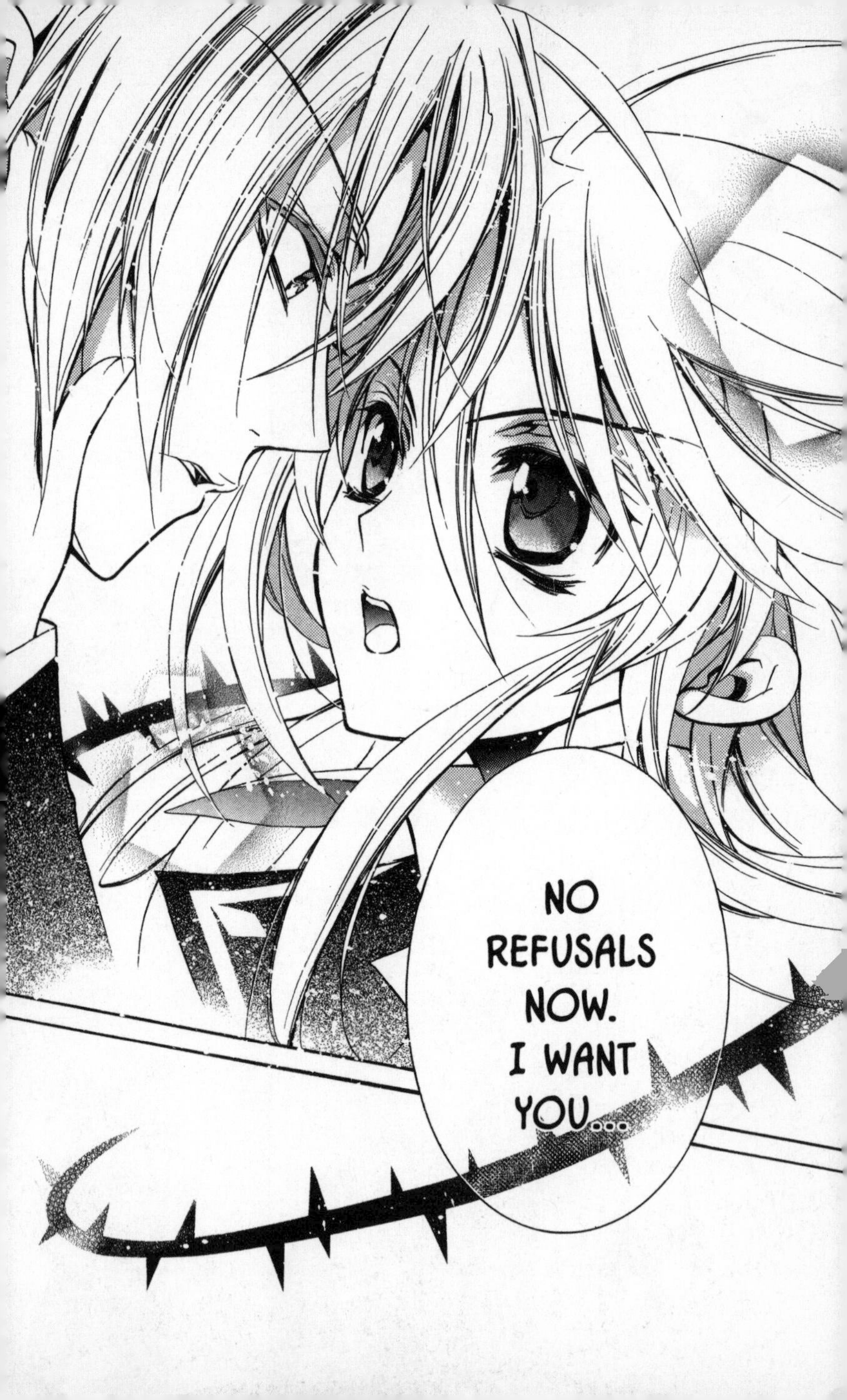
NO REFUSALS NOW. I WANT YOU...

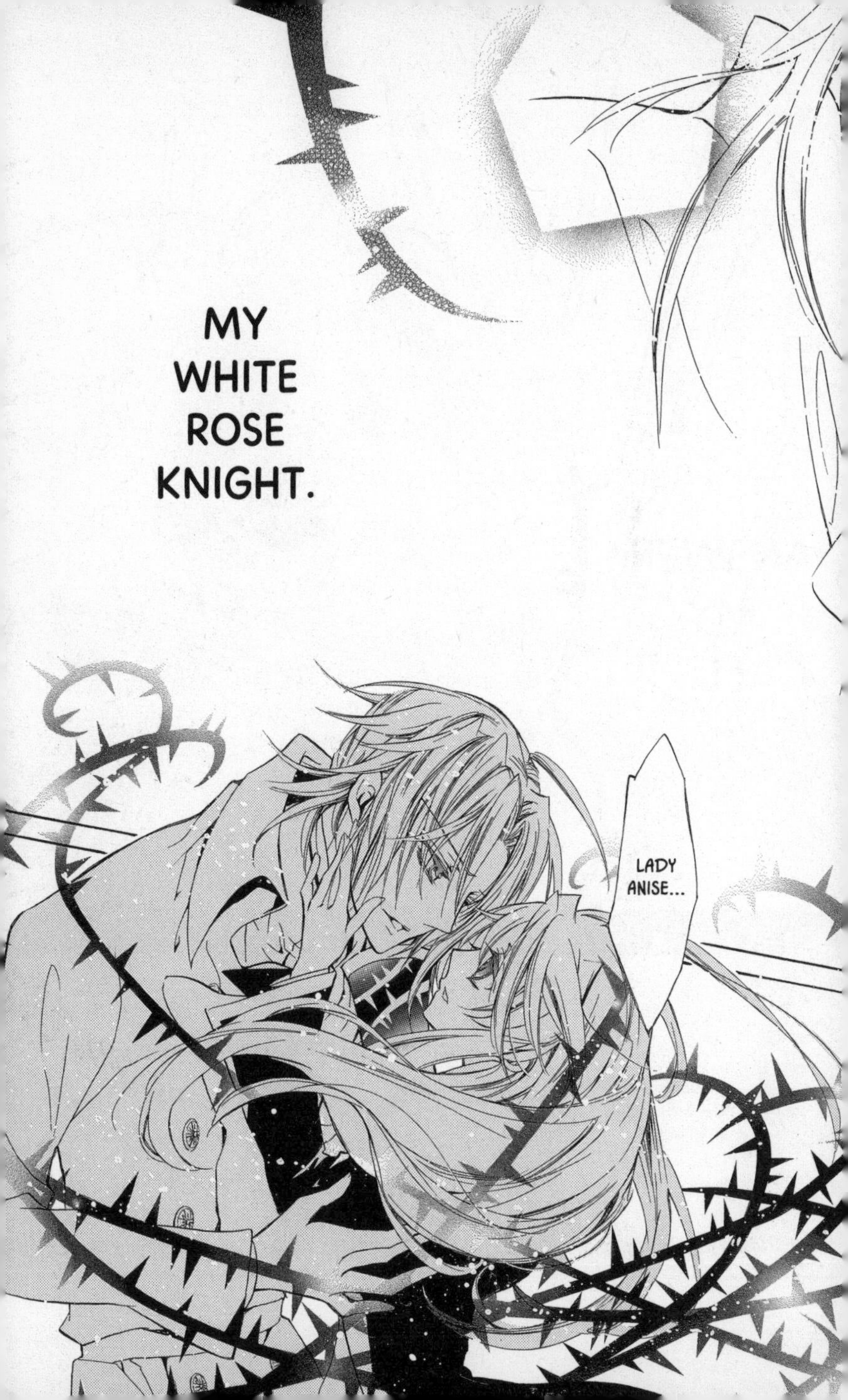
MY WHITE ROSE KNIGHT.
LADY ANISE...

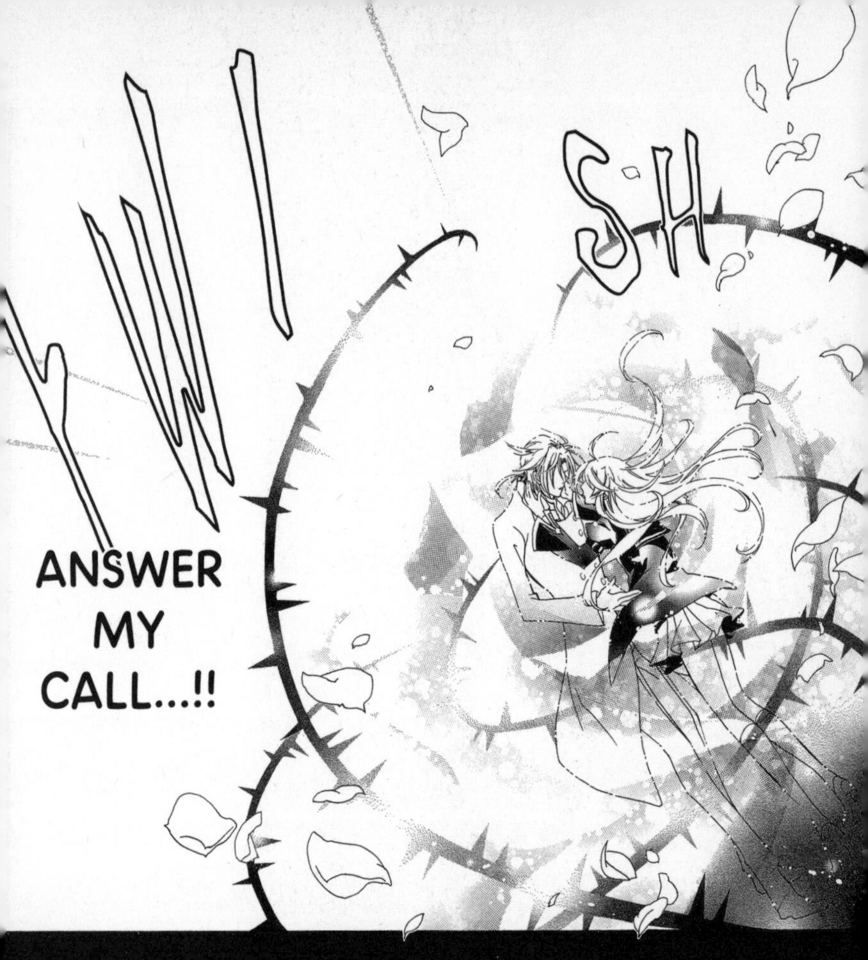
SH
ANSWER MY CALL...!!

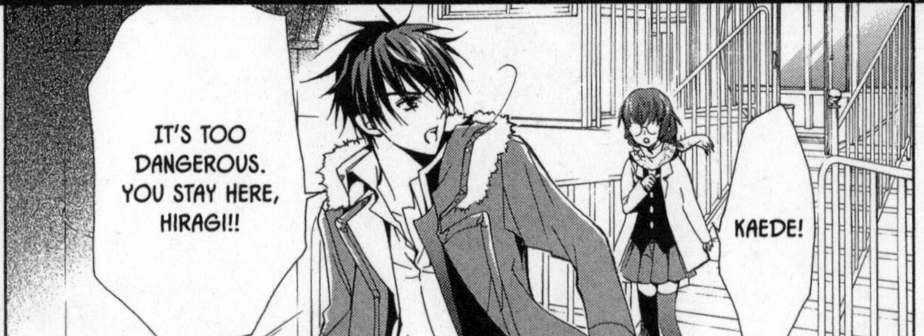
KAEDE!
IT'S TOO DANGEROUS. YOU STAY HERE, HIRAGI!!

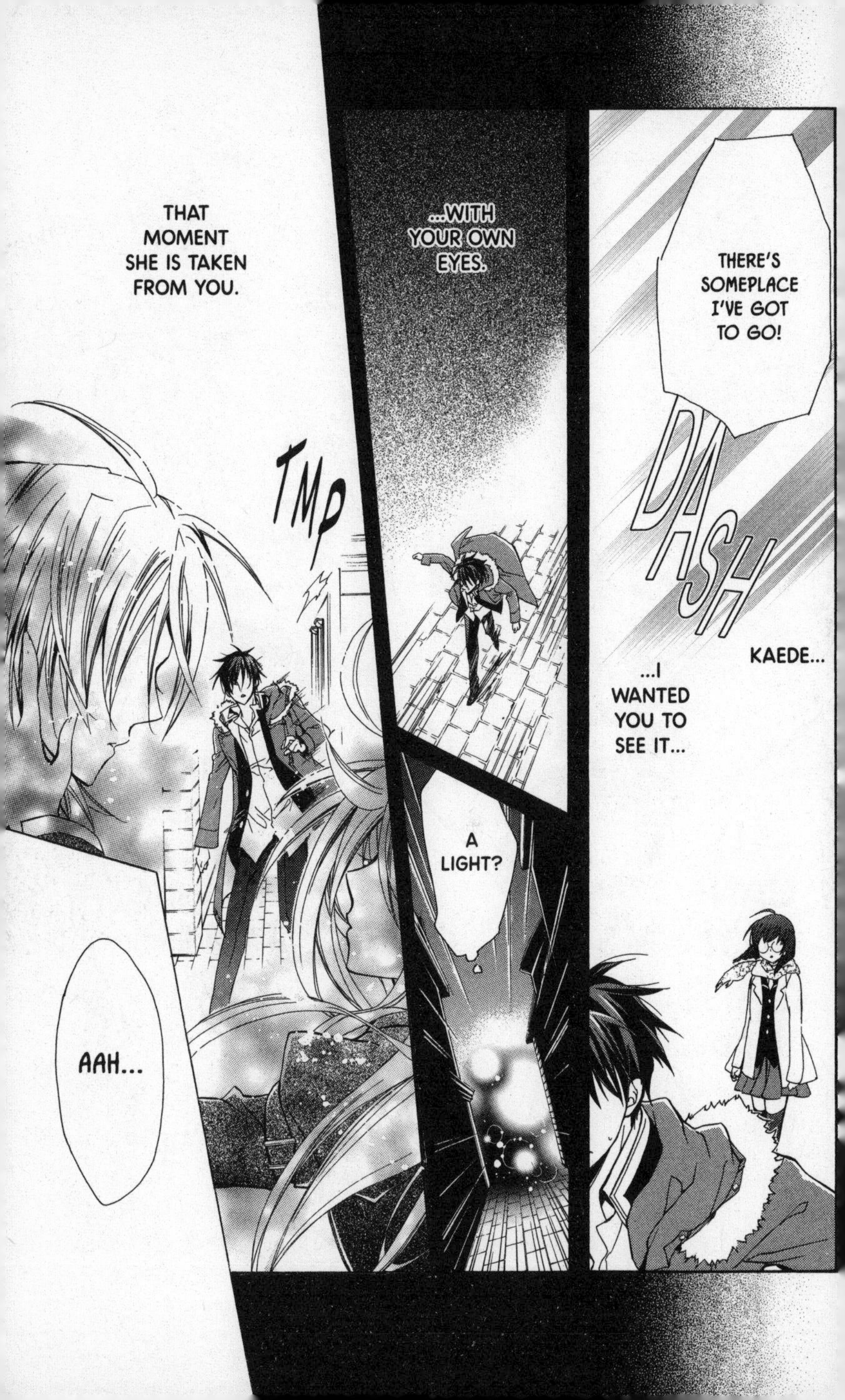

THERE'S SOMEPLACE I'VE GOT TO GO!
DASH
KAEDE...
...I WANTED YOU TO SEE IT...
...WITH YOUR OWN EYES.
A LIGHT?
THAT MOMENT SHE IS TAKEN FROM YOU.
TMP
AAH...

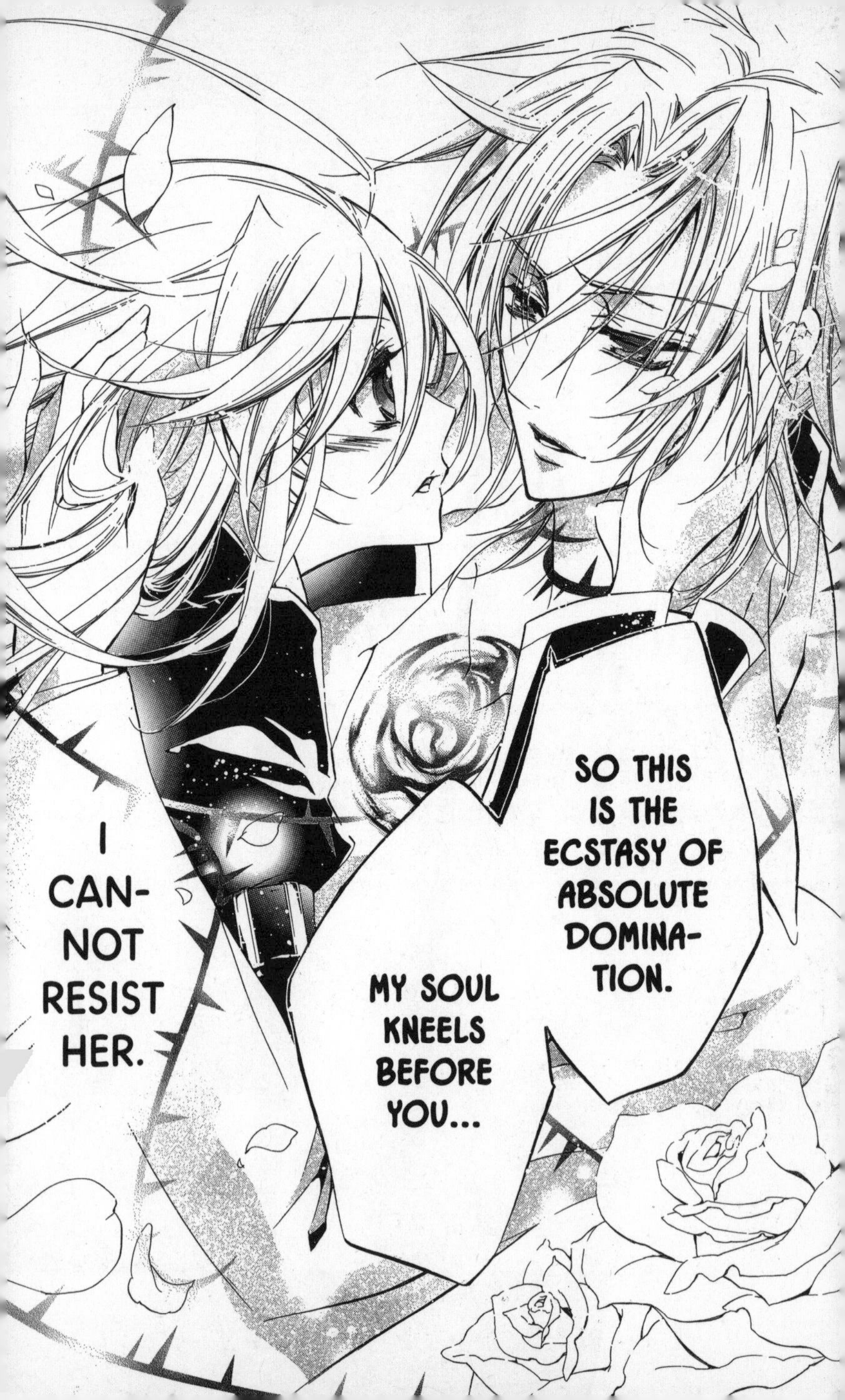
SO THIS IS THE ECSTASY OF ABSOLUTE DOMINA-TION.
MY SOUL KNEELS BEFORE YOU...
I CAN-NOT RESIST HER.

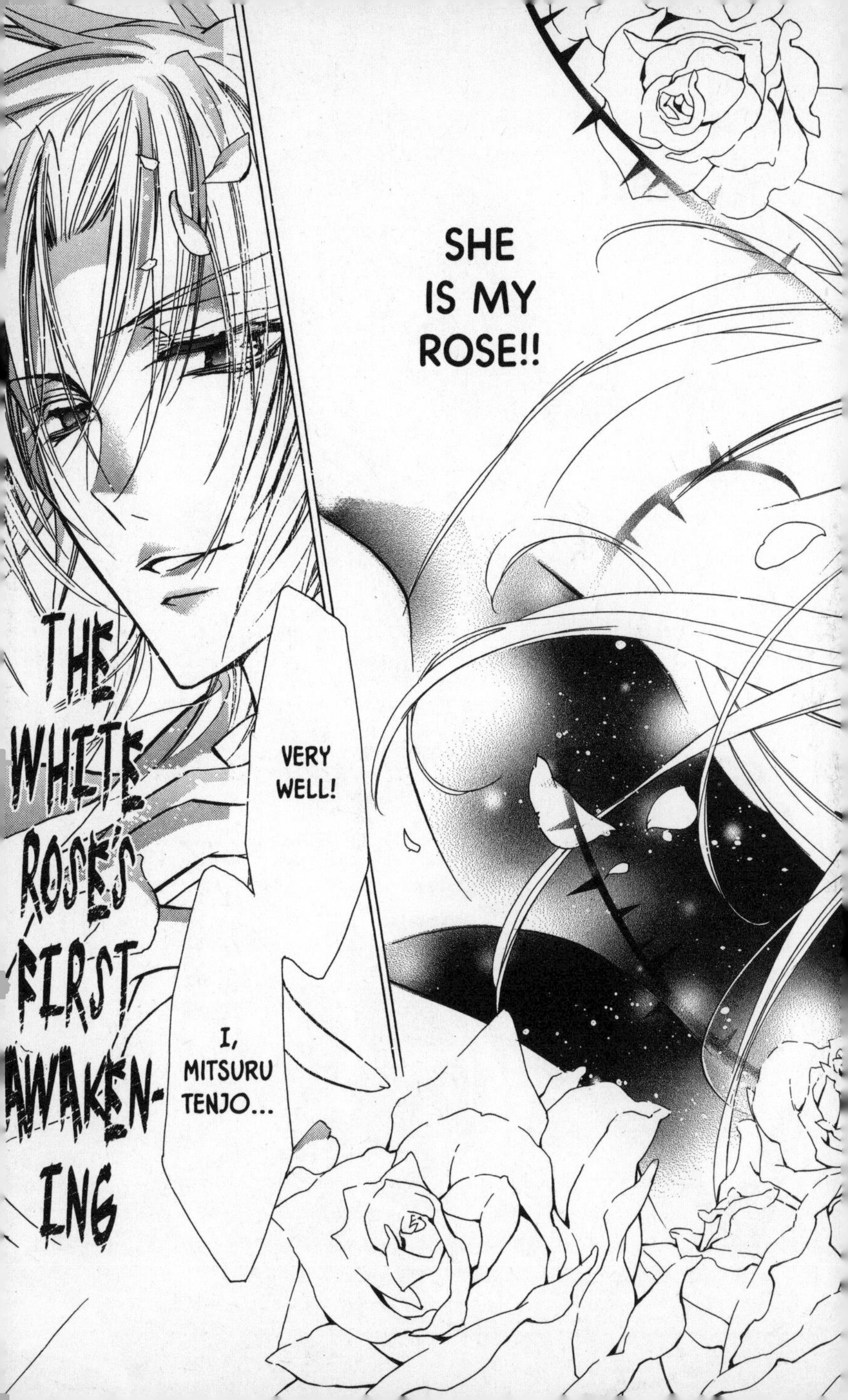
SHE IS MY ROSE!!
VERY WELL!
I, MITSURU TENJO...
THE WHITE ROSE'S FIRST AWAKENING

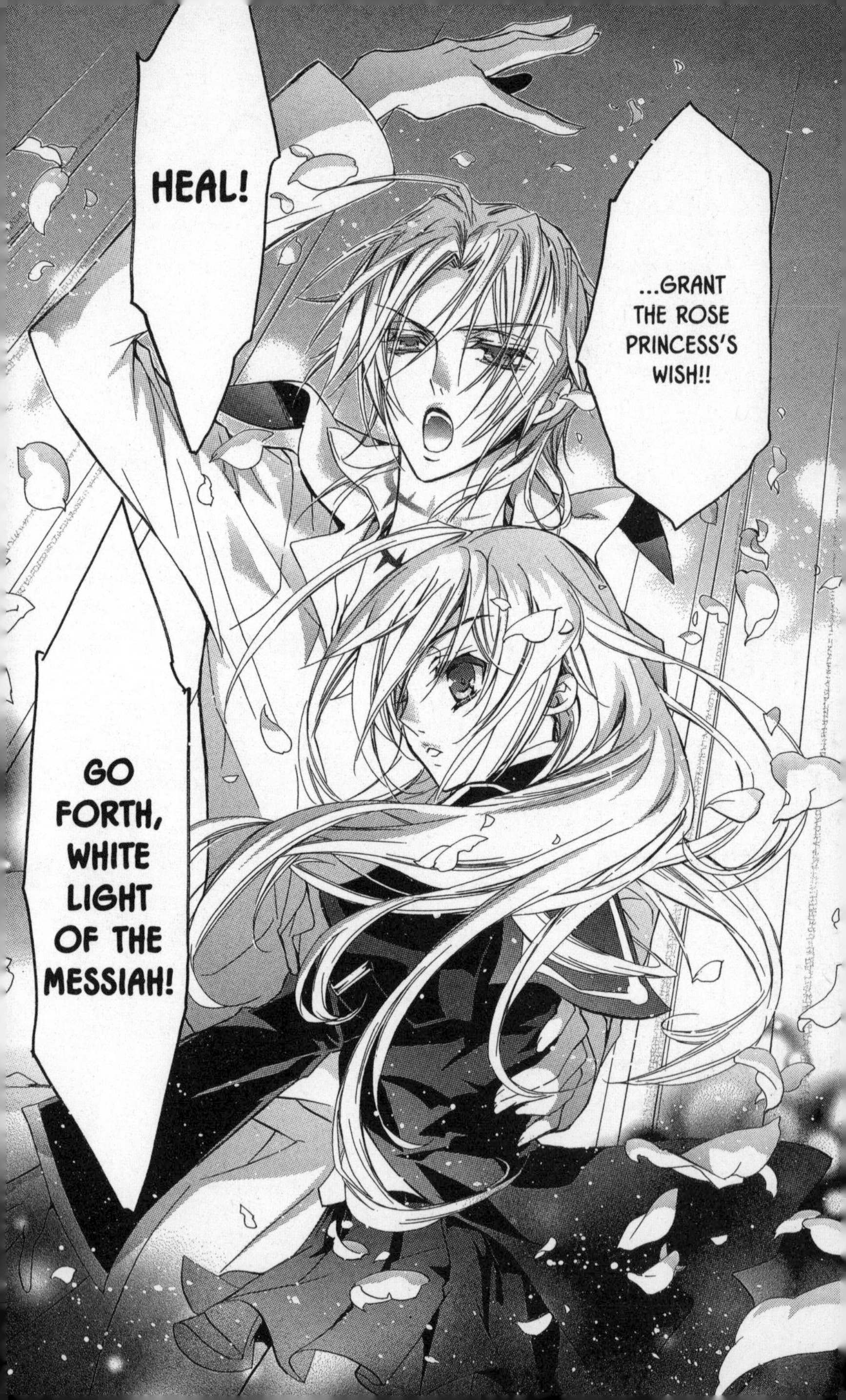
...GRANT THE ROSE PRINCESS'S WISH!!
HEAL!
GO FORTH, WHITE LIGHT OF THE MESSIAH!

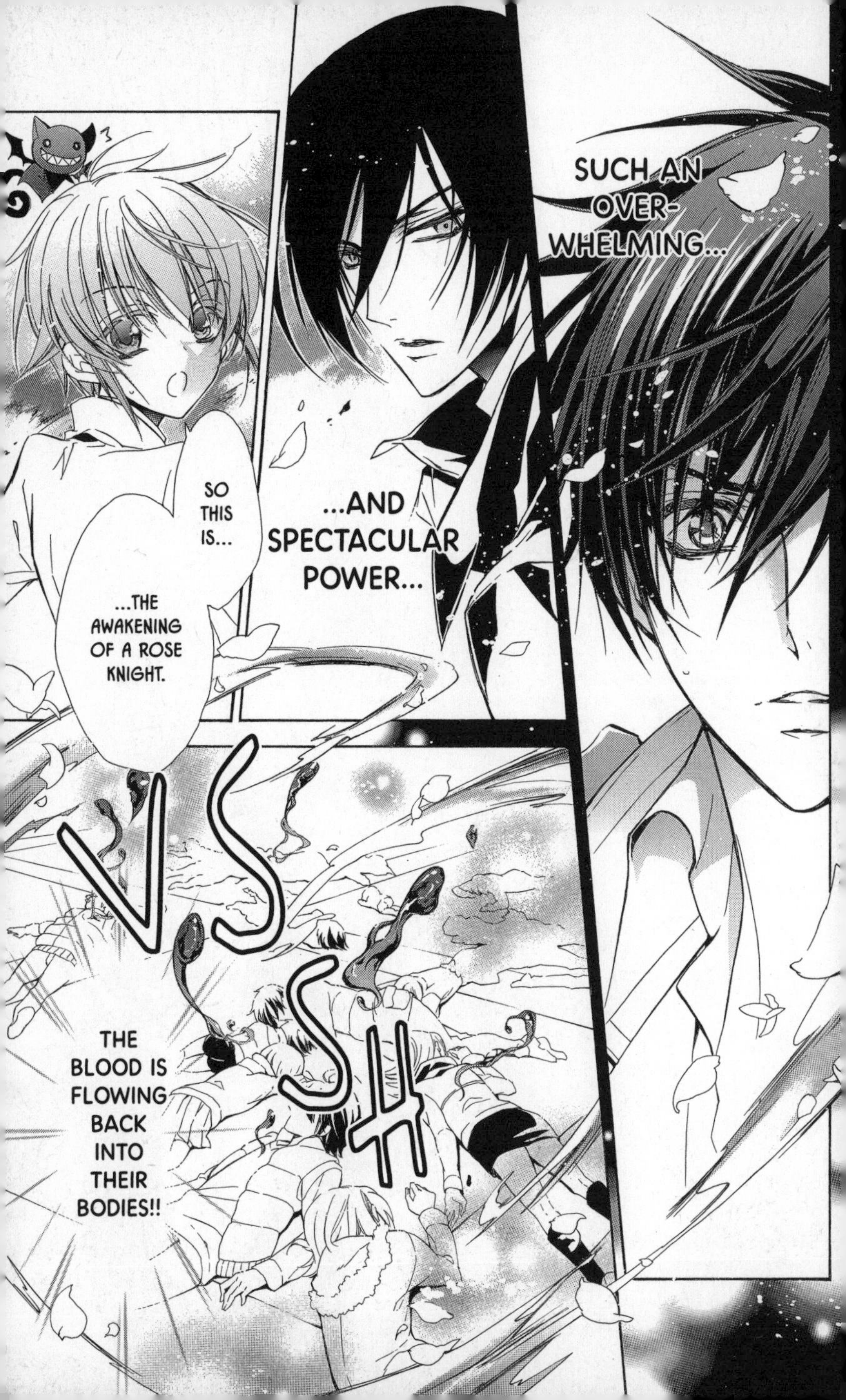
SUCH AN OVER-WHELMING...
...AND SPECTACULAR POWER...
SO THIS IS...
...THE AWAKENING OF A ROSE KNIGHT.
VSSH
THE BLOOD IS FLOWING BACK INTO THEIR BODIES!!

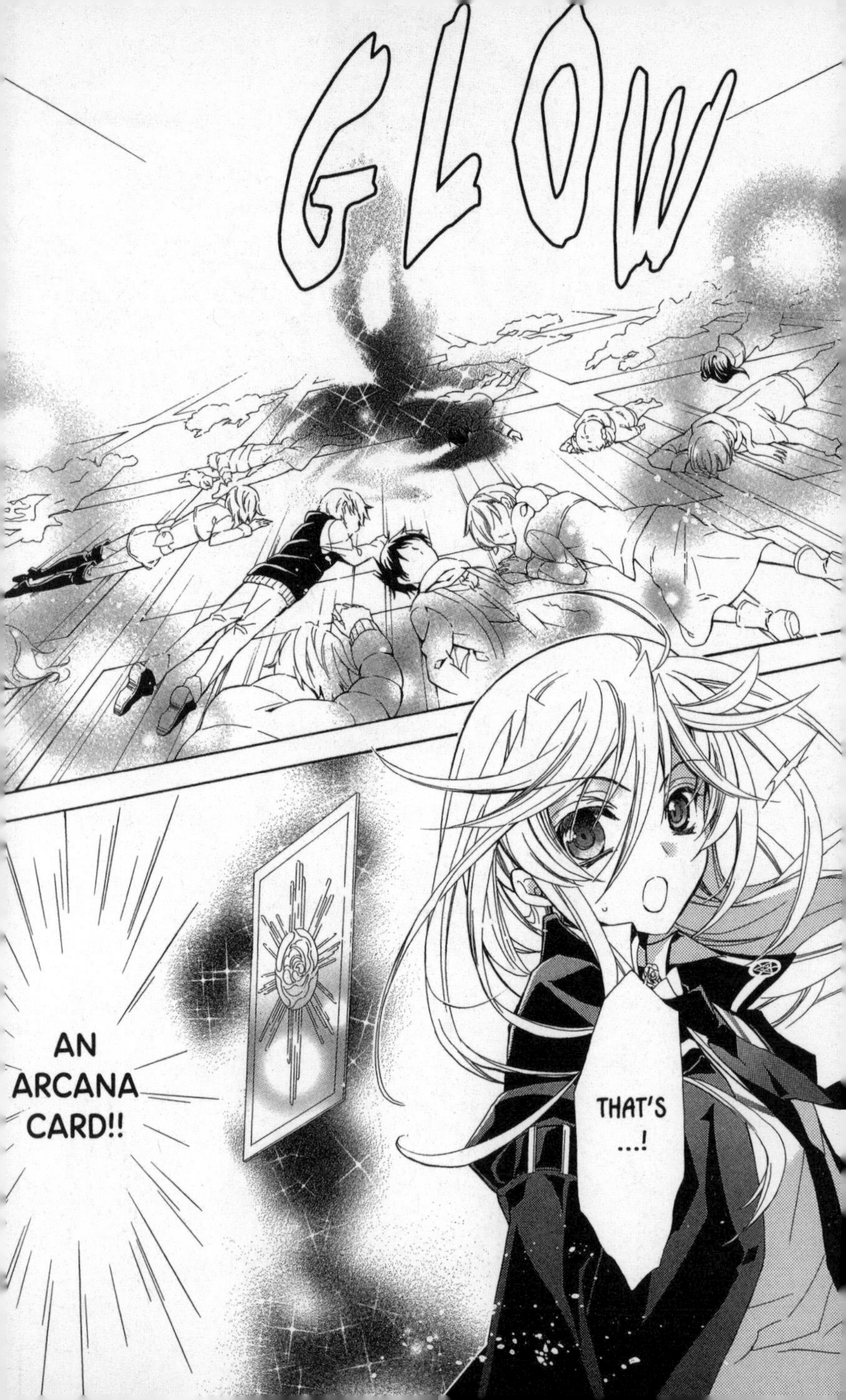
GLOW
THAT'S ...!
AN ARCANA CARD!!

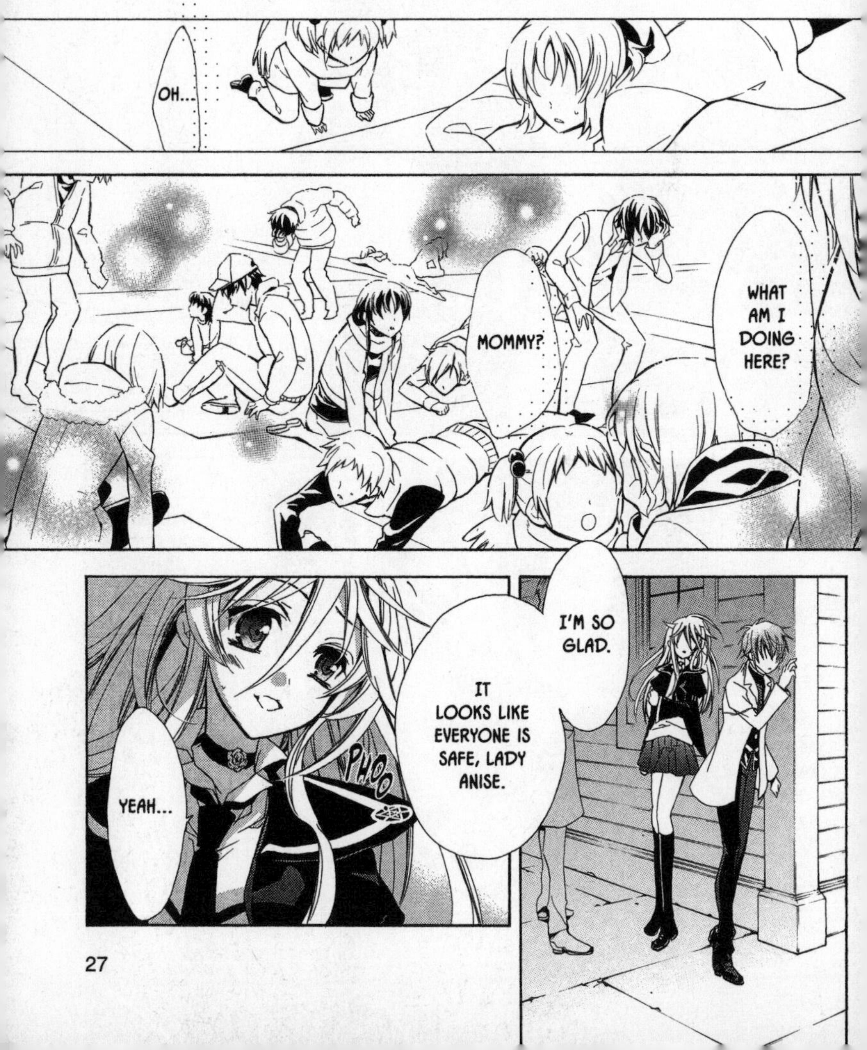
OH...
WHAT AM I DOING HERE?
MOMMY?
I'M SO GLAD.
IT LOOKS LIKE EVERYONE IS SAFE, LADY ANISE.
PHOO
YEAH...

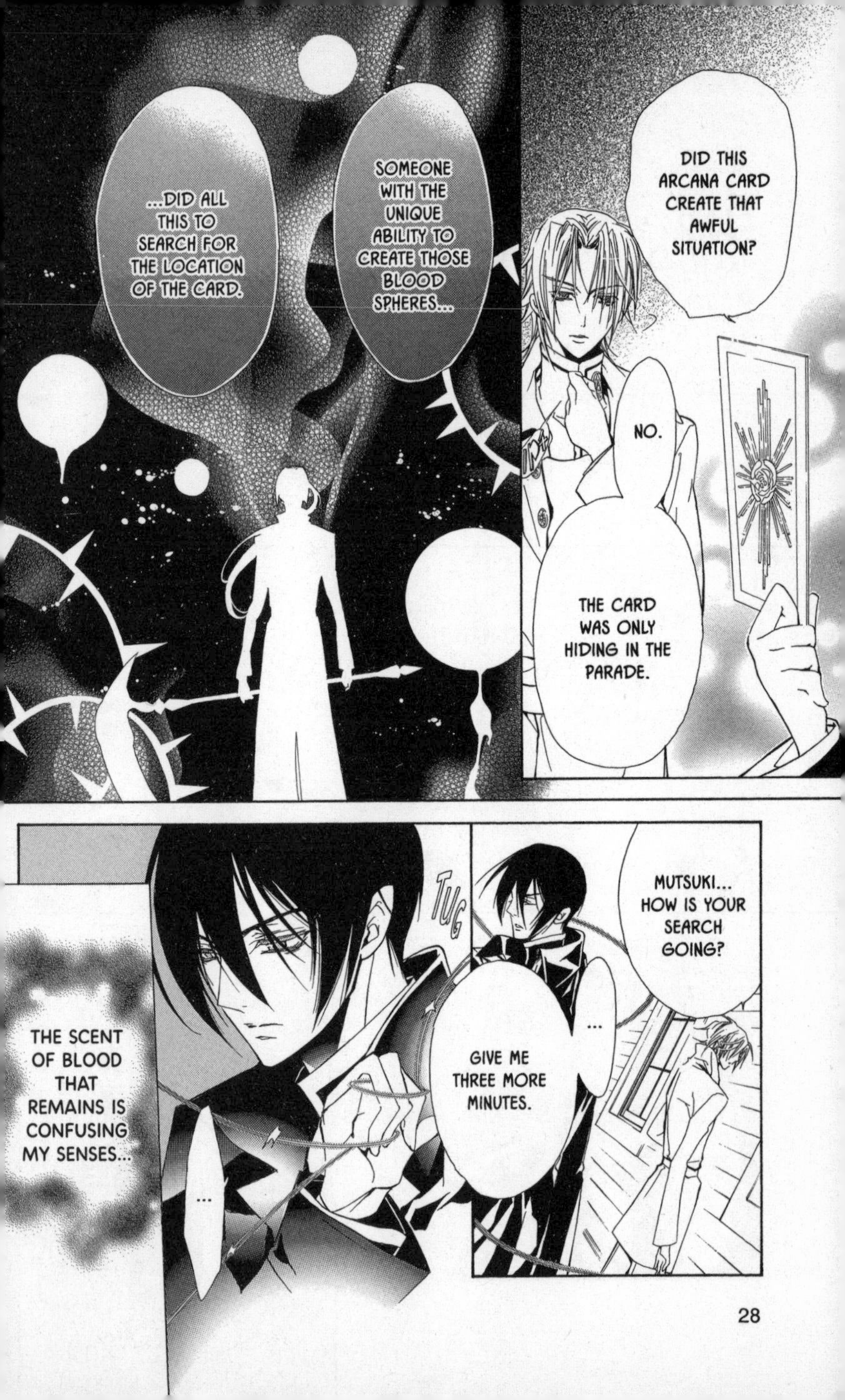
DID THIS ARCANA CARD CREATE THAT AWFUL SITUATION?
NO.
THE CARD WAS ONLY HIDING IN THE PARADE.
SOMEONE WITH THE UNIQUE ABILITY TO CREATE THOSE BLOOD SPHERES...
...DID ALL THIS TO SEARCH FOR THE LOCATION OF THE CARD.
MUTSUKI... HOW IS YOUR SEARCH GOING?
...
GIVE ME THREE MORE MINUTES.
TUG
...
THE SCENT OF BLOOD THAT REMAINS IS CONFUSING MY SENSES...

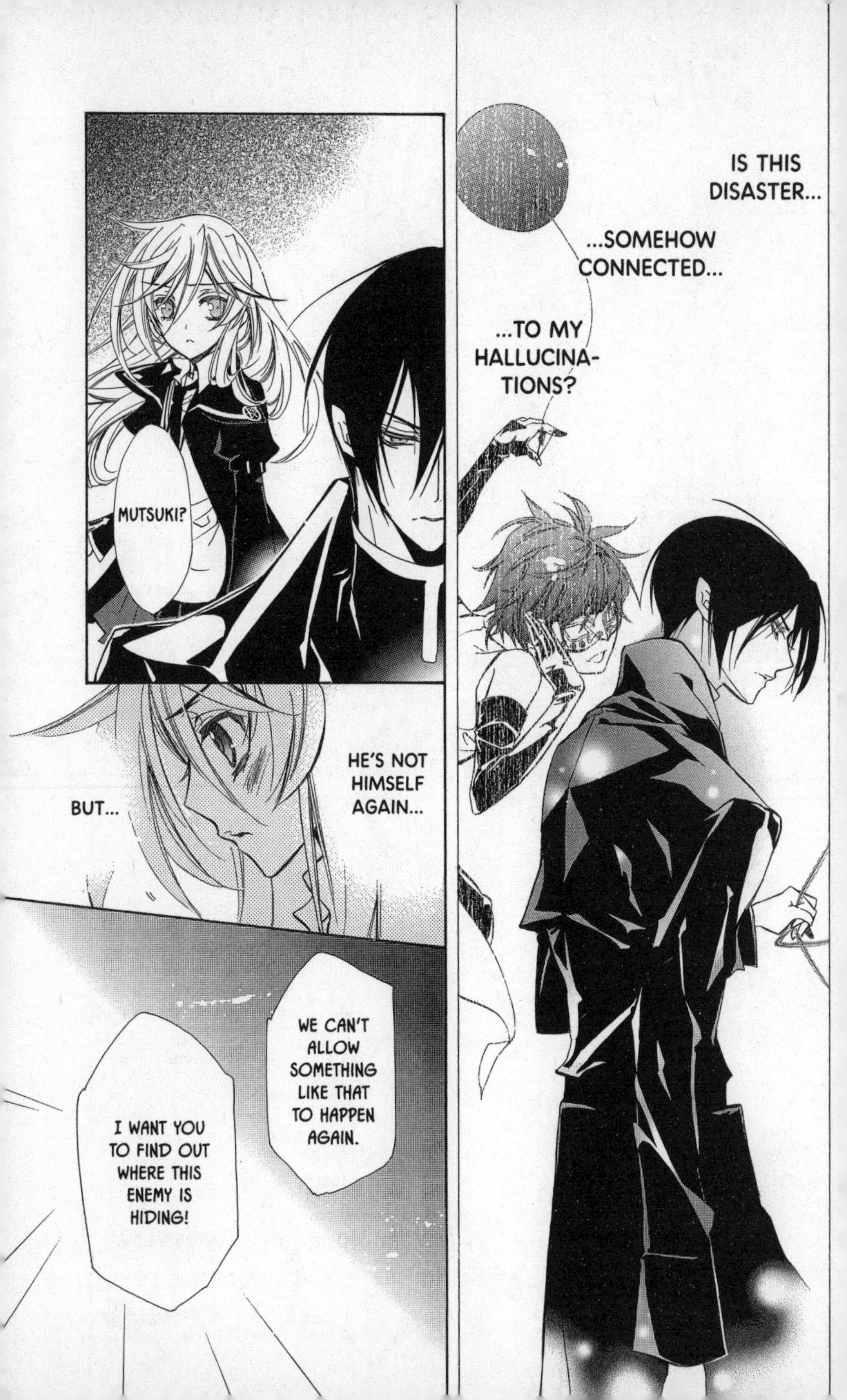
IS THIS DISASTER...
...SOMEHOW CONNECTED...
...TO MY HALLUCINATIONS?
MUTSUKI?
HE'S NOT HIMSELF AGAIN...
BUT...
WE CAN'T ALLOW SOMETHING LIKE THAT TO HAPPEN AGAIN.
I WANT YOU TO FIND OUT WHERE THIS ENEMY IS HIDING!

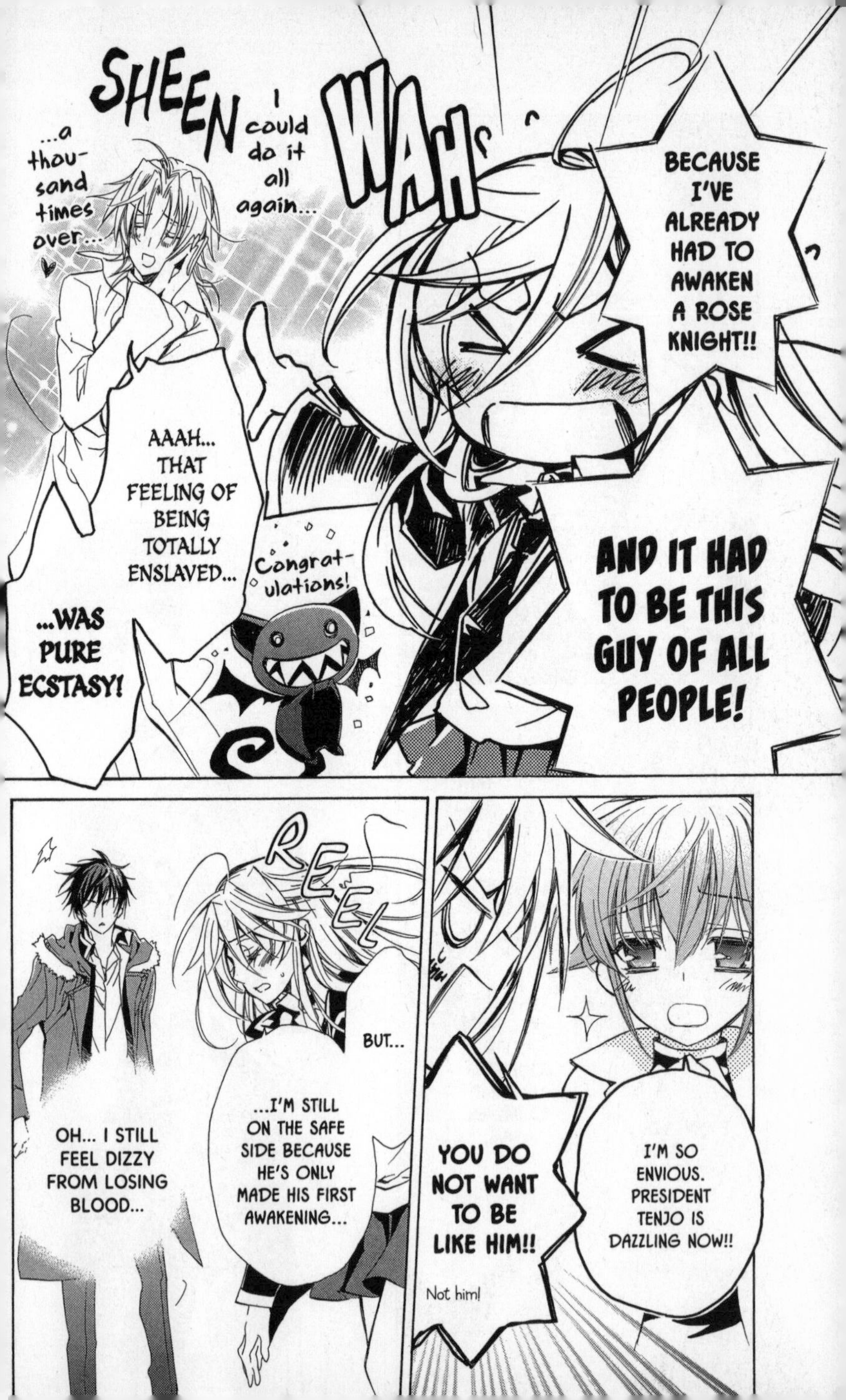
BECAUSE I'VE ALREADY HAD TO AWAKEN A ROSE KNIGHT!!
WAH
AND IT HAD TO BE THIS GUY OF ALL PEOPLE!
I could do it all again...
SHEEN
...a thousand times over...
AAAH... THAT FEELING OF BEING TOTALLY ENSLAVED...
Congratulations!
...WAS PURE ECSTASY!
I'M SO ENVIOUS. PRESIDENT TENJO IS DAZZLING NOW!!
YOU DO NOT WANT TO BE LIKE HIM!!
Not him!
REEL
BUT...
...I'M STILL ON THE SAFE SIDE BECAUSE HE'S ONLY MADE HIS FIRST AWAKENING...
OH... I STILL FEEL DIZZY FROM LOSING BLOOD...

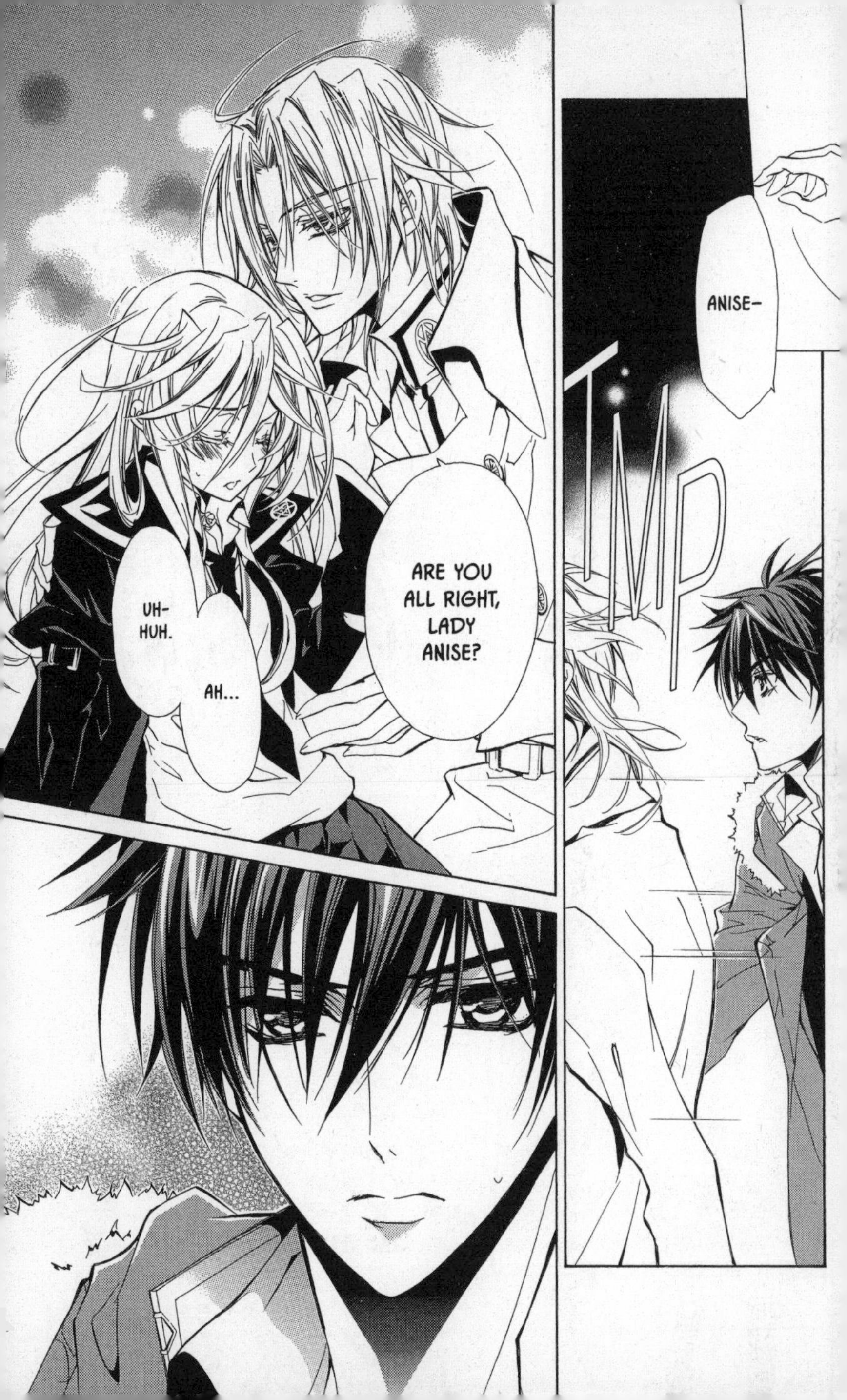
ANISE—
TMP
ARE YOU ALL RIGHT, LADY ANISE?
UH-HUH.
AH...

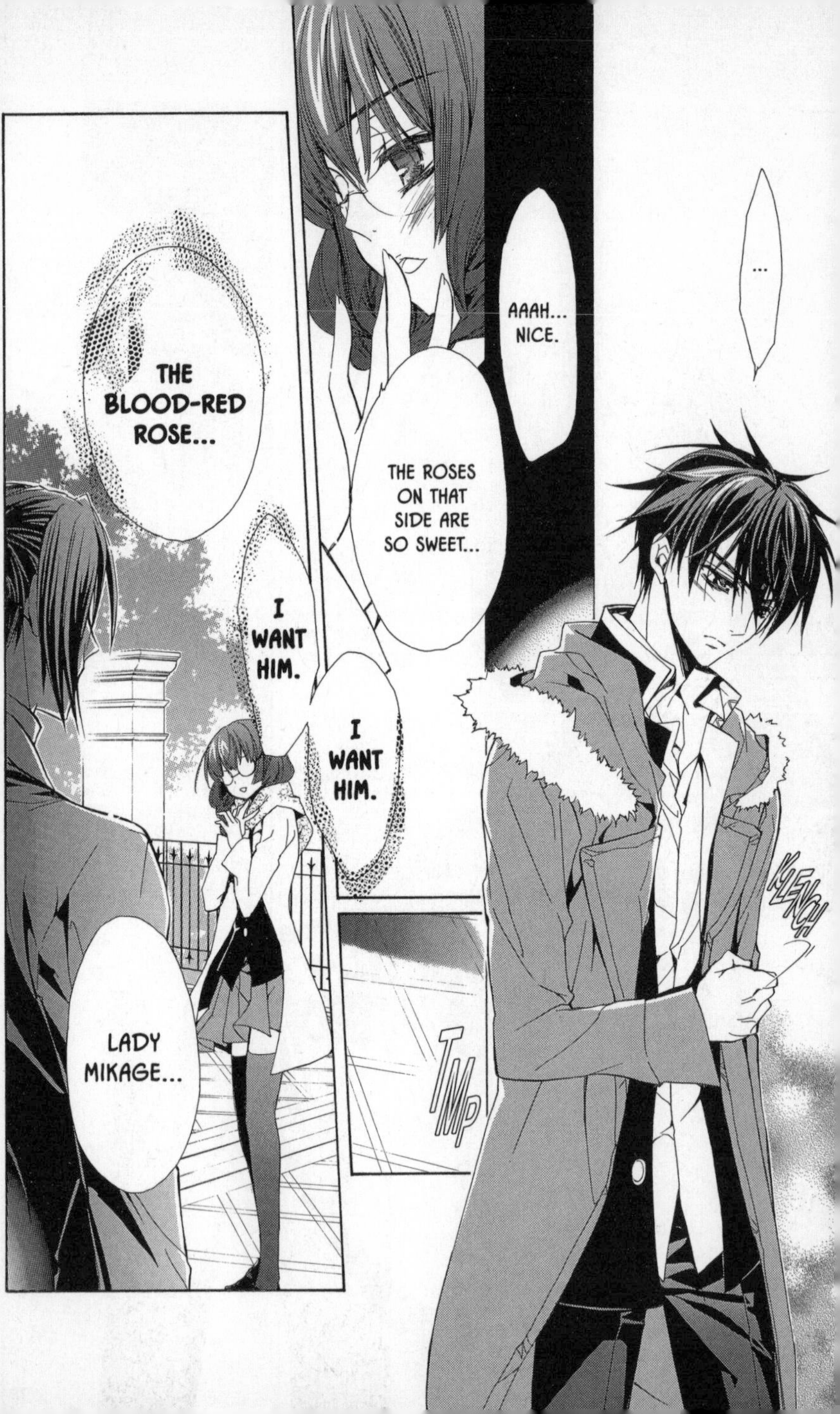
...
AAAH... NICE.
THE ROSES ON THAT SIDE ARE SO SWEET...
THE BLOOD-RED ROSE...
I WANT HIM.
I WANT HIM.
LADY MIKAGE...
TMP
KLENCH

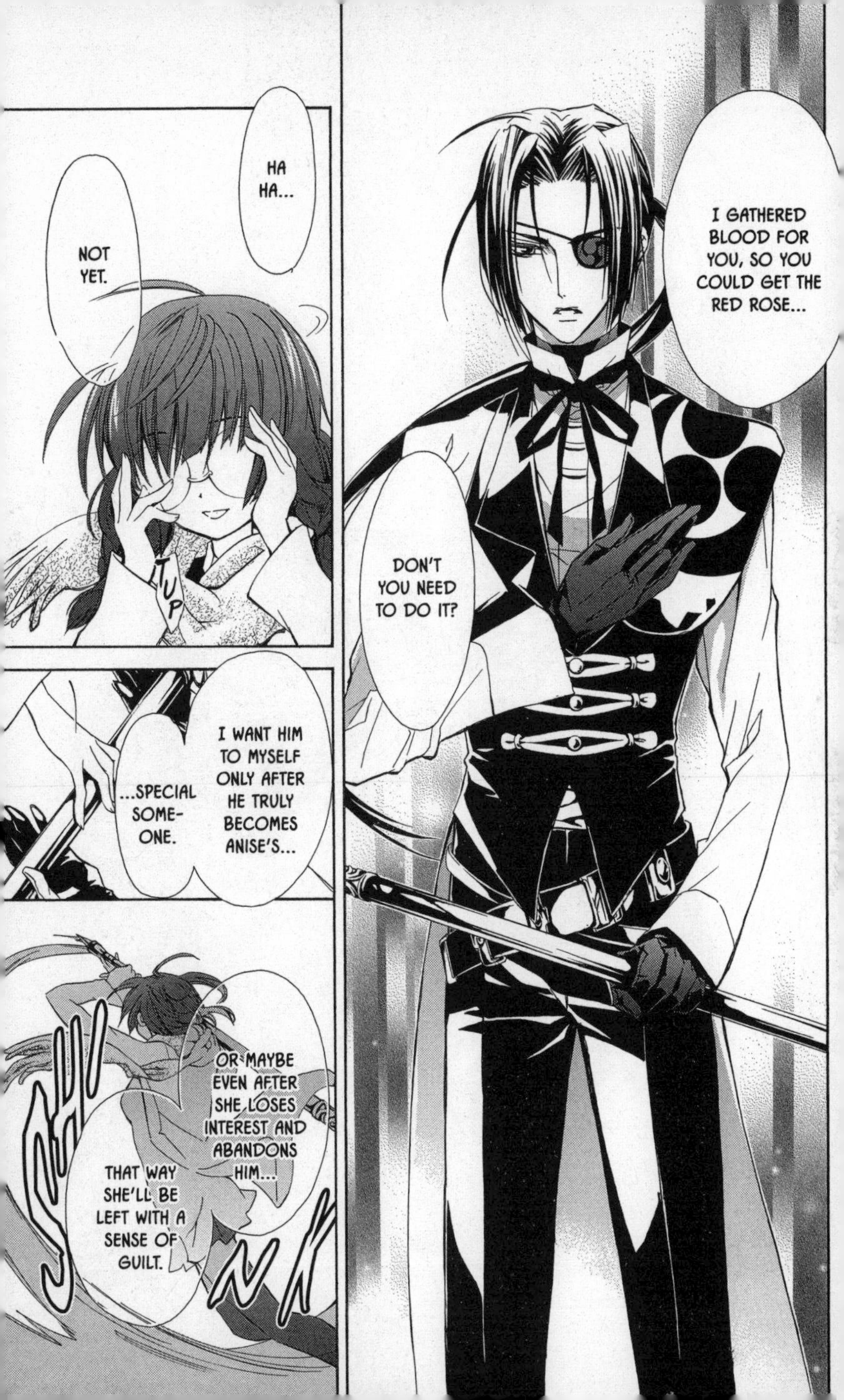
I GATHERED BLOOD FOR YOU, SO YOU COULD GET THE RED ROSE...
DON'T YOU NEED TO DO IT?
HA HA...
NOT YET.
TUP
I WANT HIM TO MYSELF ONLY AFTER HE TRULY BECOMES ANISE'S...
...SPECIAL SOMEONE.
OR MAYBE EVEN AFTER SHE LOSES INTEREST AND ABANDONS HIM...
THAT WAY SHE'LL BE LEFT WITH A SENSE OF GUILT.

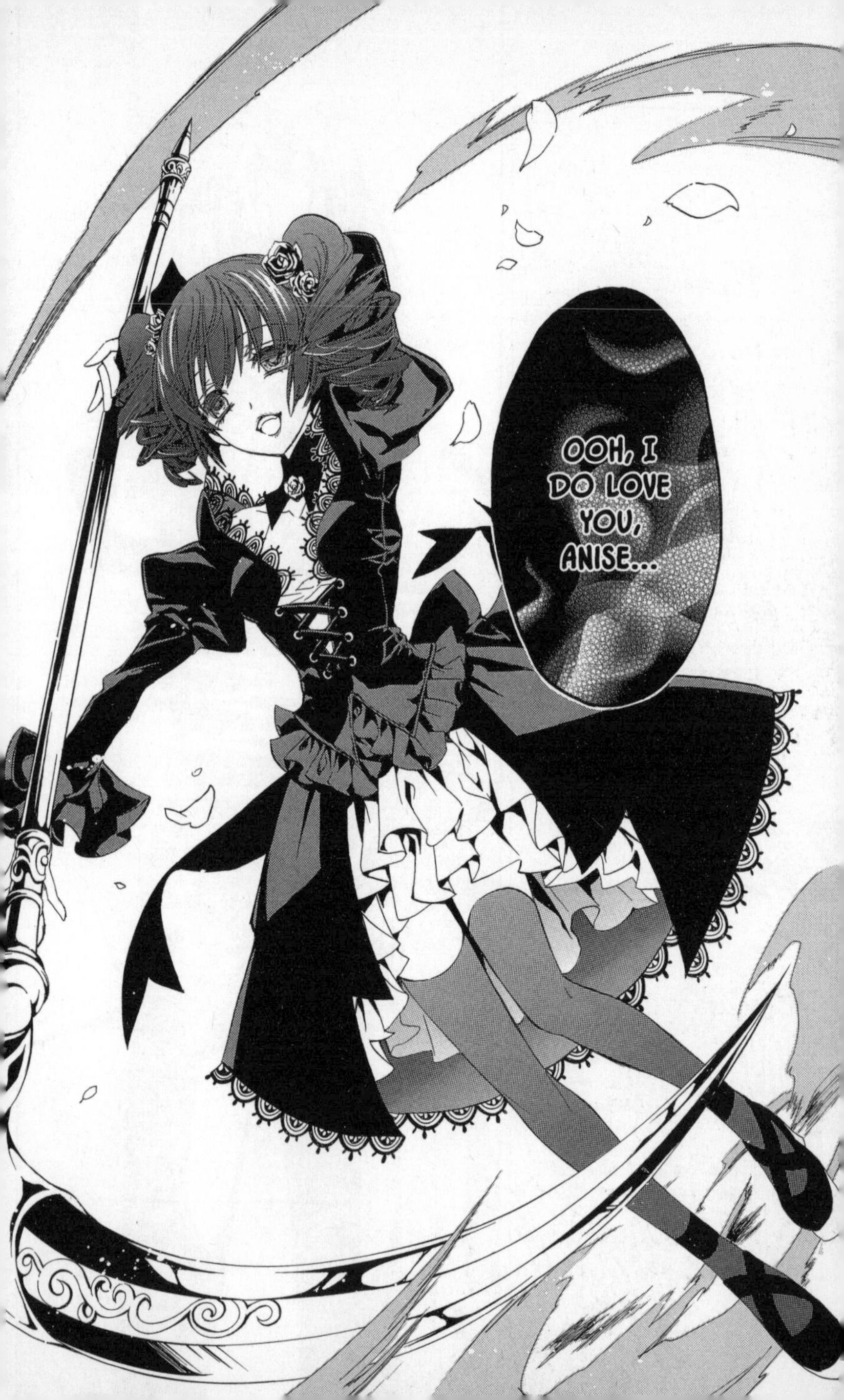
OOH, I DO LOVE YOU, ANISE...

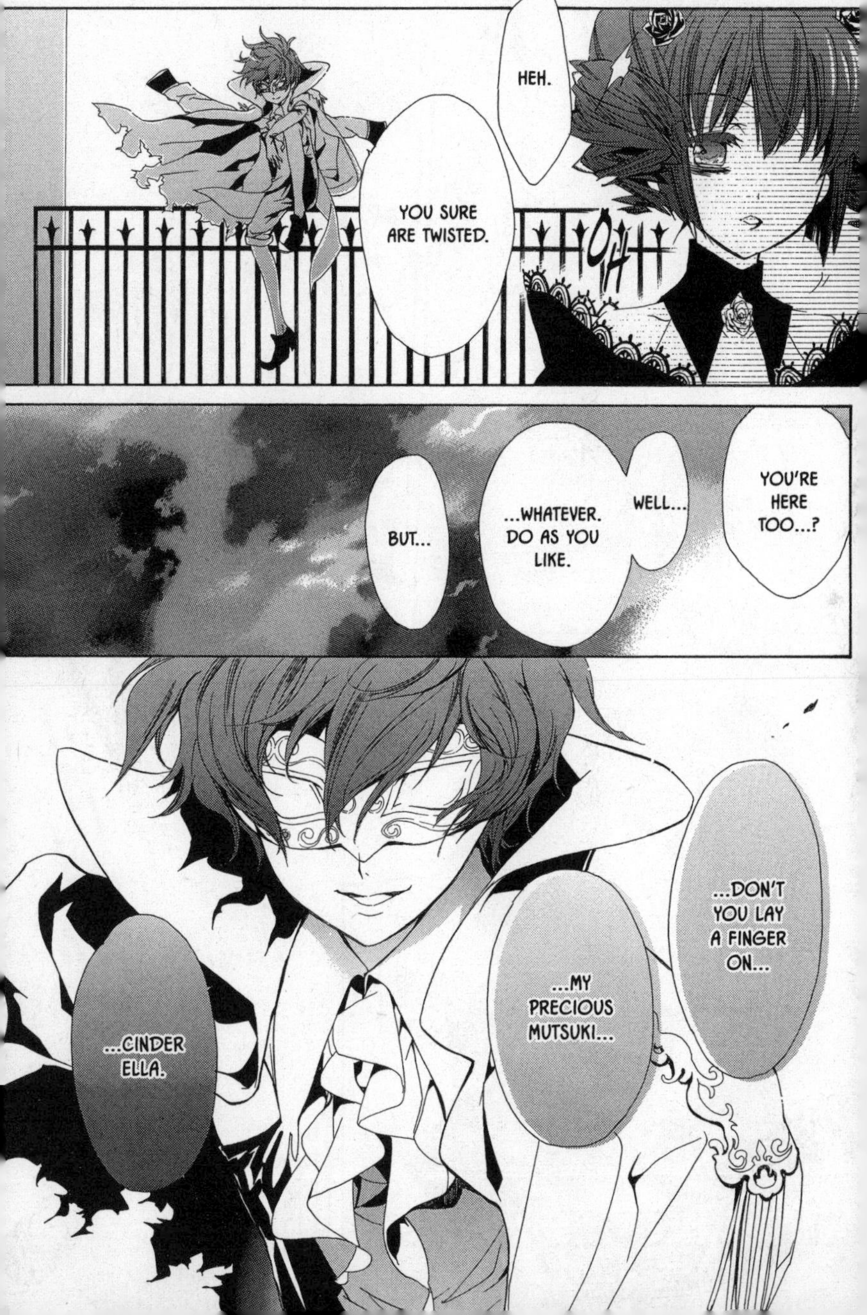
HEH.
OH
YOU SURE ARE TWISTED.
YOU'RE HERE TOO...?
WELL...
...WHATEVER. DO AS YOU LIKE.
BUT...
...DON'T YOU LAY A FINGER ON...
...MY PRECIOUS MUTSUKI...
...CINDER ELLA.

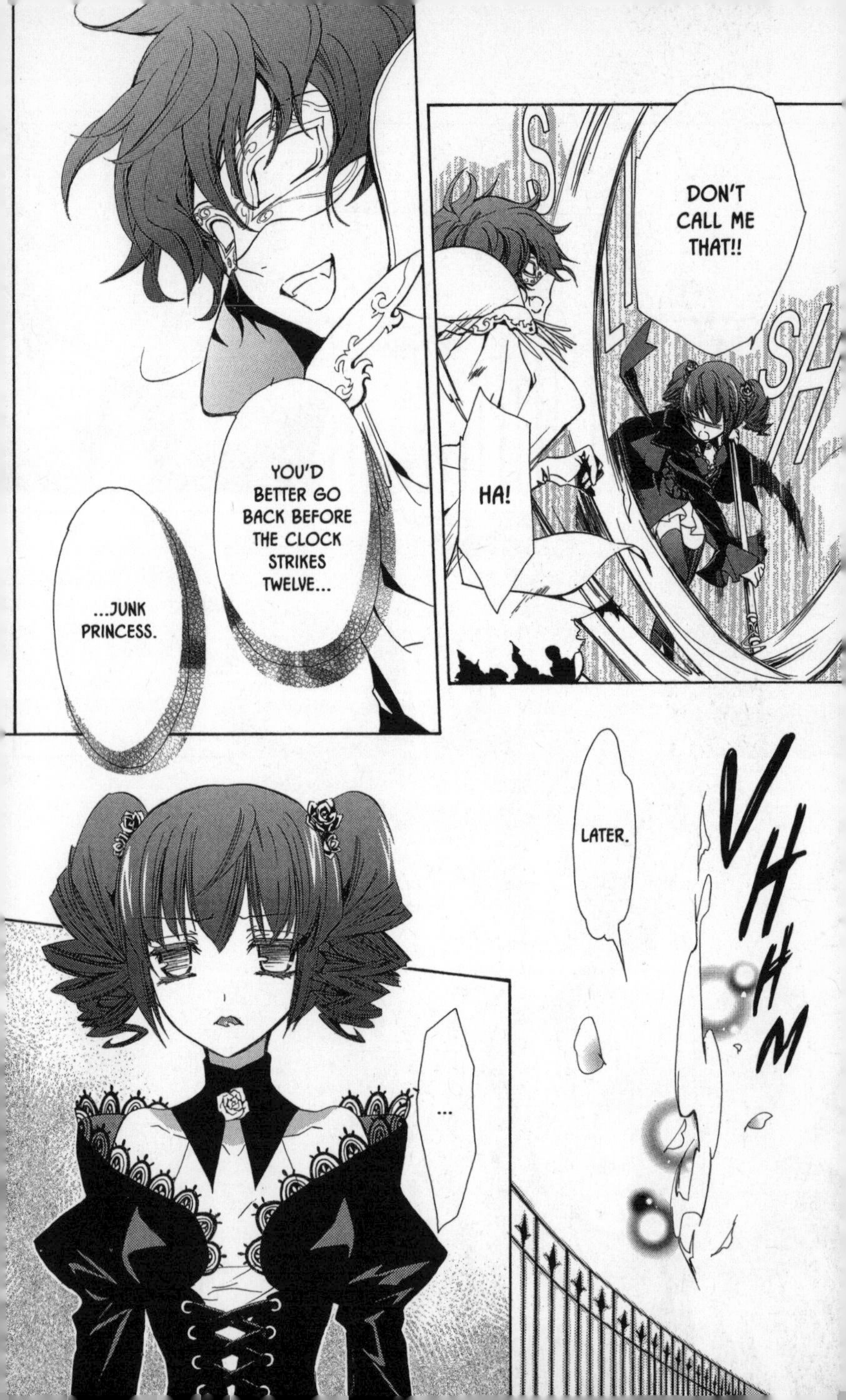
DON'T CALL ME THAT!!
HA!
YOU'D BETTER GO BACK BEFORE THE CLOCK STRIKES TWELVE...
...JUNK PRINCESS.
LATER.
VHHM
...

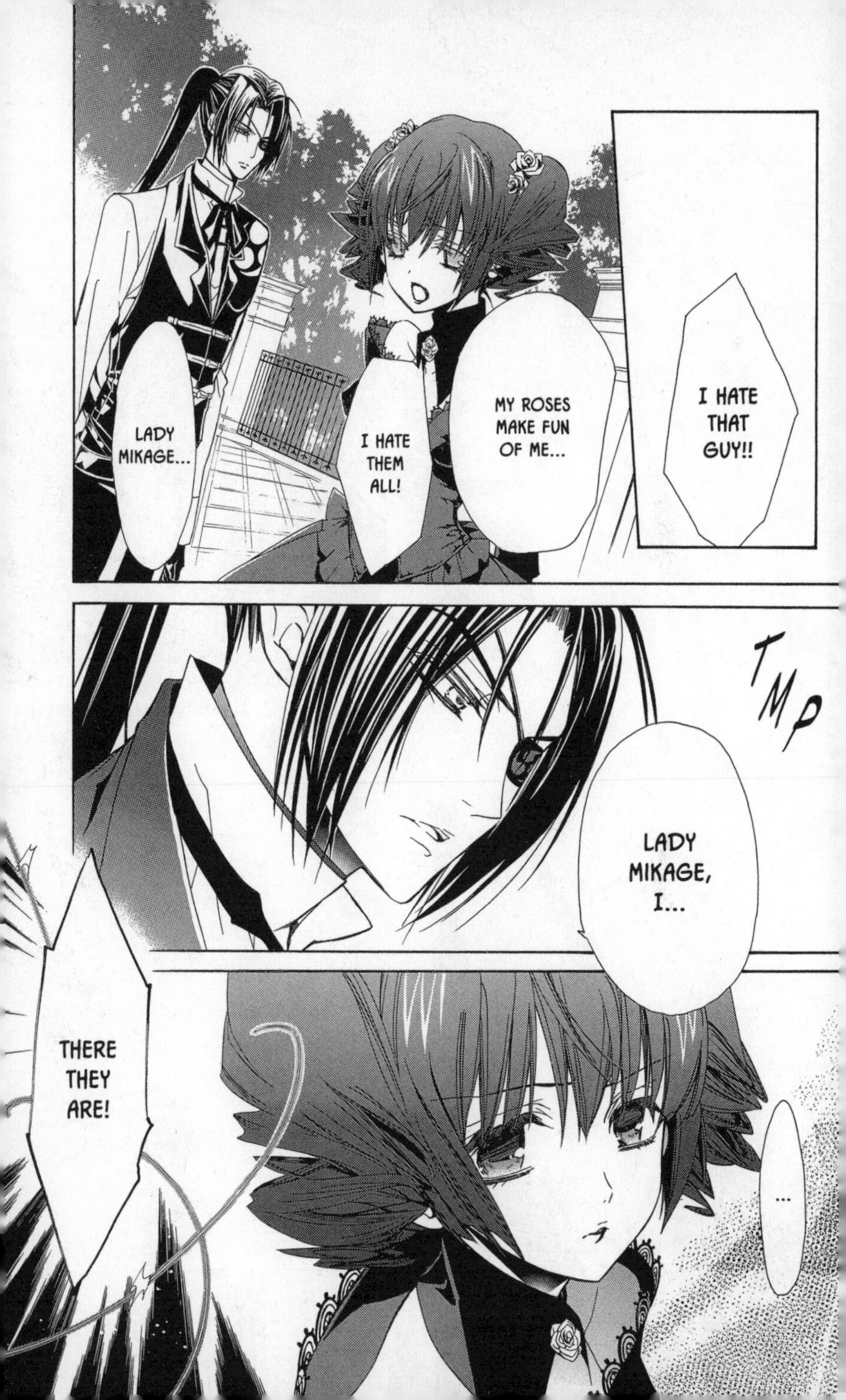
I HATE THAT GUY!!
MY ROSES MAKE FUN OF ME...
I HATE THEM ALL!
LADY MIKAGE...
TMP
LADY MIKAGE, I...
...
THERE THEY ARE!

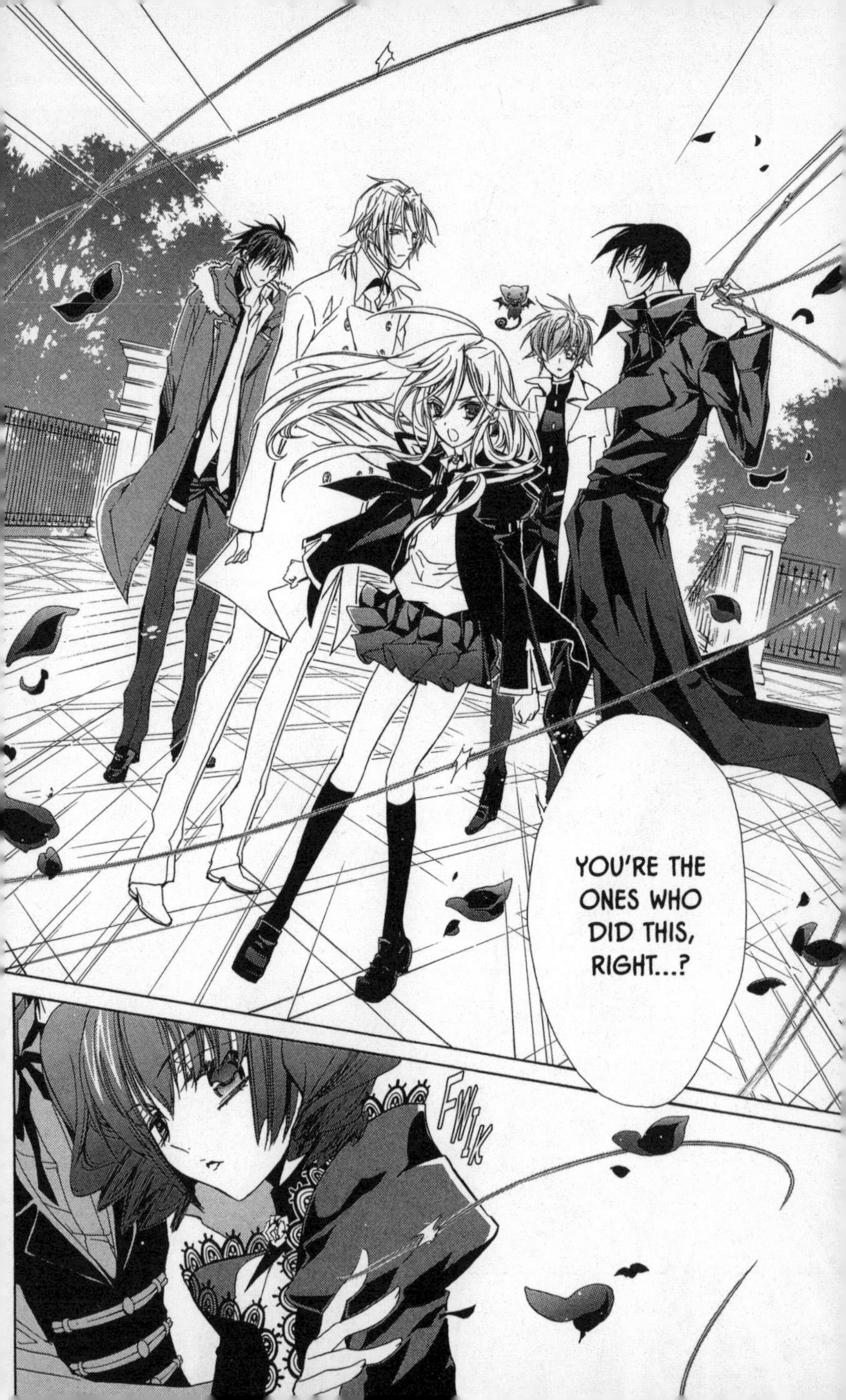
YOU'RE THE ONES WHO DID THIS, RIGHT...?
FWIK

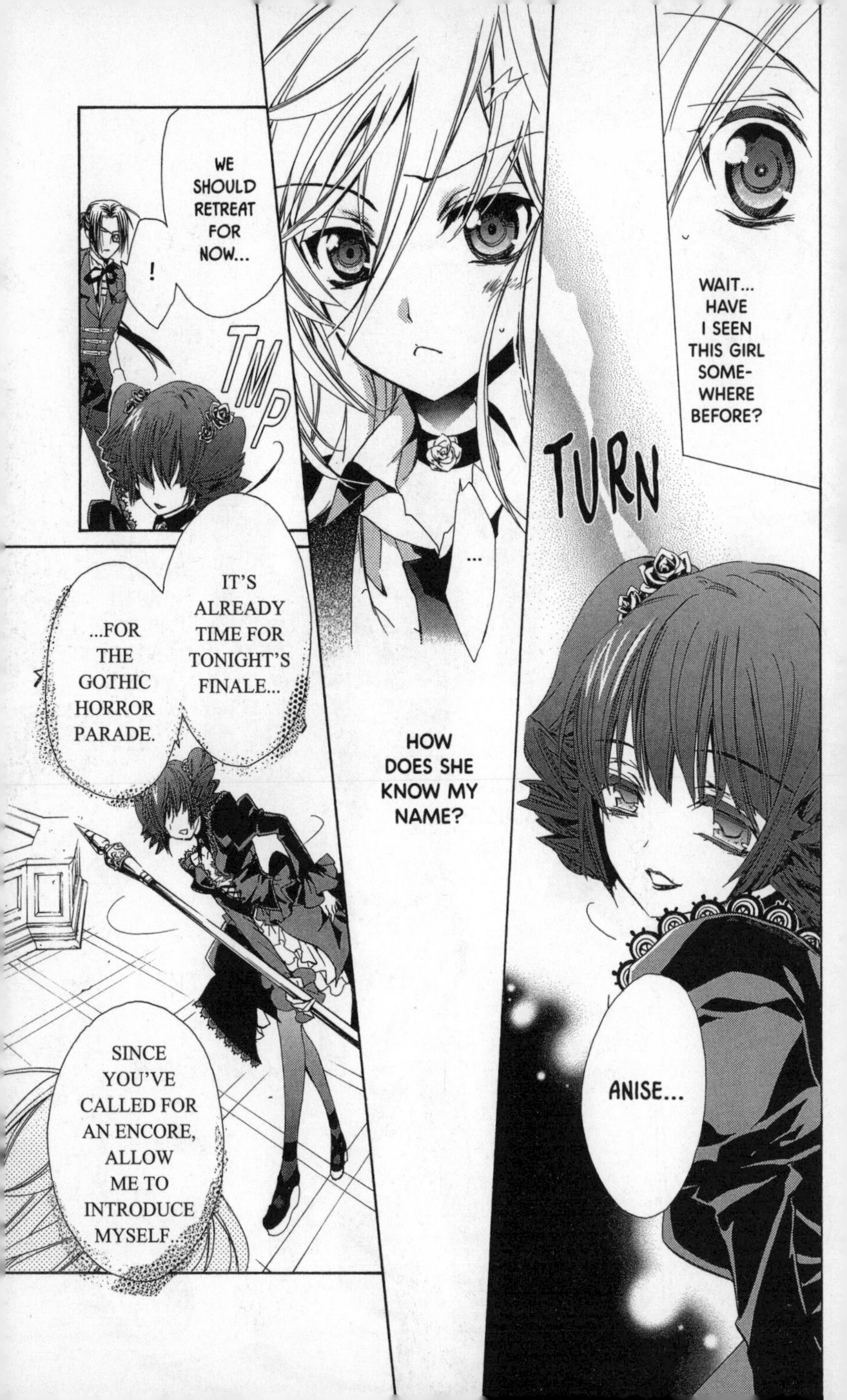
WAIT... HAVE I SEEN THIS GIRL SOME-WHERE BEFORE?
TURN
ANISE...
...
HOW DOES SHE KNOW MY NAME?
WE SHOULD RETREAT FOR NOW...
!
TMP
IT'S ALREADY TIME FOR TONIGHT'S FINALE...
...FOR THE GOTHIC HORROR PARADE.
SINCE YOU'VE CALLED FOR AN ENCORE, ALLOW ME TO INTRODUCE MYSELF.

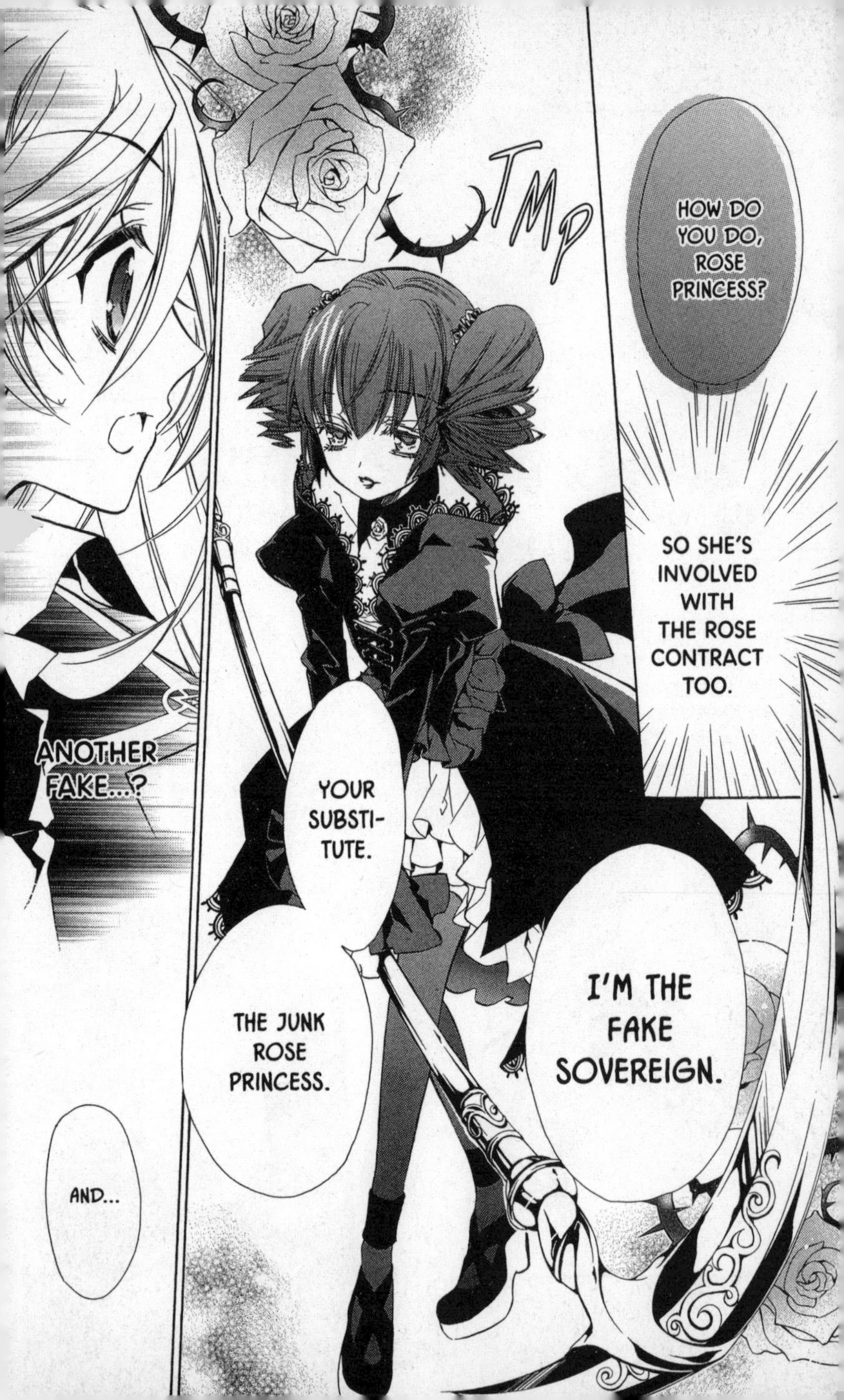
HOW DO YOU DO, ROSE PRINCESS?
SO SHE'S INVOLVED WITH THE ROSE CONTRACT TOO.
TMP
I'M THE FAKE SOVEREIGN.
YOUR SUBSTI-TUTE.
THE JUNK ROSE PRINCESS.
ANOTHER FAKE...?
AND...

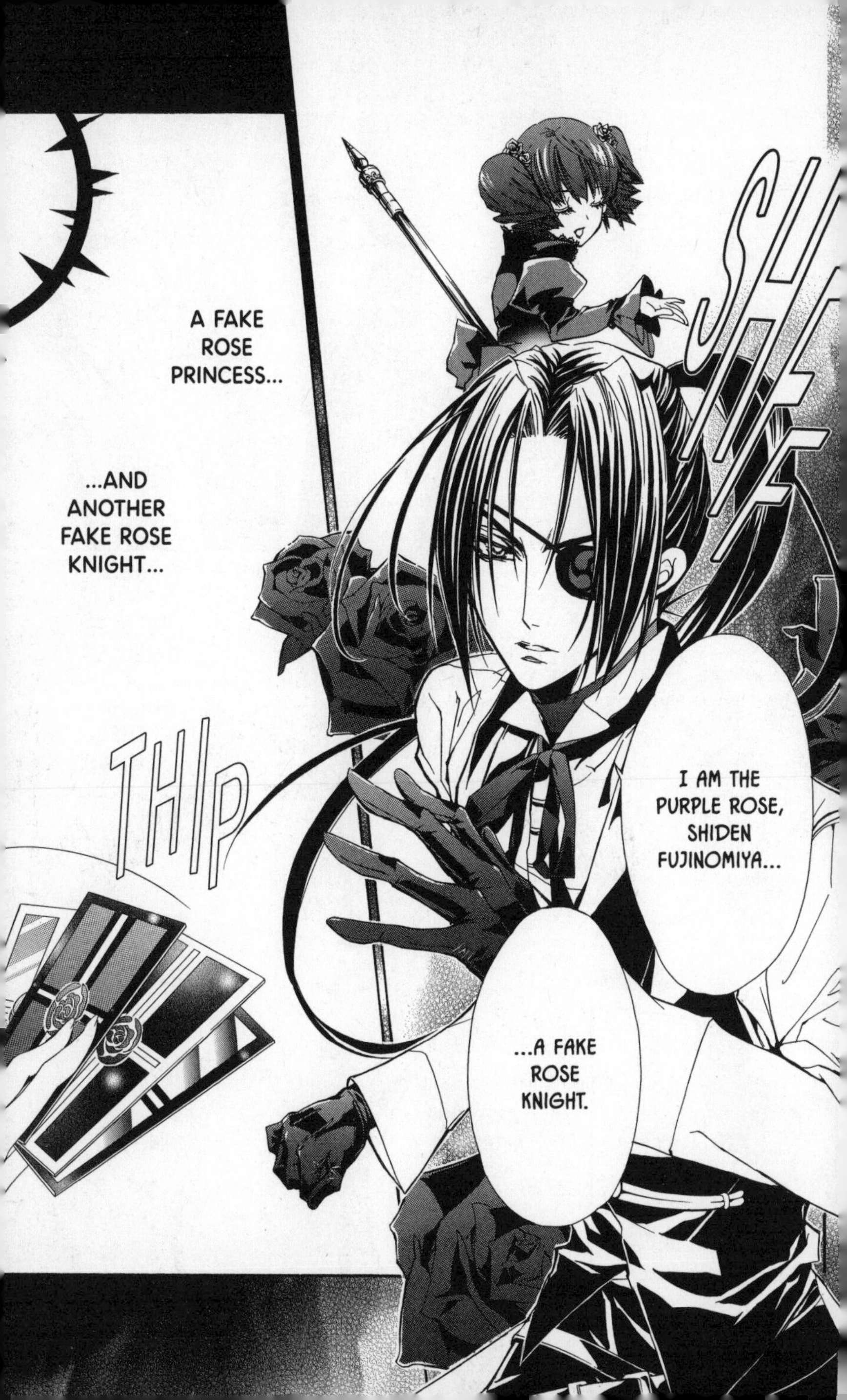
A FAKE ROSE PRINCESS...
...AND ANOTHER FAKE ROSE KNIGHT...
SHFF
THIP
I AM THE PURPLE ROSE, SHIDEN FUJINOMIYA...
...A FAKE ROSE KNIGHT.

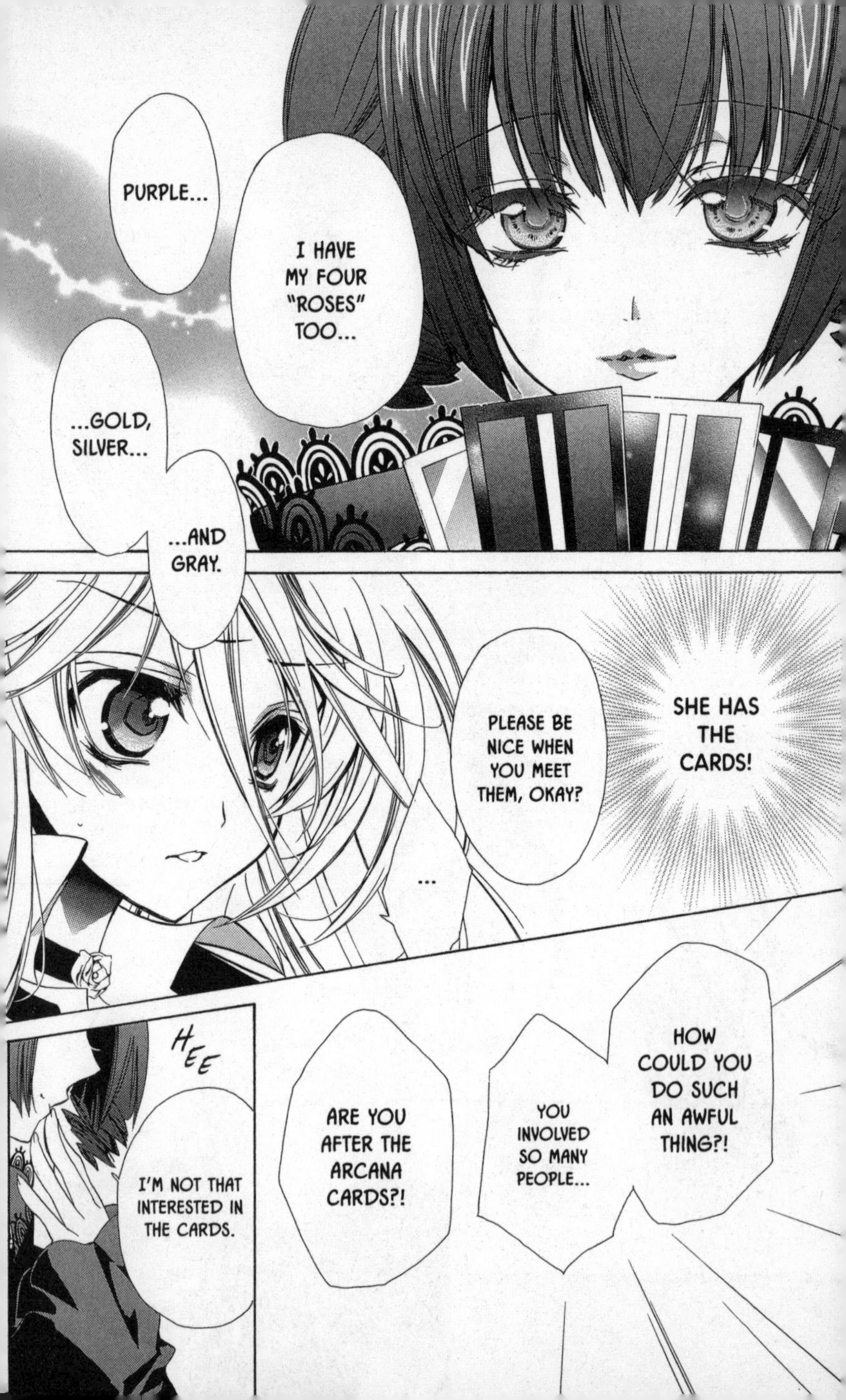
I HAVE MY FOUR "ROSES" TOO...
PURPLE...
...GOLD, SILVER...
...AND GRAY.
SHE HAS THE CARDS!
PLEASE BE NICE WHEN YOU MEET THEM, OKAY?
...
HOW COULD YOU DO SUCH AN AWFUL THING?!
YOU INVOLVED SO MANY PEOPLE...
ARE YOU AFTER THE ARCANA CARDS?!
HEE
I'M NOT THAT INTERESTED IN THE CARDS.

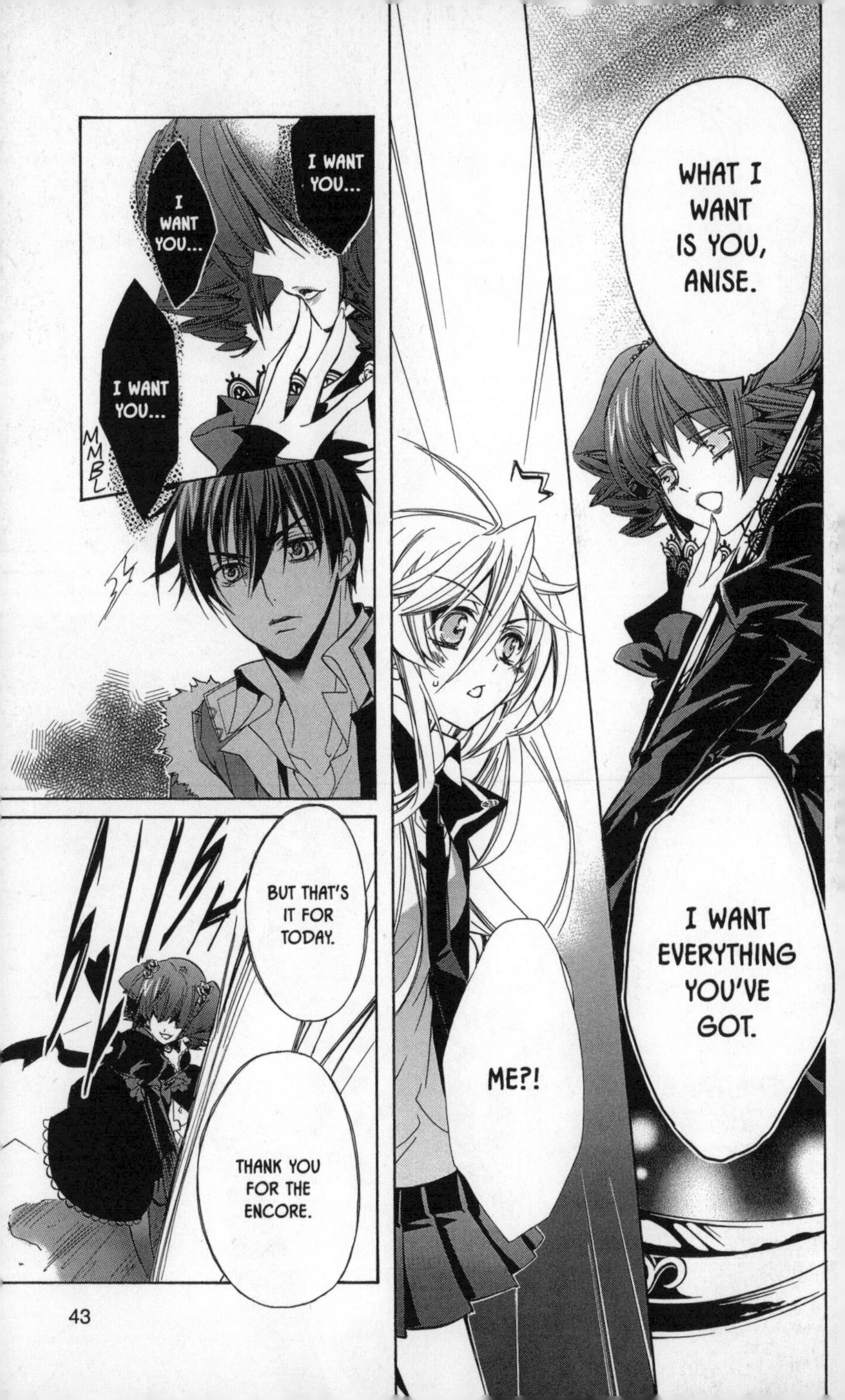
WHAT I WANT IS YOU, ANISE.
I WANT EVERYTHING YOU'VE GOT.
ME?!
I WANT YOU...
I WANT YOU...
I WANT YOU...
MMBL
BUT THAT'S IT FOR TODAY.
THANK YOU FOR THE ENCORE.

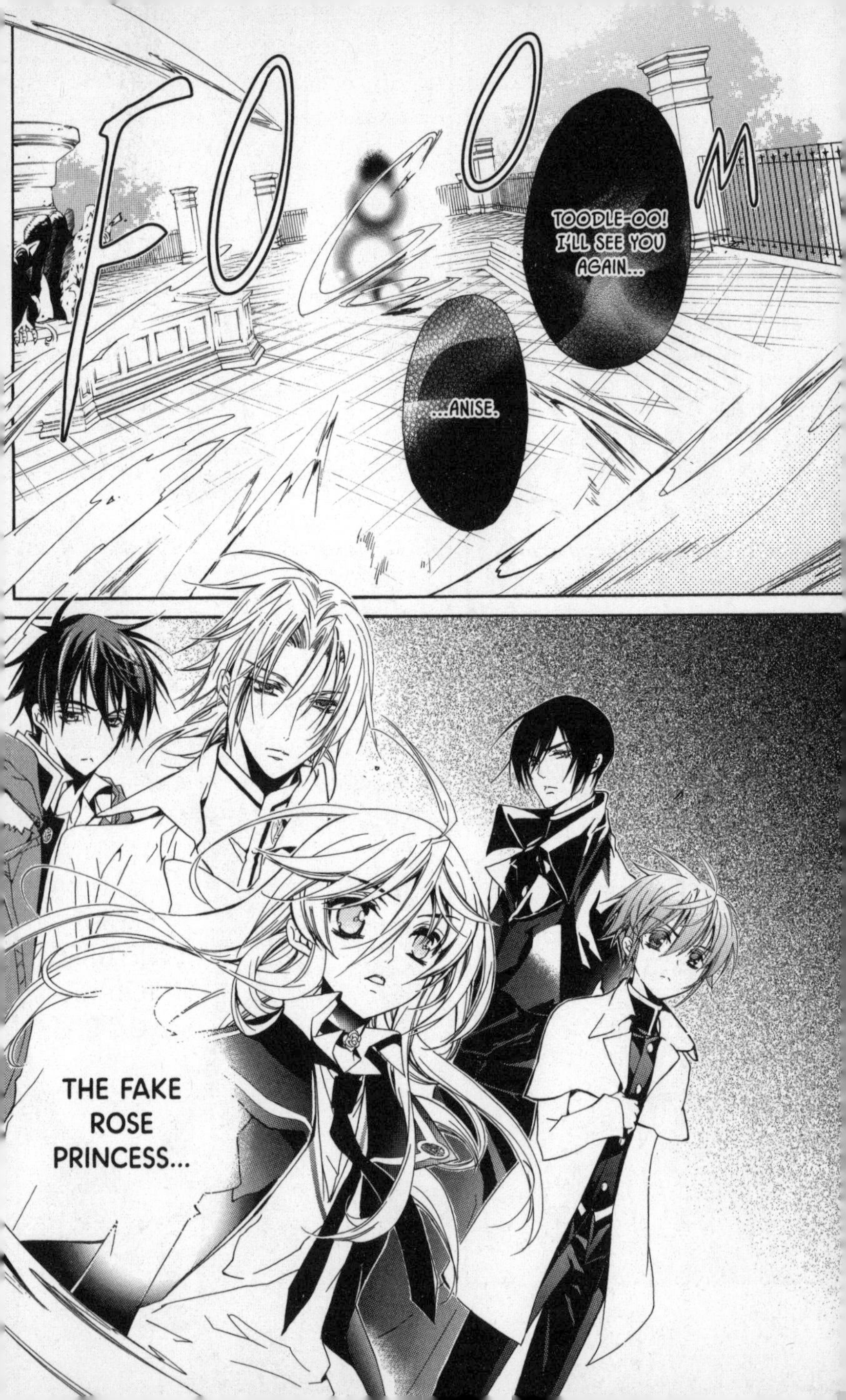
FOOOM
TOODLE-OO! I'LL SEE YOU AGAIN...
...ANISE.
THE FAKE ROSE PRINCESS...

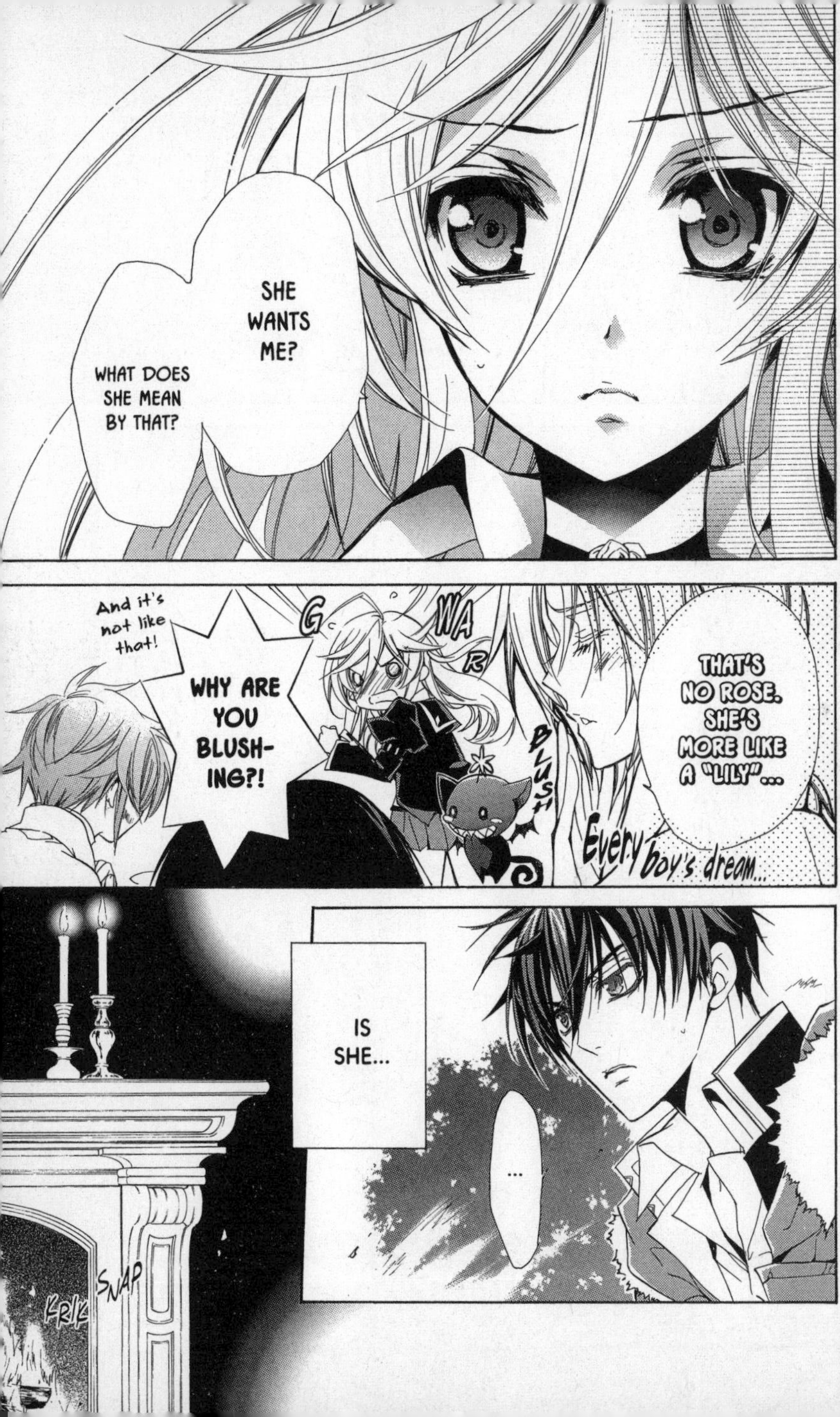
SHE WANTS ME?
WHAT DOES SHE MEAN BY THAT?
THAT'S NO ROSE. SHE'S MORE LIKE A "LILY"...
Every boy's dream...
BLUSH
GWAR
WHY ARE YOU BLUSH-ING?!
And it's not like that!
...
IS SHE...
SNAP
KRIK

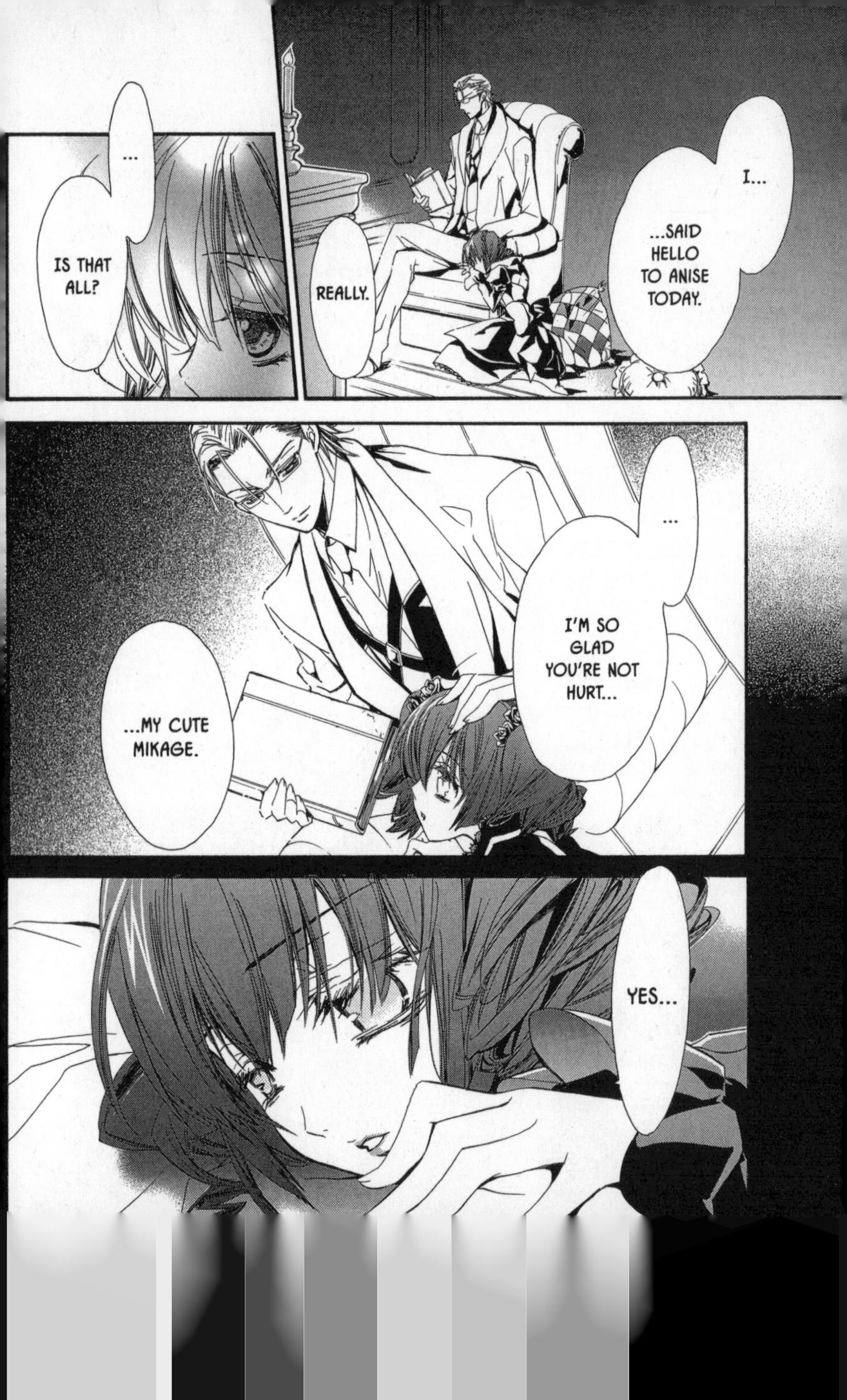
I...
...SAID HELLO TO ANISE TODAY.
REALLY.
...
IS THAT ALL?
...
I'M SO GLAD YOU'RE NOT HURT...
...MY CUTE MIKAGE.
YES...

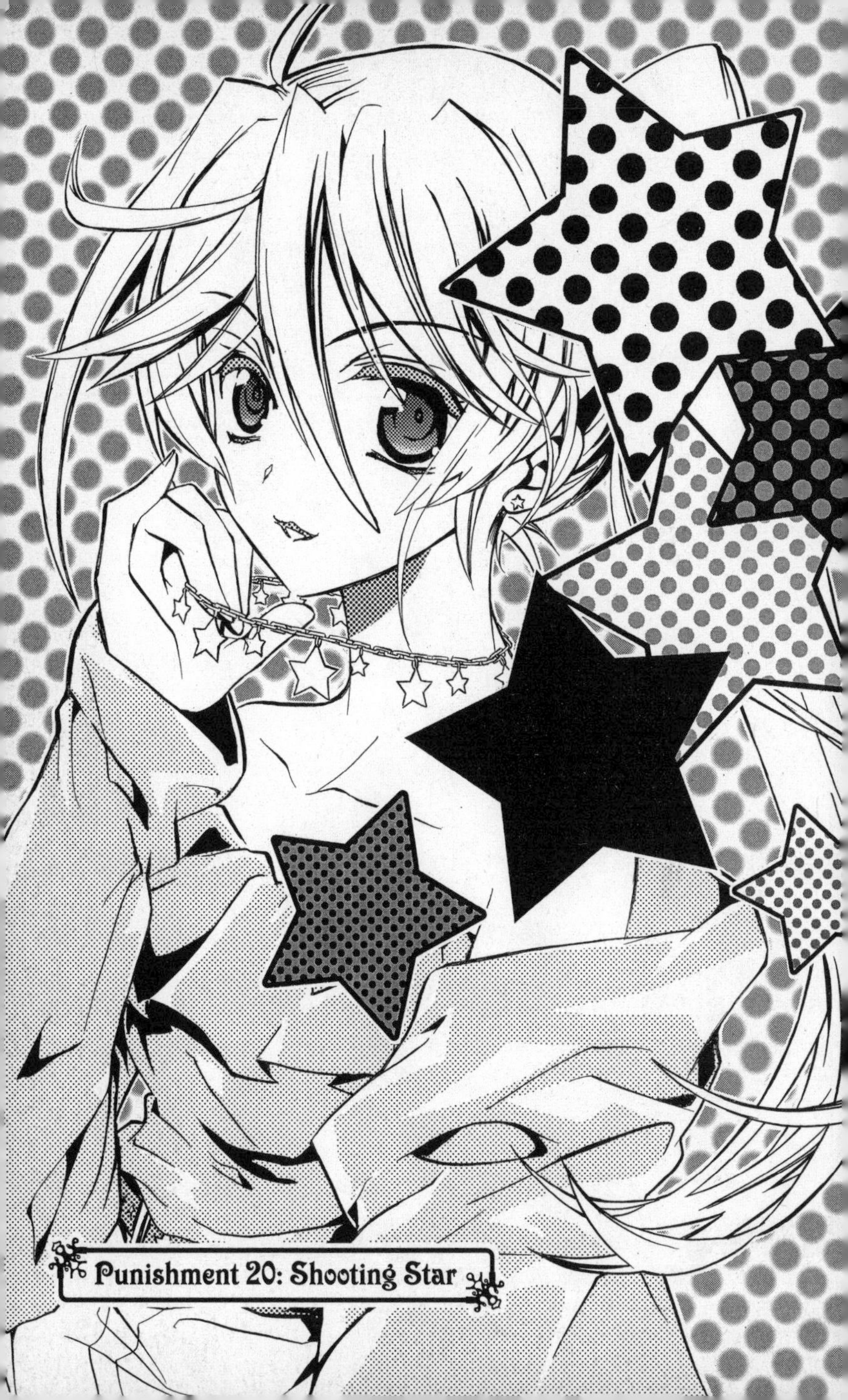
Punishment 20: Shooting Star

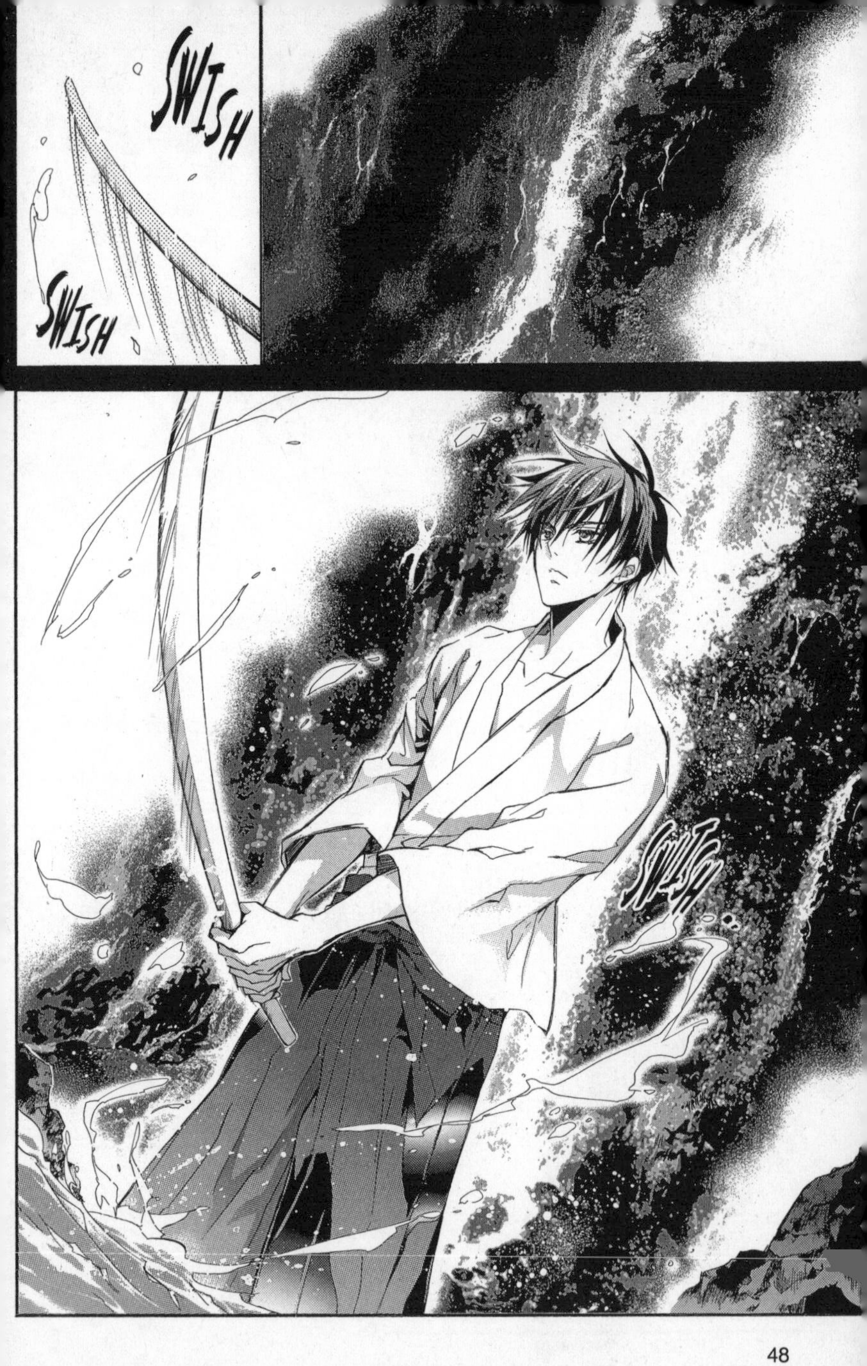
SWISH
SWISH

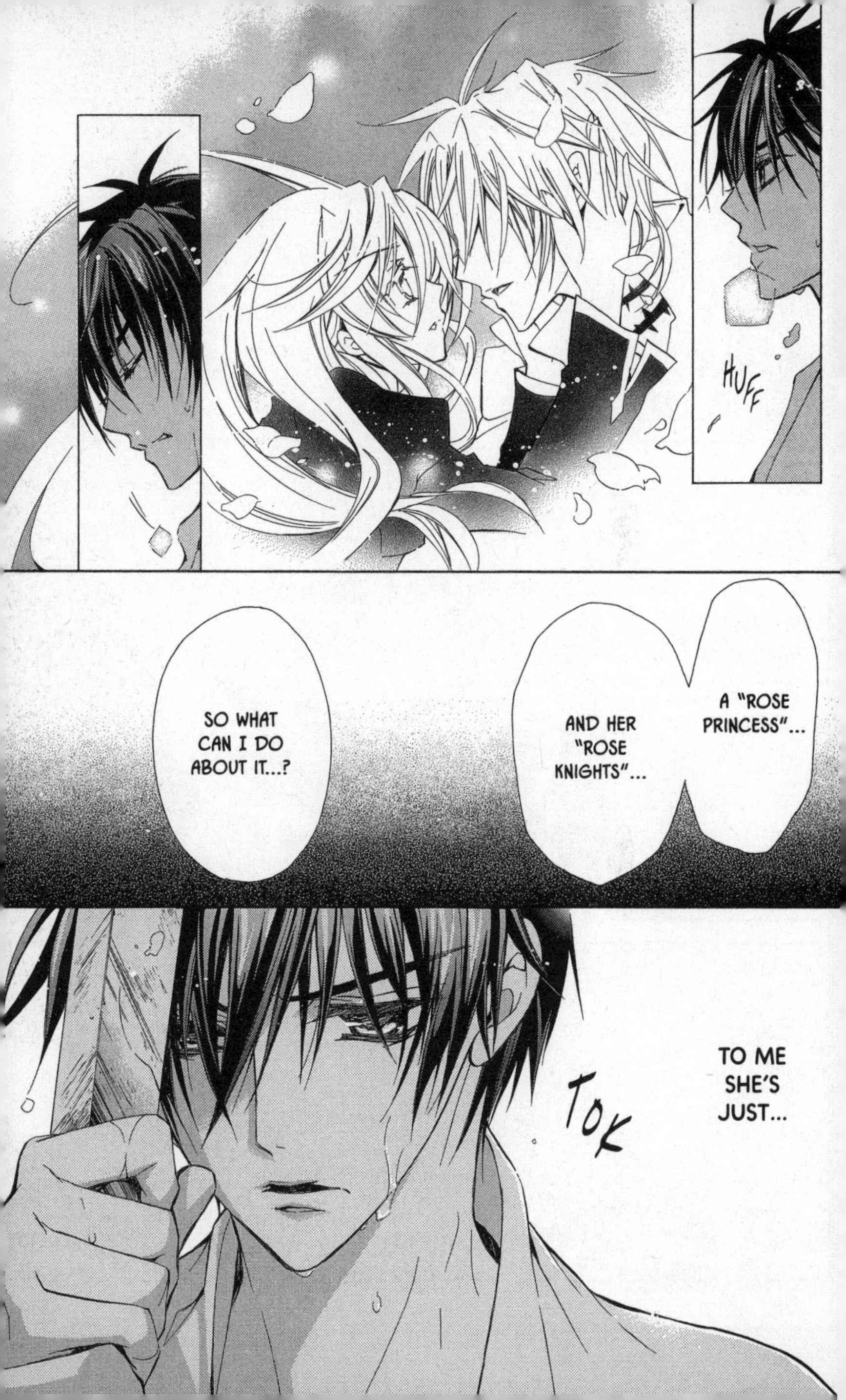
HUFF
A "ROSE PRINCESS"...
AND HER "ROSE KNIGHTS"...
SO WHAT CAN I DO ABOUT IT...?
TO ME SHE'S JUST...
TOK

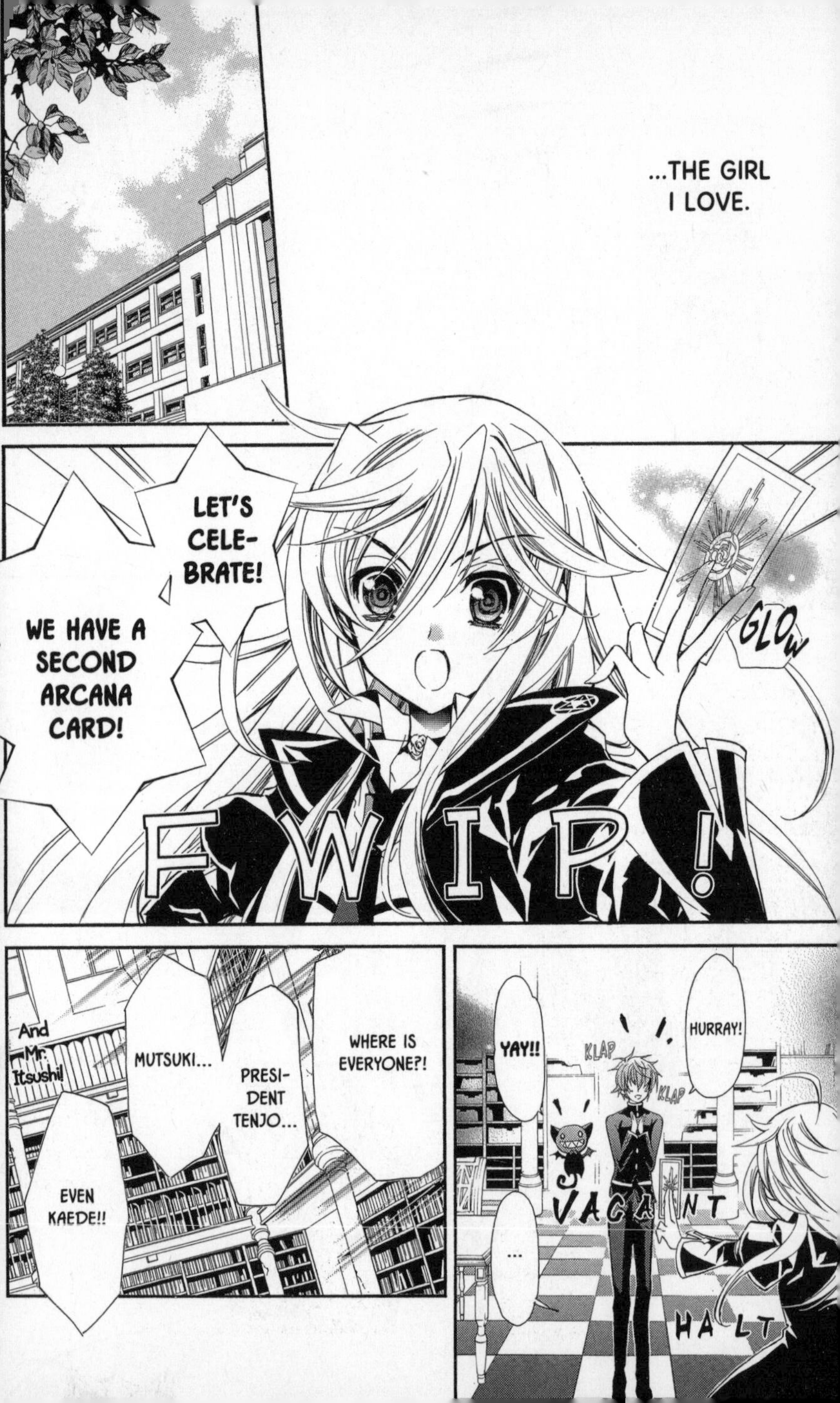
...THE GIRL I LOVE.
LET'S CELEBRATE!
GLOW
WE HAVE A SECOND ARCANA CARD!
FWIP!
HURRAY!
YAY!!
KLAP
KLAP
...
VACANT
HALT
WHERE IS EVERYONE?!
PRESIDENT TENJO...
MUTSUKI...
And Mr. Itsushi!
EVEN KAEDE!!

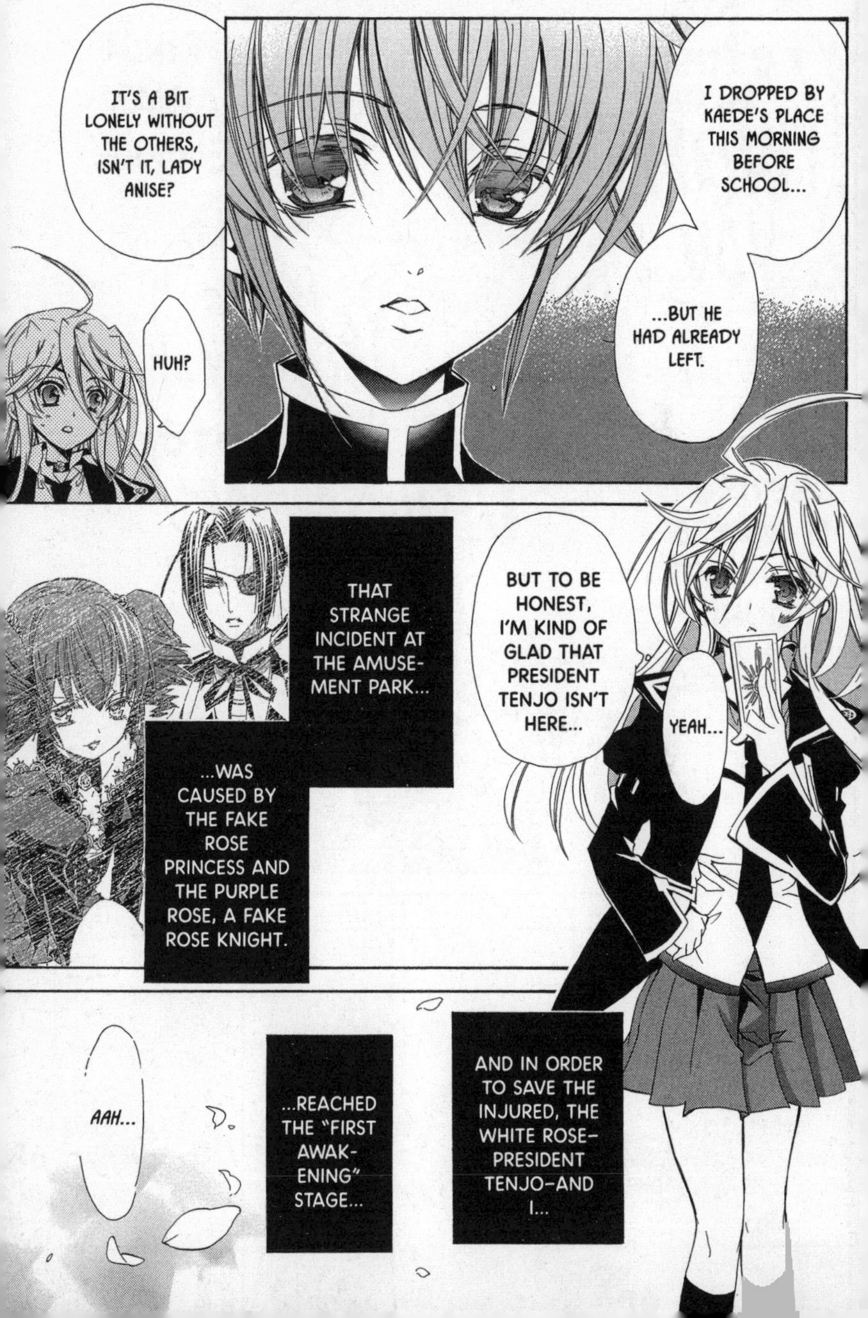
I DROPPED BY KAEDE'S PLACE THIS MORNING BEFORE SCHOOL...
...BUT HE HAD ALREADY LEFT.
IT'S A BIT LONELY WITHOUT THE OTHERS, ISN'T IT, LADY ANISE?
HUH?
BUT TO BE HONEST, I'M KIND OF GLAD THAT PRESIDENT TENJO ISN'T HERE...
YEAH...
THAT STRANGE INCIDENT AT THE AMUSEMENT PARK...
...WAS CAUSED BY THE FAKE ROSE PRINCESS AND THE PURPLE ROSE, A FAKE ROSE KNIGHT.
AND IN ORDER TO SAVE THE INJURED, THE WHITE ROSE–PRESIDENT TENJO–AND I...
...REACHED THE "FIRST AWAKENING" STAGE...
AAH...

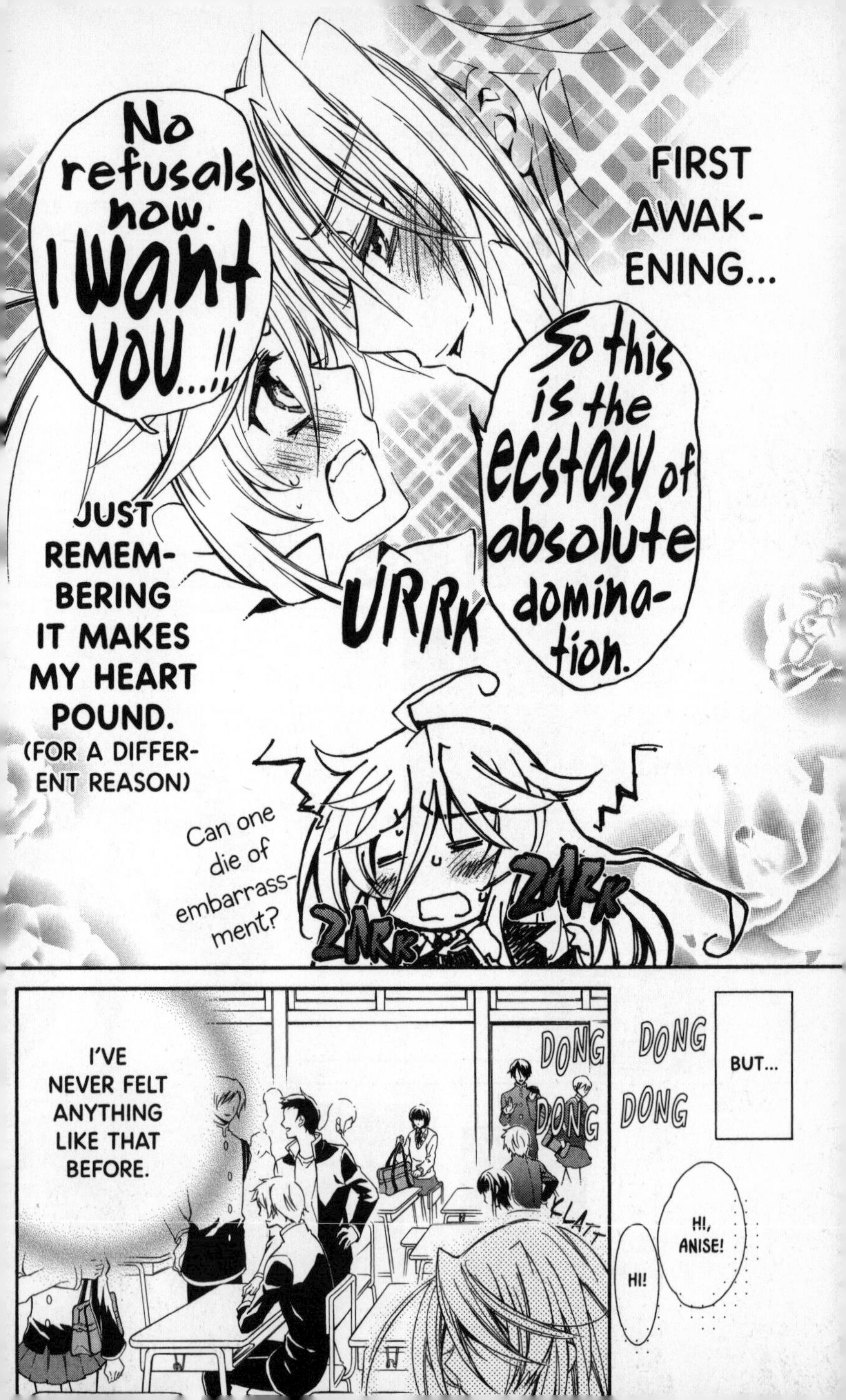
FIRST AWAK-ENING...
No refusals now. I want you...!!
So this is the ecstasy of absolute domina-tion.
URRK
JUST REMEM-BERING IT MAKES MY HEART POUND. (FOR A DIFFER-ENT REASON)
Can one die of embarrass-ment?
ZNRK
ZNRK
BUT...
DONG DONG
DONG DONG
HI, ANISE!
HI!
KLATT
I'VE NEVER FELT ANYTHING LIKE THAT BEFORE.

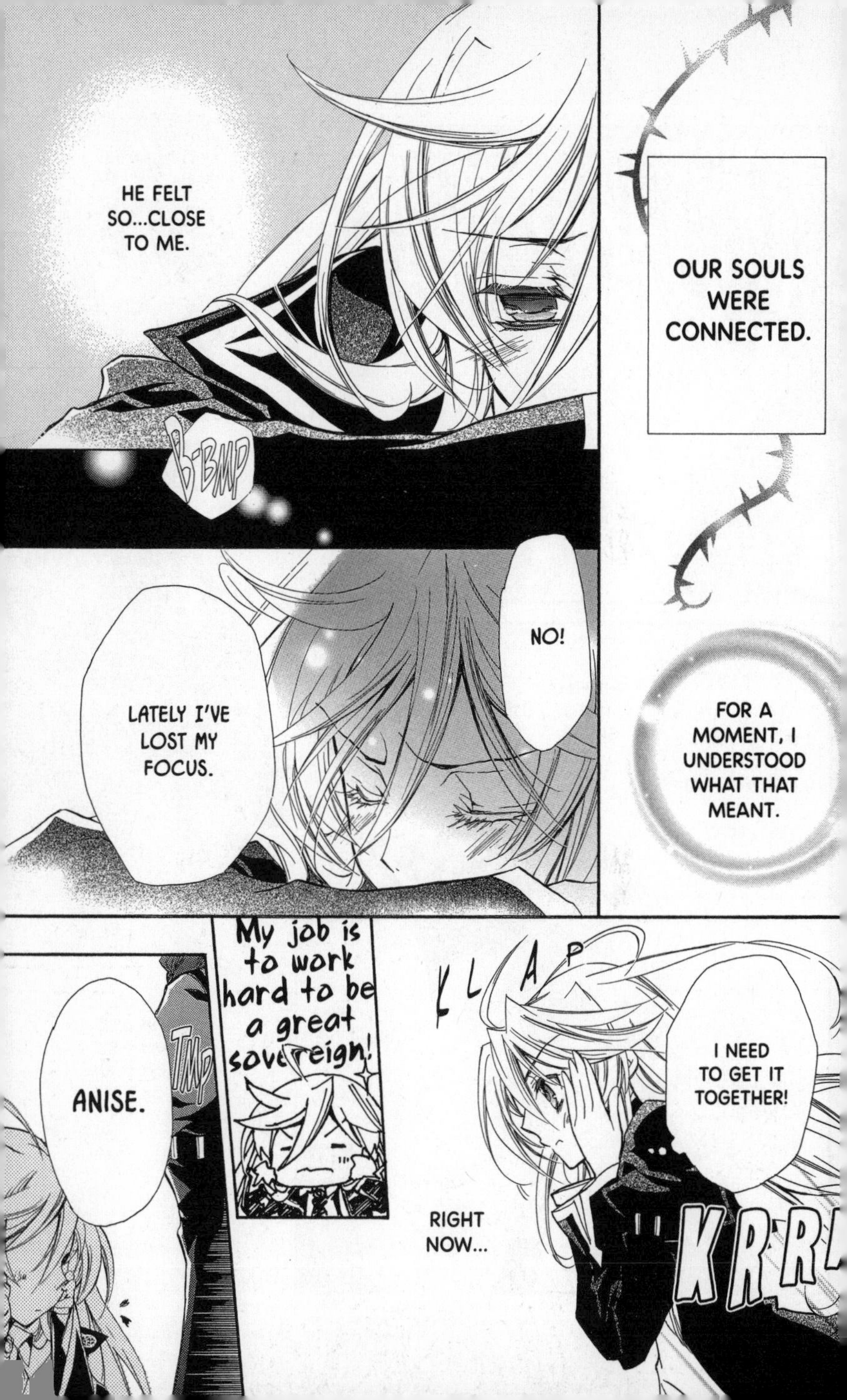
OUR SOULS WERE CONNECTED.
FOR A MOMENT, I UNDERSTOOD WHAT THAT MEANT.
HE FELT SO...CLOSE TO ME.
B-BMP
NO!
LATELY I'VE LOST MY FOCUS.
KLAP
I NEED TO GET IT TOGETHER!
KRRL
RIGHT NOW...
My job is to work hard to be a great sovereign!
TMP
ANISE.

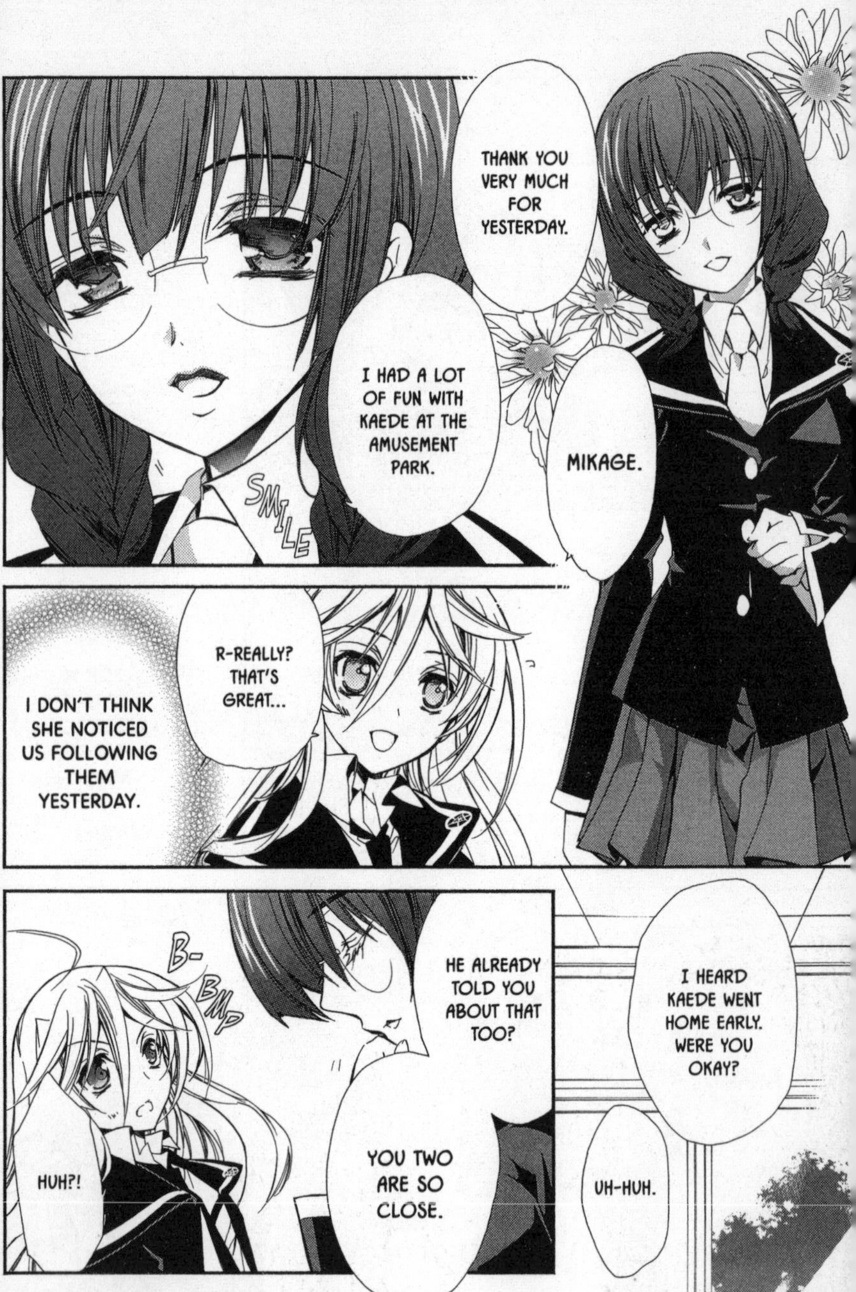
MIKAGE.
THANK YOU VERY MUCH FOR YESTERDAY.
I HAD A LOT OF FUN WITH KAEDE AT THE AMUSEMENT PARK.
SMILE
R-REALLY? THAT'S GREAT...
I DON'T THINK SHE NOTICED US FOLLOWING THEM YESTERDAY.
I HEARD KAEDE WENT HOME EARLY. WERE YOU OKAY?
UH-HUH.
HE ALREADY TOLD YOU ABOUT THAT TOO?
YOU TWO ARE SO CLOSE.
B-BMP
HUH?!

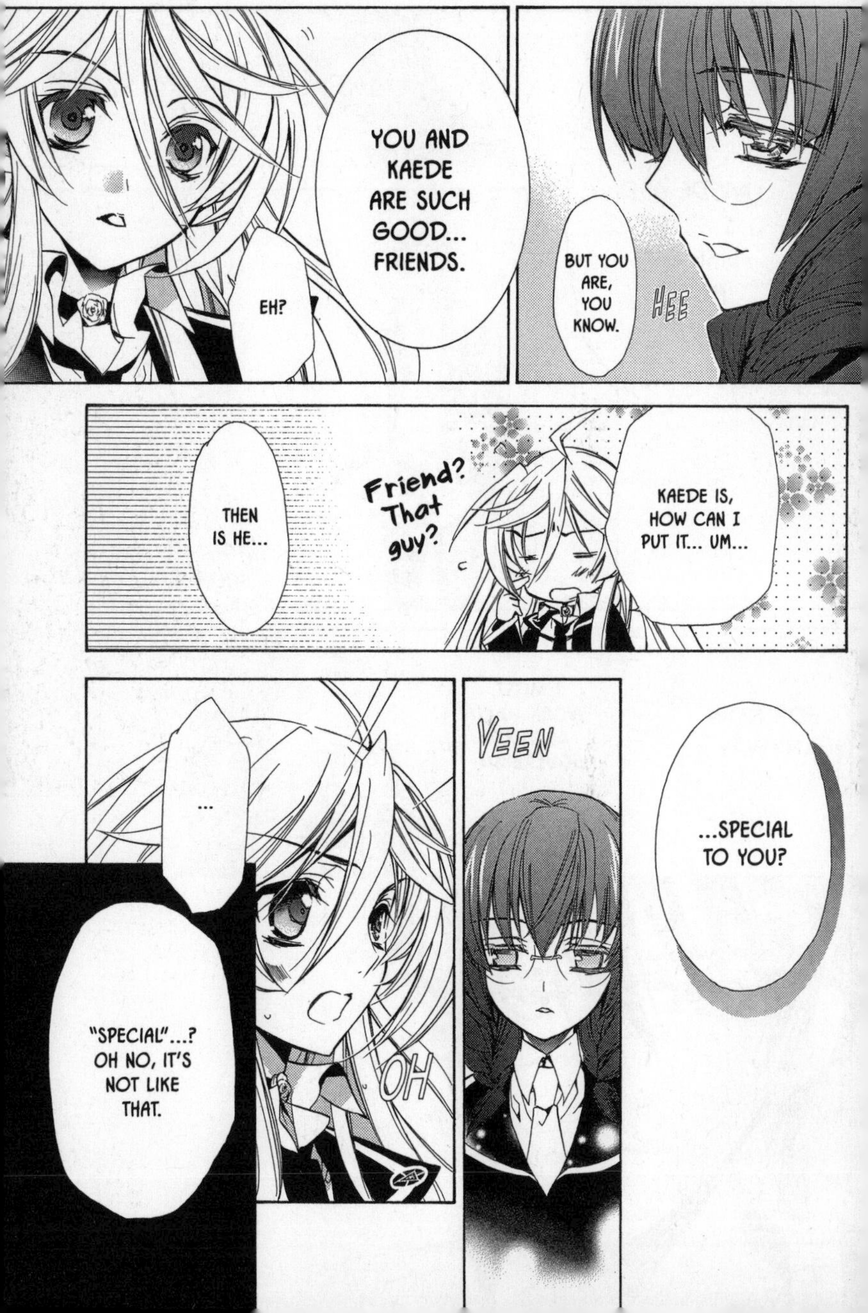
BUT YOU ARE, YOU KNOW.
HEE
YOU AND KAEDE ARE SUCH GOOD... FRIENDS.
EH?
KAEDE IS, HOW CAN I PUT IT... UM...
Friend? That guy?
THEN IS HE...
...SPECIAL TO YOU?
VEEN
...
OH
"SPECIAL"...? OH NO, IT'S NOT LIKE THAT.

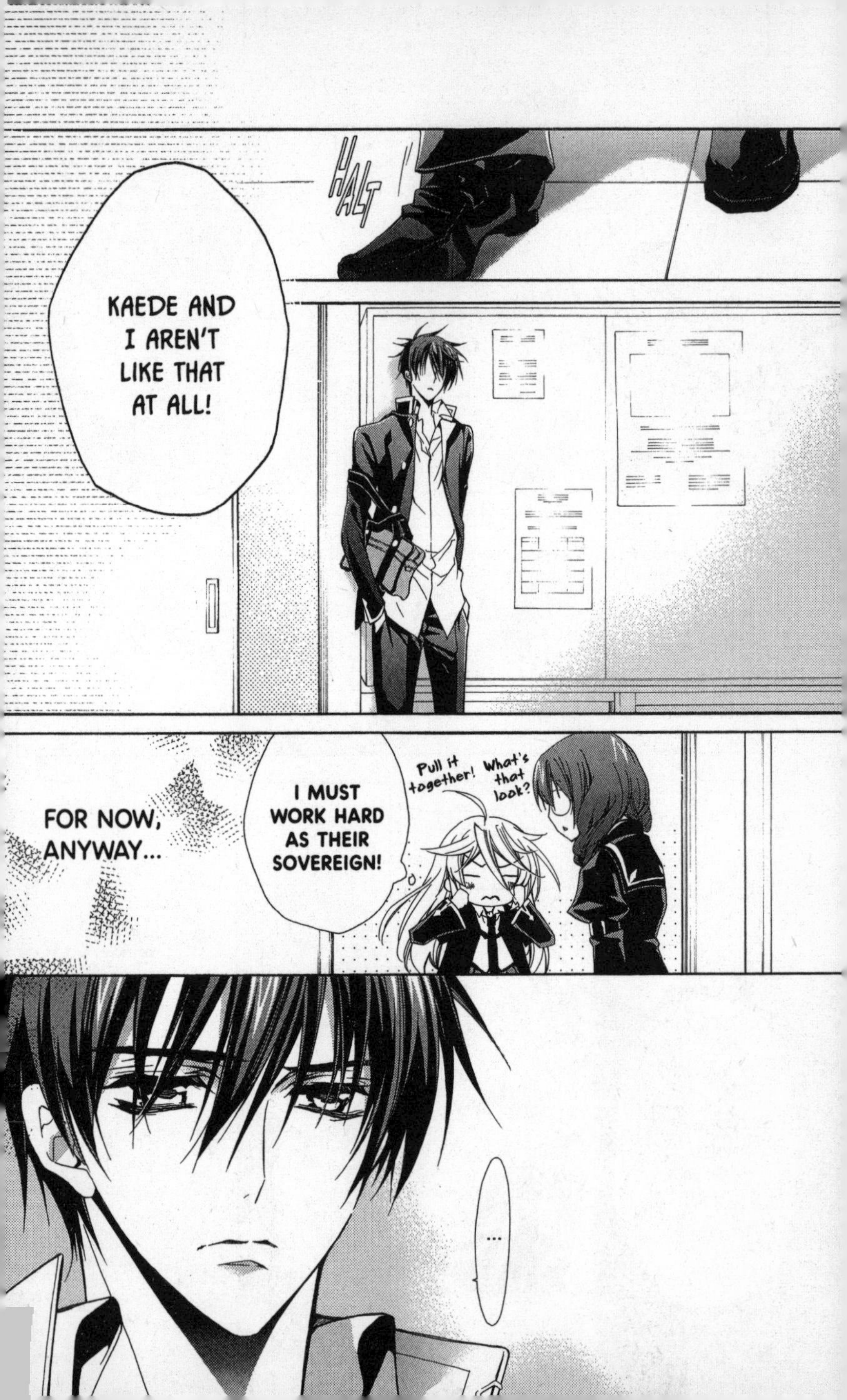
HALT
KAEDE AND I AREN'T LIKE THAT AT ALL!
What's that look?
Pull it together!
I MUST WORK HARD AS THEIR SOVEREIGN!
FOR NOW, ANYWAY...
...

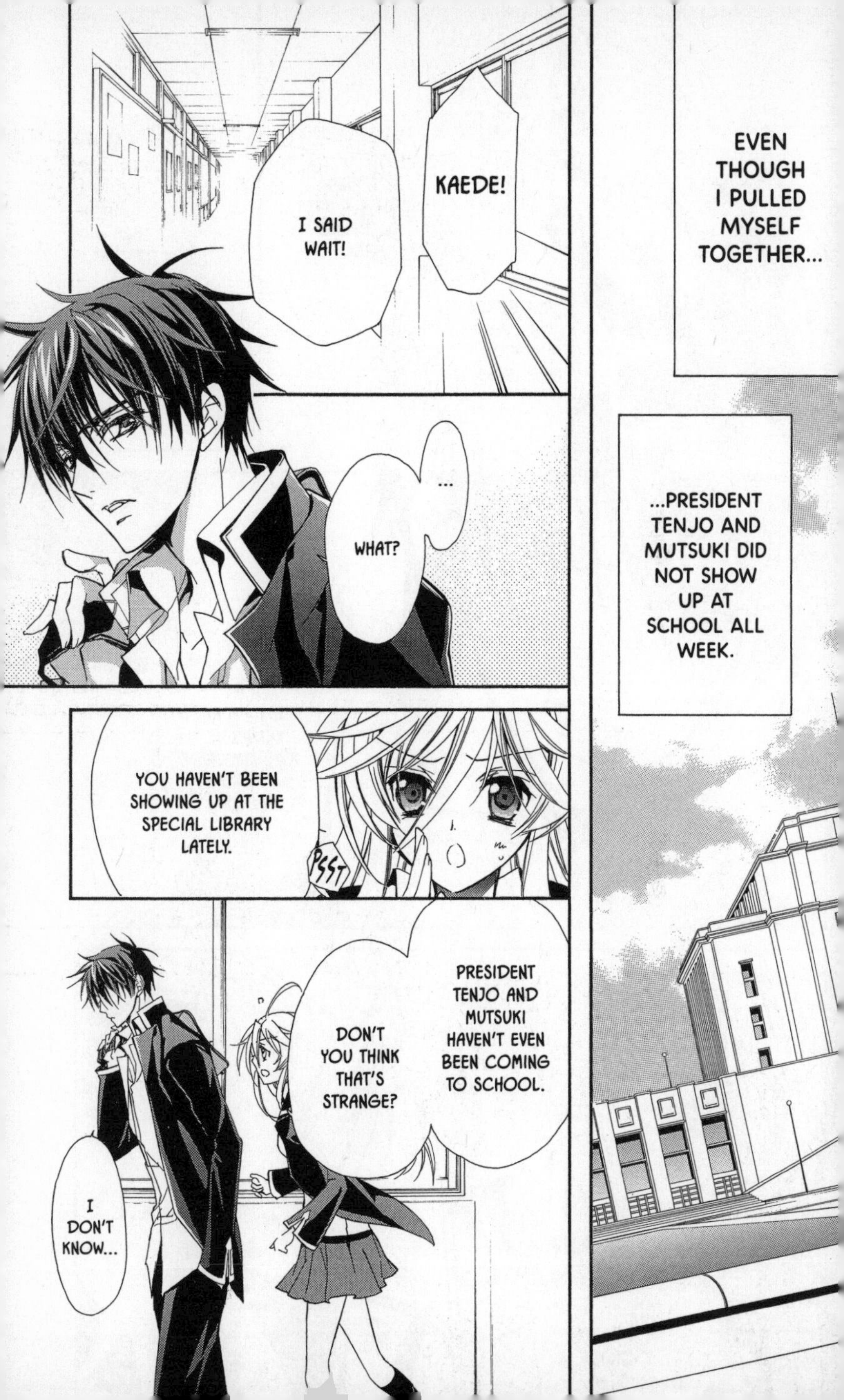
EVEN THOUGH I PULLED MYSELF TOGETHER...
...PRESIDENT TENJO AND MUTSUKI DID NOT SHOW UP AT SCHOOL ALL WEEK.
KAEDE!
I SAID WAIT!
...
WHAT?
PSST
YOU HAVEN'T BEEN SHOWING UP AT THE SPECIAL LIBRARY LATELY.
PRESIDENT TENJO AND MUTSUKI HAVEN'T EVEN BEEN COMING TO SCHOOL.
DON'T YOU THINK THAT'S STRANGE?
I DON'T KNOW...

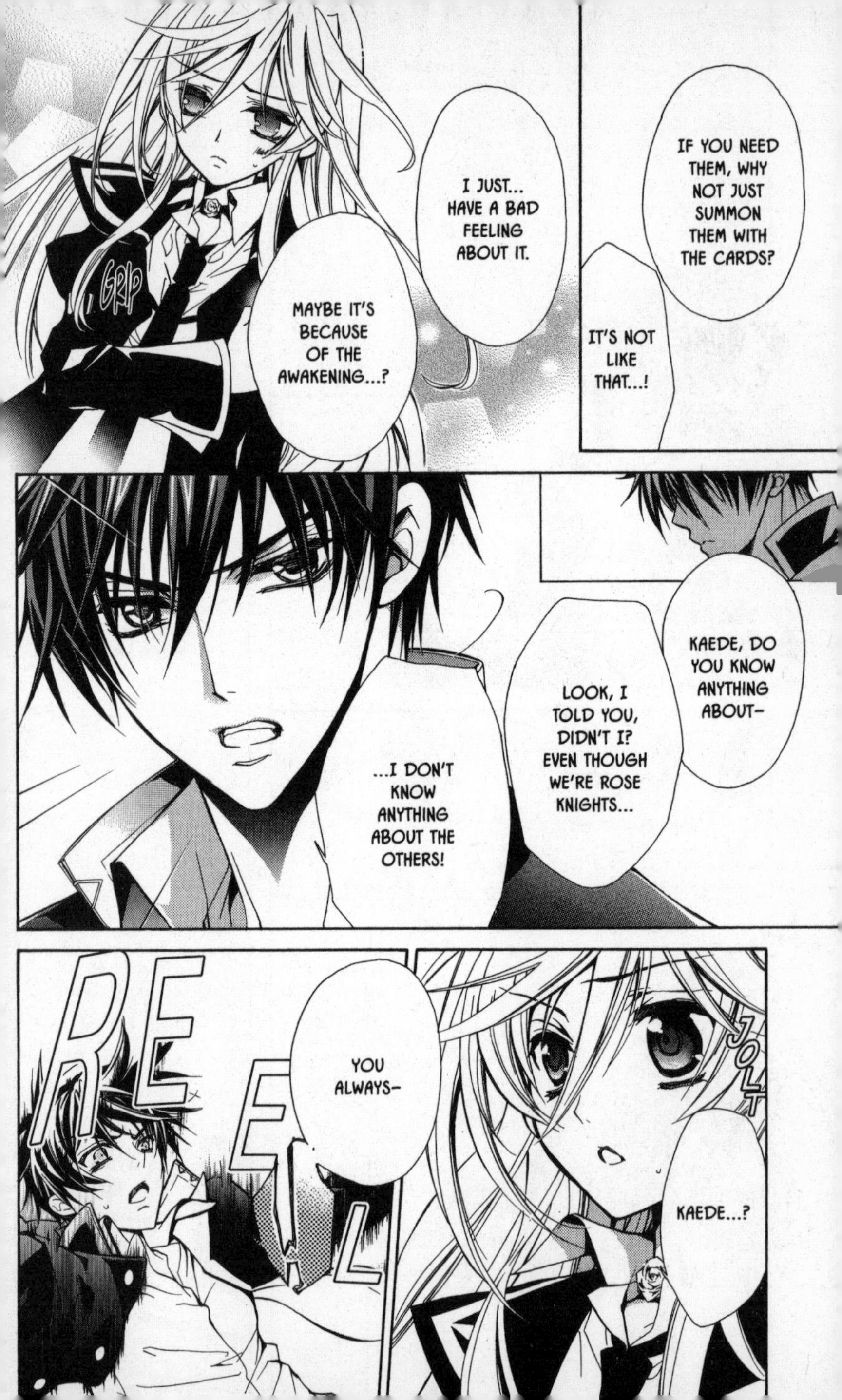
IF YOU NEED THEM, WHY NOT JUST SUMMON THEM WITH THE CARDS?
IT'S NOT LIKE THAT...!
I JUST... HAVE A BAD FEELING ABOUT IT.
GRIP
MAYBE IT'S BECAUSE OF THE AWAKENING...?
KAEDE, DO YOU KNOW ANYTHING ABOUT-
LOOK, I TOLD YOU, DIDN'T I? EVEN THOUGH WE'RE ROSE KNIGHTS...
...I DON'T KNOW ANYTHING ABOUT THE OTHERS!
YOU ALWAYS-
JOLT
KAEDE...?
REEL

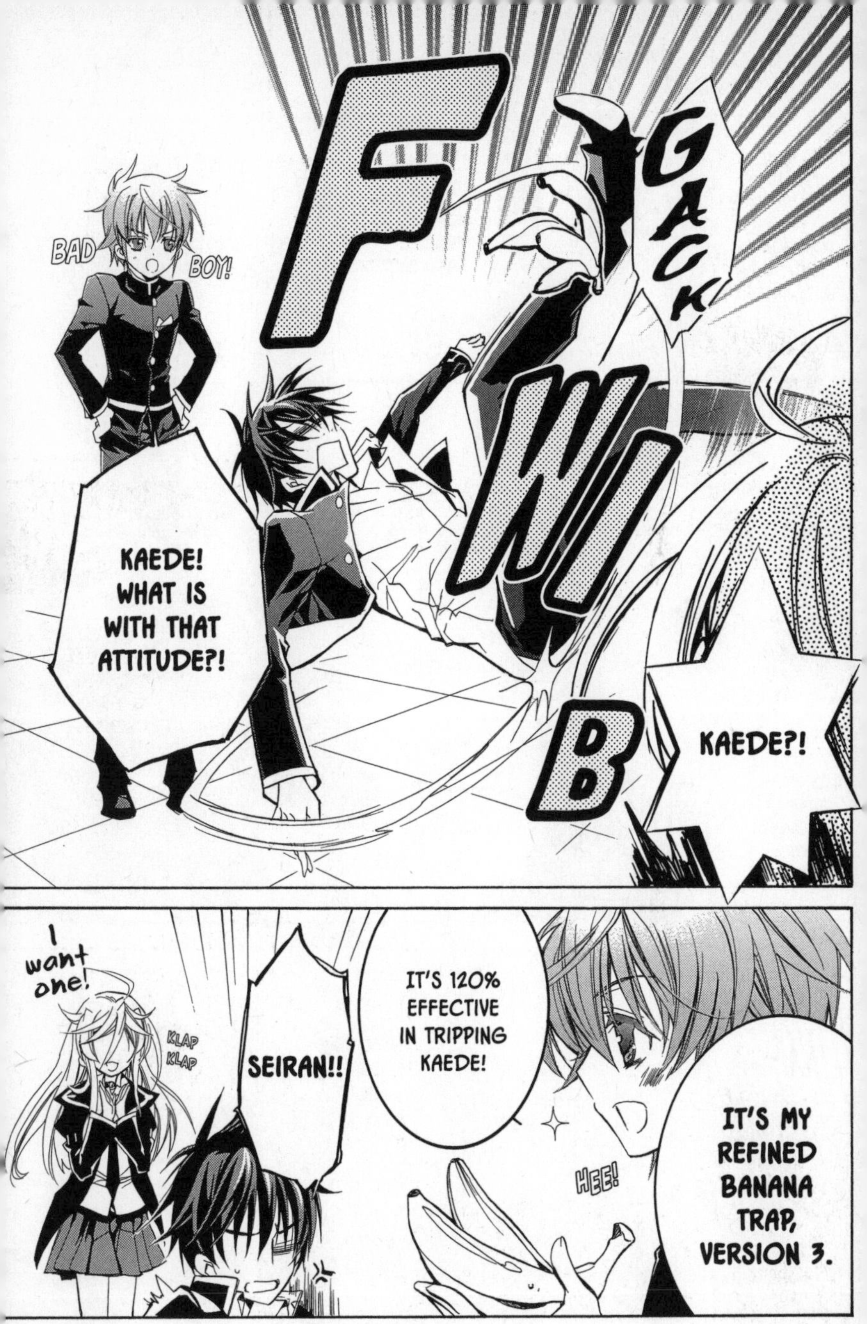
GACK
FWIBB
KAEDE?!
BAD BOY!
KAEDE! WHAT IS WITH THAT ATTITUDE?!
IT'S MY REFINED BANANA TRAP, VERSION 3.
HEE!
IT'S 120% EFFECTIVE IN TRIPPING KAEDE!
SEIRAN!!
KLAP KLAP
I want one!

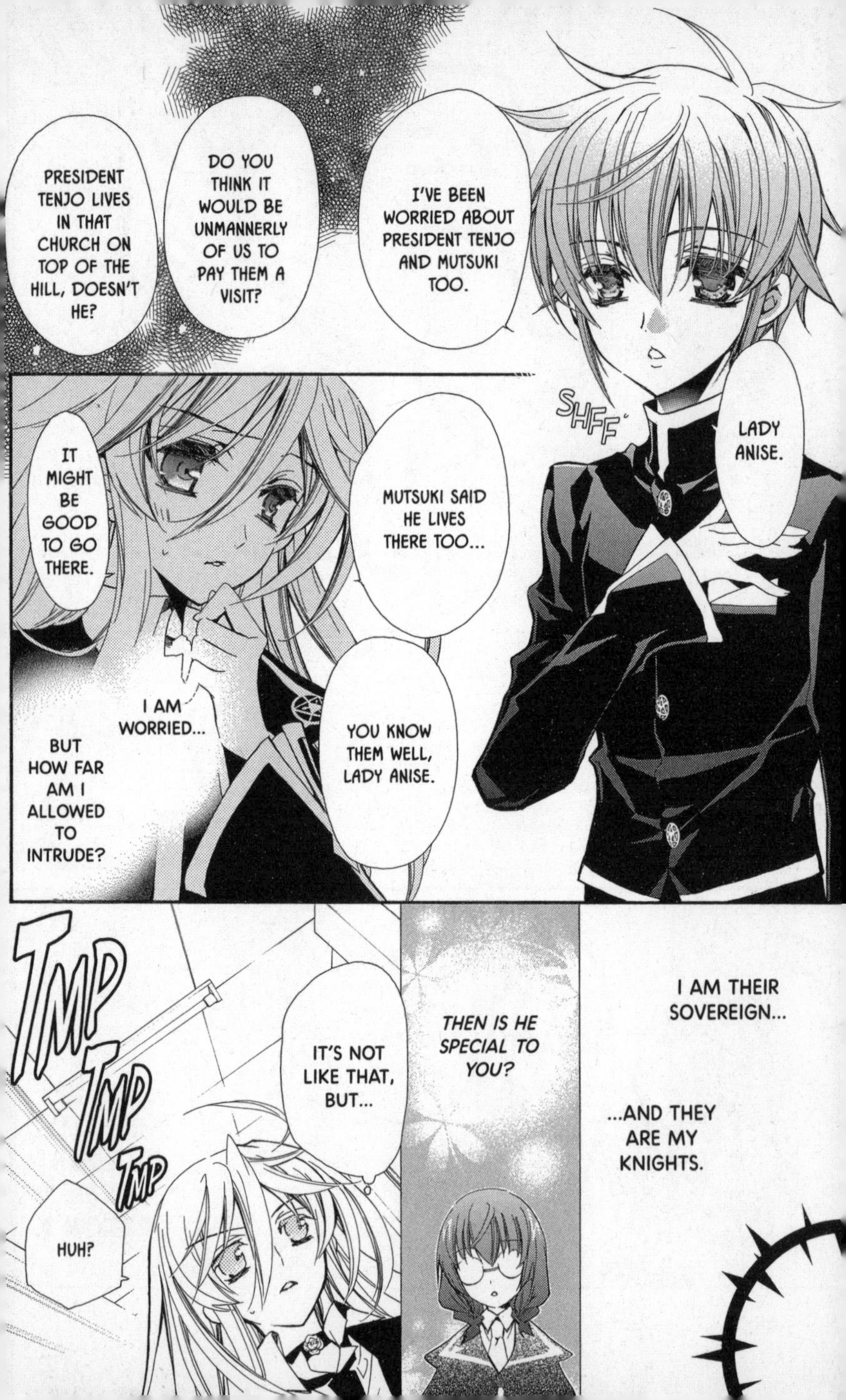
SHFF
LADY ANISE.
I'VE BEEN WORRIED ABOUT PRESIDENT TENJO AND MUTSUKI TOO.
DO YOU THINK IT WOULD BE UNMANNERLY OF US TO PAY THEM A VISIT?
PRESIDENT TENJO LIVES IN THAT CHURCH ON TOP OF THE HILL, DOESN'T HE?
MUTSUKI SAID HE LIVES THERE TOO...
IT MIGHT BE GOOD TO GO THERE.
YOU KNOW THEM WELL, LADY ANISE.
I AM WORRIED...
BUT HOW FAR AM I ALLOWED TO INTRUDE?
I AM THEIR SOVEREIGN...
...AND THEY ARE MY KNIGHTS.
THEN IS HE SPECIAL TO YOU?
IT'S NOT LIKE THAT, BUT...
TMP
TMP
TMP
HUH?

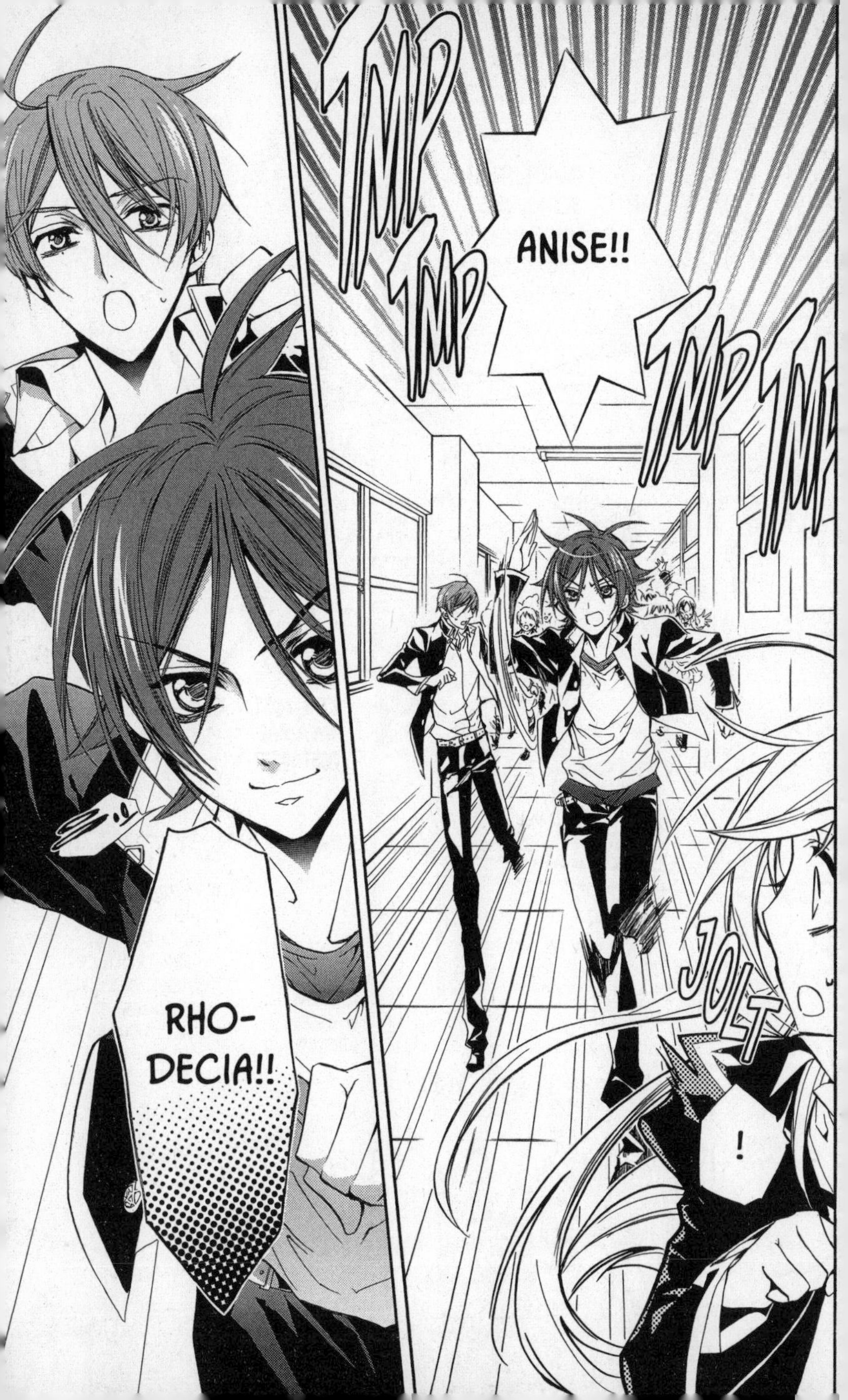

TMP TM
ANISE!!
TMP TMP
JOLT
!
RHO-
DECIA!!

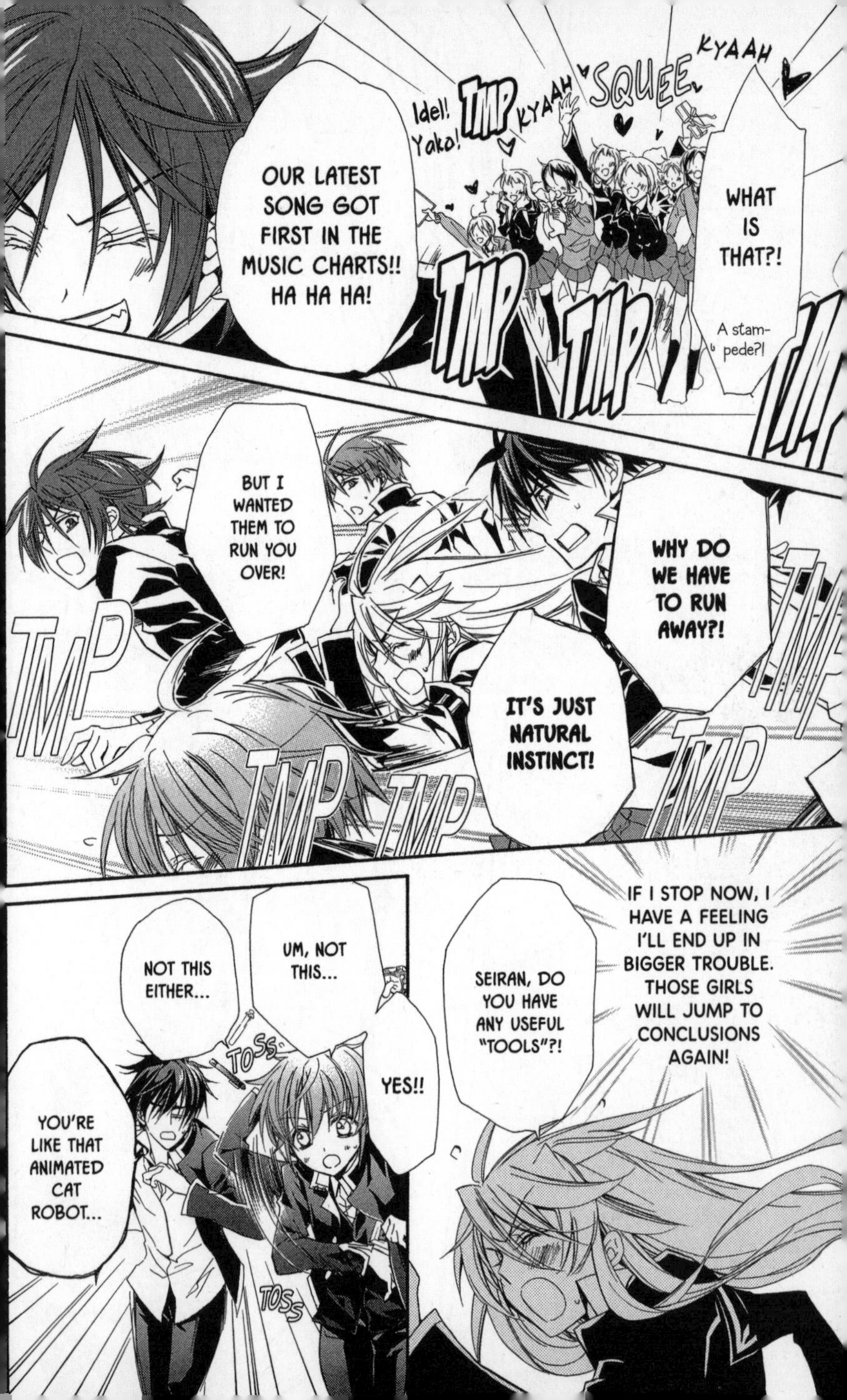
KYAAH
WHAT IS THAT?!
A stampede?!
SQUEE
KYAAH
TMP
Idol! Yako!
TMP
TMP
OUR LATEST SONG GOT FIRST IN THE MUSIC CHARTS!! HA HA HA!
TMP
TMP
WHY DO WE HAVE TO RUN AWAY?!
IT'S JUST NATURAL INSTINCT!
TMP
BUT I WANTED THEM TO RUN YOU OVER!
TMP
TMP
TMP
IF I STOP NOW, I HAVE A FEELING I'LL END UP IN BIGGER TROUBLE. THOSE GIRLS WILL JUMP TO CONCLUSIONS AGAIN!
SEIRAN, DO YOU HAVE ANY USEFUL "TOOLS"?!
YES!!
UM, NOT THIS...
NOT THIS EITHER...
TOSS
TOSS
YOU'RE LIKE THAT ANIMATED CAT ROBOT...

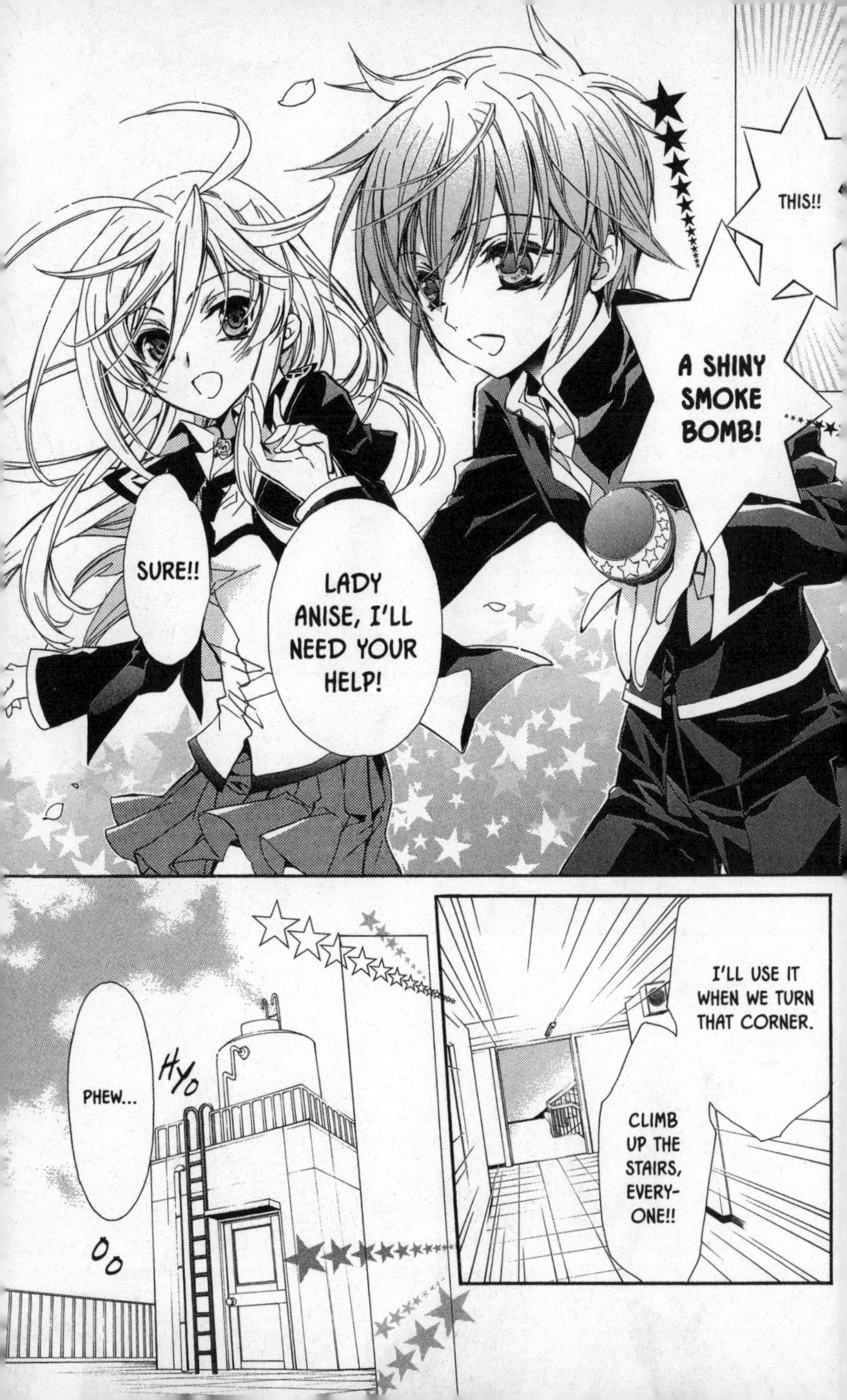
THIS!!
A SHINY SMOKE BOMB!
LADY ANISE, I'LL NEED YOUR HELP!
SURE!!
I'LL USE IT WHEN WE TURN THAT CORNER.
CLIMB UP THE STAIRS, EVERY-ONE!!
HYO
PHEW...

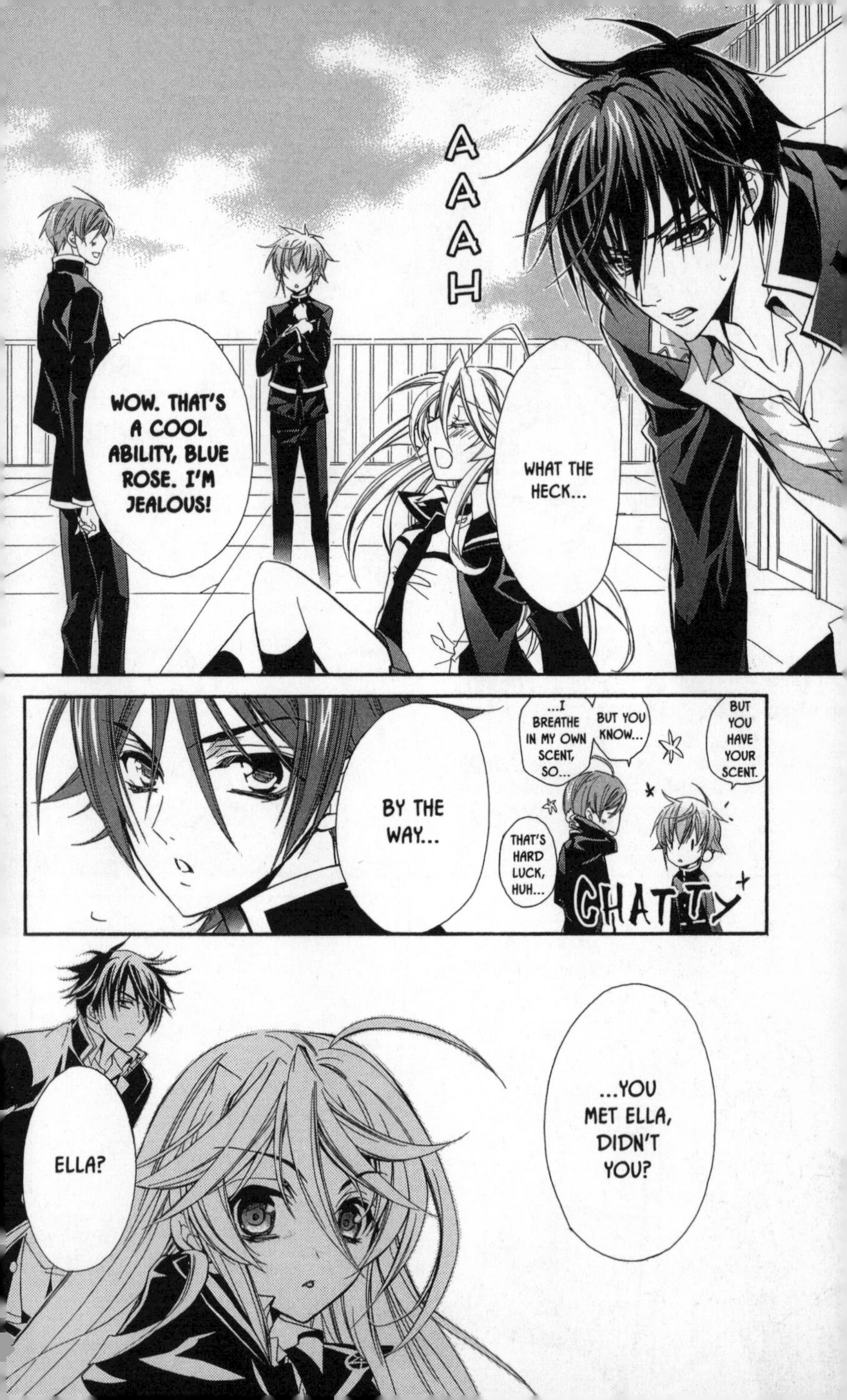
AAAH
WHAT THE HECK...
WOW. THAT'S A COOL ABILITY, BLUE ROSE. I'M JEALOUS!
BUT YOU HAVE YOUR SCENT.
BUT YOU KNOW...
...I BREATHE IN MY OWN SCENT, SO...
THAT'S HARD LUCK, HUH...
CHATTY
BY THE WAY...
...YOU MET ELLA, DIDN'T YOU?
ELLA?

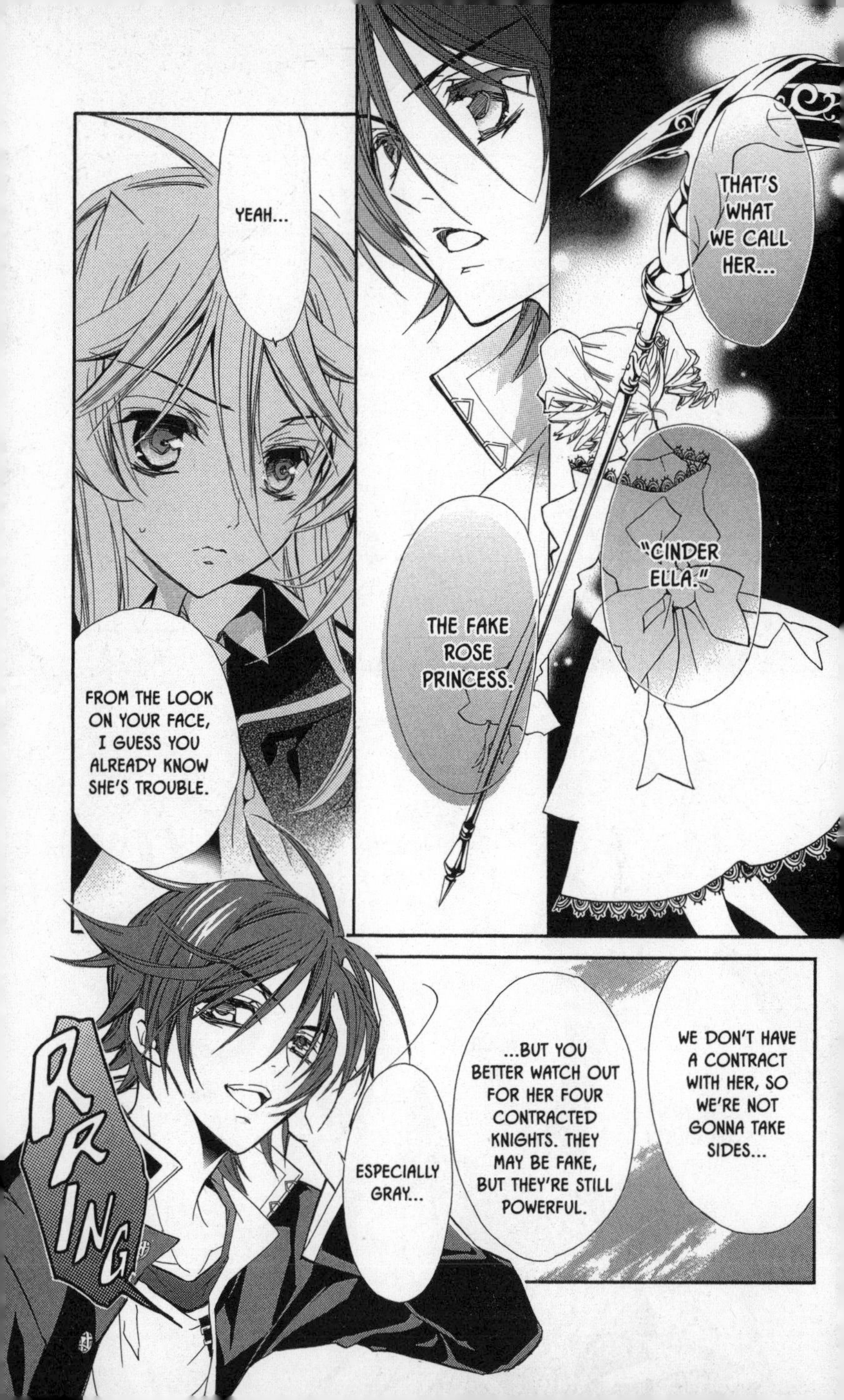
THAT'S WHAT WE CALL HER...
"CINDER ELLA."
THE FAKE ROSE PRINCESS.
YEAH...
FROM THE LOOK ON YOUR FACE, I GUESS YOU ALREADY KNOW SHE'S TROUBLE.
WE DON'T HAVE A CONTRACT WITH HER, SO WE'RE NOT GONNA TAKE SIDES...
...BUT YOU BETTER WATCH OUT FOR HER FOUR CONTRACTED KNIGHTS. THEY MAY BE FAKE, BUT THEY'RE STILL POWERFUL.
ESPECIALLY GRAY...
RRING

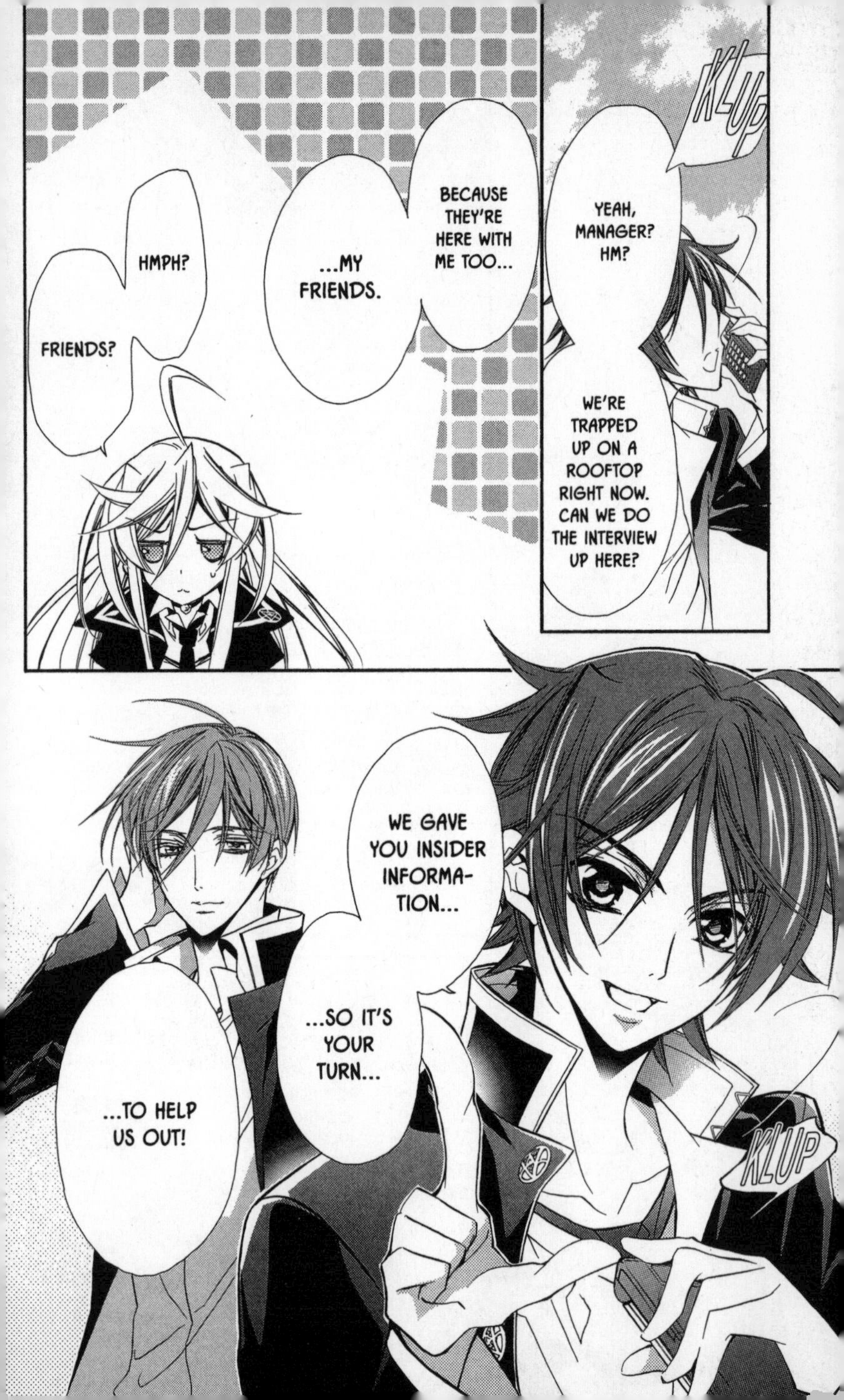
KLUP
YEAH, MANAGER? HM?
WE'RE TRAPPED UP ON A ROOFTOP RIGHT NOW. CAN WE DO THE INTERVIEW UP HERE?
BECAUSE THEY'RE HERE WITH ME TOO...
...MY FRIENDS.
HMPH?
FRIENDS?
WE GAVE YOU INSIDER INFORMATION...
...SO IT'S YOUR TURN...
...TO HELP US OUT!
KLUP

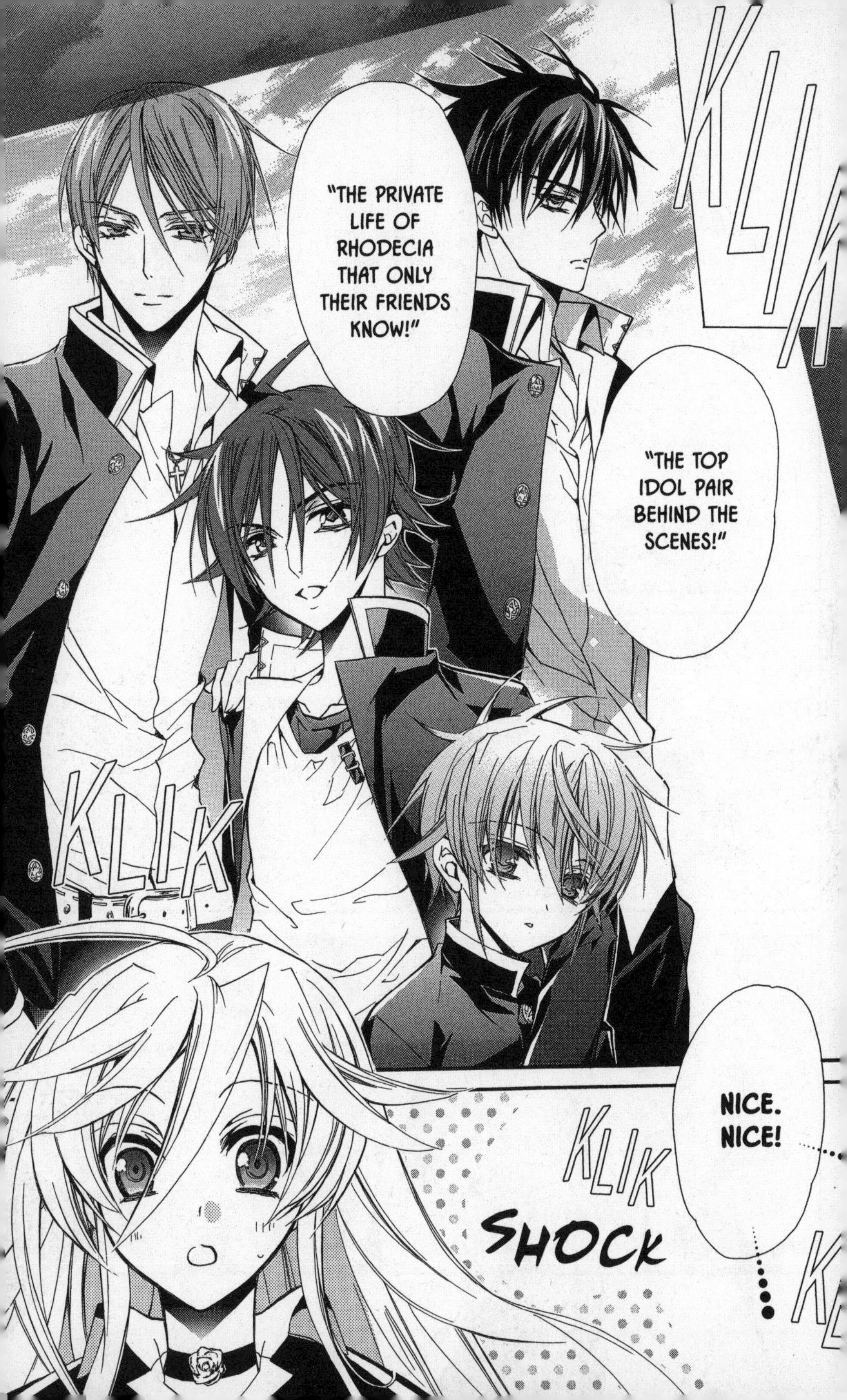
KLIK
"THE PRIVATE LIFE OF RHODECIA THAT ONLY THEIR FRIENDS KNOW!"
"THE TOP IDOL PAIR BEHIND THE SCENES!"
KLIK
NICE. NICE!
KLIK
SHOCK

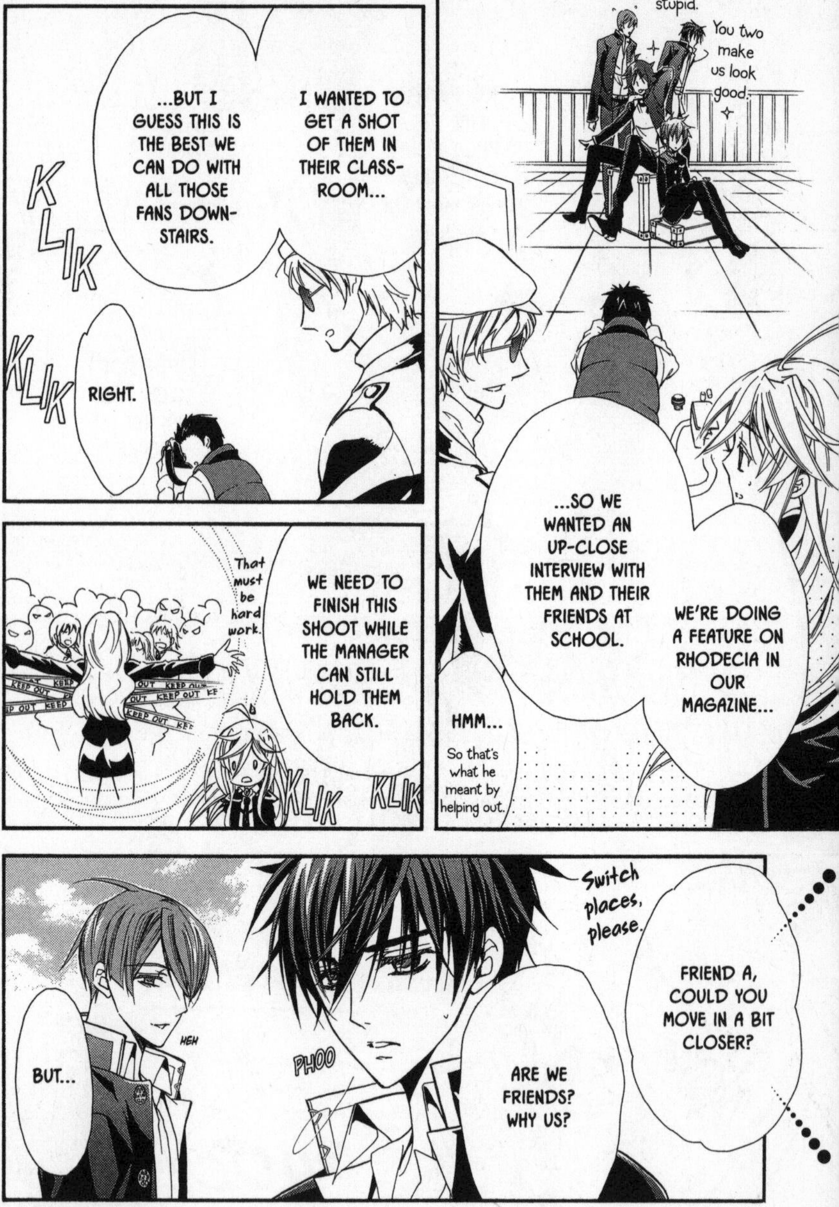
How stupid.
You two make us look good.
WE'RE DOING A FEATURE ON RHODECIA IN OUR MAGAZINE...
...SO WE WANTED AN UP-CLOSE INTERVIEW WITH THEM AND THEIR FRIENDS AT SCHOOL.
HMM...
So that's what he meant by helping out.
I WANTED TO GET A SHOT OF THEM IN THEIR CLASSROOM...
...BUT I GUESS THIS IS THE BEST WE CAN DO WITH ALL THOSE FANS DOWN-STAIRS.
KLIK
KLIK
RIGHT.
WE NEED TO FINISH THIS SHOOT WHILE THE MANAGER CAN STILL HOLD THEM BACK.
That must be hard work.
KEEP OUT
KLIK
KLIK
FRIEND A, COULD YOU MOVE IN A BIT CLOSER?
Switch places, please.
ARE WE FRIENDS? WHY US?
PHOO
HEH
BUT...

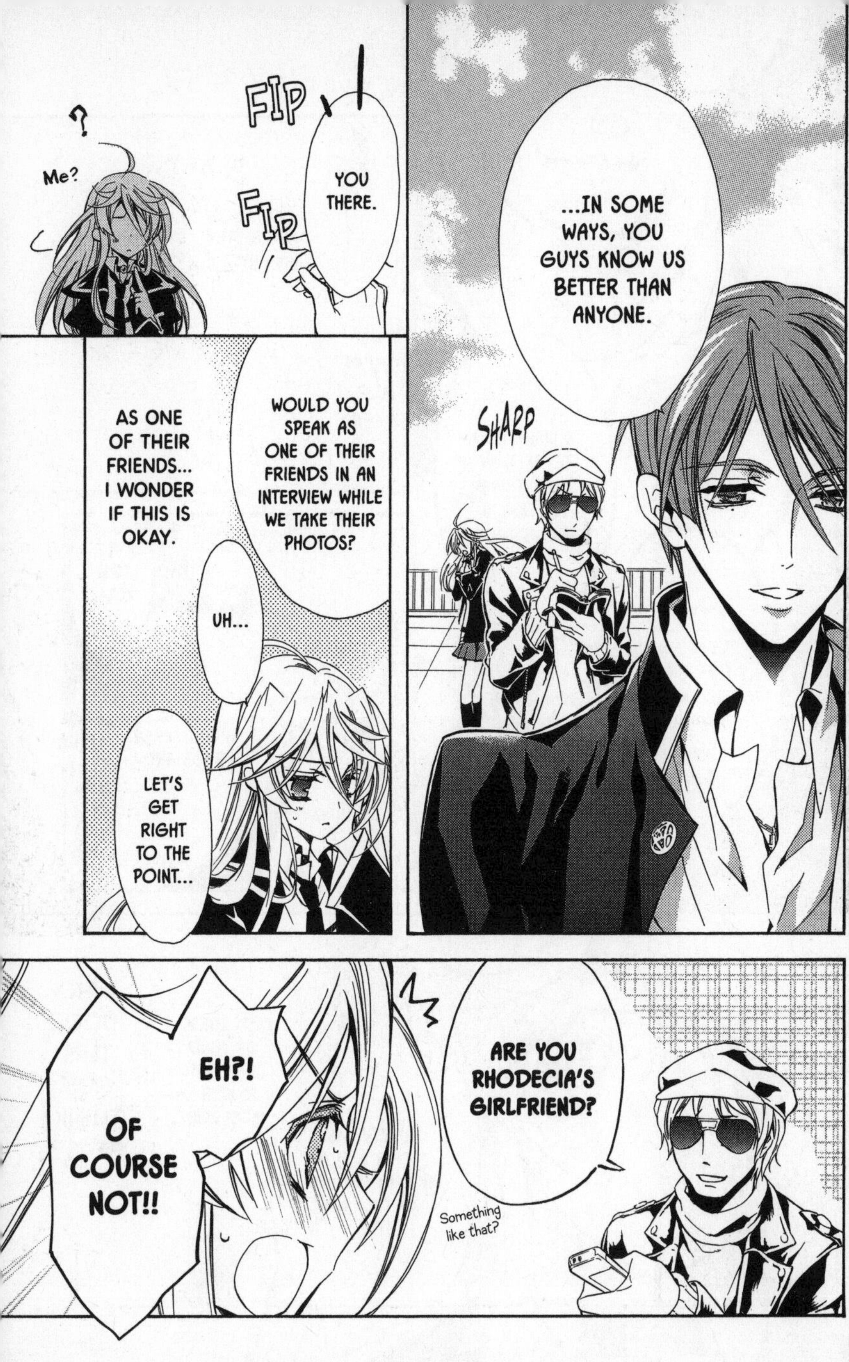
...IN SOME WAYS, YOU GUYS KNOW US BETTER THAN ANYONE.
SHARP
FIP
YOU THERE.
FIP
Me?
WOULD YOU SPEAK AS ONE OF THEIR FRIENDS IN AN INTERVIEW WHILE WE TAKE THEIR PHOTOS?
AS ONE OF THEIR FRIENDS... I WONDER IF THIS IS OKAY.
UH...
LET'S GET RIGHT TO THE POINT...
ARE YOU RHODECIA'S GIRLFRIEND?
Something like that?
EH?!
OF COURSE NOT!!

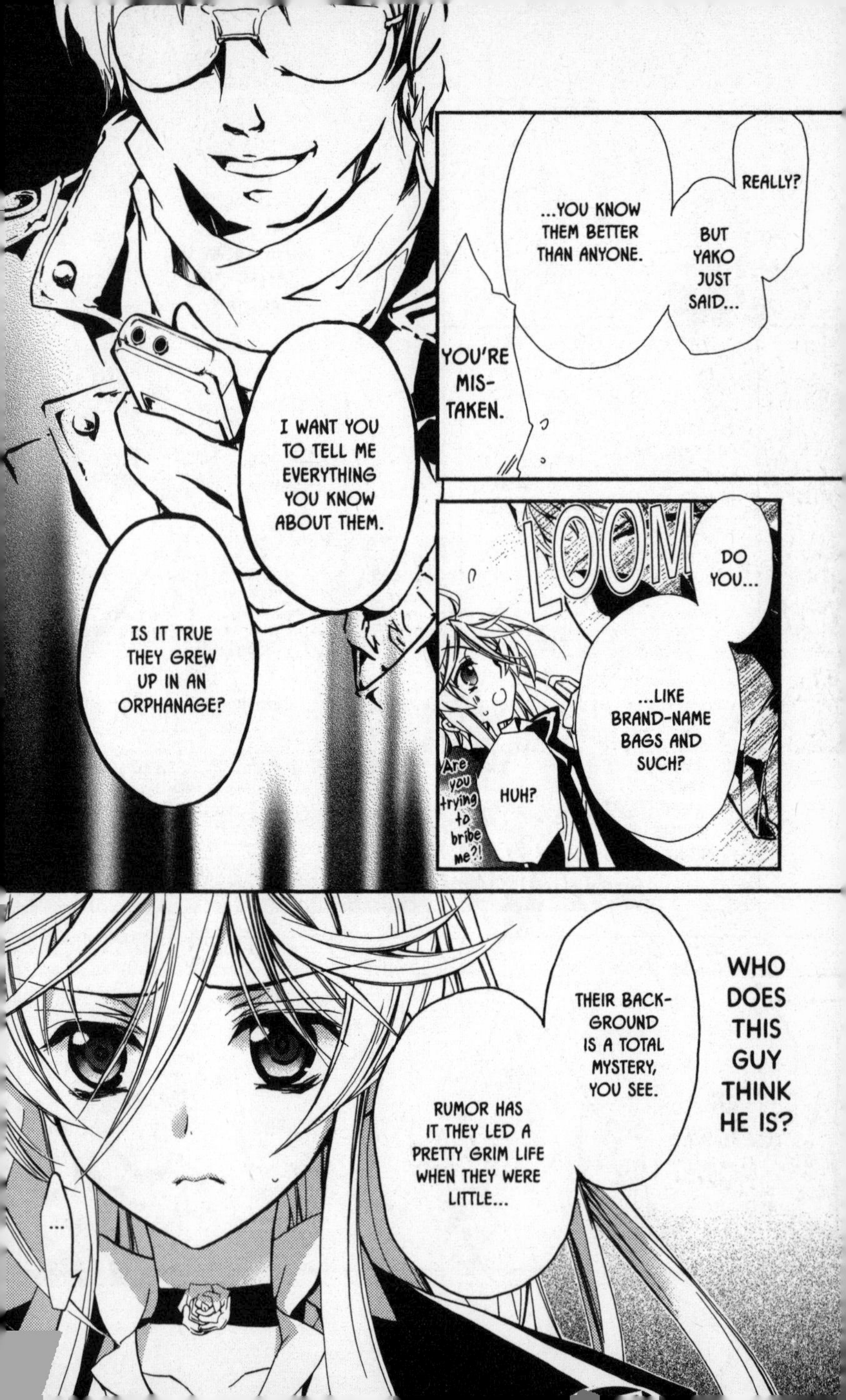
REALLY?
BUT YAKO JUST SAID...
...YOU KNOW THEM BETTER THAN ANYONE.
YOU'RE MIS- TAKEN.
LOOM
DO YOU...
...LIKE BRAND-NAME BAGS AND SUCH?
HUH?
Are you trying to bribe me?!
I WANT YOU TO TELL ME EVERYTHING YOU KNOW ABOUT THEM.
IS IT TRUE THEY GREW UP IN AN ORPHANAGE?
WHO DOES THIS GUY THINK HE IS?
THEIR BACK- GROUND IS A TOTAL MYSTERY, YOU SEE.
RUMOR HAS IT THEY LED A PRETTY GRIM LIFE WHEN THEY WERE LITTLE...
...

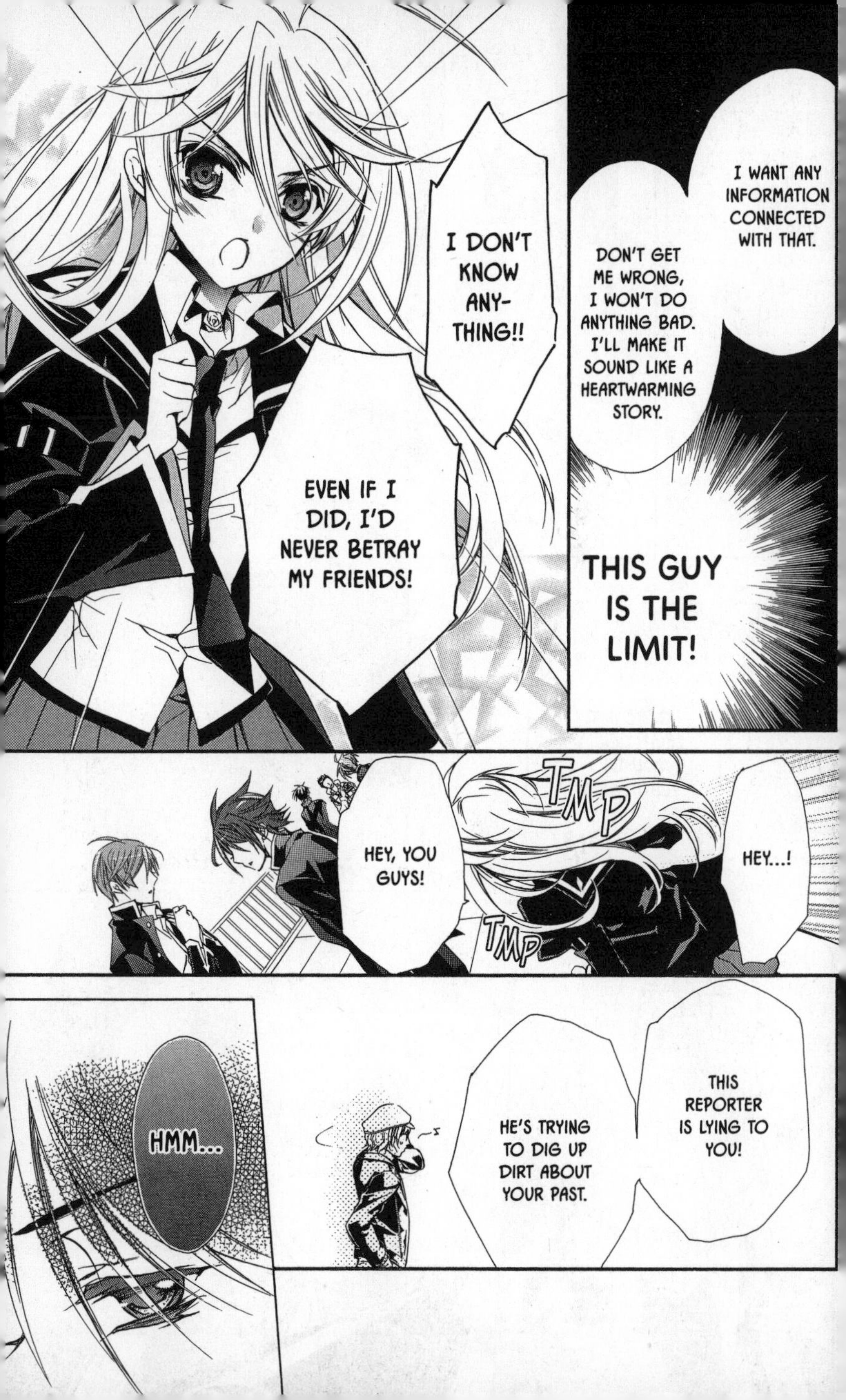
I WANT ANY INFORMATION CONNECTED WITH THAT.
DON'T GET ME WRONG, I WON'T DO ANYTHING BAD. I'LL MAKE IT SOUND LIKE A HEARTWARMING STORY.
THIS GUY IS THE LIMIT!
I DON'T KNOW ANY-THING!!
EVEN IF I DID, I'D NEVER BETRAY MY FRIENDS!
HEY...!
TMP
HEY, YOU GUYS!
TMP
THIS REPORTER IS LYING TO YOU!
HE'S TRYING TO DIG UP DIRT ABOUT YOUR PAST.
HMM...

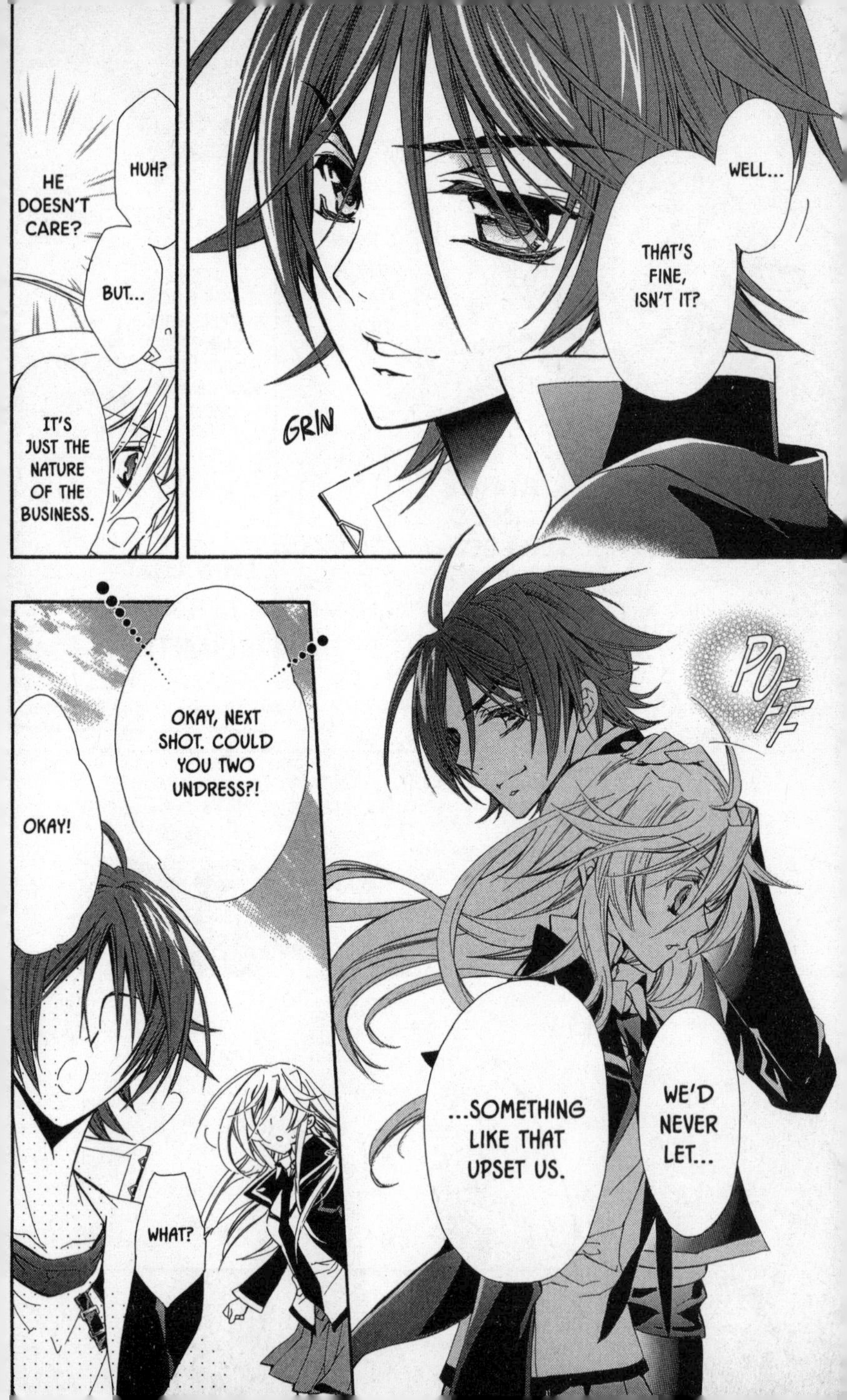
WELL...
THAT'S FINE, ISN'T IT?
GRIN
HUH?
HE DOESN'T CARE?
BUT...
IT'S JUST THE NATURE OF THE BUSINESS.
POFF
WE'D NEVER LET...
...SOMETHING LIKE THAT UPSET US.
......
OKAY, NEXT SHOT. COULD YOU TWO UNDRESS?!
OKAY!
WHAT?

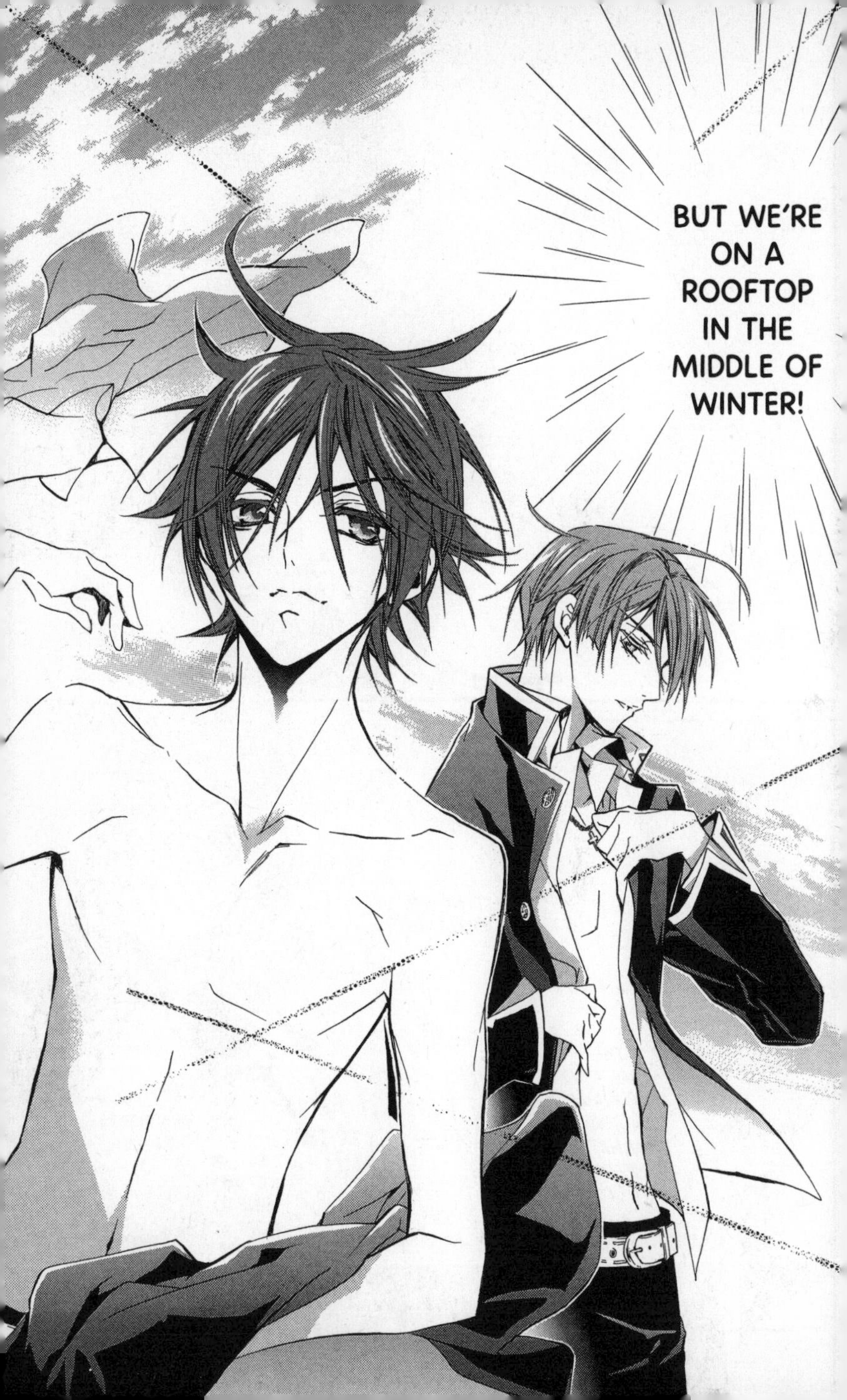
BUT WE'RE ON A ROOFTOP IN THE MIDDLE OF WINTER!

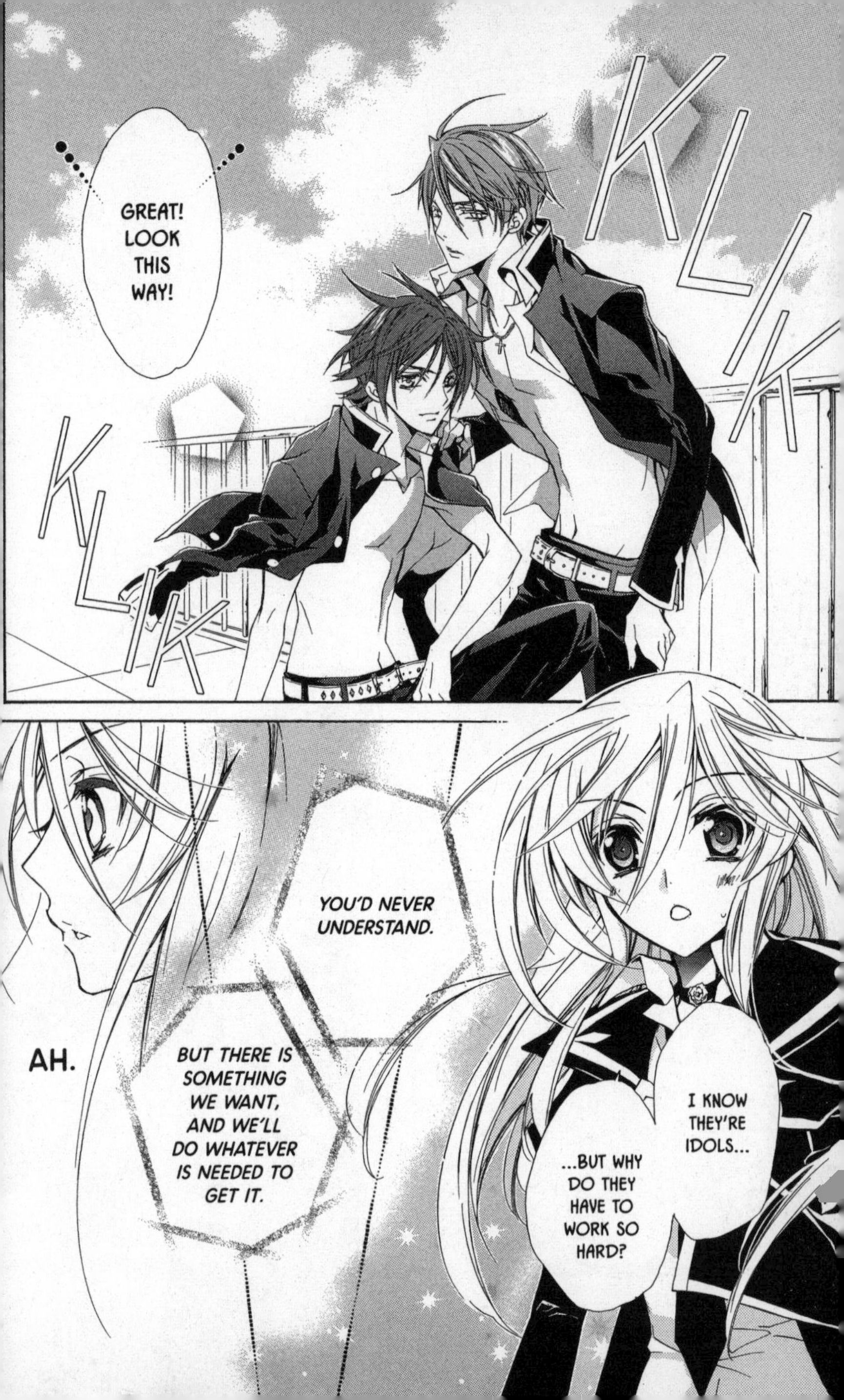
KLIK
GREAT! LOOK THIS WAY!
KLIK
I KNOW THEY'RE IDOLS...
...BUT WHY DO THEY HAVE TO WORK SO HARD?
YOU'D NEVER UNDERSTAND.
BUT THERE IS SOMETHING WE WANT, AND WE'LL DO WHATEVER IS NEEDED TO GET IT.
AH.

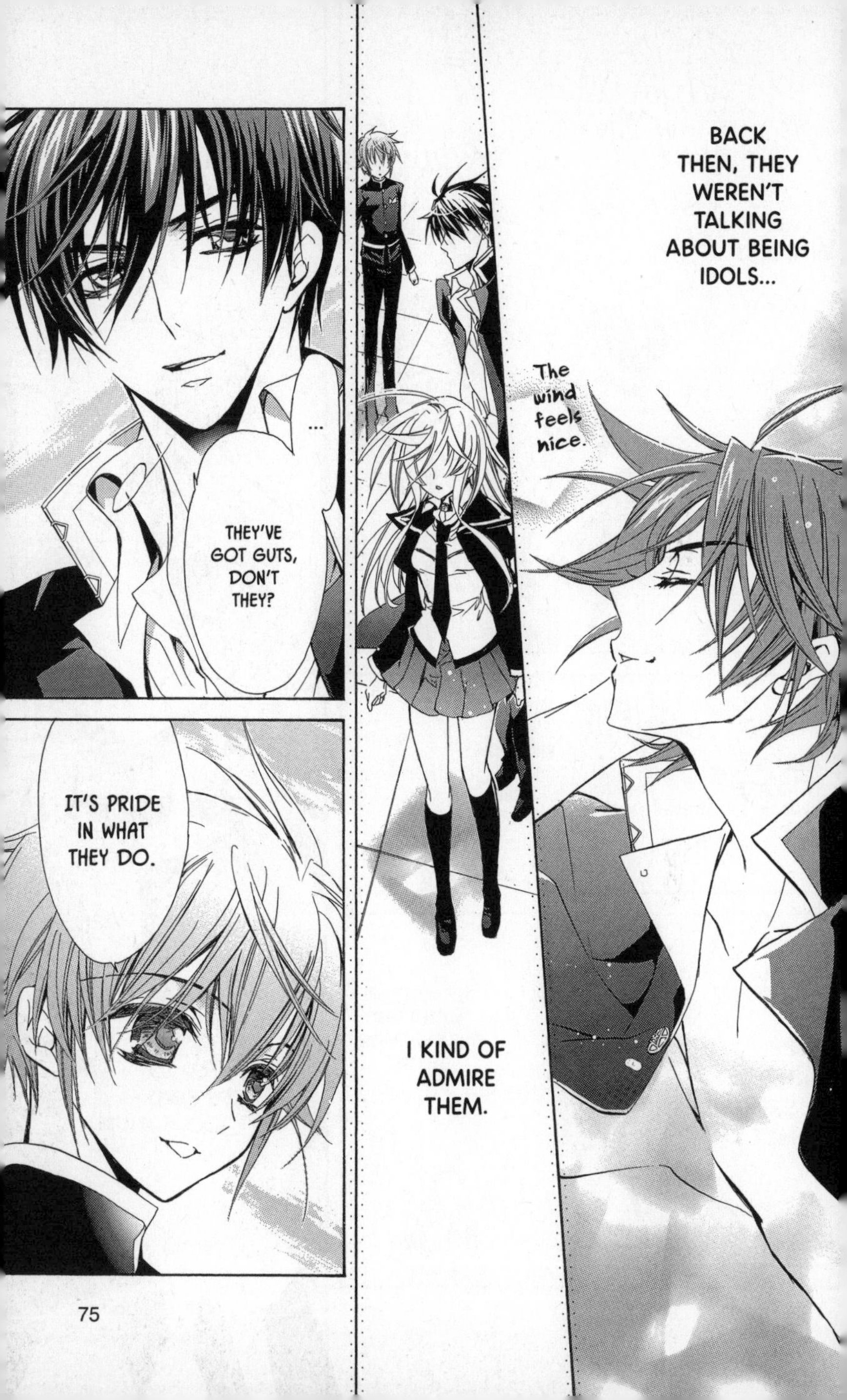
BACK THEN, THEY WEREN'T TALKING ABOUT BEING IDOLS...
The wind feels nice.
I KIND OF ADMIRE THEM.
...
THEY'VE GOT GUTS, DON'T THEY?
IT'S PRIDE IN WHAT THEY DO.

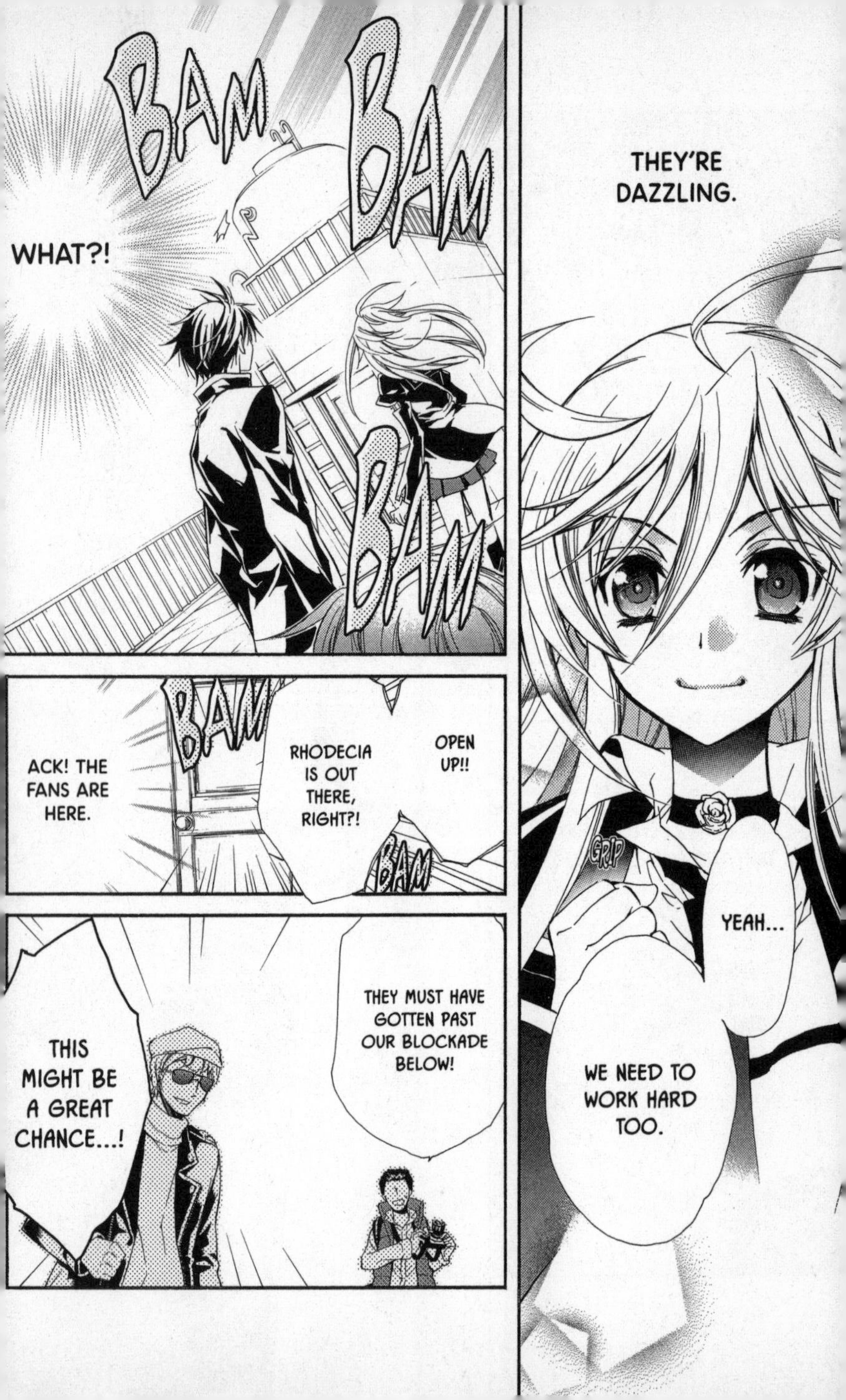
THEY'RE DAZZLING.
GRIP
YEAH...
WE NEED TO WORK HARD TOO.
BAM
BAM
WHAT?!
BAM
BAM
OPEN UP!!
RHODECIA IS OUT THERE, RIGHT?!
ACK! THE FANS ARE HERE.
BAM
THEY MUST HAVE GOTTEN PAST OUR BLOCKADE BELOW!
THIS MIGHT BE A GREAT CHANCE...!

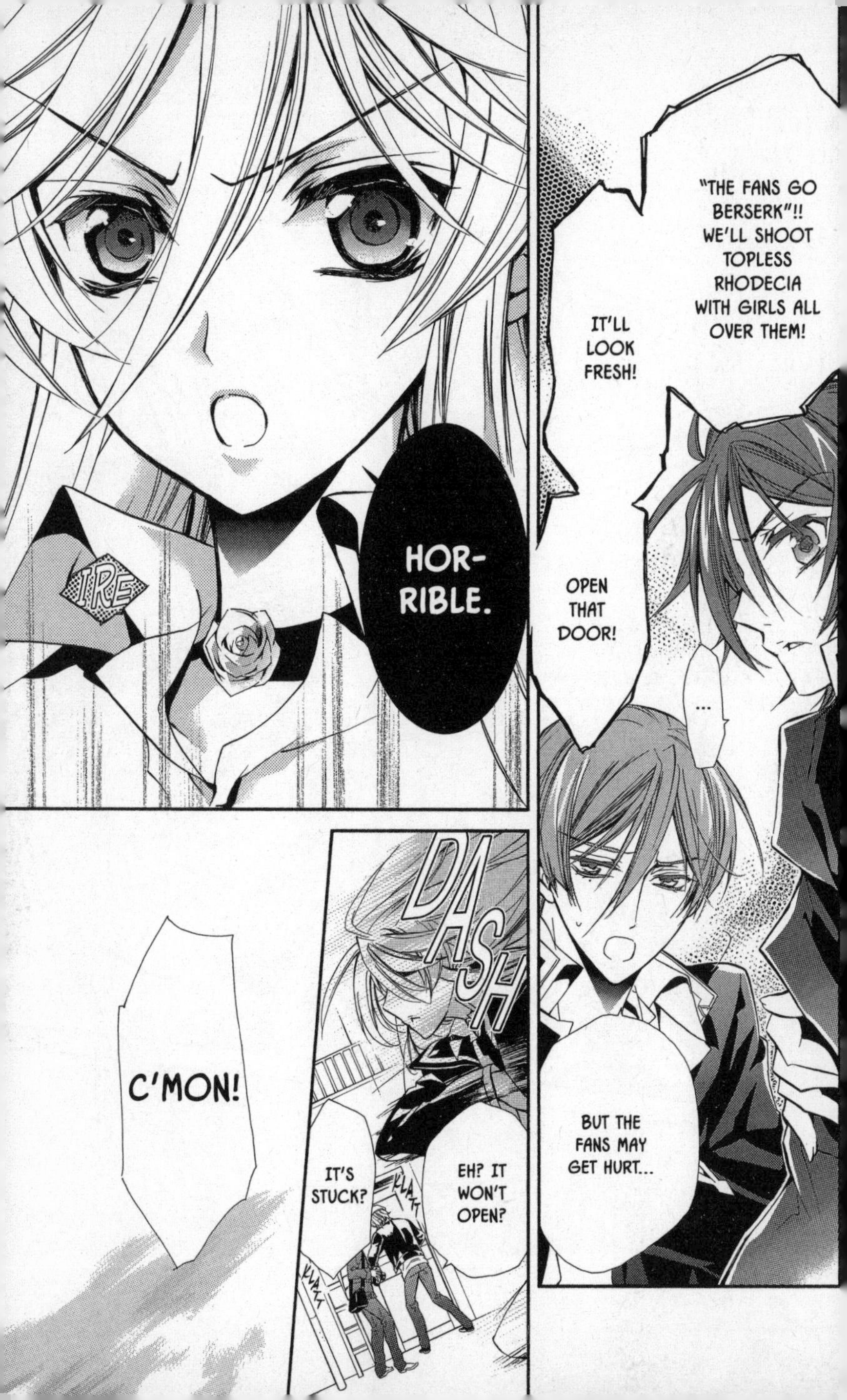
"THE FANS GO BERSERK"!! WE'LL SHOOT TOPLESS RHODECIA WITH GIRLS ALL OVER THEM!
IT'LL LOOK FRESH!
OPEN THAT DOOR!
...
BUT THE FANS MAY GET HURT...
IRE
HOR-RIBLE.
DASH
EH? IT WON'T OPEN?
IT'S STUCK?
C'MON!

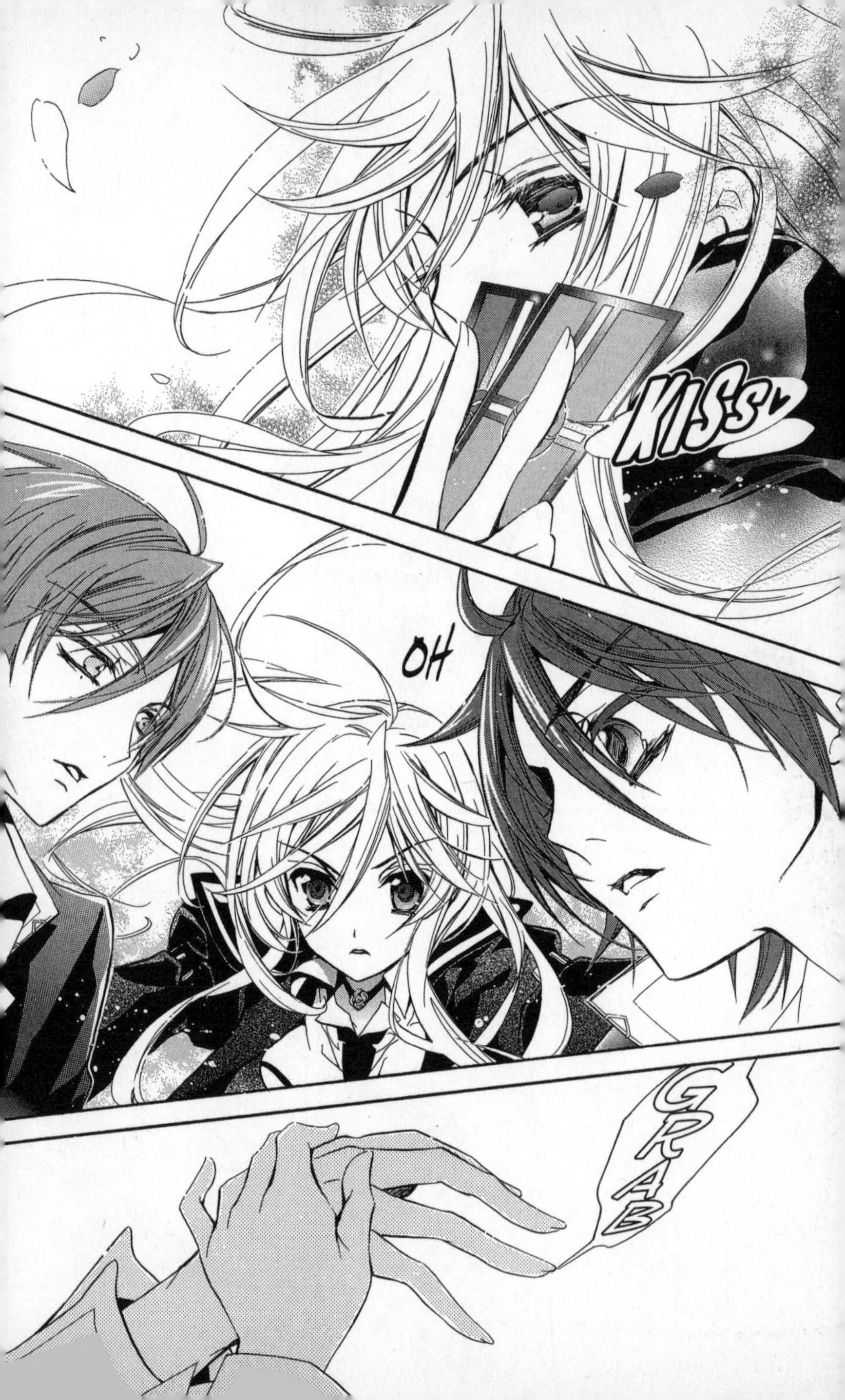
KISS♥
OH
GRAB

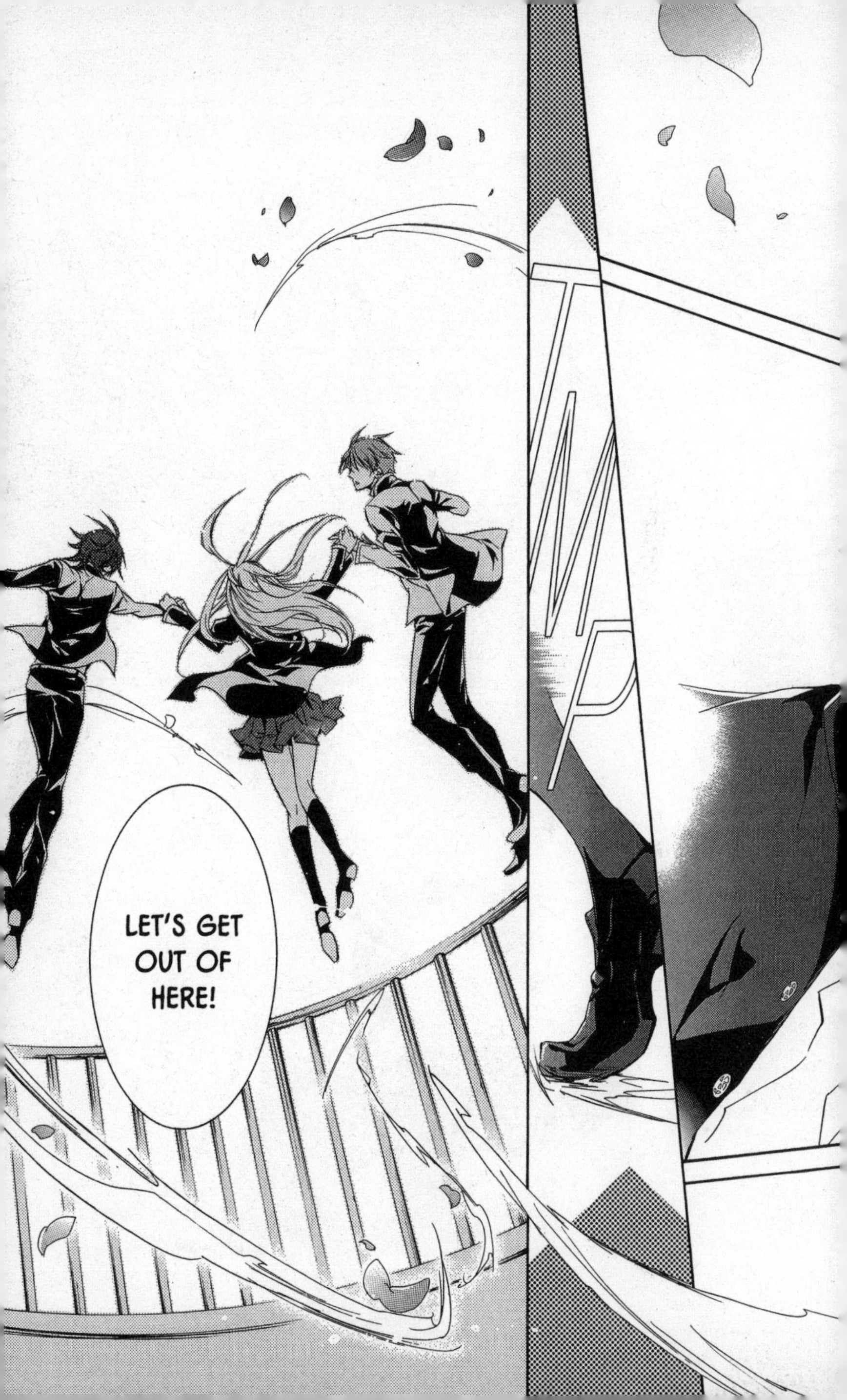
LET'S GET OUT OF HERE!

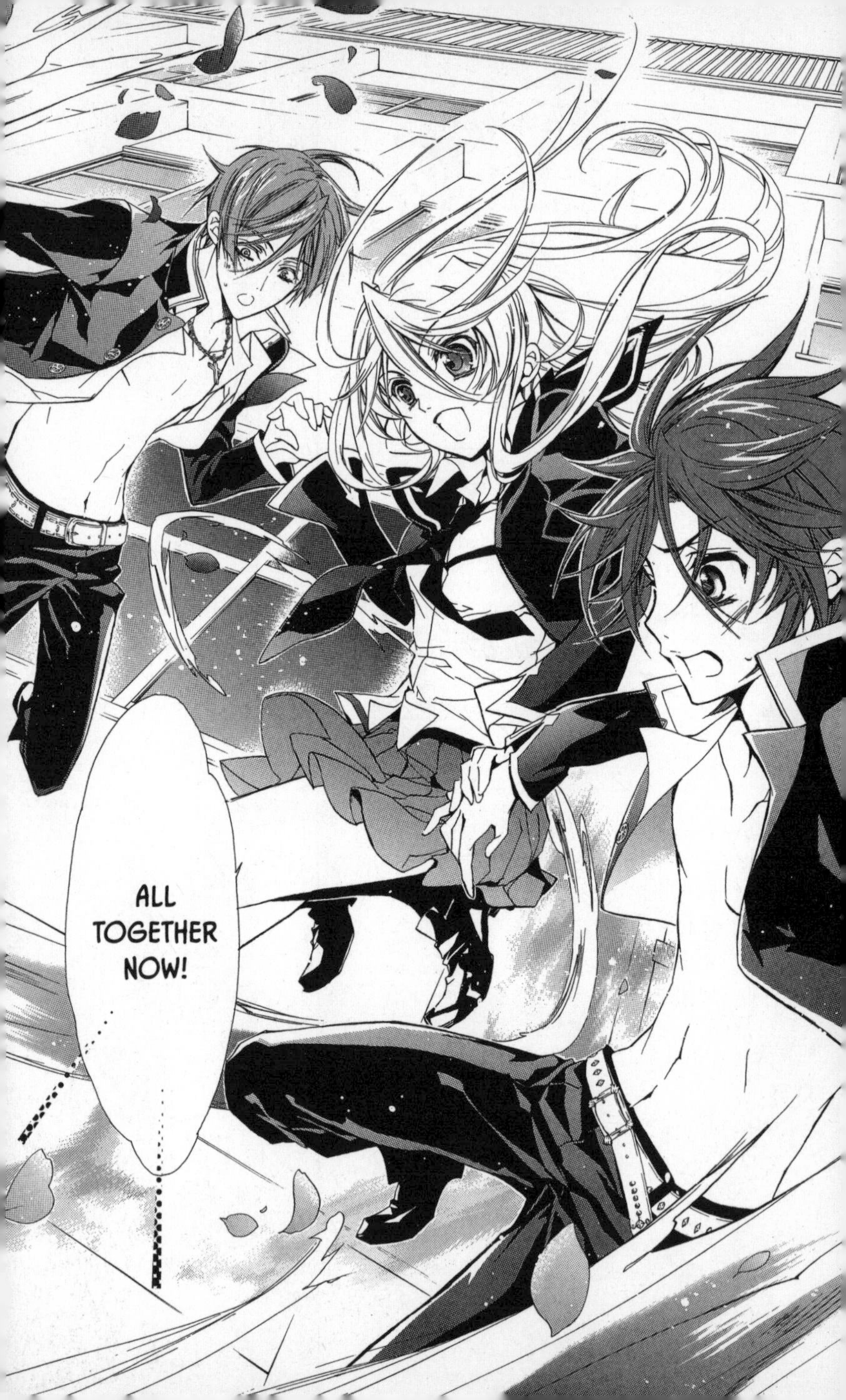
ALL TOGETHER NOW!

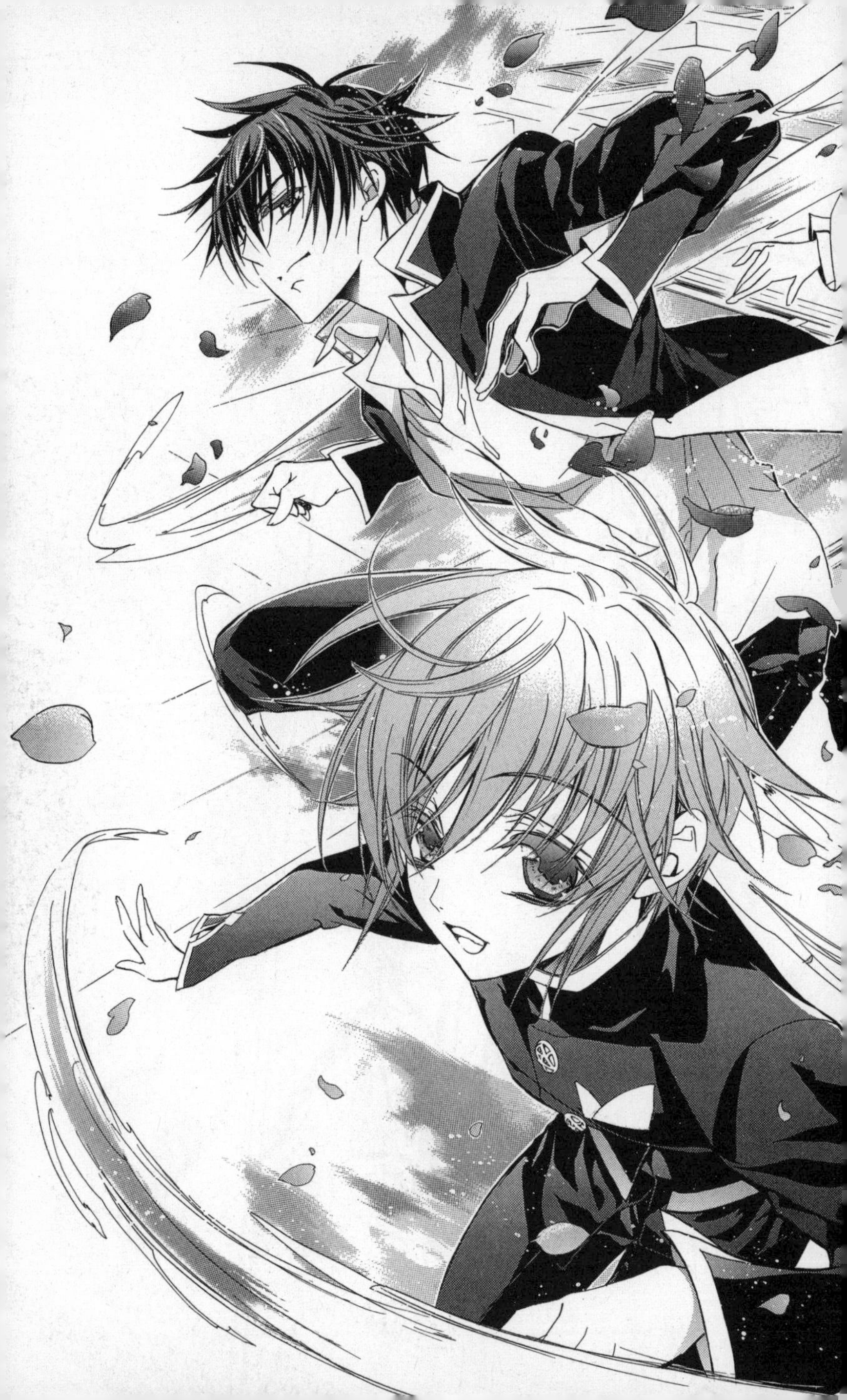

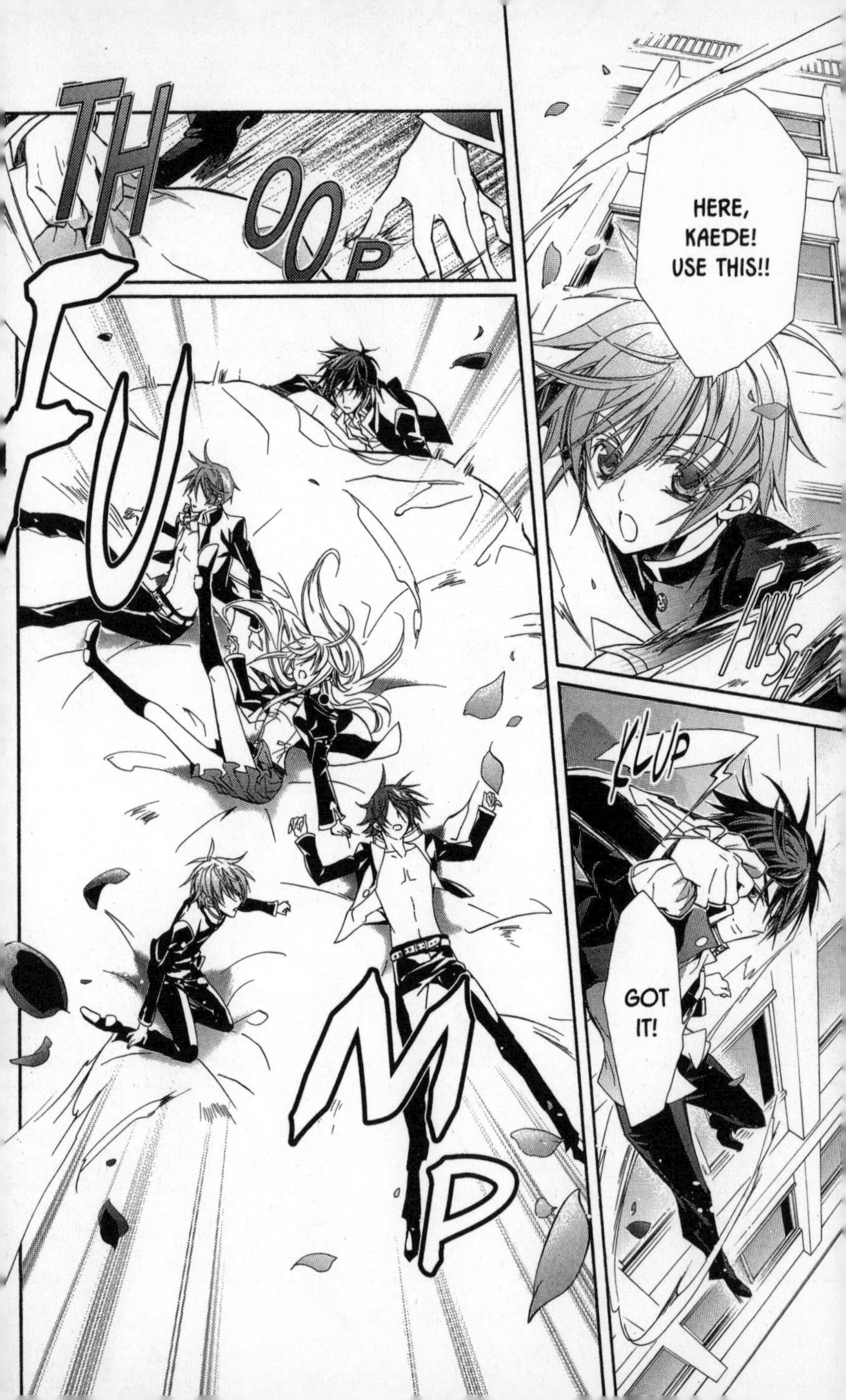
HERE, KAEDE! USE THIS!!
FWISH
KLUP
GOT IT!
THOOOP
FUMP

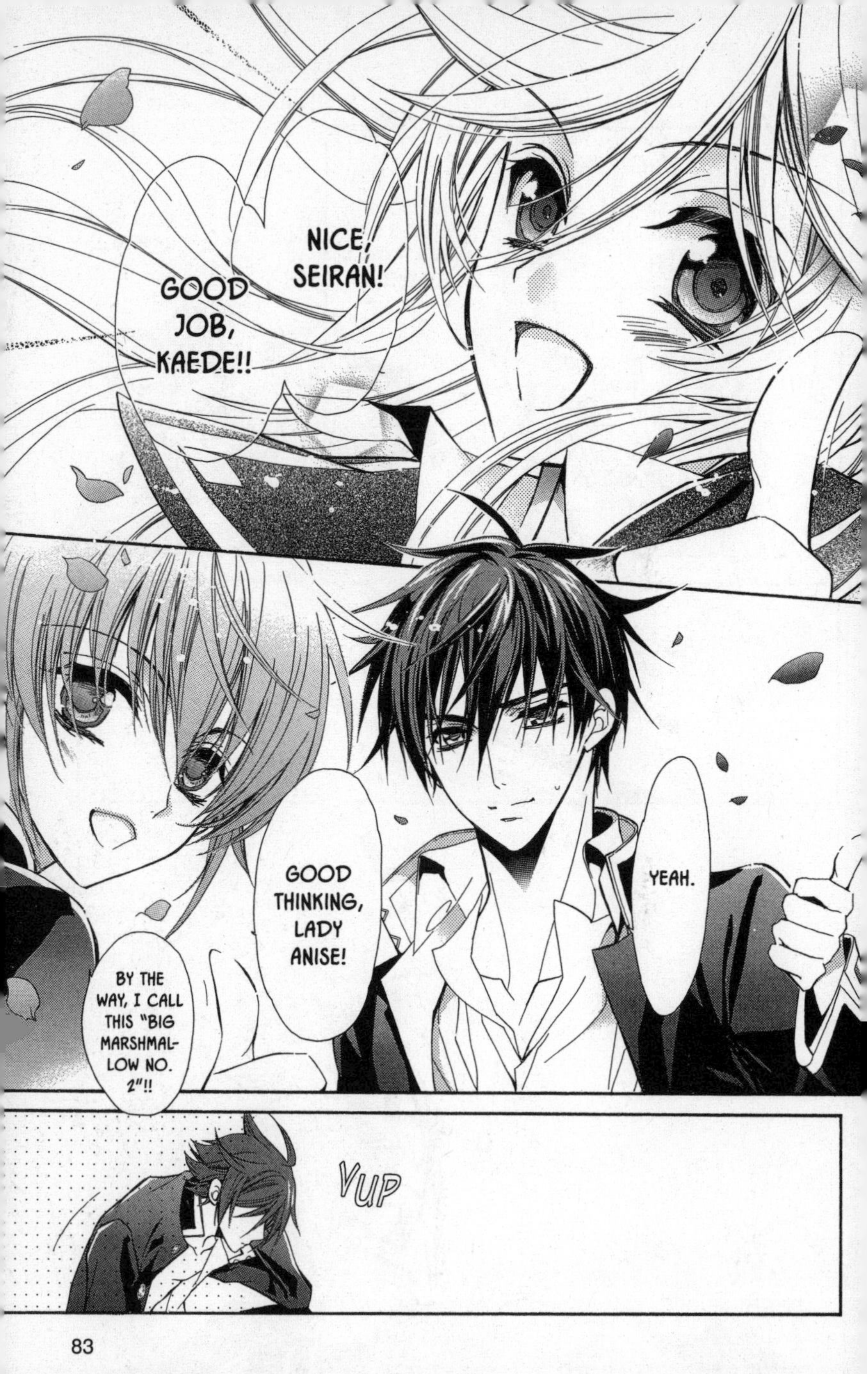
NICE, SEIRAN!
GOOD JOB, KAEDE!!
YEAH.
GOOD THINKING, LADY ANISE!
BY THE WAY, I CALL THIS "BIG MARSHMAL-LOW NO. 2"!!
VUP

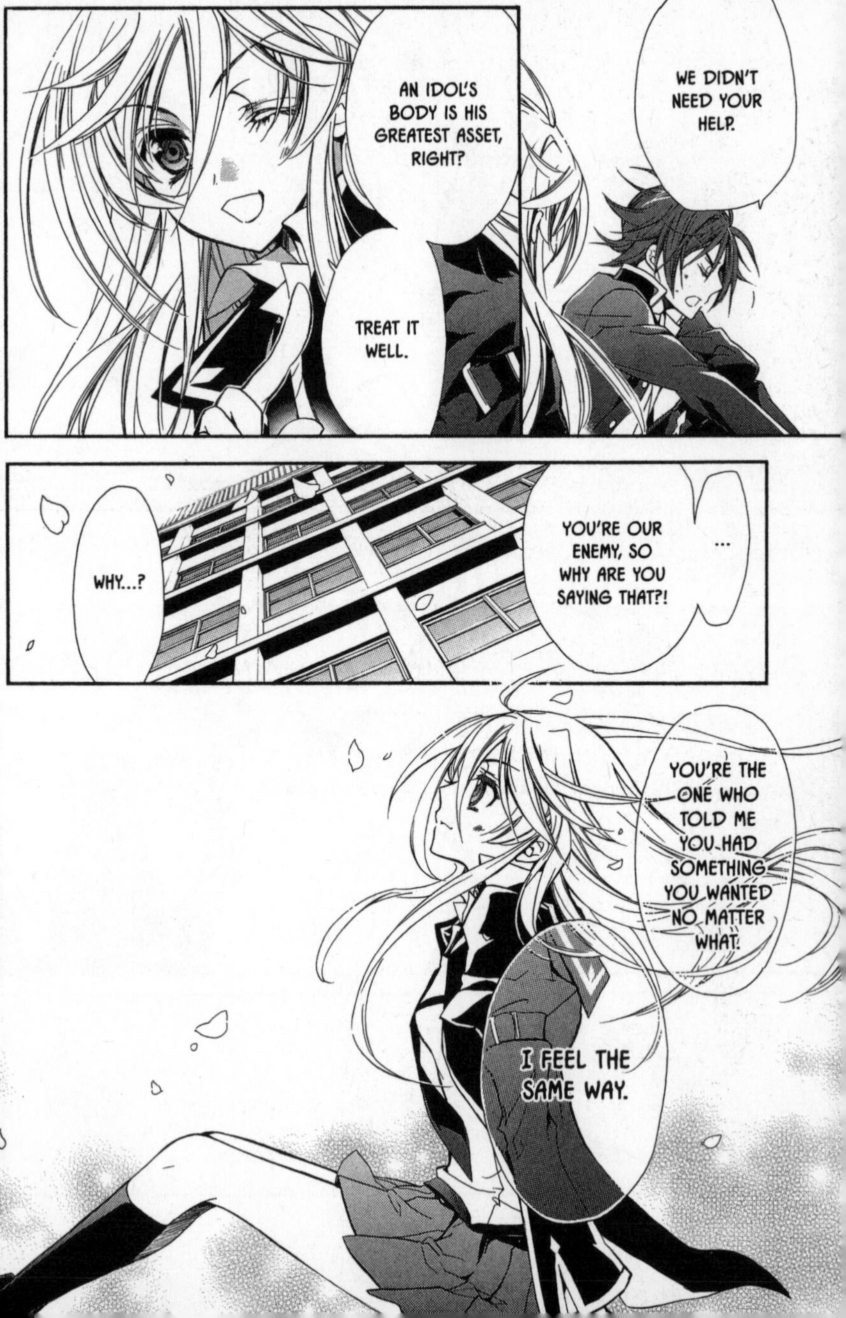
WE DIDN'T NEED YOUR HELP.
AN IDOL'S BODY IS HIS GREATEST ASSET, RIGHT?
TREAT IT WELL.
...
YOU'RE OUR ENEMY, SO WHY ARE YOU SAYING THAT?!
WHY...?
YOU'RE THE ONE WHO TOLD ME YOU HAD SOMETHING YOU WANTED NO MATTER WHAT.
I FEEL THE SAME WAY.

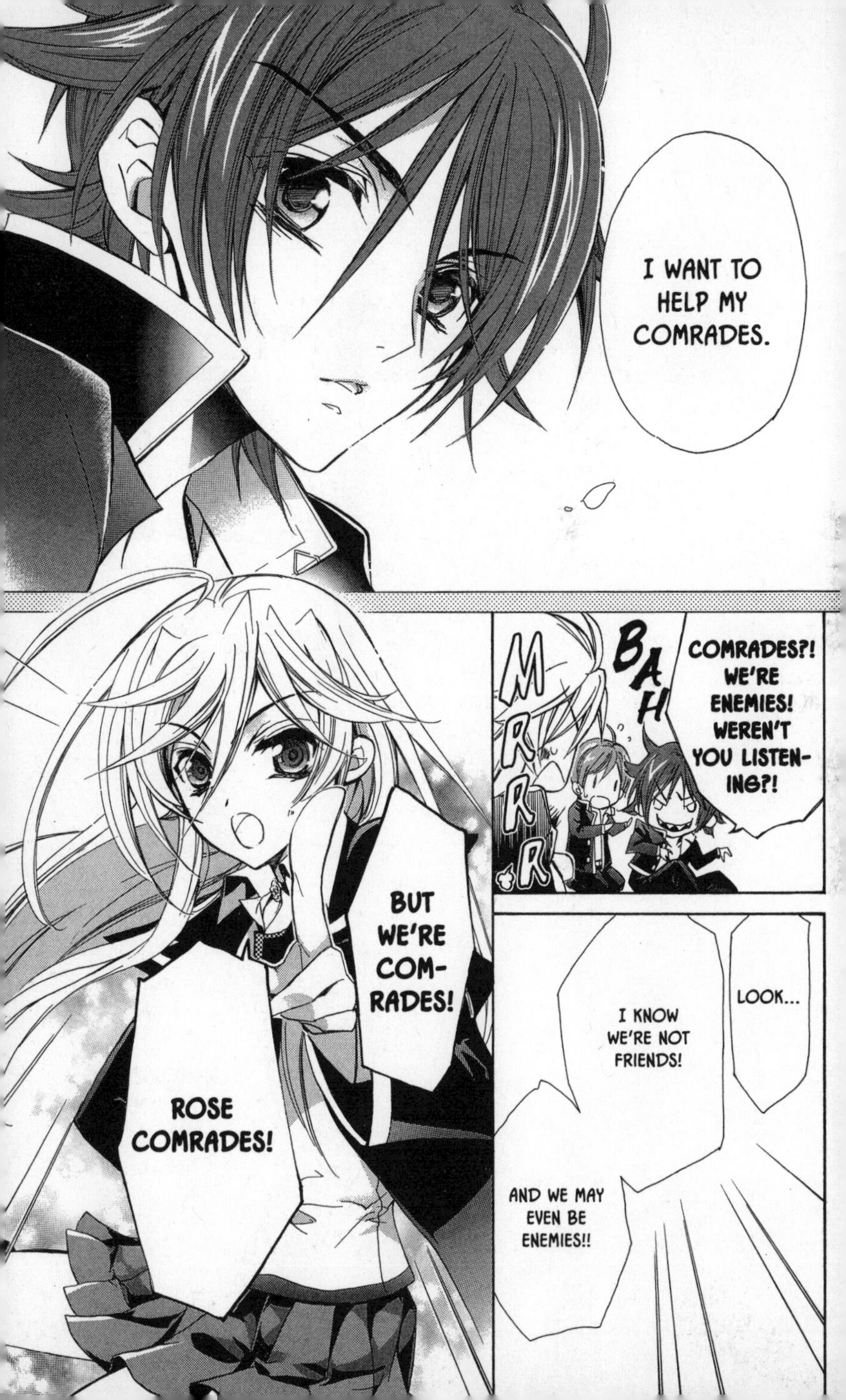
I WANT TO HELP MY COMRADES.
COMRADES?! WE'RE ENEMIES! WEREN'T YOU LISTEN-ING?!
BAH
MRRRR
LOOK...
I KNOW WE'RE NOT FRIENDS!
AND WE MAY EVEN BE ENEMIES!!
BUT WE'RE COM-RADES!
ROSE COMRADES!

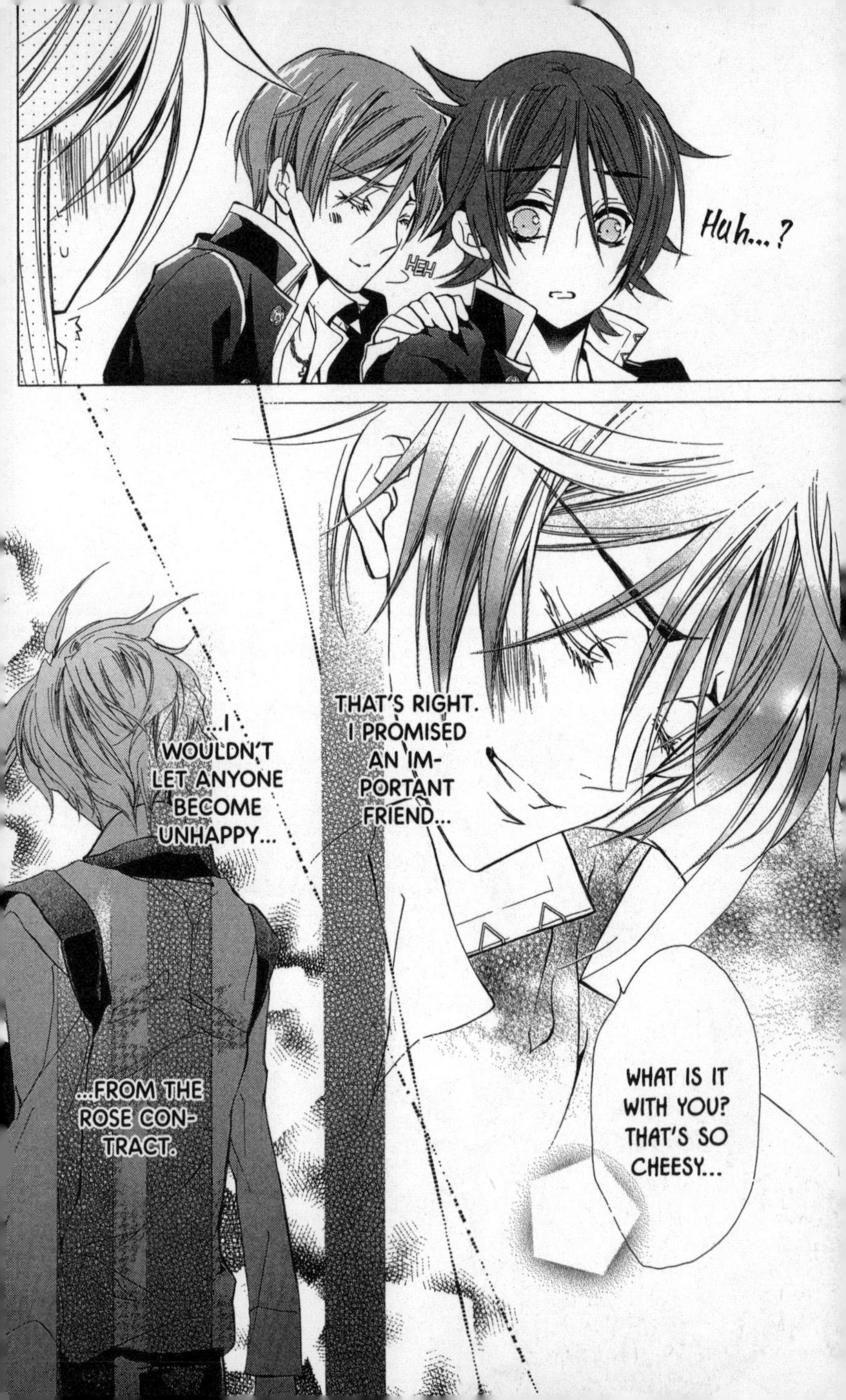
Huh...?
HEH
THAT'S RIGHT. I PROMISED AN IM-PORTANT FRIEND...
WHAT IS IT WITH YOU? THAT'S SO CHEESY...
...I WOULDN'T LET ANYONE BECOME UNHAPPY...
...FROM THE ROSE CON-TRACT.

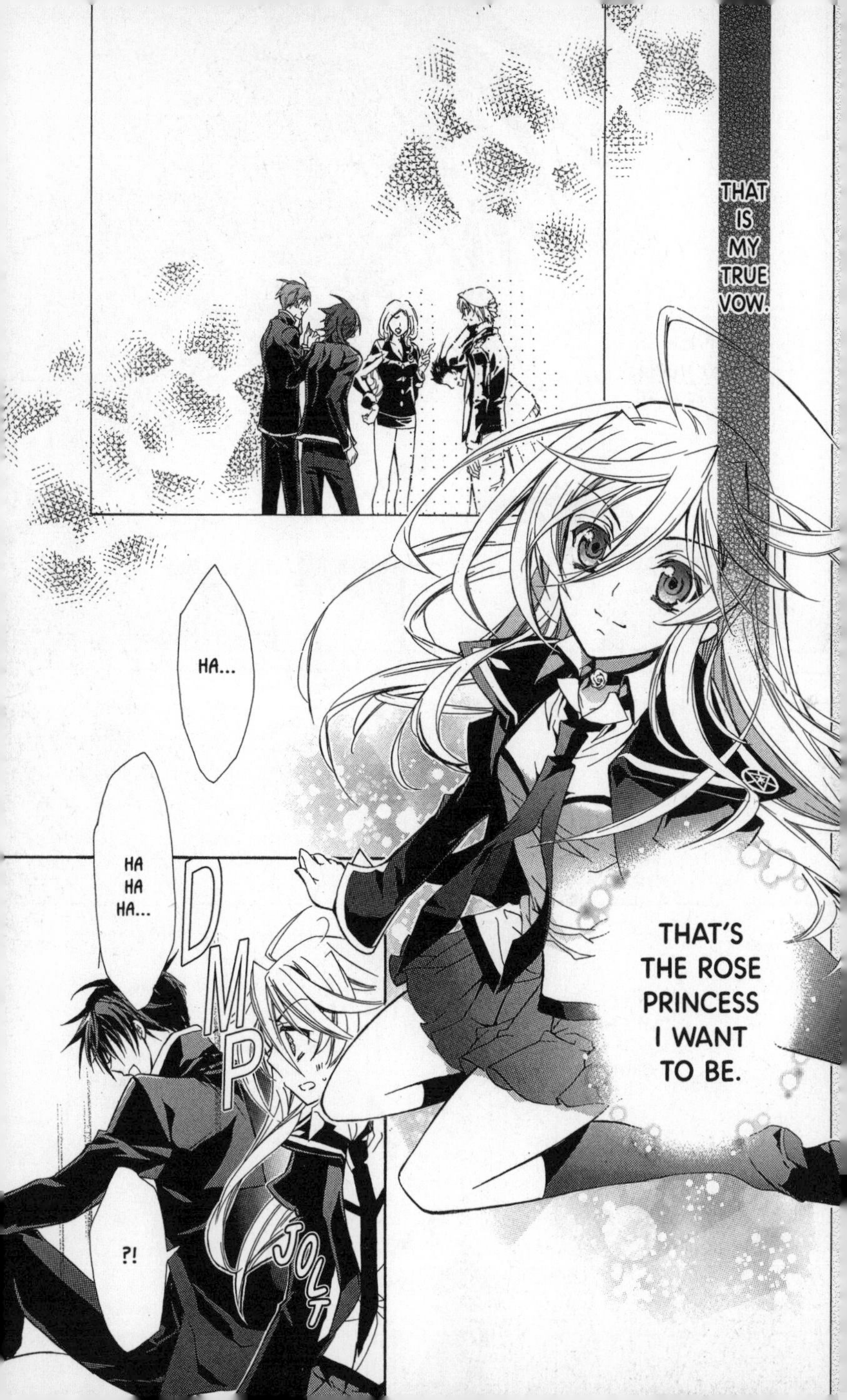
THAT IS MY TRUE VOW.
THAT'S THE ROSE PRINCESS I WANT TO BE.
HA...
HA HA HA...
DMP
JOLT
?!

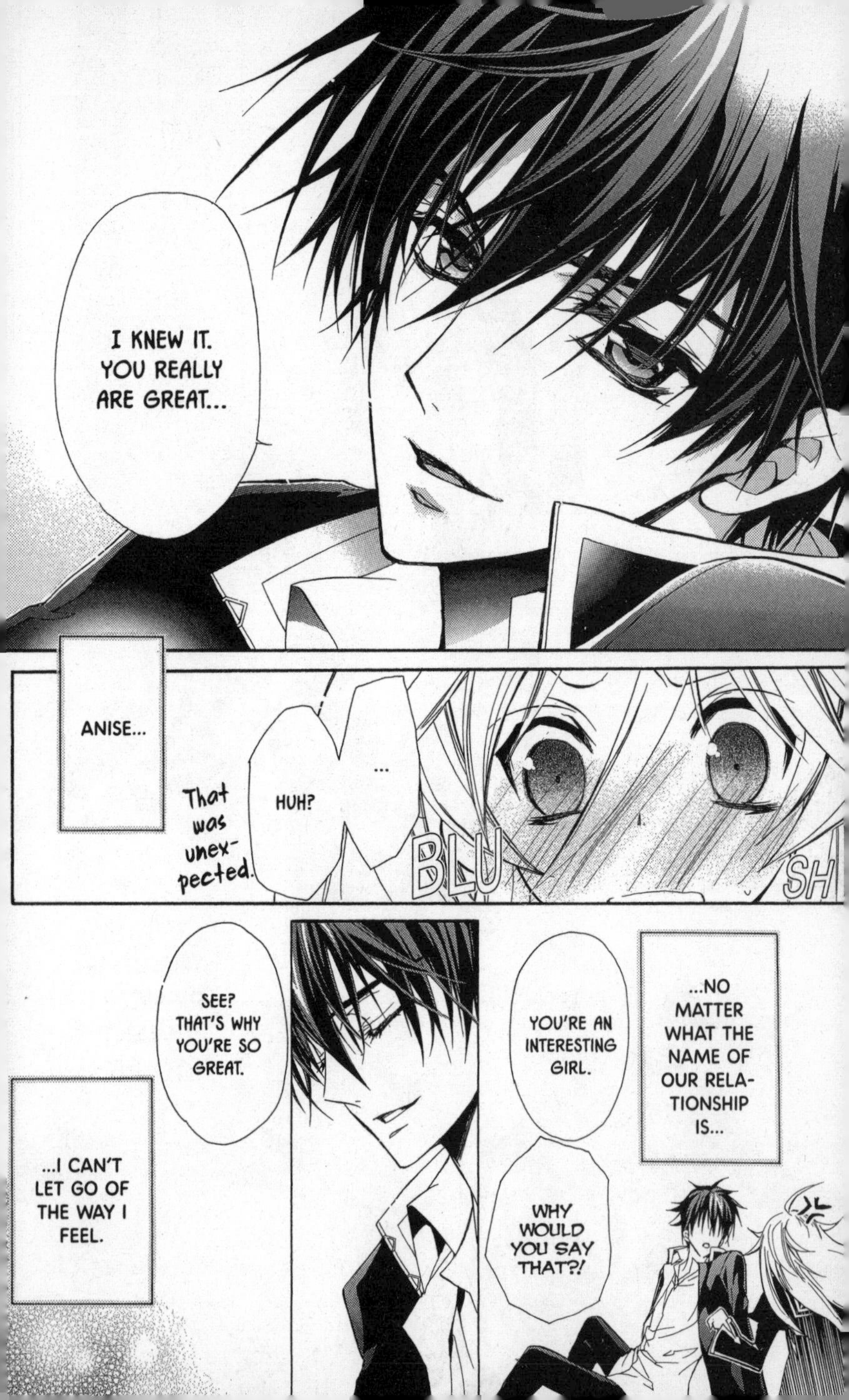
I KNEW IT. YOU REALLY ARE GREAT...
...
HUH?
ANISE...
That was unexpected.
BLUSH
...NO MATTER WHAT THE NAME OF OUR RELATIONSHIP IS...
YOU'RE AN INTERESTING GIRL.
WHY WOULD YOU SAY THAT?!
SEE? THAT'S WHY YOU'RE SO GREAT.
...I CAN'T LET GO OF THE WAY I FEEL.

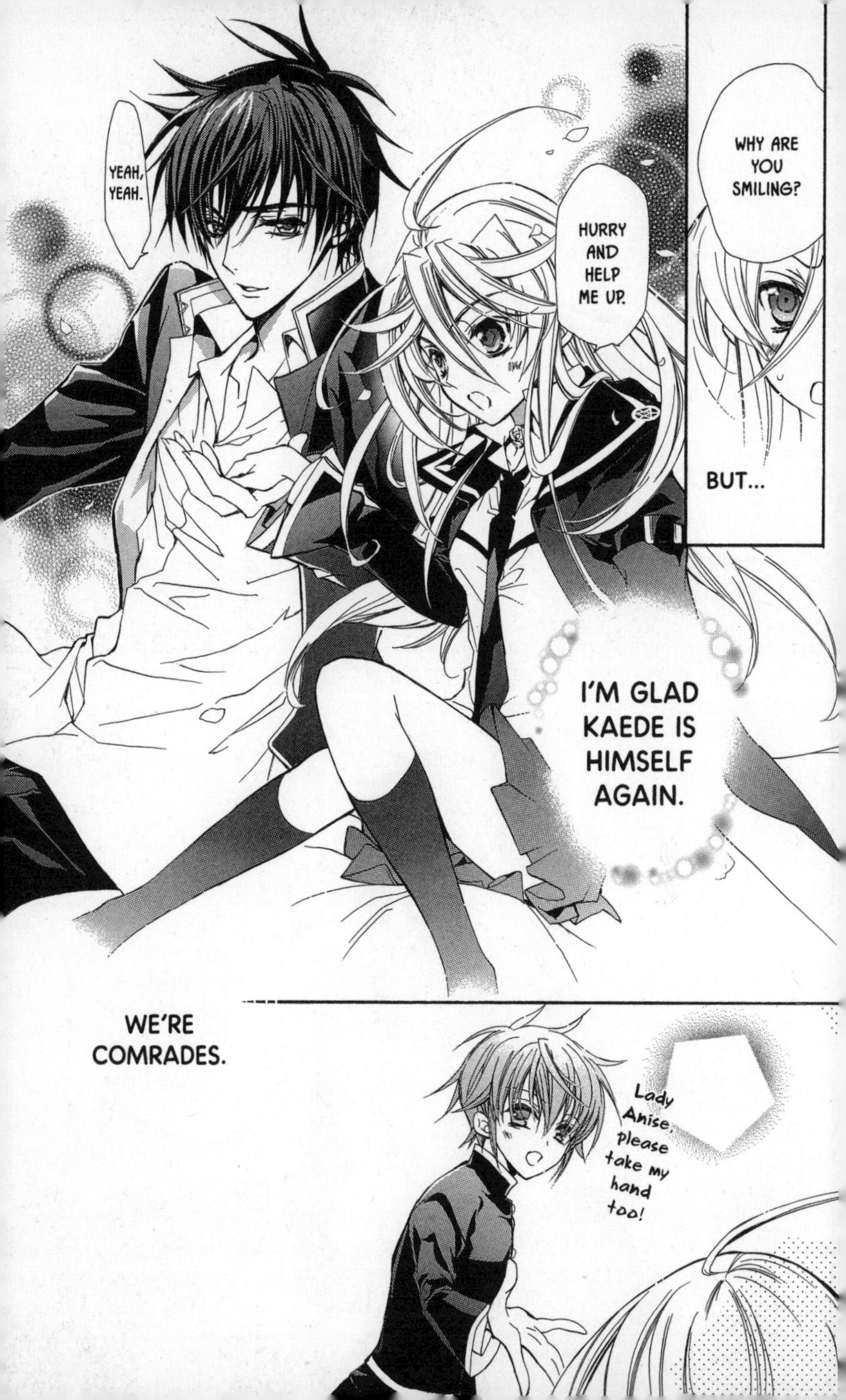
WHY ARE YOU SMILING?
BUT...
HURRY AND HELP ME UP.
YEAH, YEAH.
I'M GLAD KAEDE IS HIMSELF AGAIN.
Lady Anise, please take my hand too!
WE'RE COMRADES.

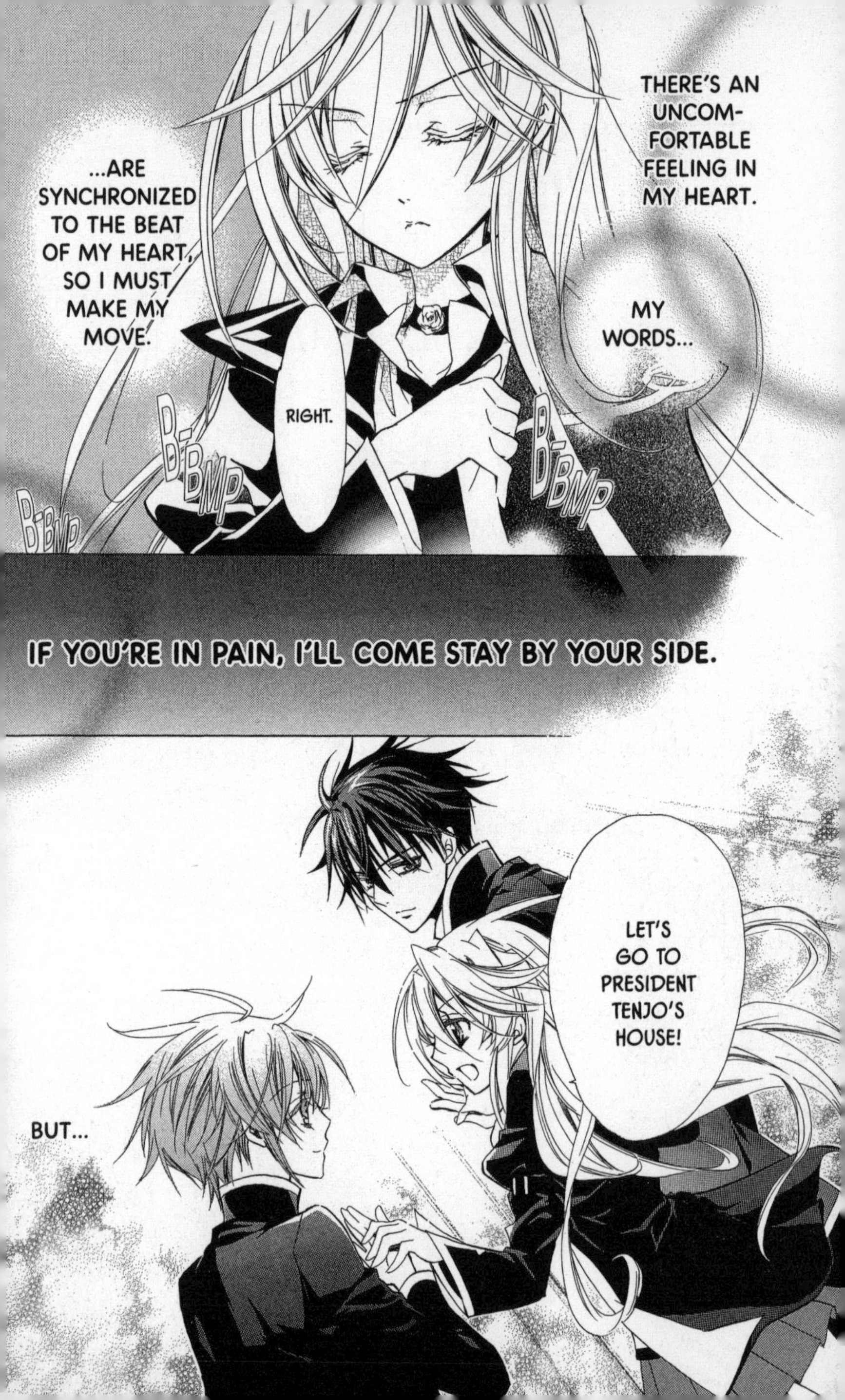
THERE'S AN UNCOMFORTABLE FEELING IN MY HEART.
MY WORDS...
RIGHT.
...ARE SYNCHRONIZED TO THE BEAT OF MY HEART, SO I MUST MAKE MY MOVE.
B-BMP
B-BMP
B-BMP
IF YOU'RE IN PAIN, I'LL COME STAY BY YOUR SIDE.
LET'S GO TO PRESIDENT TENJO'S HOUSE!
BUT...

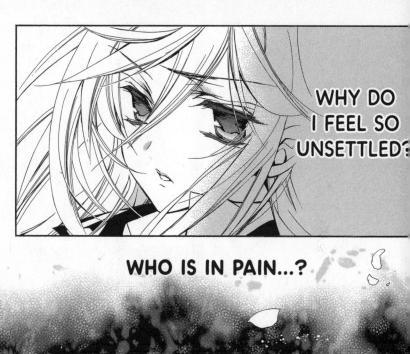

WHY DO
I FEEL SO
UNSETTLED?

WHO IS IN PAIN...?

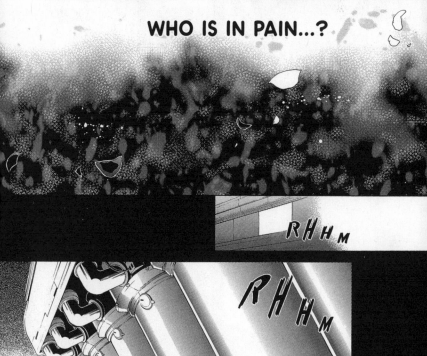

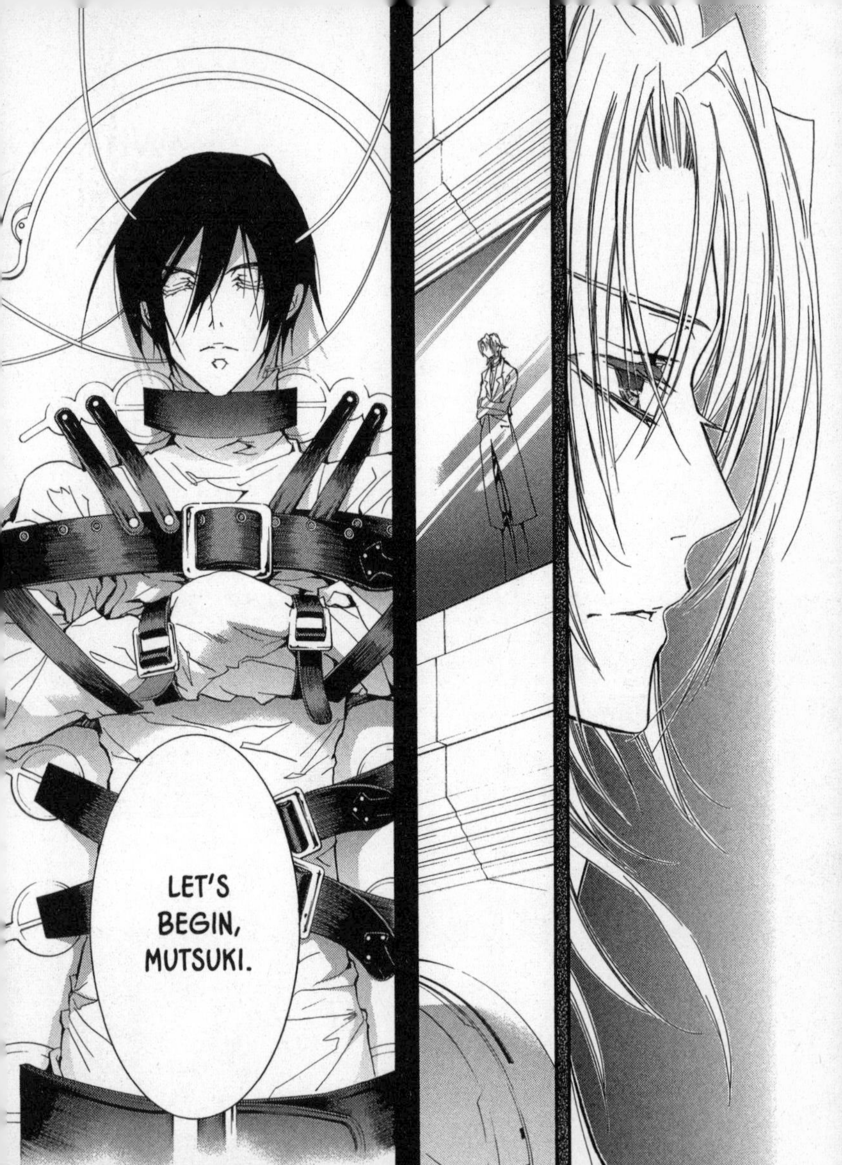
LET'S BEGIN, MUTSUKI.

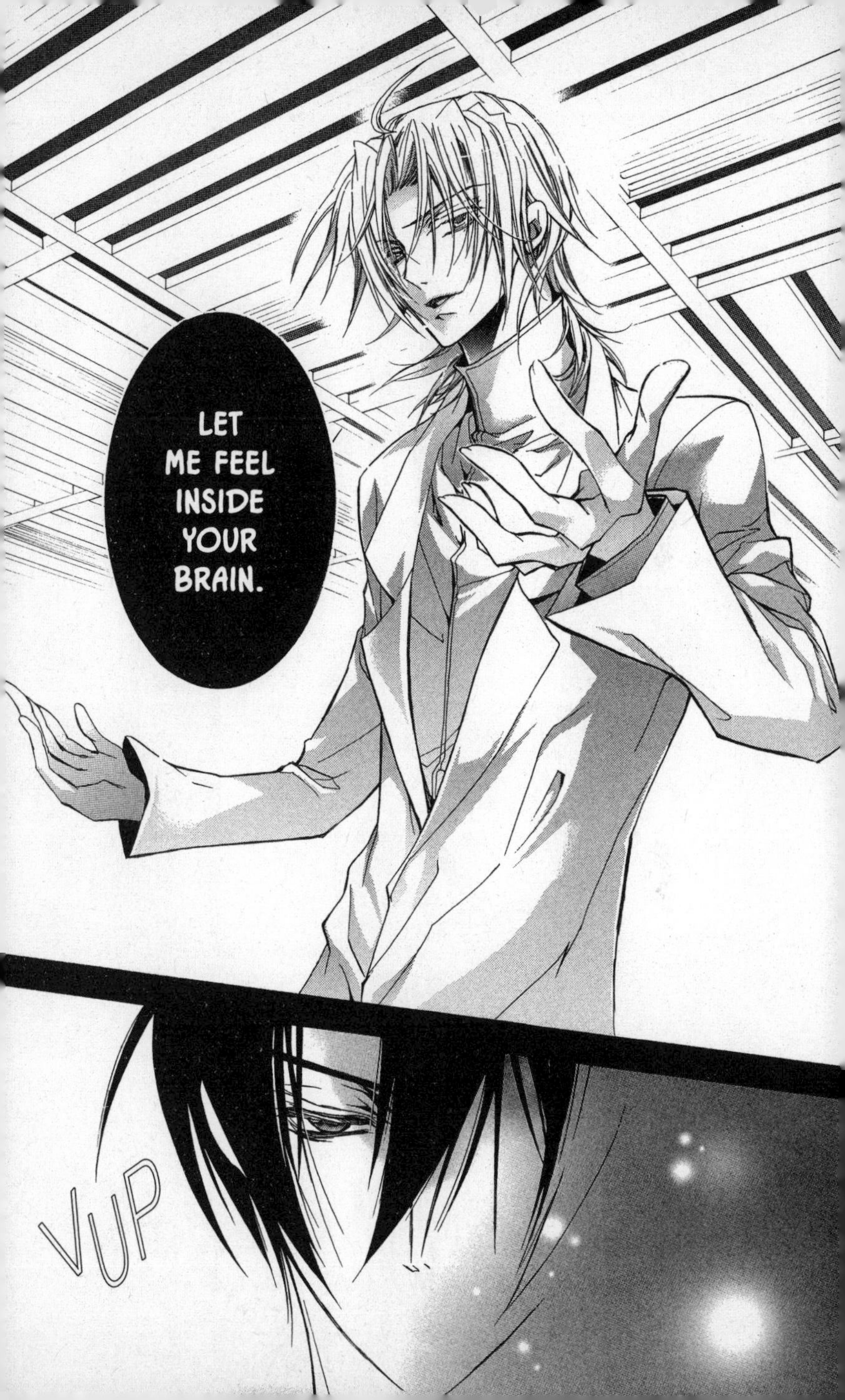
LET ME FEEL INSIDE YOUR BRAIN.
VUP

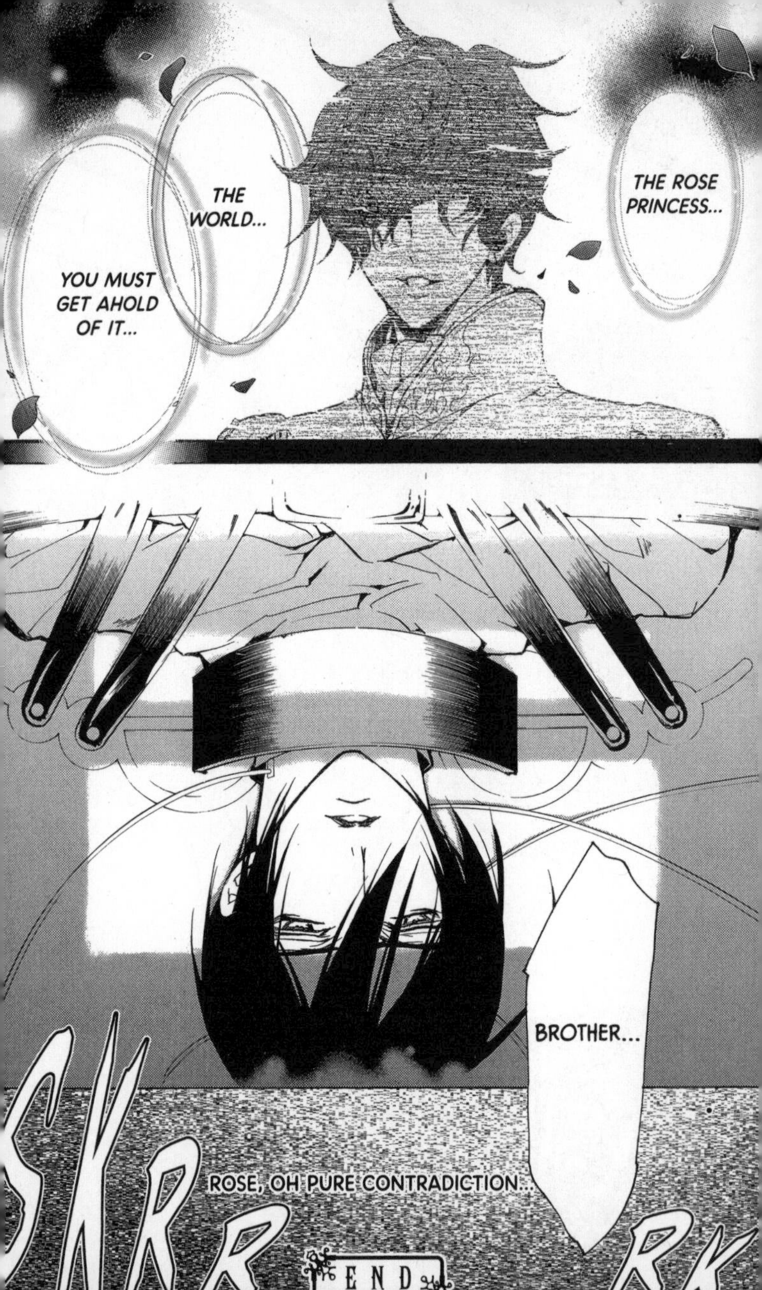
THE ROSE PRINCESS...
THE WORLD...
YOU MUST GET AHOLD OF IT...
BROTHER...
ROSE, OH PURE CONTRADICTION...
SKRR
RK
END

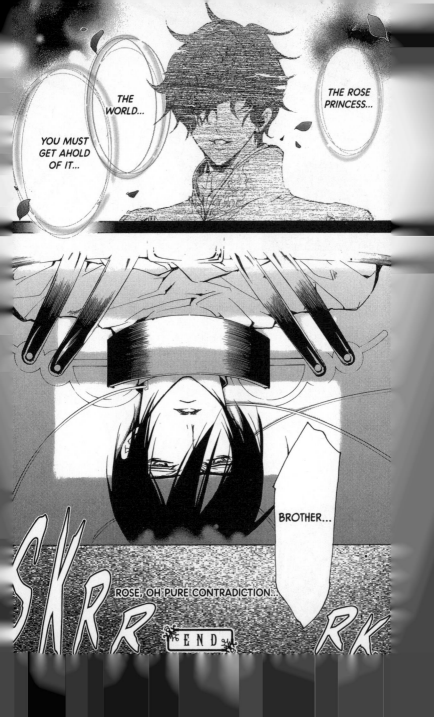

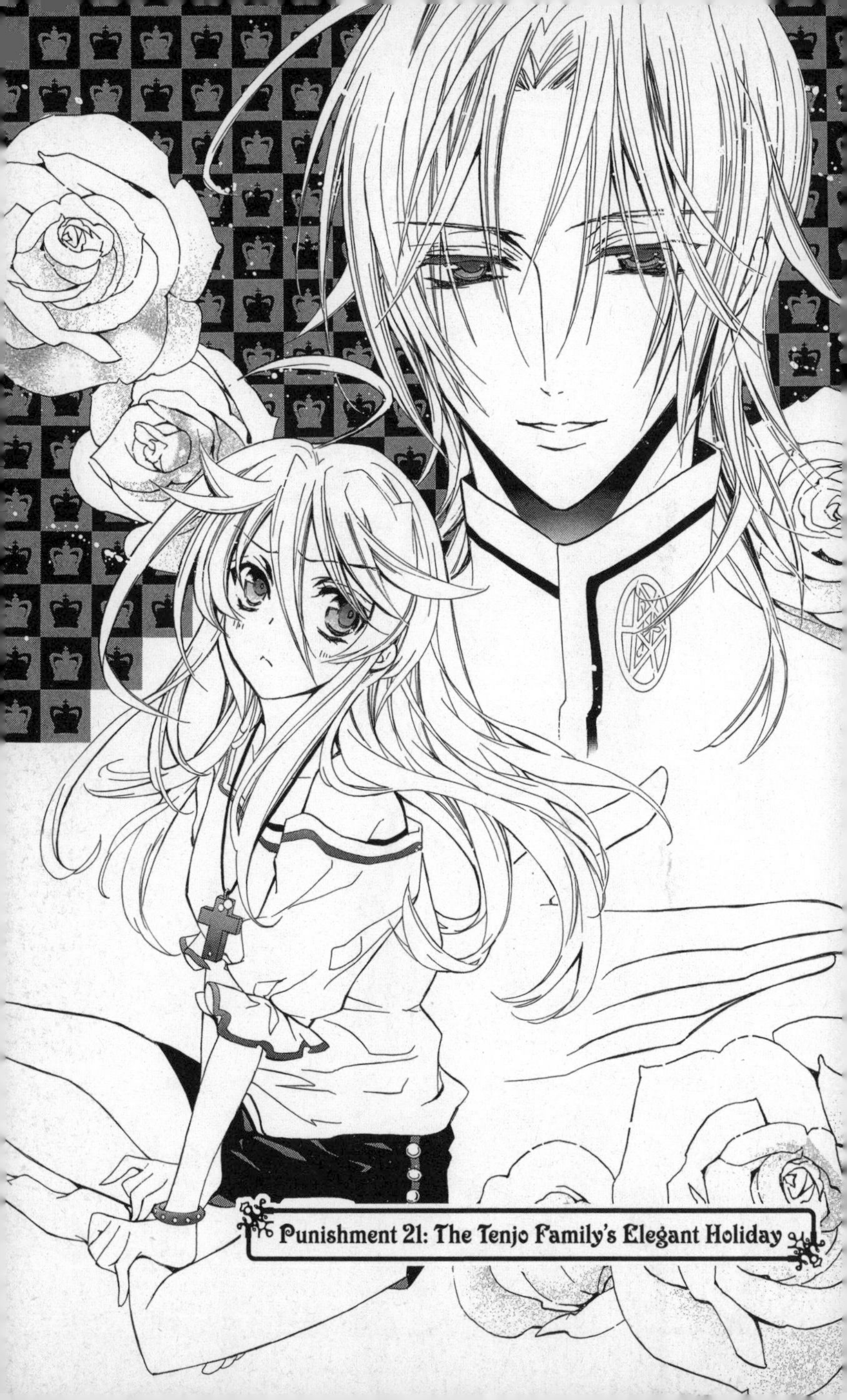
Punishment 21: The Tenjo Family's Elegant Holiday

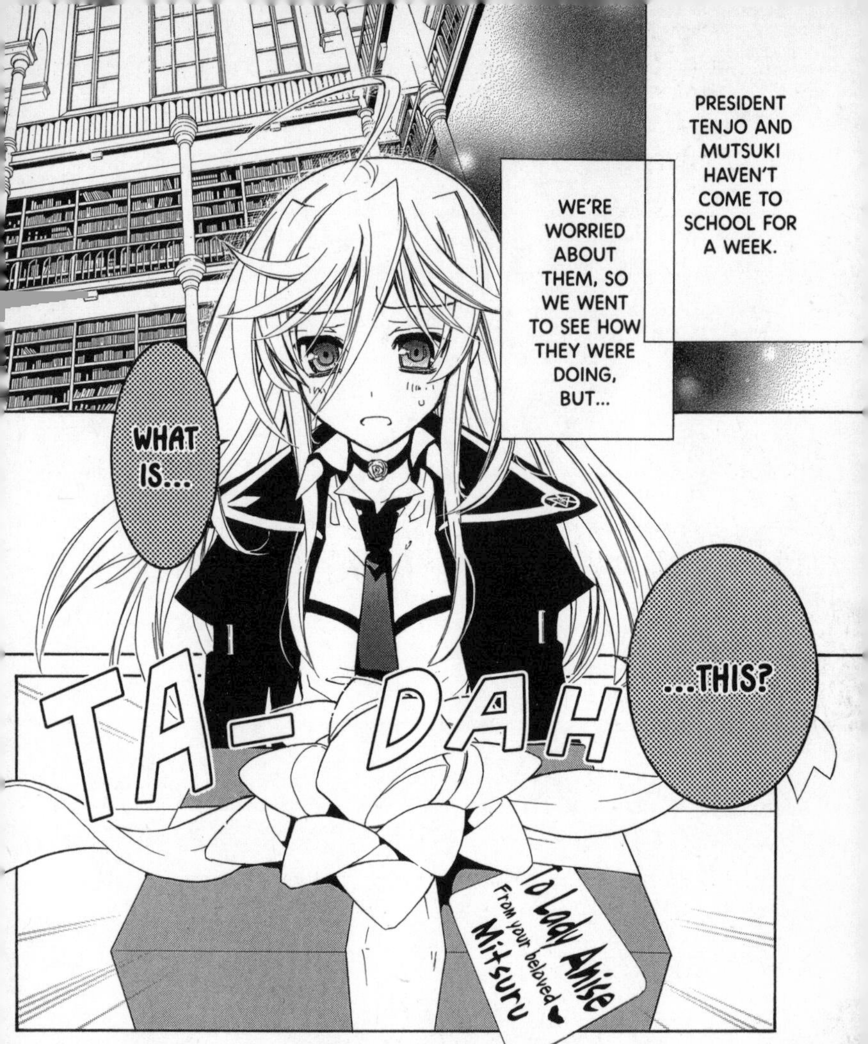
PRESIDENT TENJO AND MUTSUKI HAVEN'T COME TO SCHOOL FOR A WEEK.
WE'RE WORRIED ABOUT THEM, SO WE WENT TO SEE HOW THEY WERE DOING, BUT...
WHAT IS...
...THIS?
TA-DAH
To Lady Anise
From your beloved
Mitsuru

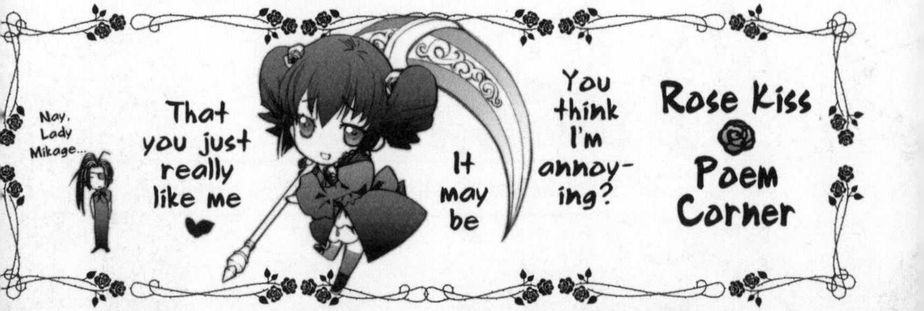
Rose Kiss Poem Corner
You think I'm annoy-ing?
It may be
That you just really like me
Nay, Lady Mikage...

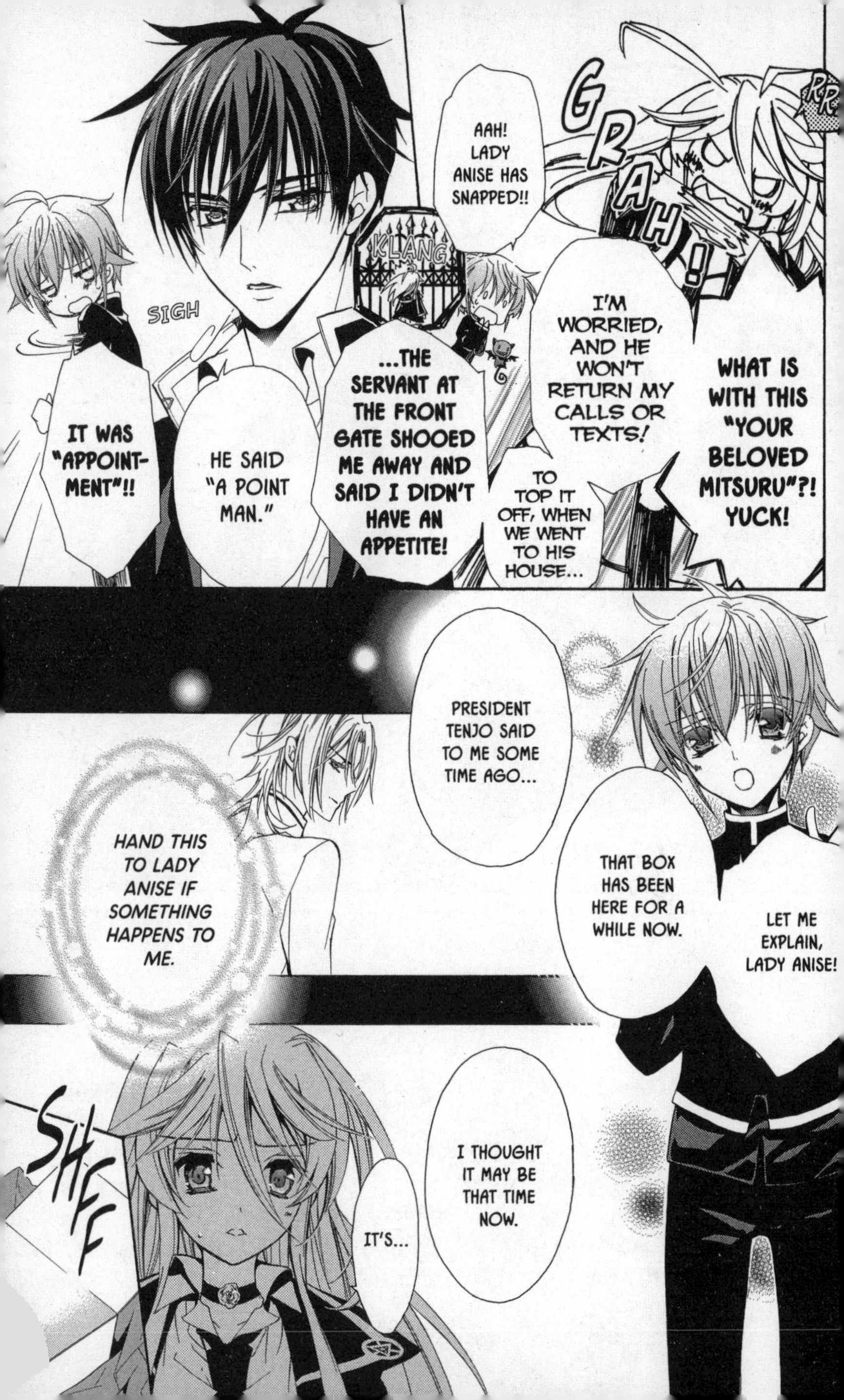
RRR
GRAH!
AAH! LADY ANISE HAS SNAPPED!!
WHAT IS WITH THIS "YOUR BELOVED MITSURU"?! YUCK!
I'M WORRIED, AND HE WON'T RETURN MY CALLS OR TEXTS!
TO TOP IT OFF, WHEN WE WENT TO HIS HOUSE...
KLANG
...THE SERVANT AT THE FRONT GATE SHOOED ME AWAY AND SAID I DIDN'T HAVE AN APPETITE!
HE SAID "A POINT MAN."
SIGH
IT WAS "APPOINT-MENT"!!
LET ME EXPLAIN, LADY ANISE!
THAT BOX HAS BEEN HERE FOR A WHILE NOW.
PRESIDENT TENJO SAID TO ME SOME TIME AGO...
HAND THIS TO LADY ANISE IF SOMETHING HAPPENS TO ME.
I THOUGHT IT MAY BE THAT TIME NOW.
SHFF
IT'S...

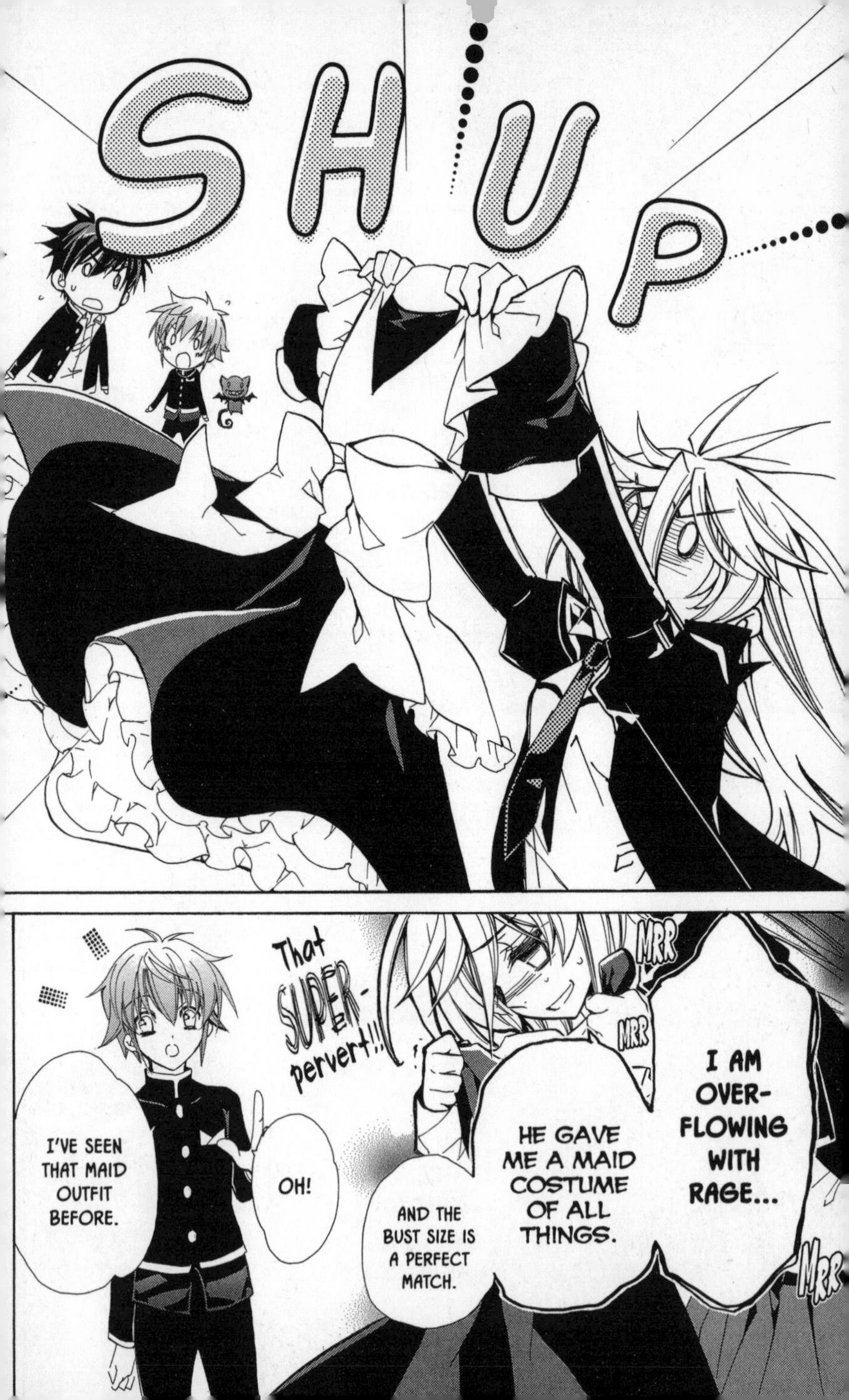
SHUP
MRR
I AM OVER-FLOWING WITH RAGE...
MRR
HE GAVE ME A MAID COSTUME OF ALL THINGS.
AND THE BUST SIZE IS A PERFECT MATCH.
MRR
That SUPER-pervert!!
OH!
I'VE SEEN THAT MAID OUTFIT BEFORE.

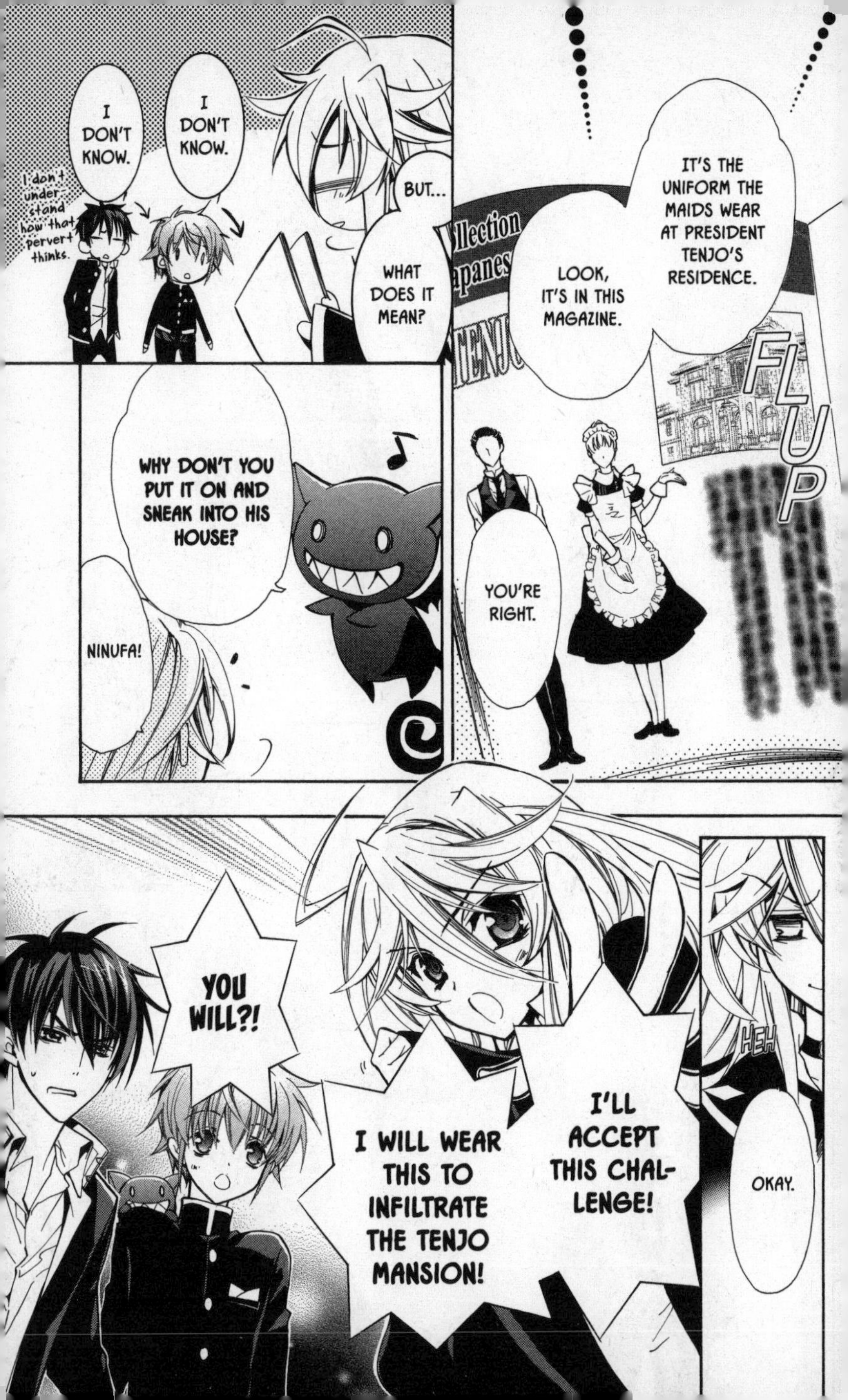
IT'S THE UNIFORM THE MAIDS WEAR AT PRESIDENT TENJO'S RESIDENCE.
LOOK, IT'S IN THIS MAGAZINE.
FLUP
YOU'RE RIGHT.
BUT...
WHAT DOES IT MEAN?
I DON'T KNOW.
I DON'T KNOW.
I don't understand how that pervert thinks.
WHY DON'T YOU PUT IT ON AND SNEAK INTO HIS HOUSE?
NINUFA!
OKAY.
HEH
I'LL ACCEPT THIS CHAL-LENGE!
I WILL WEAR THIS TO INFILTRATE THE TENJO MANSION!
YOU WILL?!

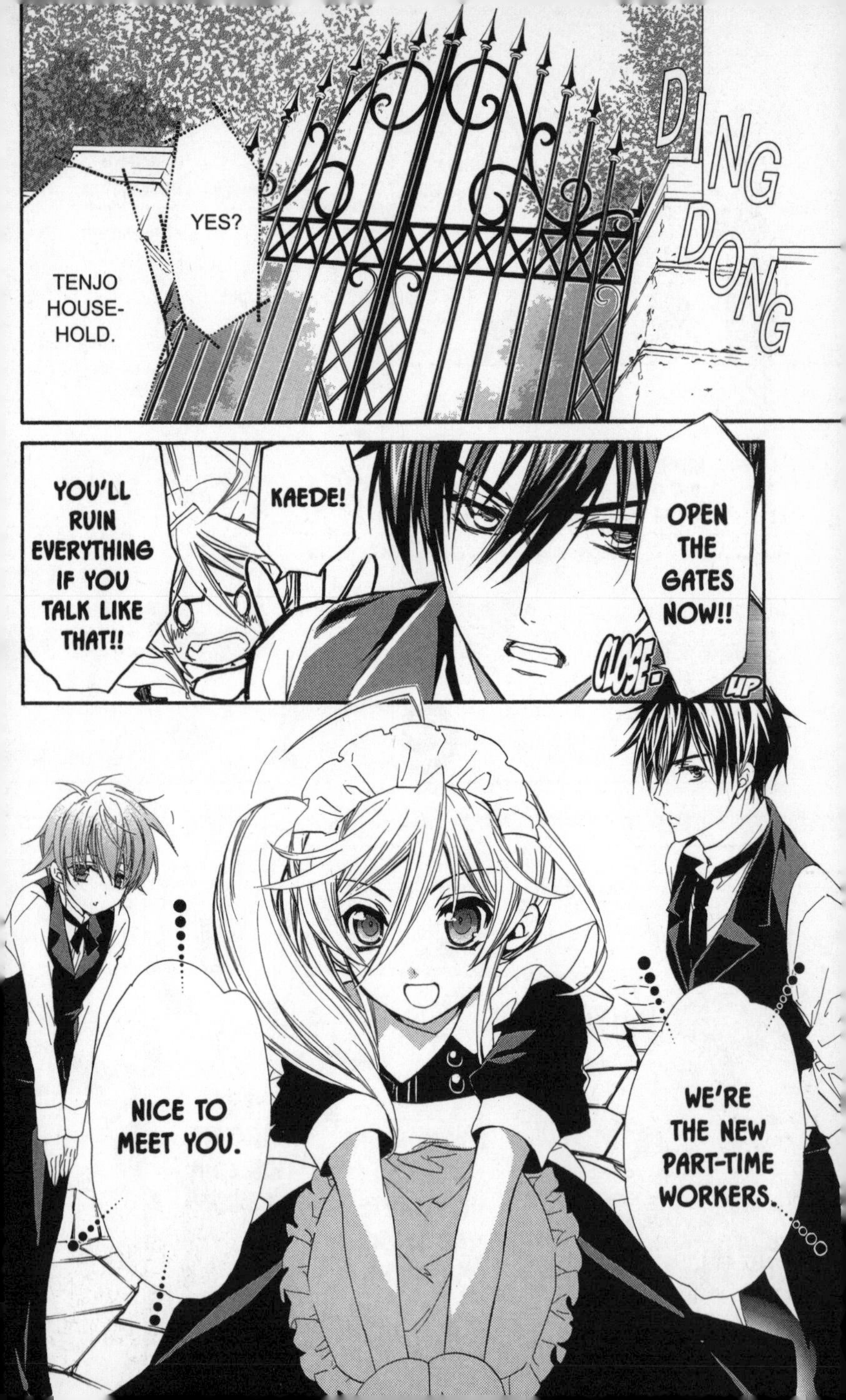
DING DONG
YES?
TENJO HOUSE-HOLD.
OPEN THE GATES NOW!!
CLOSE-UP
KAEDE!
YOU'LL RUIN EVERYTHING IF YOU TALK LIKE THAT!!
WE'RE THE NEW PART-TIME WORKERS.
NICE TO MEET YOU.

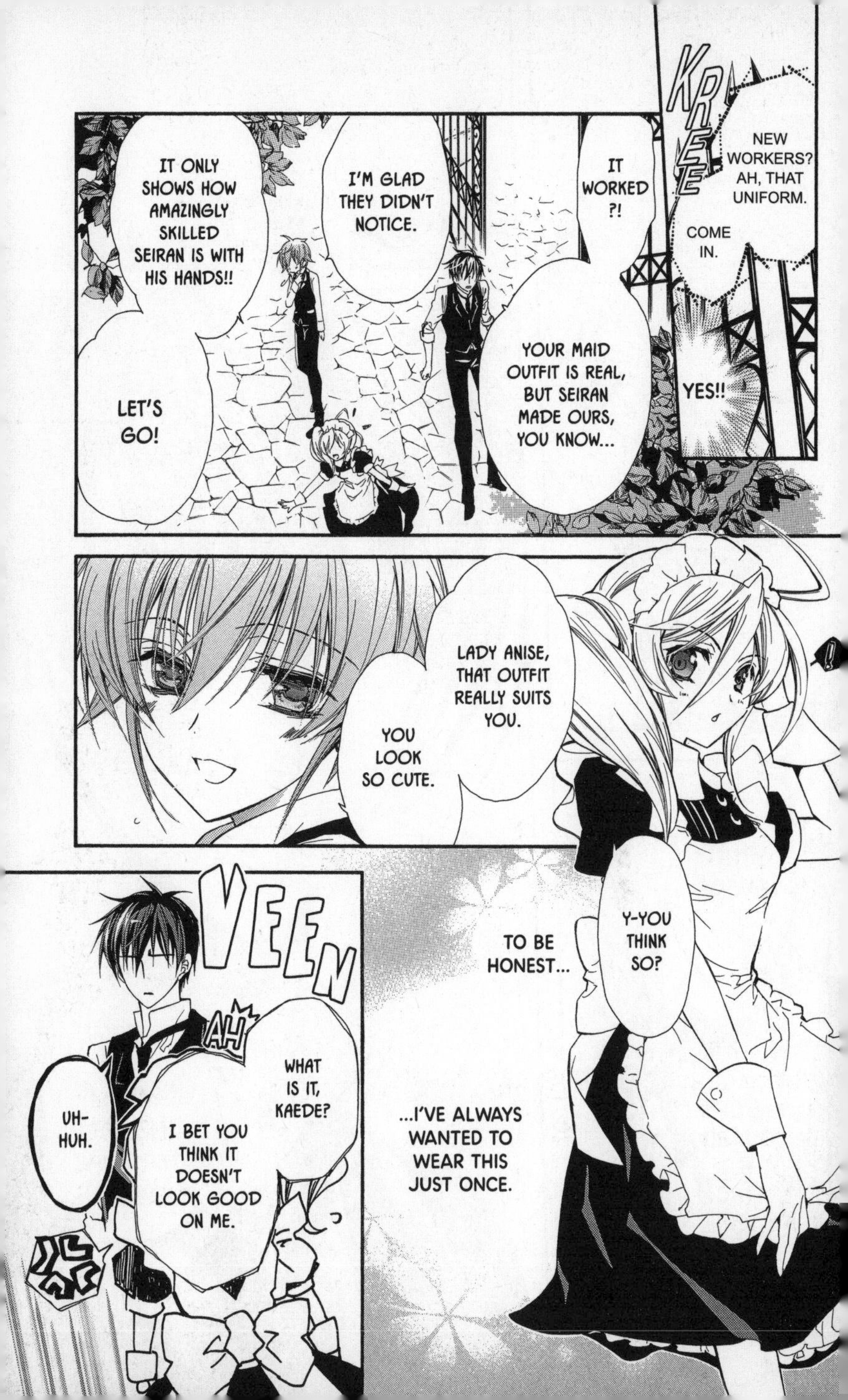
KREE
NEW WORKERS? AH, THAT UNIFORM.
COME IN.
YES!!
IT WORKED?!
YOUR MAID OUTFIT IS REAL, BUT SEIRAN MADE OURS, YOU KNOW...
I'M GLAD THEY DIDN'T NOTICE.
IT ONLY SHOWS HOW AMAZINGLY SKILLED SEIRAN IS WITH HIS HANDS!!
LET'S GO!
LADY ANISE, THAT OUTFIT REALLY SUITS YOU.
YOU LOOK SO CUTE.
Y-YOU THINK SO?
TO BE HONEST...
...I'VE ALWAYS WANTED TO WEAR THIS JUST ONCE.
VEEN
AH
WHAT IS IT, KAEDE?
I BET YOU THINK IT DOESN'T LOOK GOOD ON ME.
UH-HUH.

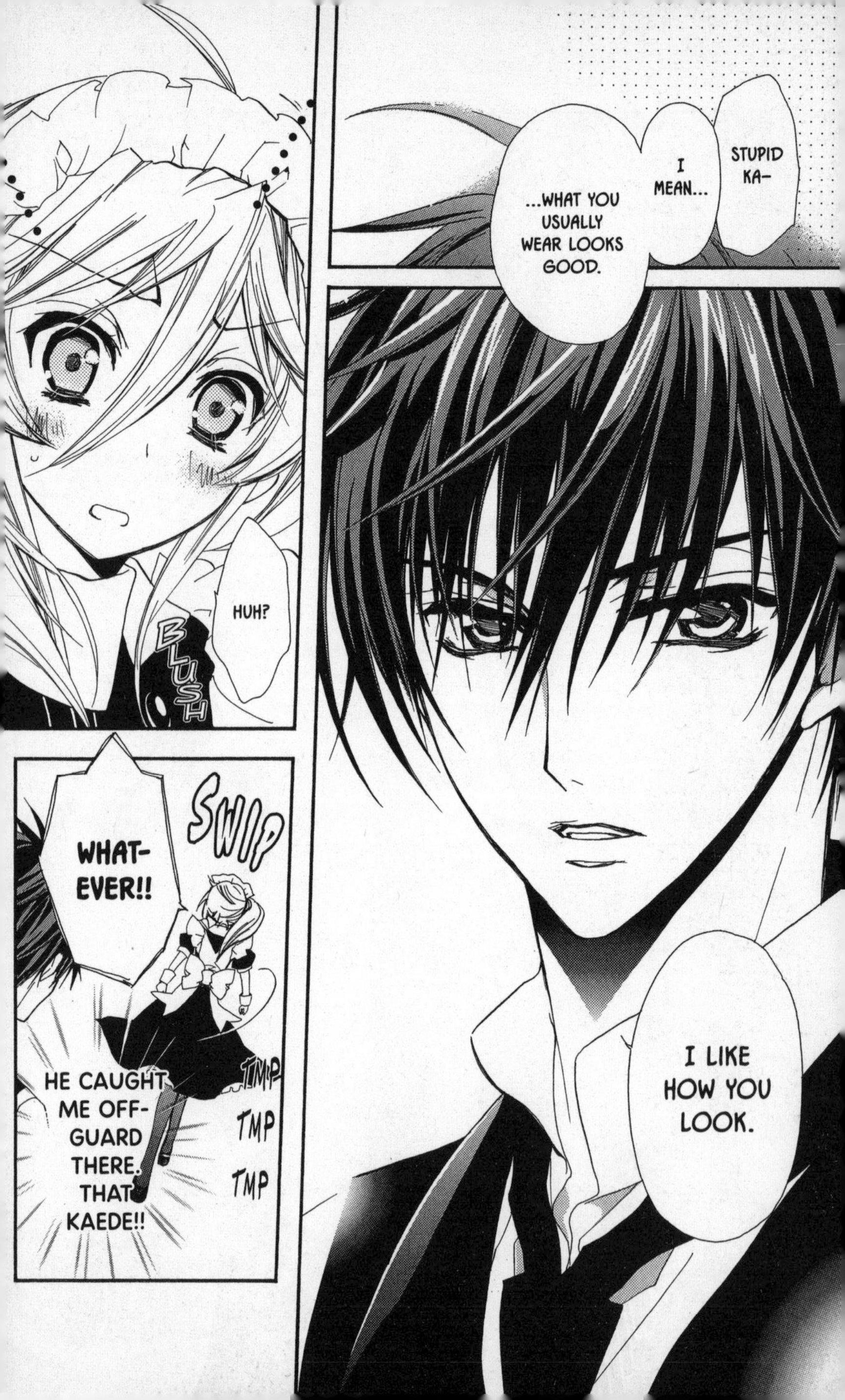
STUPID KA-
I MEAN...
...WHAT YOU USUALLY WEAR LOOKS GOOD.
I LIKE HOW YOU LOOK.
HUH?
BLUSH
SWIP
WHAT-EVER!!
TMP
TMP
TMP
HE CAUGHT ME OFF-GUARD THERE. THAT KAEDE!!

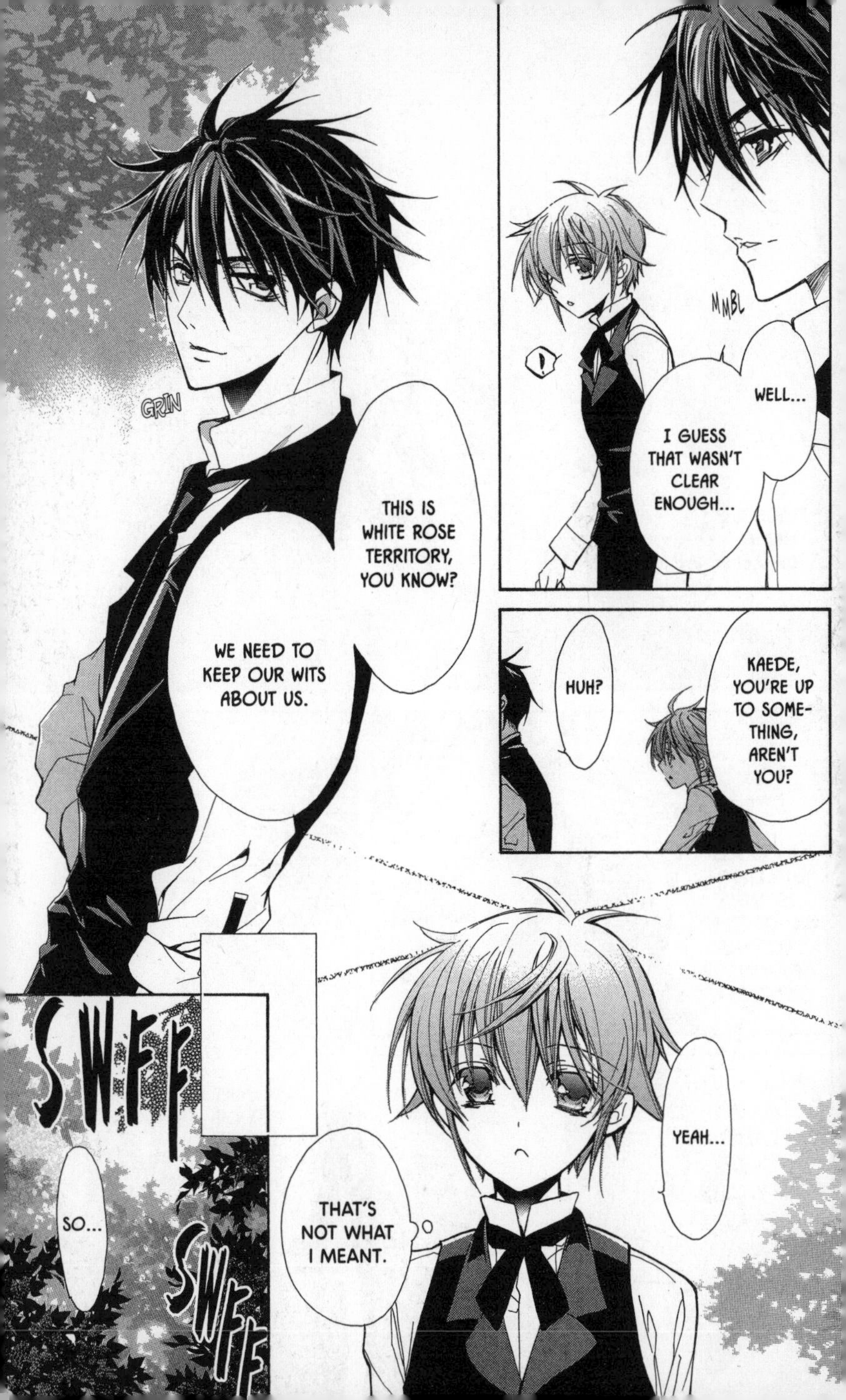
!
MMBL
WELL...
I GUESS THAT WASN'T CLEAR ENOUGH...
KAEDE, YOU'RE UP TO SOME-THING, AREN'T YOU?
HUH?
GRIN
THIS IS WHITE ROSE TERRITORY, YOU KNOW?
WE NEED TO KEEP OUR WITS ABOUT US.
YEAH...
THAT'S NOT WHAT I MEANT.
SWFF
SO...
SWFF

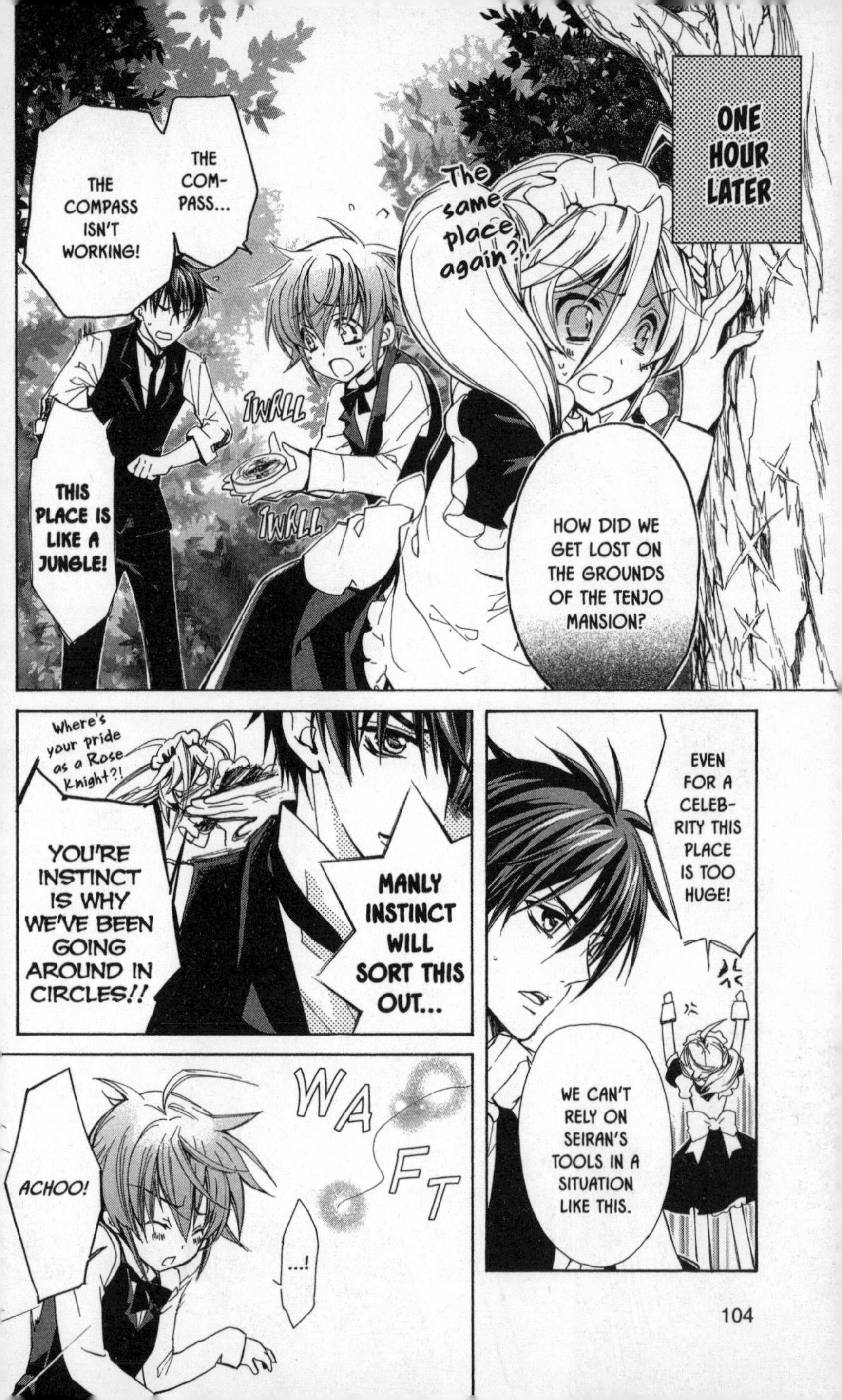
ONE HOUR LATER
The same place again?!
HOW DID WE GET LOST ON THE GROUNDS OF THE TENJO MANSION?
THE COM-PASS...
THE COMPASS ISN'T WORKING!
IWRLL
IWRLL
THIS PLACE IS LIKE A JUNGLE!
EVEN FOR A CELEB-RITY THIS PLACE IS TOO HUGE!
WE CAN'T RELY ON SEIRAN'S TOOLS IN A SITUATION LIKE THIS.
MANLY INSTINCT WILL SORT THIS OUT...
Where's your pride as a Rose Knight?!
YOU'RE INSTINCT IS WHY WE'VE BEEN GOING AROUND IN CIRCLES!!
WAFT
...!
ACHOO!

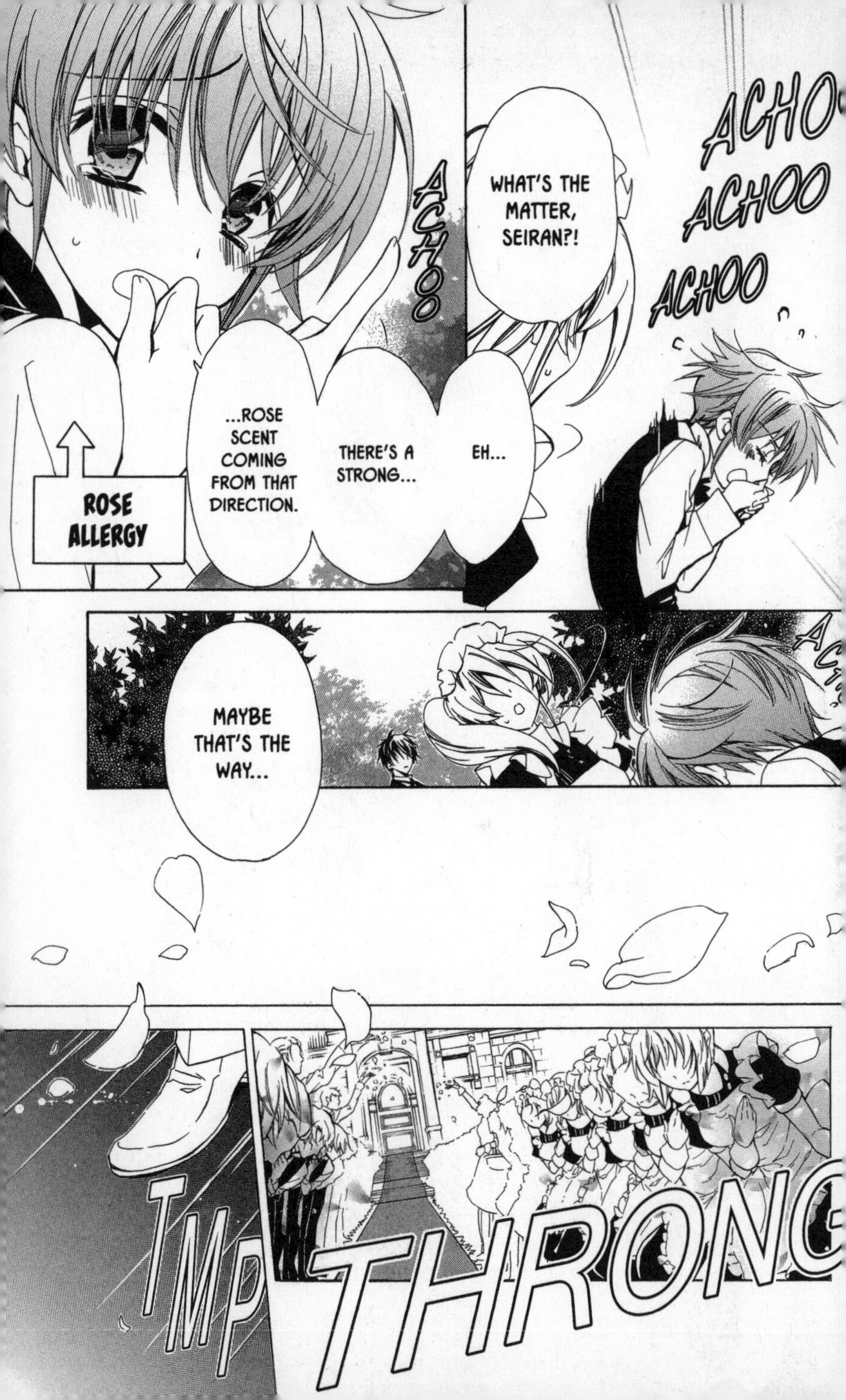

ACHO
ACHOO
ACHOO
WHAT'S THE MATTER, SEIRAN?!
ACHOO
EH...
THERE'S A STRONG...
...ROSE SCENT COMING FROM THAT DIRECTION.
ROSE ALLERGY
MAYBE THAT'S THE WAY...
THRONG
TMP

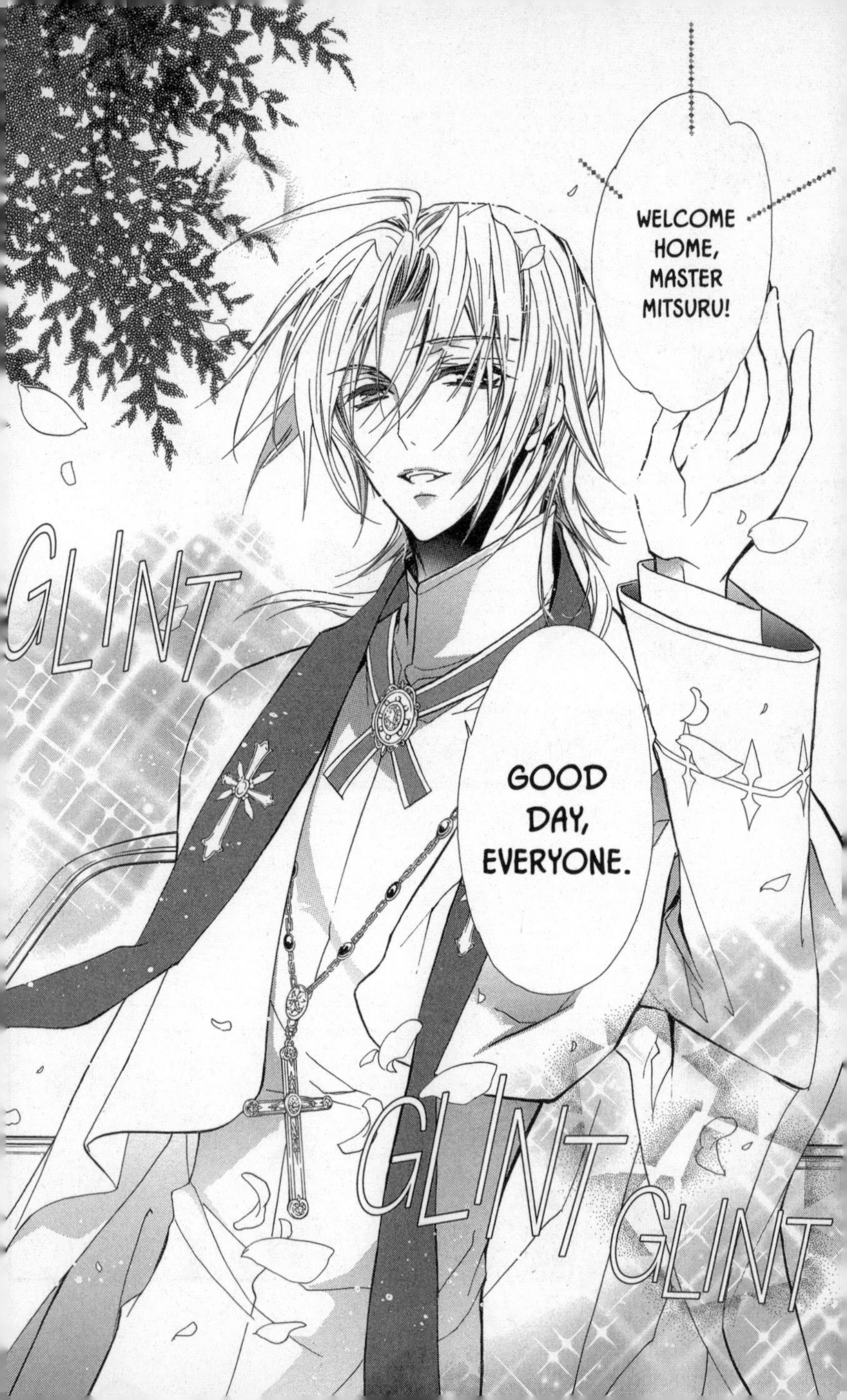
WELCOME HOME, MASTER MITSURU!
GLINT
GOOD DAY, EVERYONE.
GLINT
GLINT
GLINT

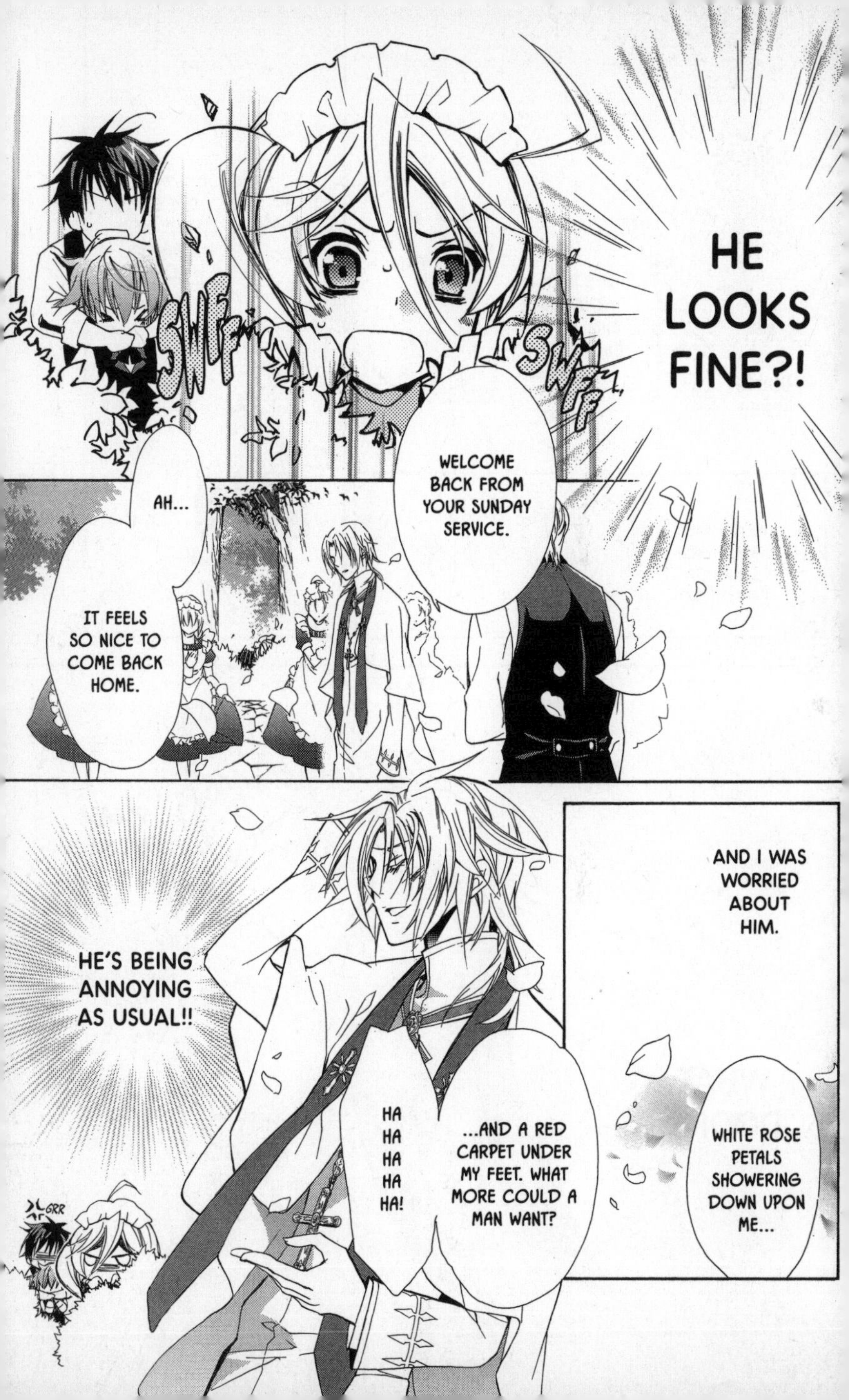
HE LOOKS FINE?!
SWFF
SWF
WELCOME BACK FROM YOUR SUNDAY SERVICE.
AH...
IT FEELS SO NICE TO COME BACK HOME.
AND I WAS WORRIED ABOUT HIM.
WHITE ROSE PETALS SHOWERING DOWN UPON ME...
...AND A RED CARPET UNDER MY FEET. WHAT MORE COULD A MAN WANT?
HA HA HA HA HA!
HE'S BEING ANNOYING AS USUAL!!
GRR

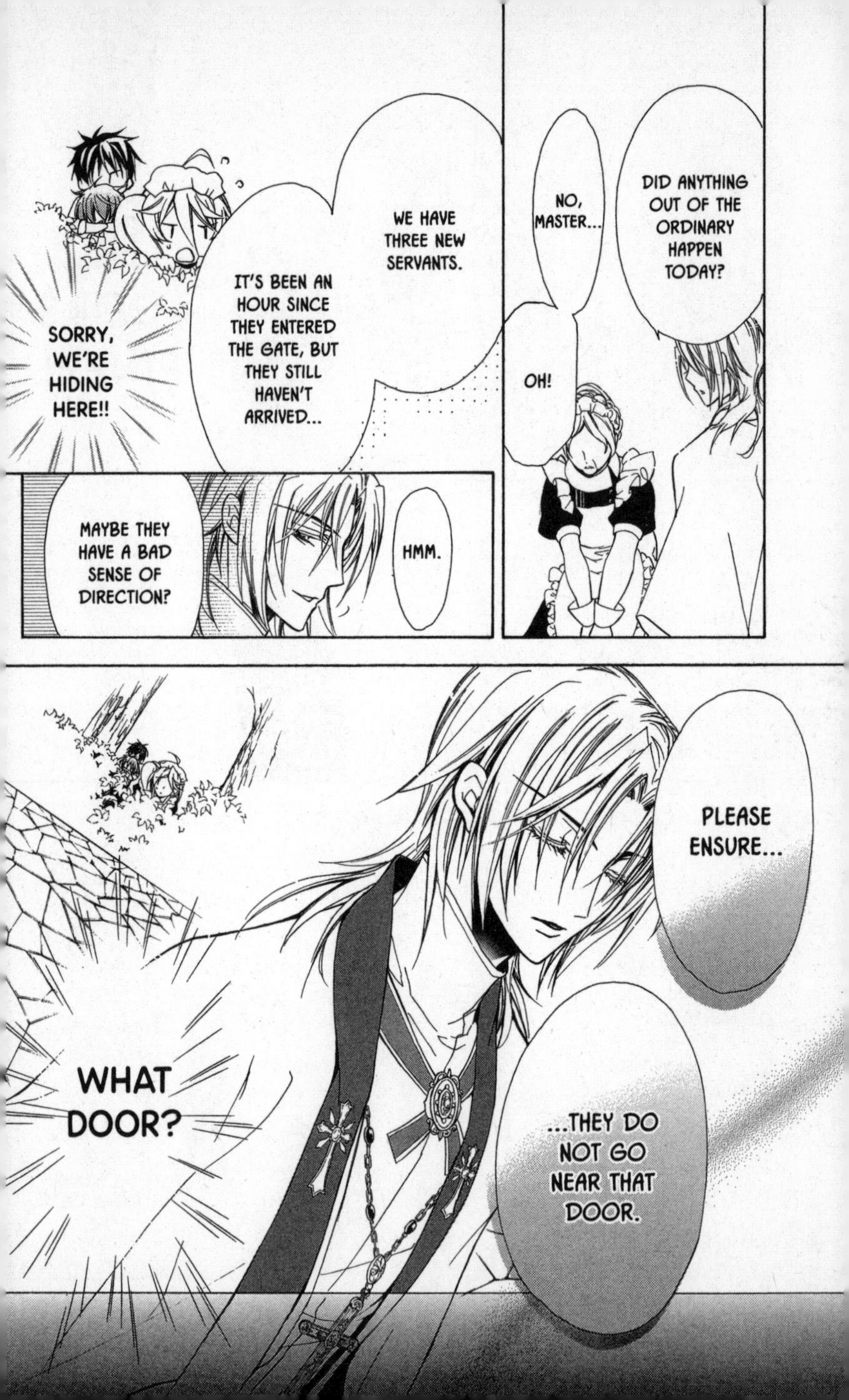
DID ANYTHING OUT OF THE ORDINARY HAPPEN TODAY?
NO, MASTER...
OH!
WE HAVE THREE NEW SERVANTS.
IT'S BEEN AN HOUR SINCE THEY ENTERED THE GATE, BUT THEY STILL HAVEN'T ARRIVED...
SORRY, WE'RE HIDING HERE!!
HMM.
MAYBE THEY HAVE A BAD SENSE OF DIRECTION?
PLEASE ENSURE...
...THEY DO NOT GO NEAR THAT DOOR.
WHAT DOOR?

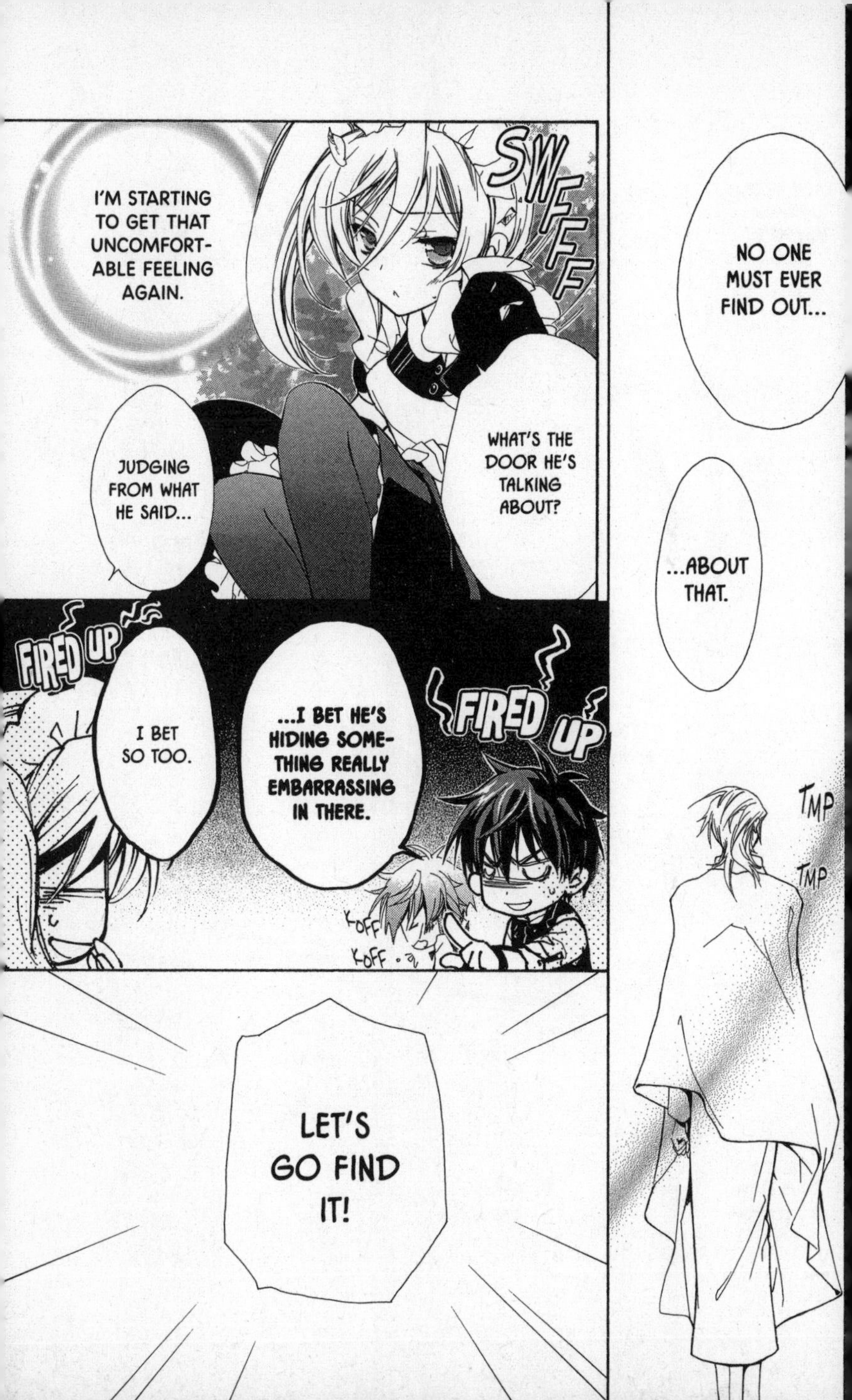
NO ONE MUST EVER FIND OUT...
...ABOUT THAT.
TMP
TMP
SWFFF
I'M STARTING TO GET THAT UNCOMFORTABLE FEELING AGAIN.
WHAT'S THE DOOR HE'S TALKING ABOUT?
JUDGING FROM WHAT HE SAID...
FIRED UP
...I BET HE'S HIDING SOMETHING REALLY EMBARRASSING IN THERE.
KOFF
KOFF
I BET SO TOO.
FIRED UP
LET'S GO FIND IT!

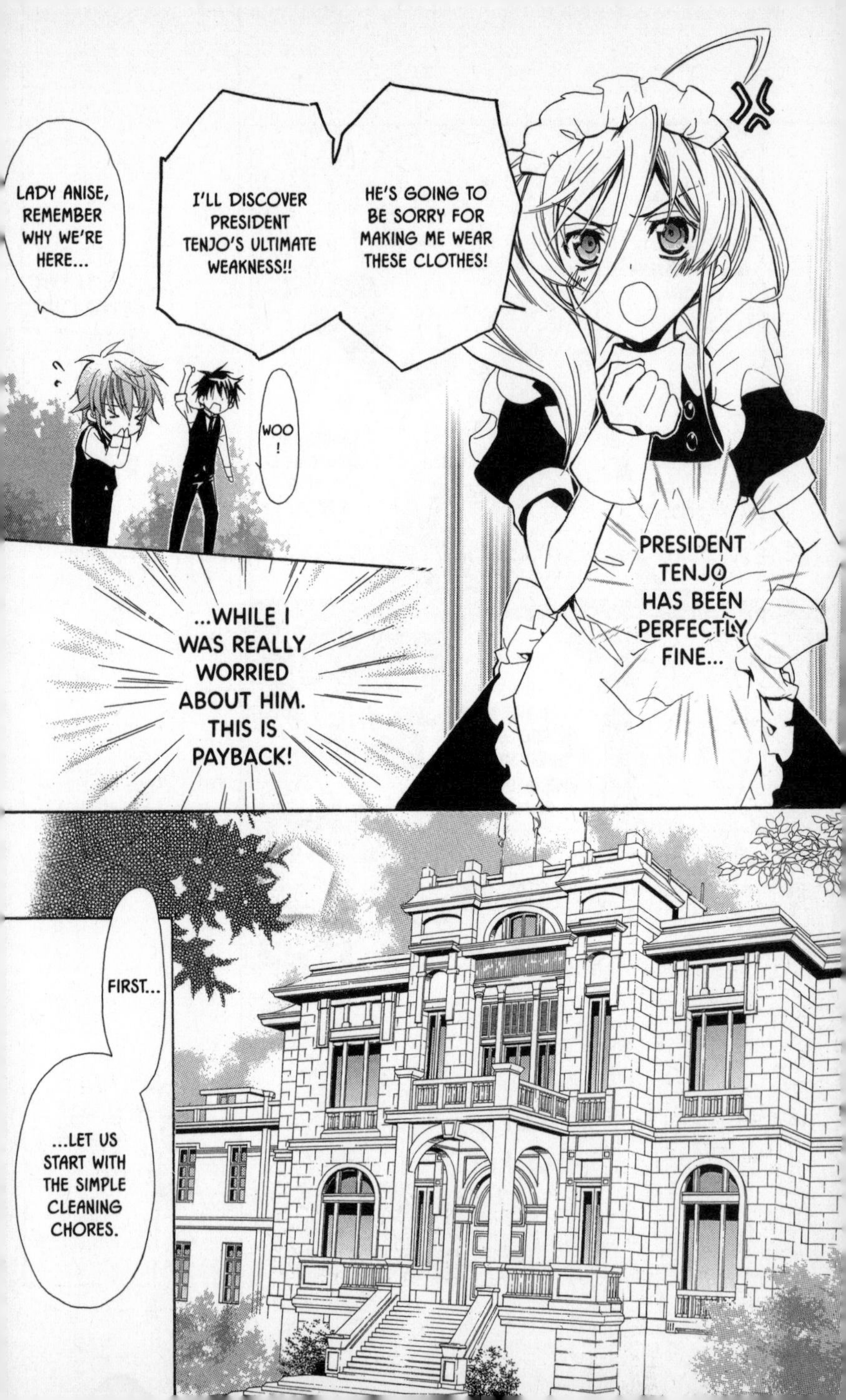

HE'S GOING TO BE SORRY FOR MAKING ME WEAR THESE CLOTHES!
I'LL DISCOVER PRESIDENT TENJO'S ULTIMATE WEAKNESS!!
PRESIDENT TENJO HAS BEEN PERFECTLY FINE...
LADY ANISE, REMEMBER WHY WE'RE HERE...
WOO!
...WHILE I WAS REALLY WORRIED ABOUT HIM. THIS IS PAYBACK!
FIRST...
...LET US START WITH THE SIMPLE CLEANING CHORES.

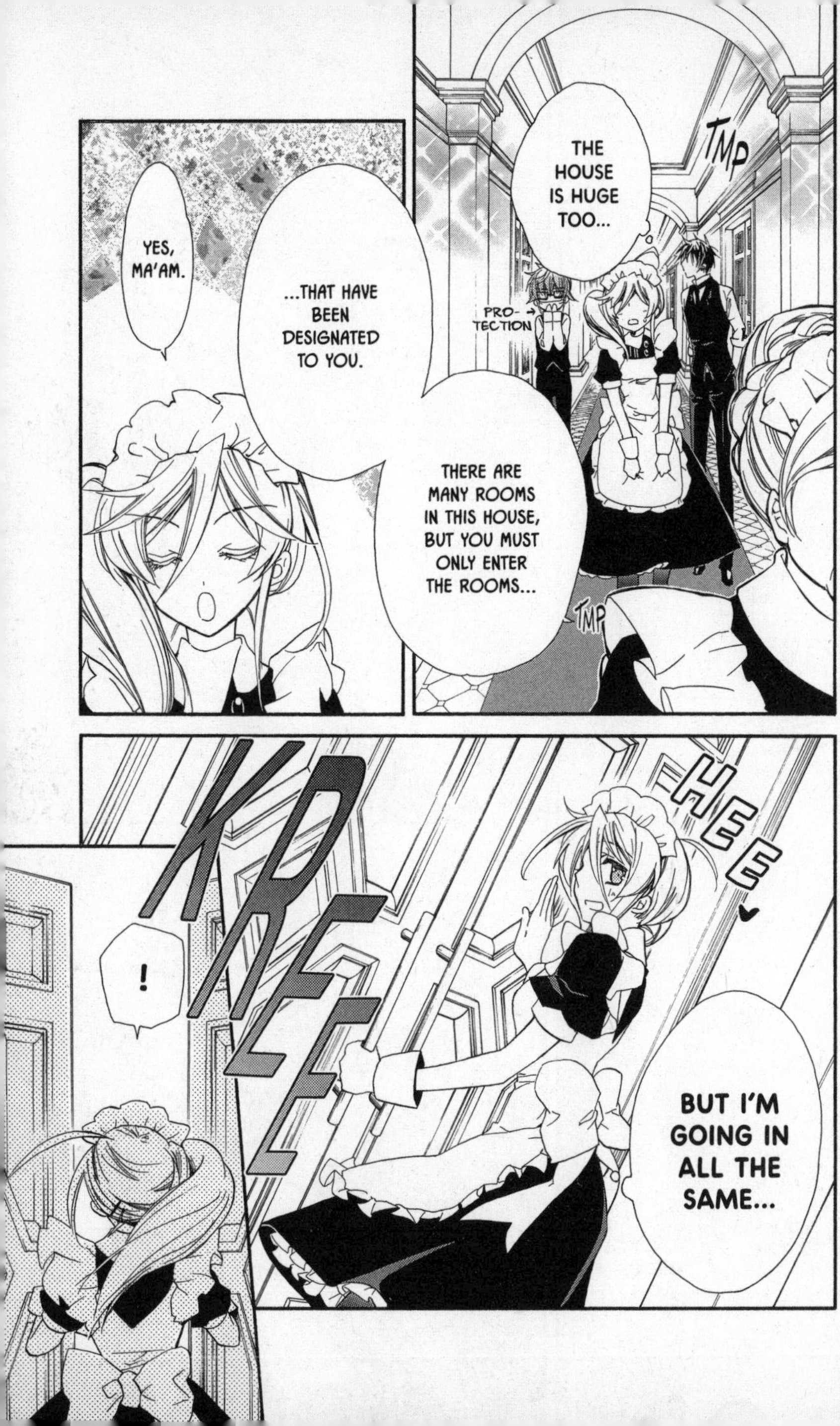
TMP
THE HOUSE IS HUGE TOO...
PRO- TECTION
THERE ARE MANY ROOMS IN THIS HOUSE, BUT YOU MUST ONLY ENTER THE ROOMS...
TMP
...THAT HAVE BEEN DESIGNATED TO YOU.
YES, MA'AM.
HEE
KREEE
BUT I'M GOING IN ALL THE SAME...
!

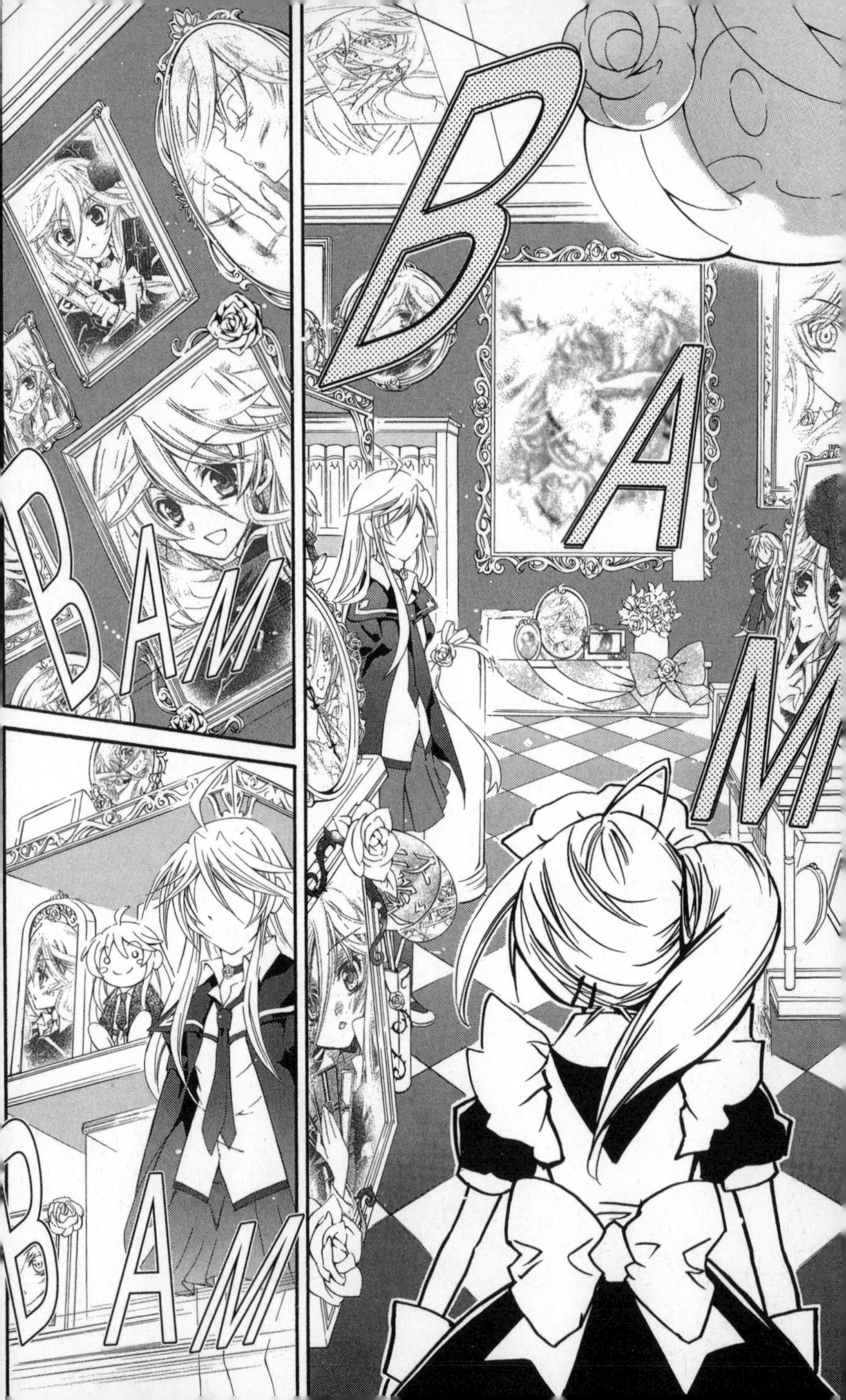
BAM
BAM
BAM

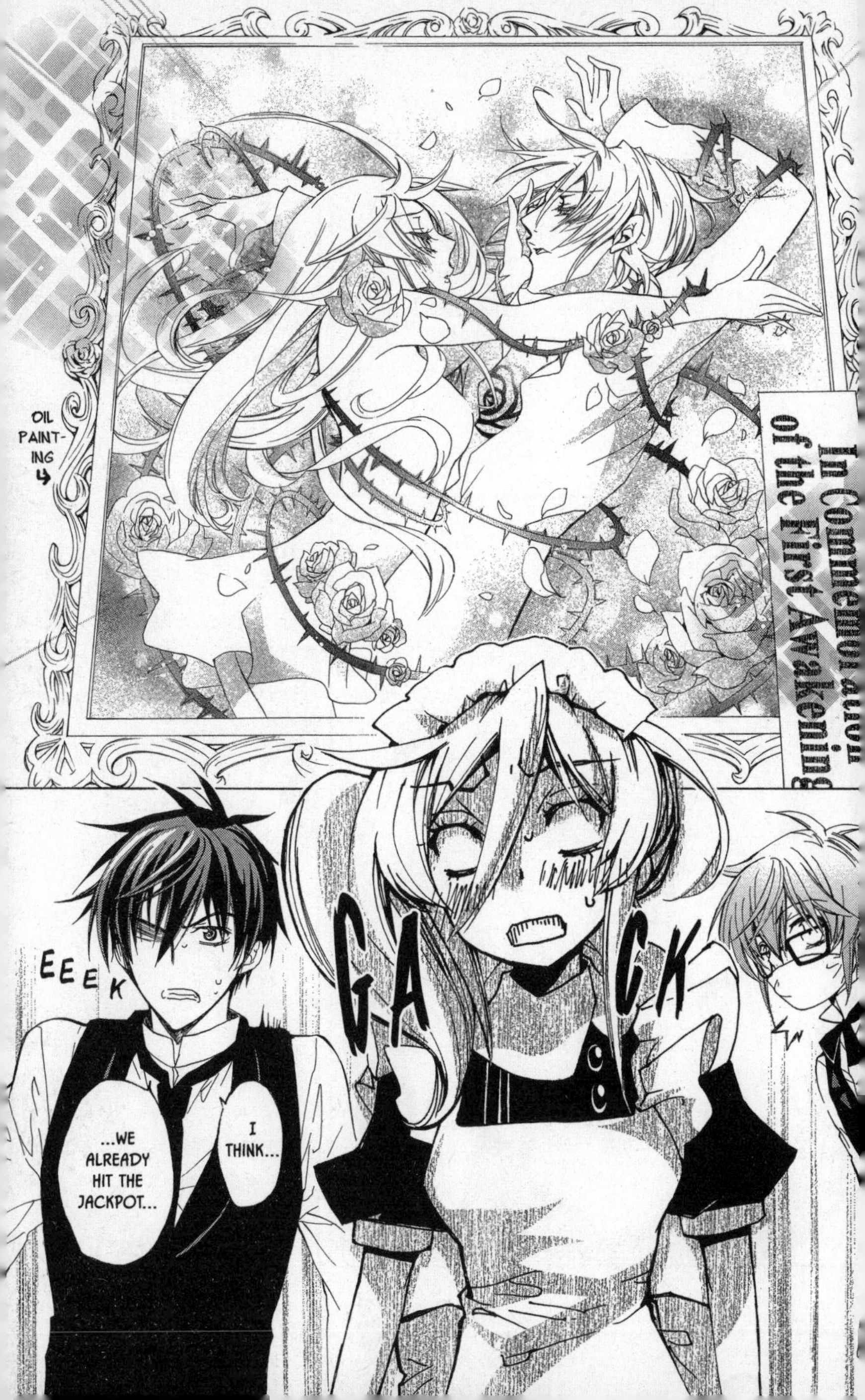
In Commemoration of the First Awakening
OIL PAINT-ING
GACK
I THINK...
...WE ALREADY HIT THE JACKPOT...
EEEK

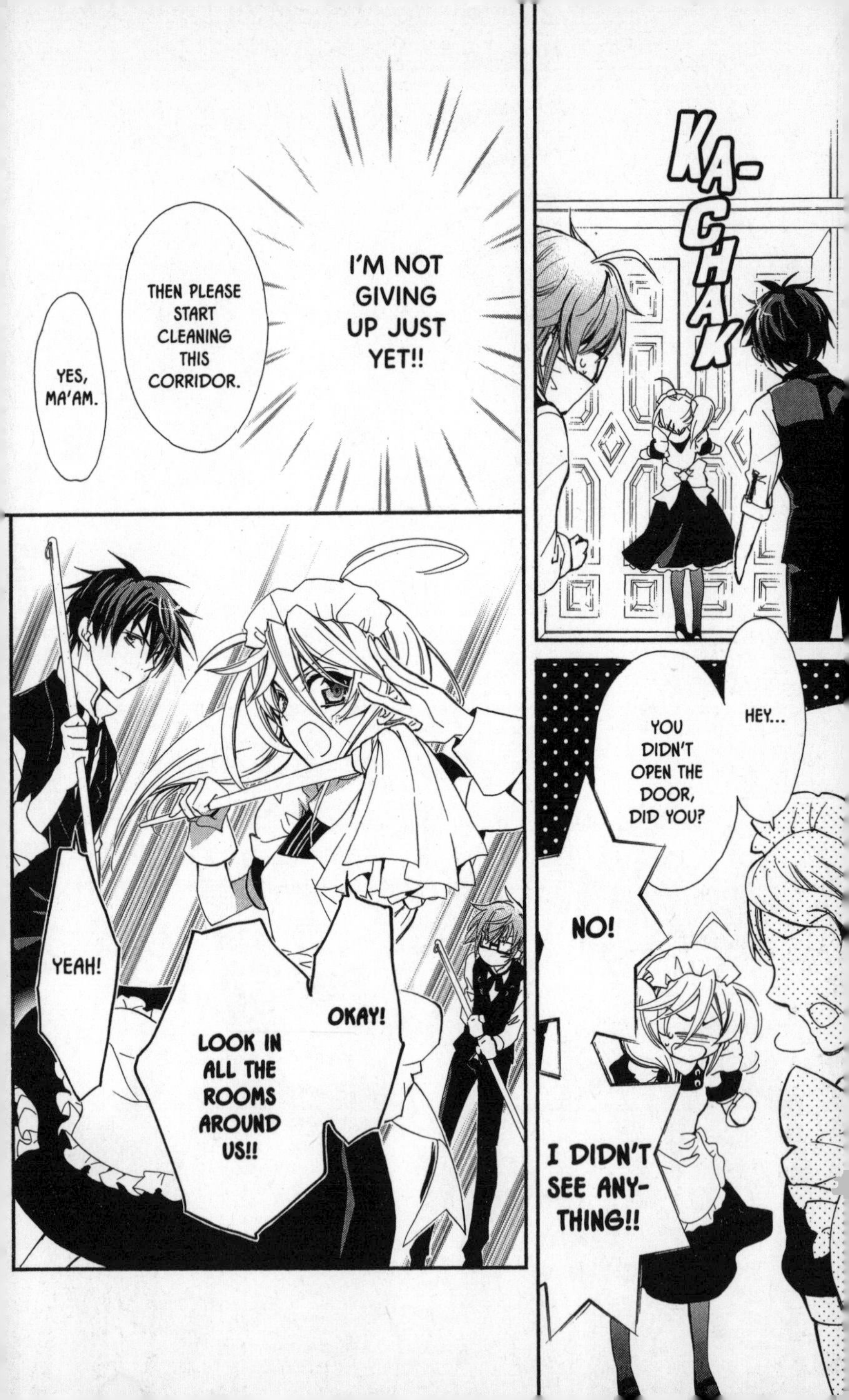
KA-CHAK
HEY...
YOU DIDN'T OPEN THE DOOR, DID YOU?
NO!
I DIDN'T SEE ANY-THING!!
I'M NOT GIVING UP JUST YET!!
THEN PLEASE START CLEANING THIS CORRIDOR.
YES, MA'AM.
LOOK IN ALL THE ROOMS AROUND US!!
OKAY!
YEAH!

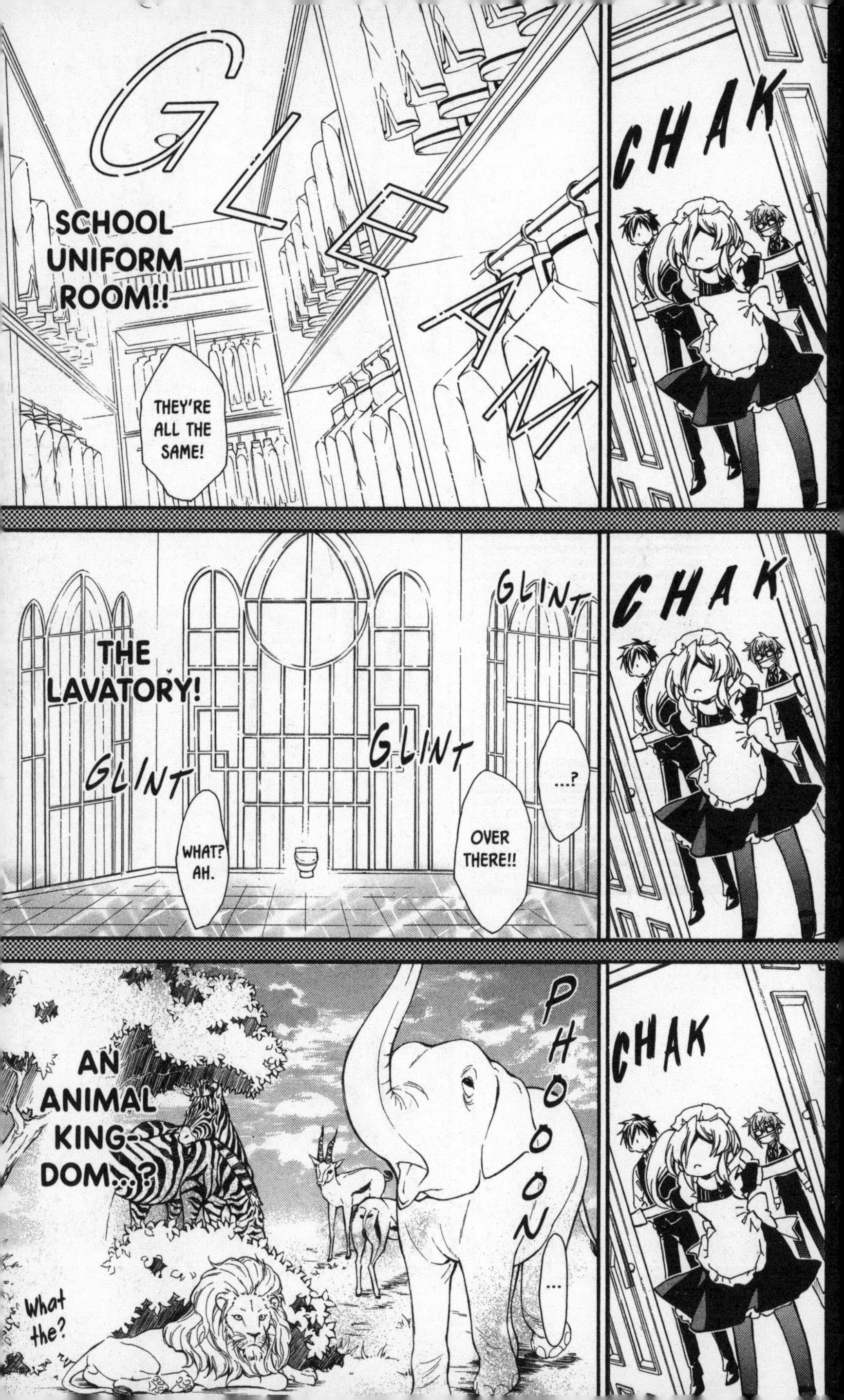
CHAK
GLEAM
SCHOOL UNIFORM ROOM!!
THEY'RE ALL THE SAME!
CHAK
GLINT
THE LAVATORY!
...?
OVER THERE!!
GLINT
WHAT? AH.
GLINT
CHAK
PHOOOON
AN ANIMAL KING-DOM...?
...
What the?

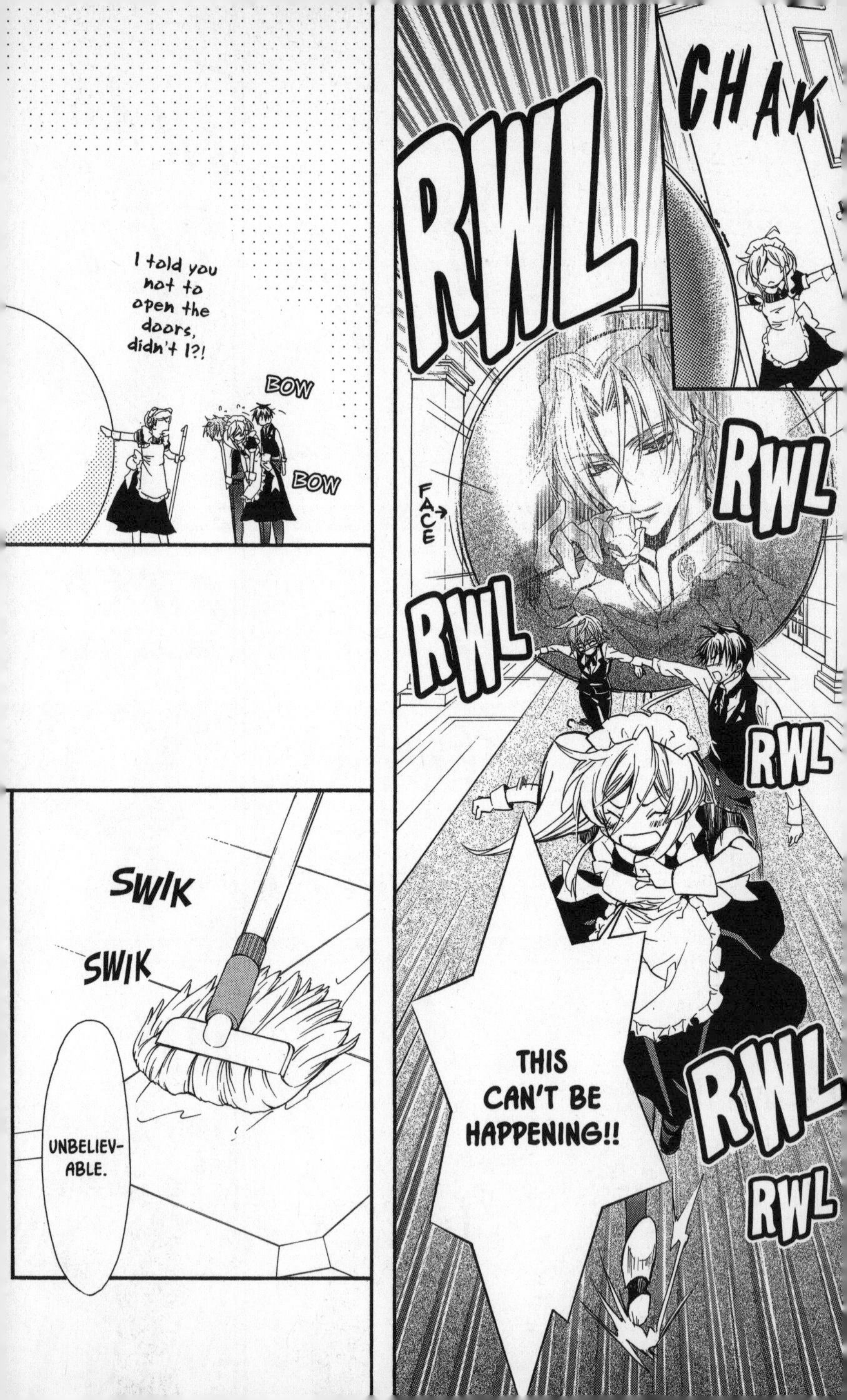
CHAK
RWL
RWL
FACE→
RWL
RWL
THIS CAN'T BE HAPPENING!!
RWL
RWL
I told you not to open the doors, didn't I?!
BOW
BOW
SWIK
SWIK
UNBELIEV-ABLE.

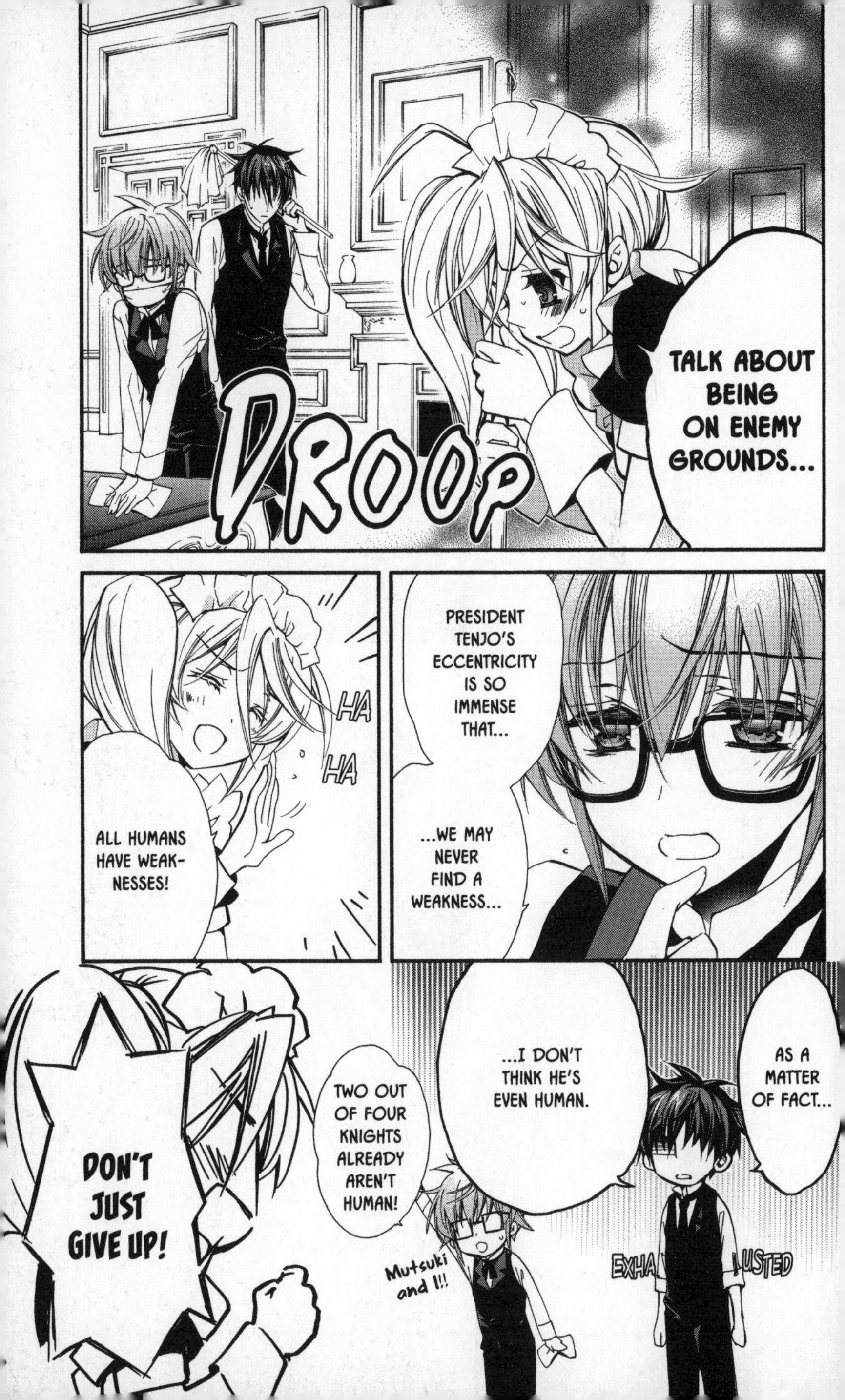
TALK ABOUT BEING ON ENEMY GROUNDS...
DROOP
PRESIDENT TENJO'S ECCENTRICITY IS SO IMMENSE THAT...
...WE MAY NEVER FIND A WEAKNESS...
HA
HA
ALL HUMANS HAVE WEAK-NESSES!
AS A MATTER OF FACT...
...I DON'T THINK HE'S EVEN HUMAN.
EXHAUSTED
TWO OUT OF FOUR KNIGHTS ALREADY AREN'T HUMAN!
Mutsuki and I!!
DON'T JUST GIVE UP!

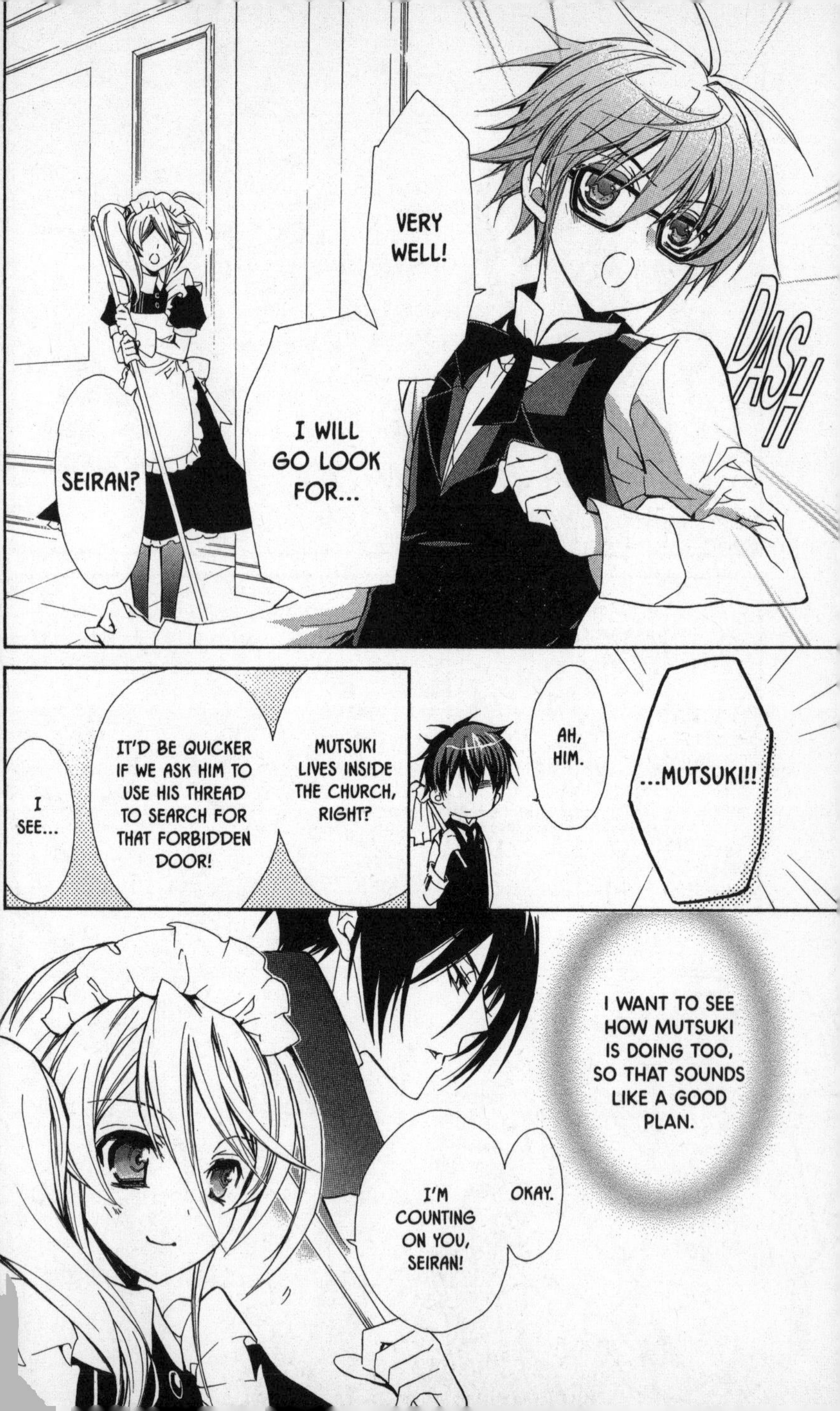
DASH
VERY WELL!
I WILL GO LOOK FOR...
SEIRAN?
...MUTSUKI!!
AH, HIM.
MUTSUKI LIVES INSIDE THE CHURCH, RIGHT?
IT'D BE QUICKER IF WE ASK HIM TO USE HIS THREAD TO SEARCH FOR THAT FORBIDDEN DOOR!
I SEE...
I WANT TO SEE HOW MUTSUKI IS DOING TOO, SO THAT SOUNDS LIKE A GOOD PLAN.
OKAY.
I'M COUNTING ON YOU, SEIRAN!

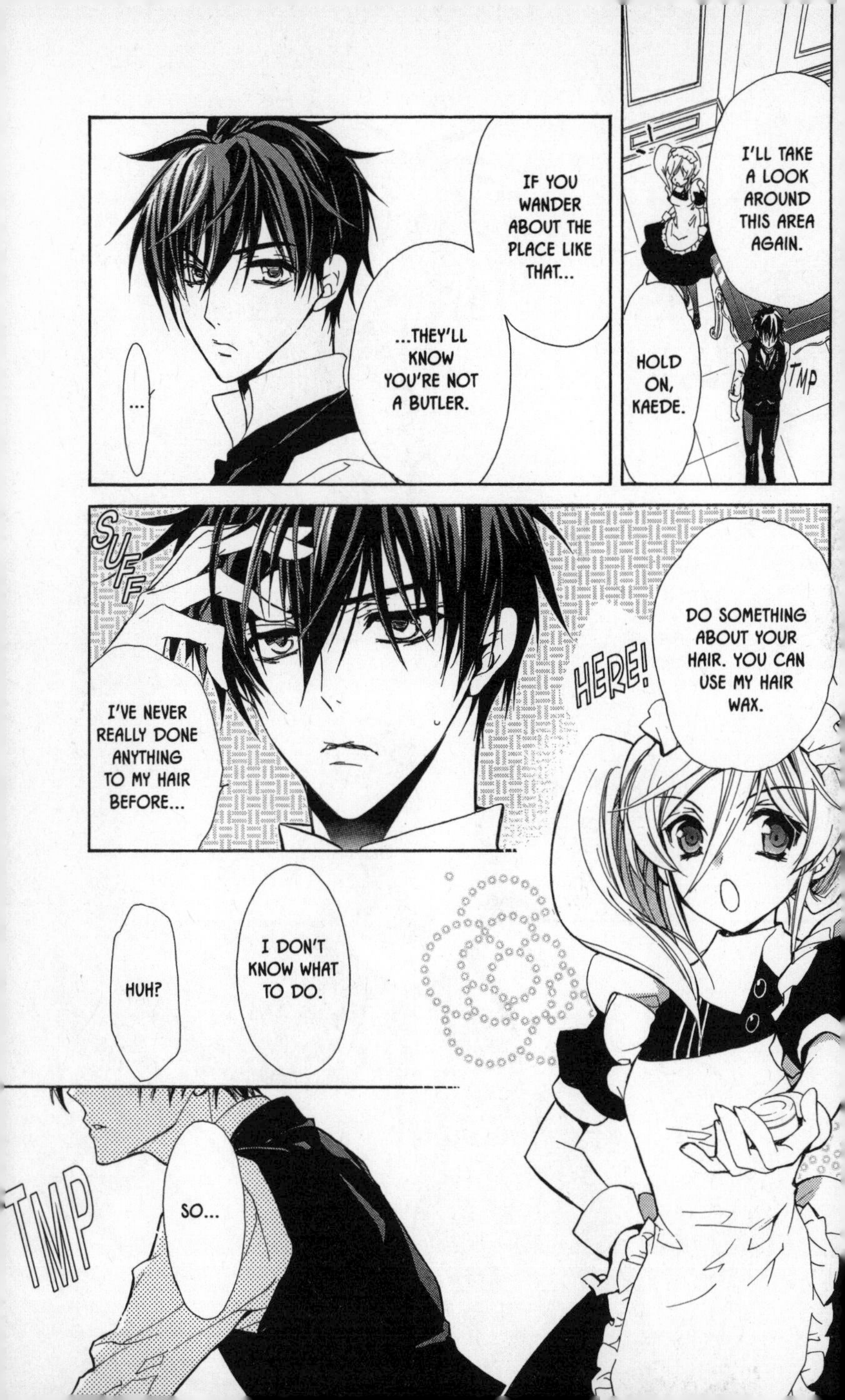
I'LL TAKE A LOOK AROUND THIS AREA AGAIN.
HOLD ON, KAEDE.
TMP
IF YOU WANDER ABOUT THE PLACE LIKE THAT...
...THEY'LL KNOW YOU'RE NOT A BUTLER.
...
DO SOMETHING ABOUT YOUR HAIR. YOU CAN USE MY HAIR WAX.
HERE!
SUFF
I'VE NEVER REALLY DONE ANYTHING TO MY HAIR BEFORE...
I DON'T KNOW WHAT TO DO.
HUH?
SO...
TMP

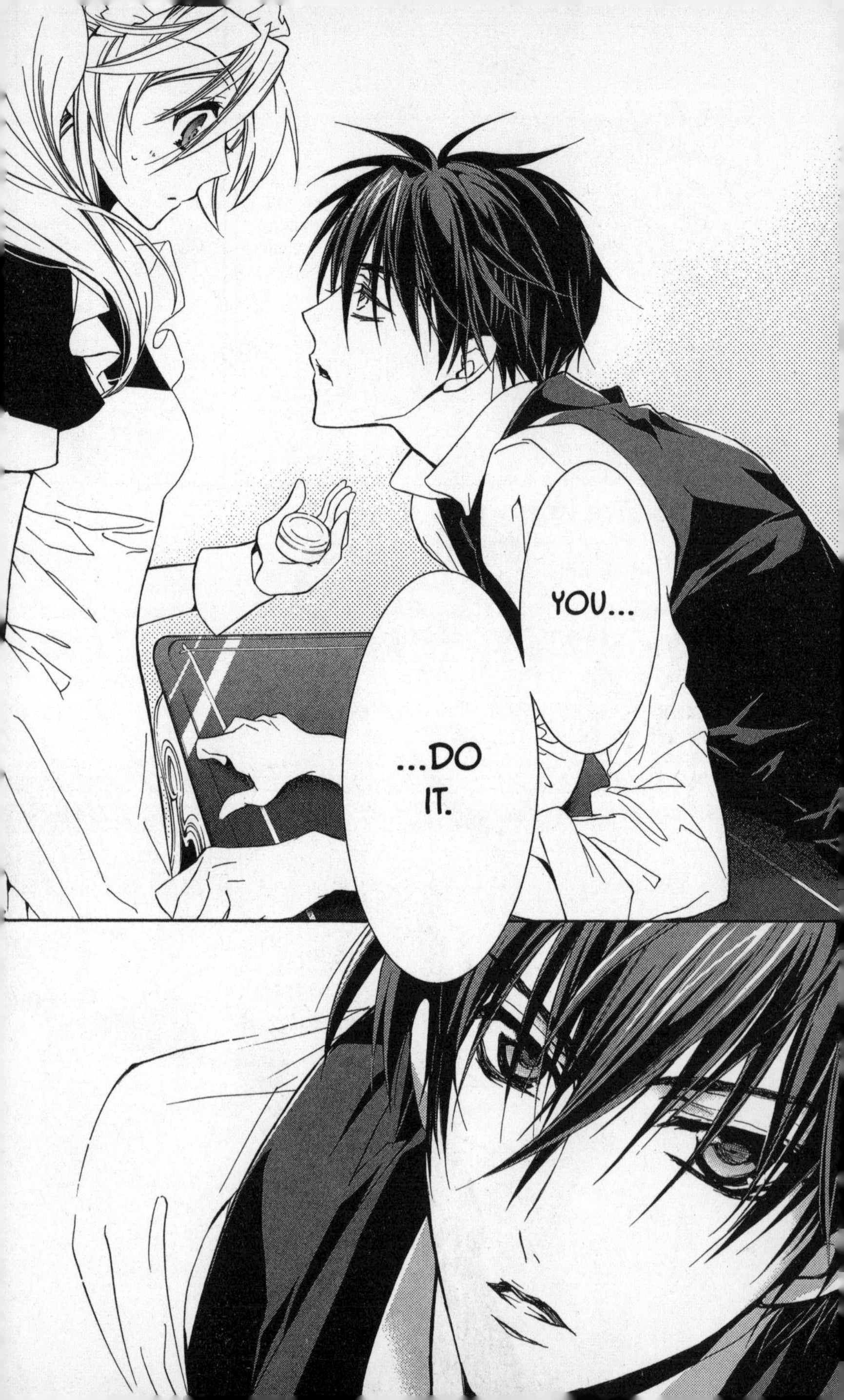
YOU...
...DO IT.

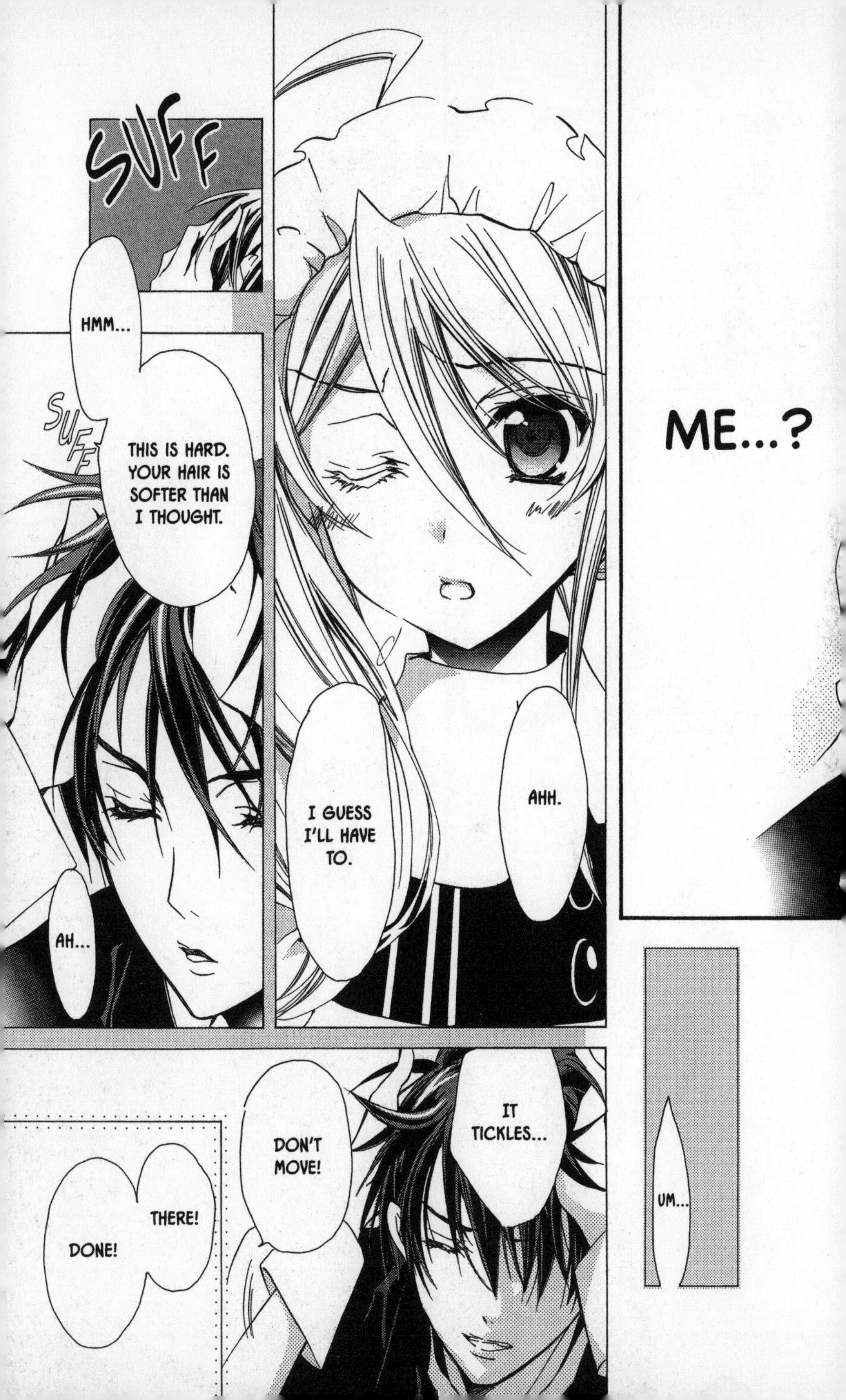
ME...?
AHH.
I GUESS I'LL HAVE TO.
SUFF
HMM...
SUFF
THIS IS HARD. YOUR HAIR IS SOFTER THAN I THOUGHT.
AH...
UM...
IT TICKLES...
DON'T MOVE!
THERE!
DONE!

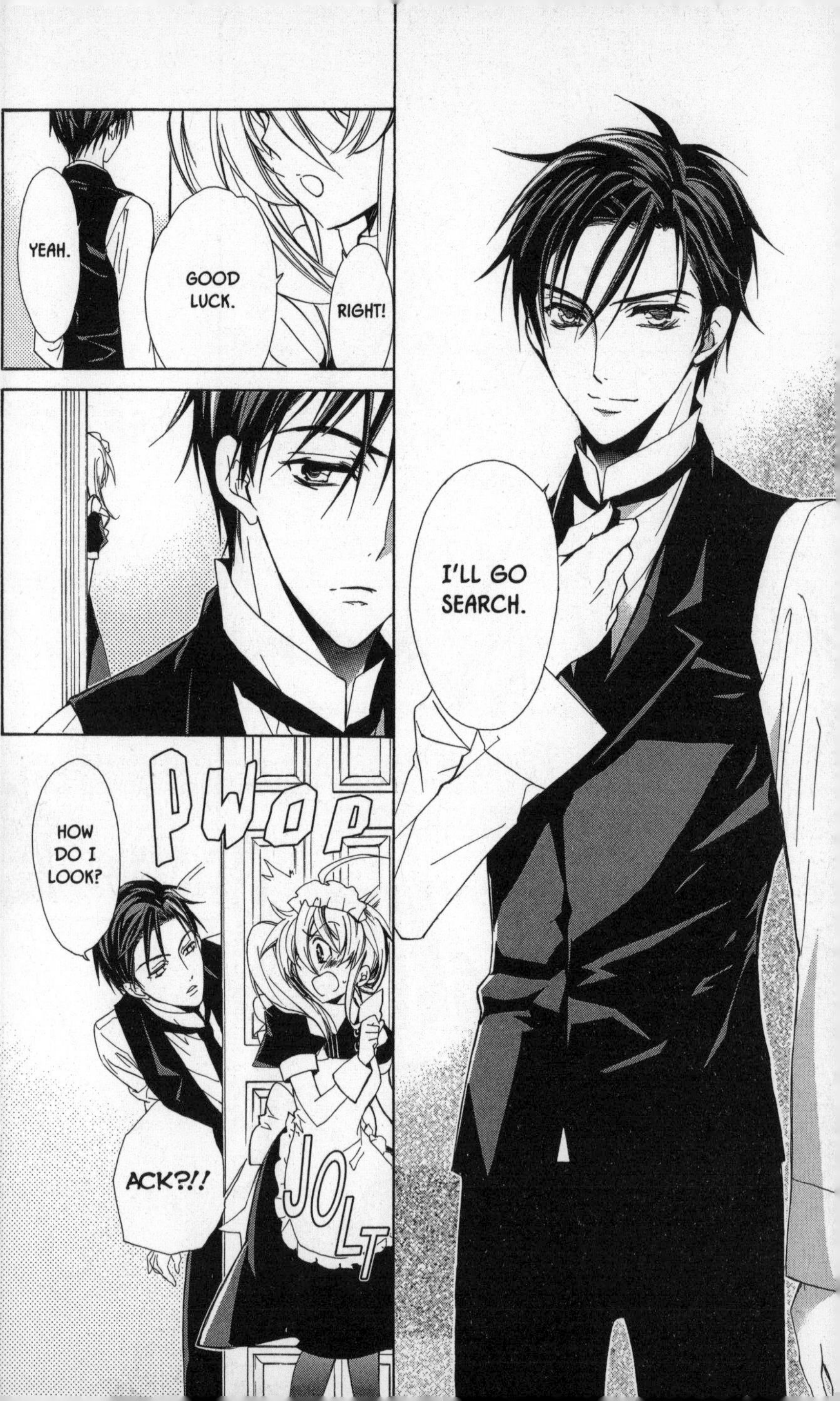
I'LL GO SEARCH.
RIGHT!
GOOD LUCK.
YEAH.
PWOP
HOW DO I LOOK?
JOLT
ACK?!!

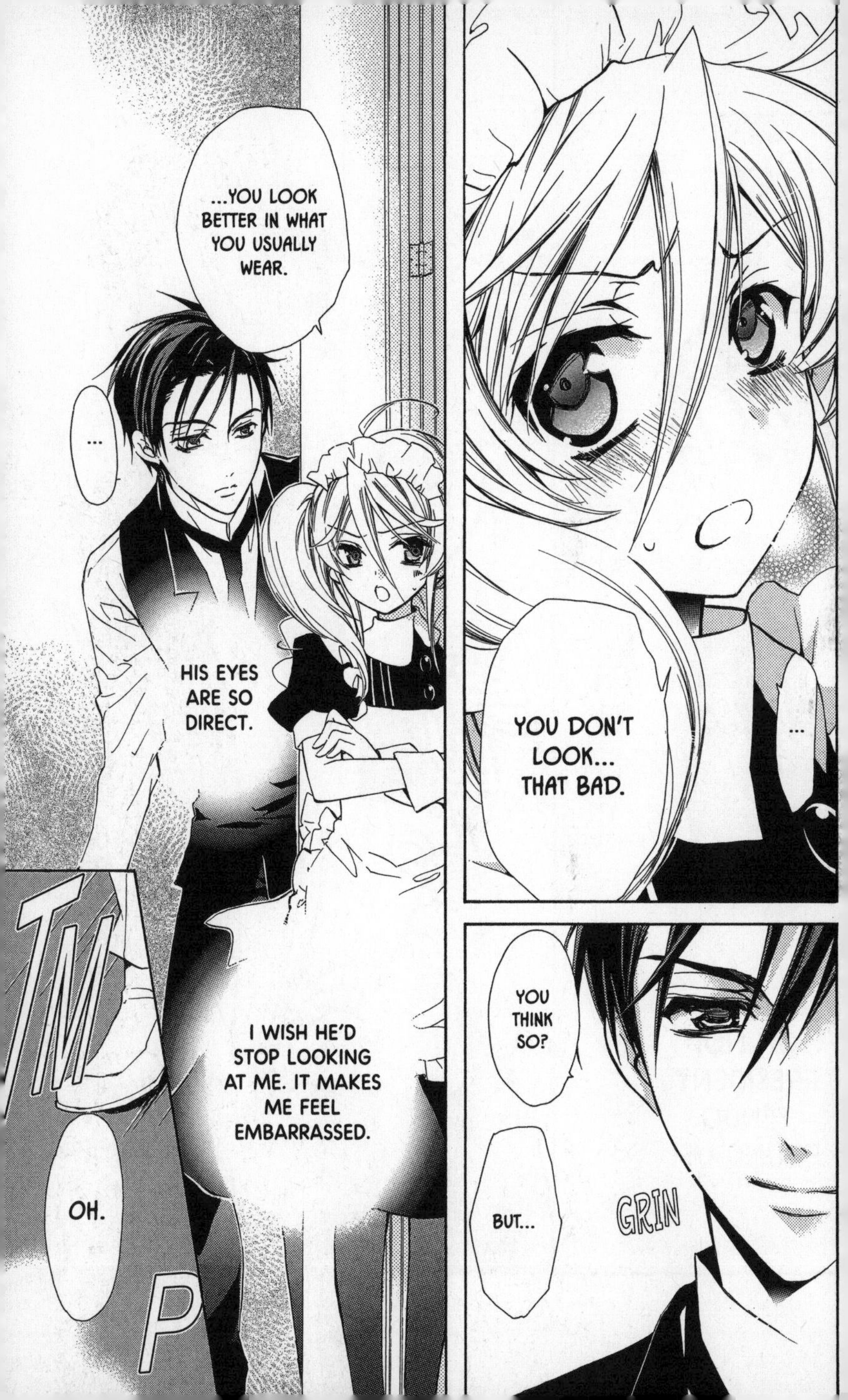
...
YOU DON'T LOOK... THAT BAD.
YOU THINK SO?
GRIN
BUT...
...YOU LOOK BETTER IN WHAT YOU USUALLY WEAR.
...
HIS EYES ARE SO DIRECT.
I WISH HE'D STOP LOOKING AT ME. IT MAKES ME FEEL EMBARRASSED.
TMP
OH.

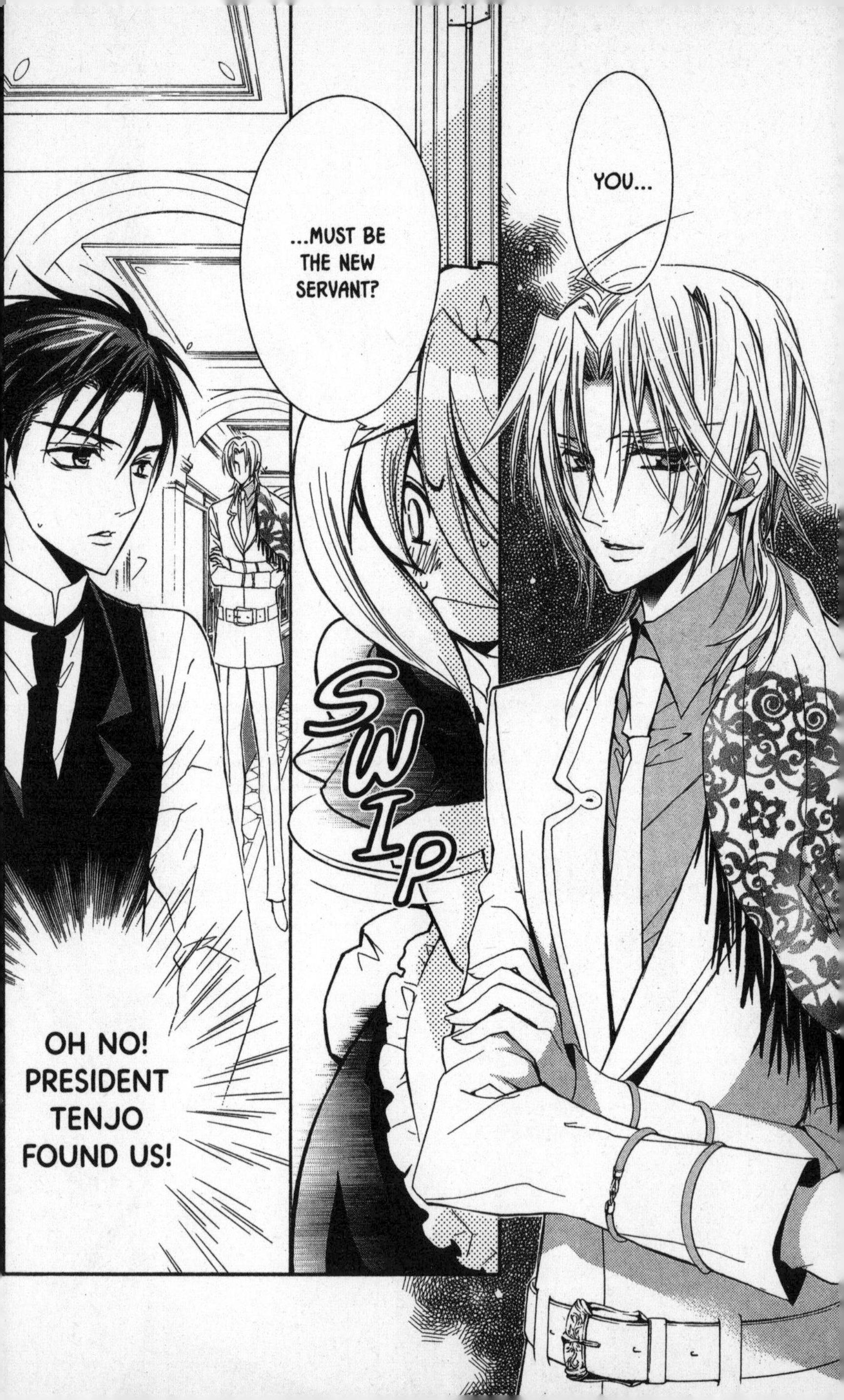
YOU...
...MUST BE THE NEW SERVANT?
SWIP
OH NO! PRESIDENT TENJO FOUND US!

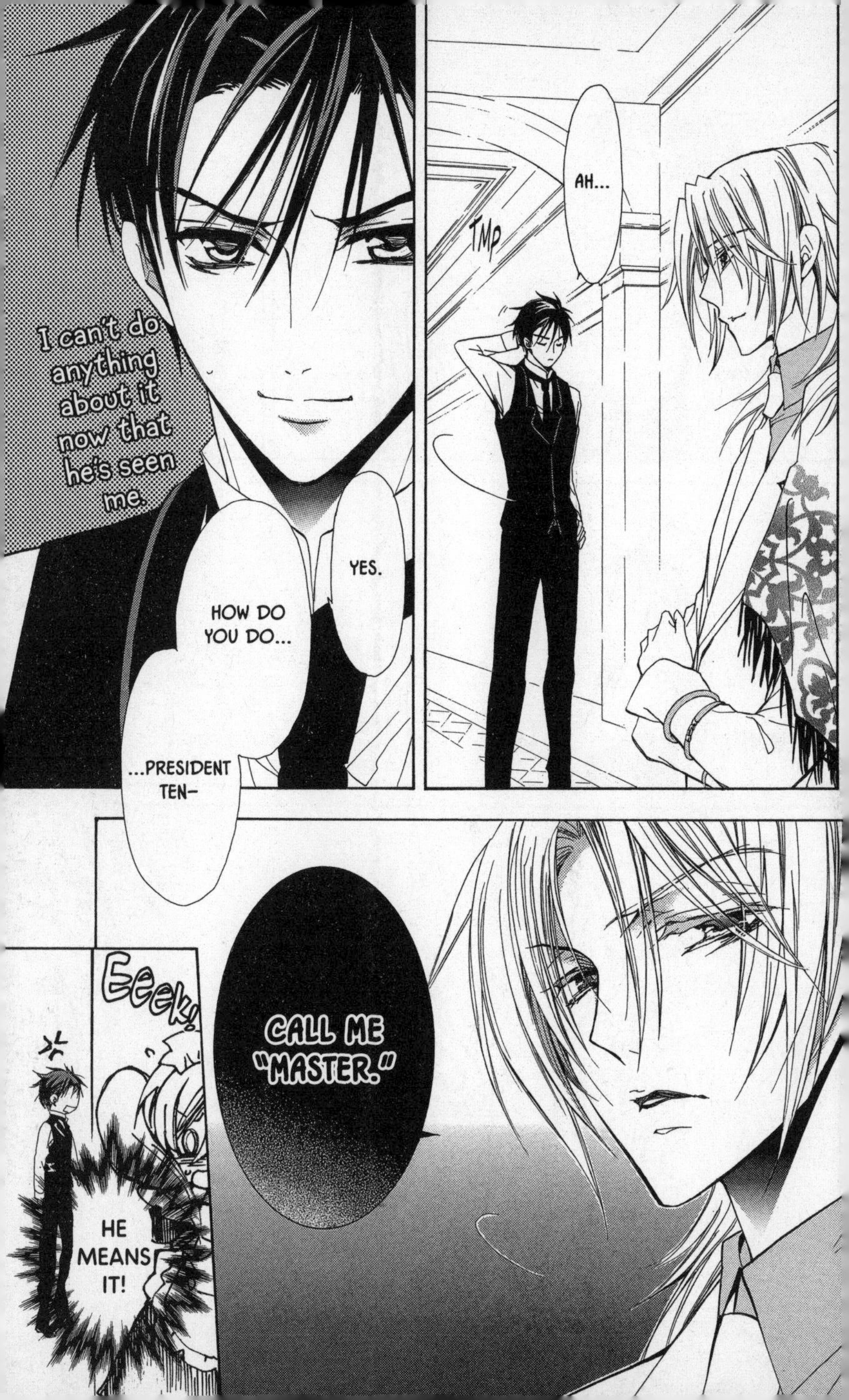
AH...
TMP
I can't do anything about it now that he's seen me.
YES.
HOW DO YOU DO...
...PRESIDENT TEN–
CALL ME "MASTER."
Eeek!
HE MEANS IT!

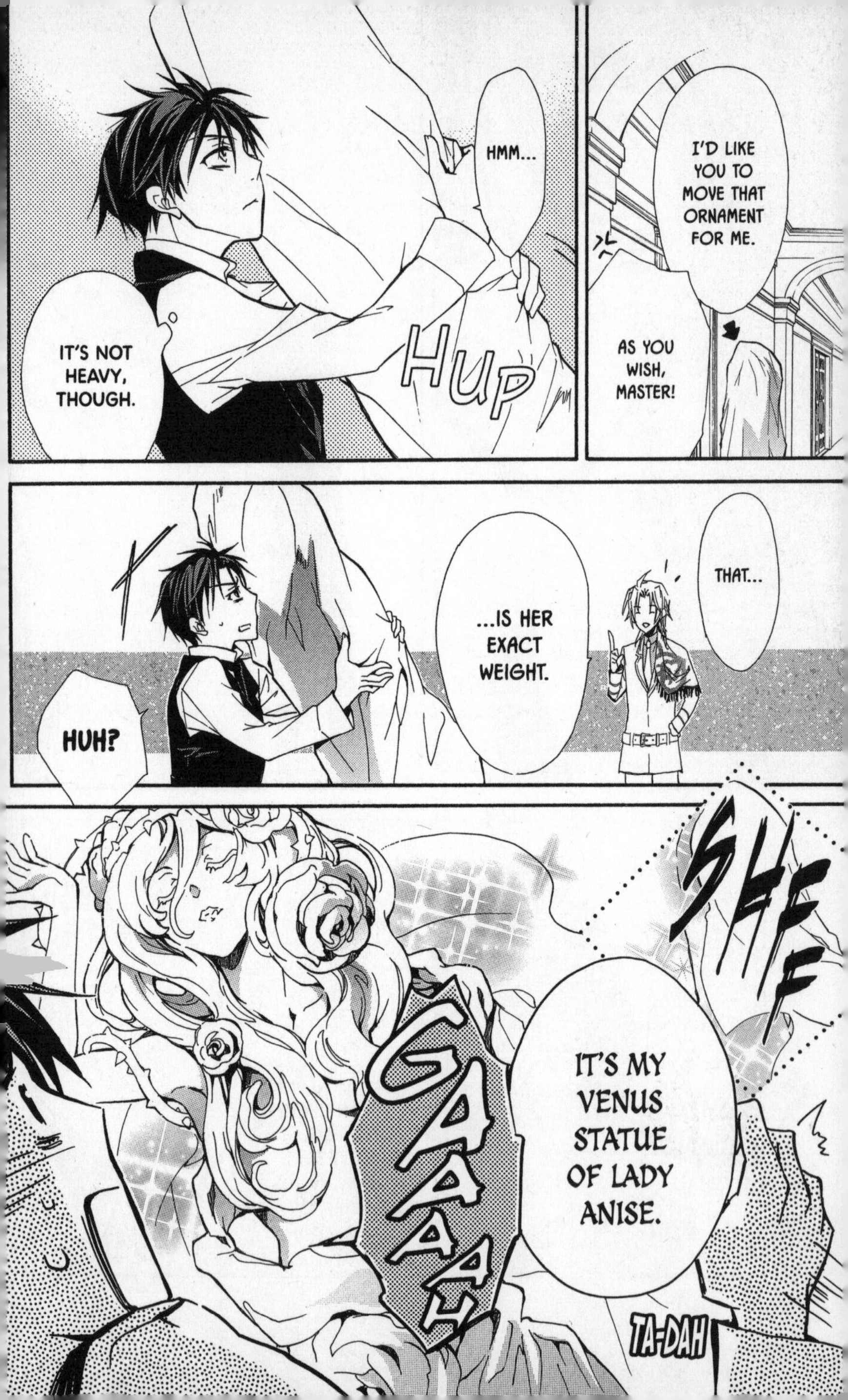
I'D LIKE YOU TO MOVE THAT ORNAMENT FOR ME.
AS YOU WISH, MASTER!
HMM...
HUP
IT'S NOT HEAVY, THOUGH.
THAT...
...IS HER EXACT WEIGHT.
HUH?
SHFF
IT'S MY VENUS STATUE OF LADY ANISE.
TA-DAH
GAAAH

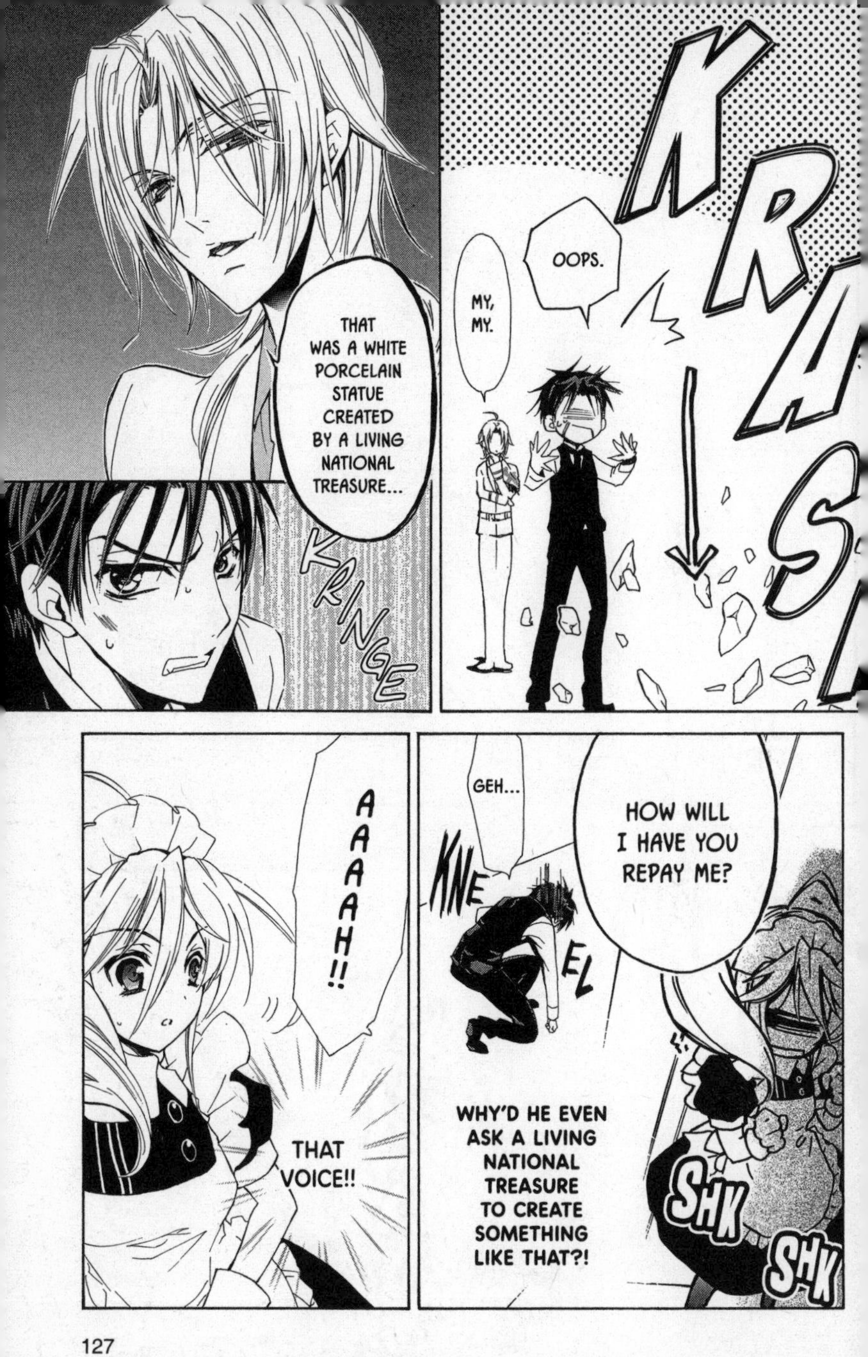
KRAS
OOPS.
MY, MY.
THAT WAS A WHITE PORCELAIN STATUE CREATED BY A LIVING NATIONAL TREASURE...
KRINGE
HOW WILL I HAVE YOU REPAY ME?
GEH...
KNEEL
WHY'D HE EVEN ASK A LIVING NATIONAL TREASURE TO CREATE SOMETHING LIKE THAT?!
SHK
SHK
AAAAAH!!
THAT VOICE!!

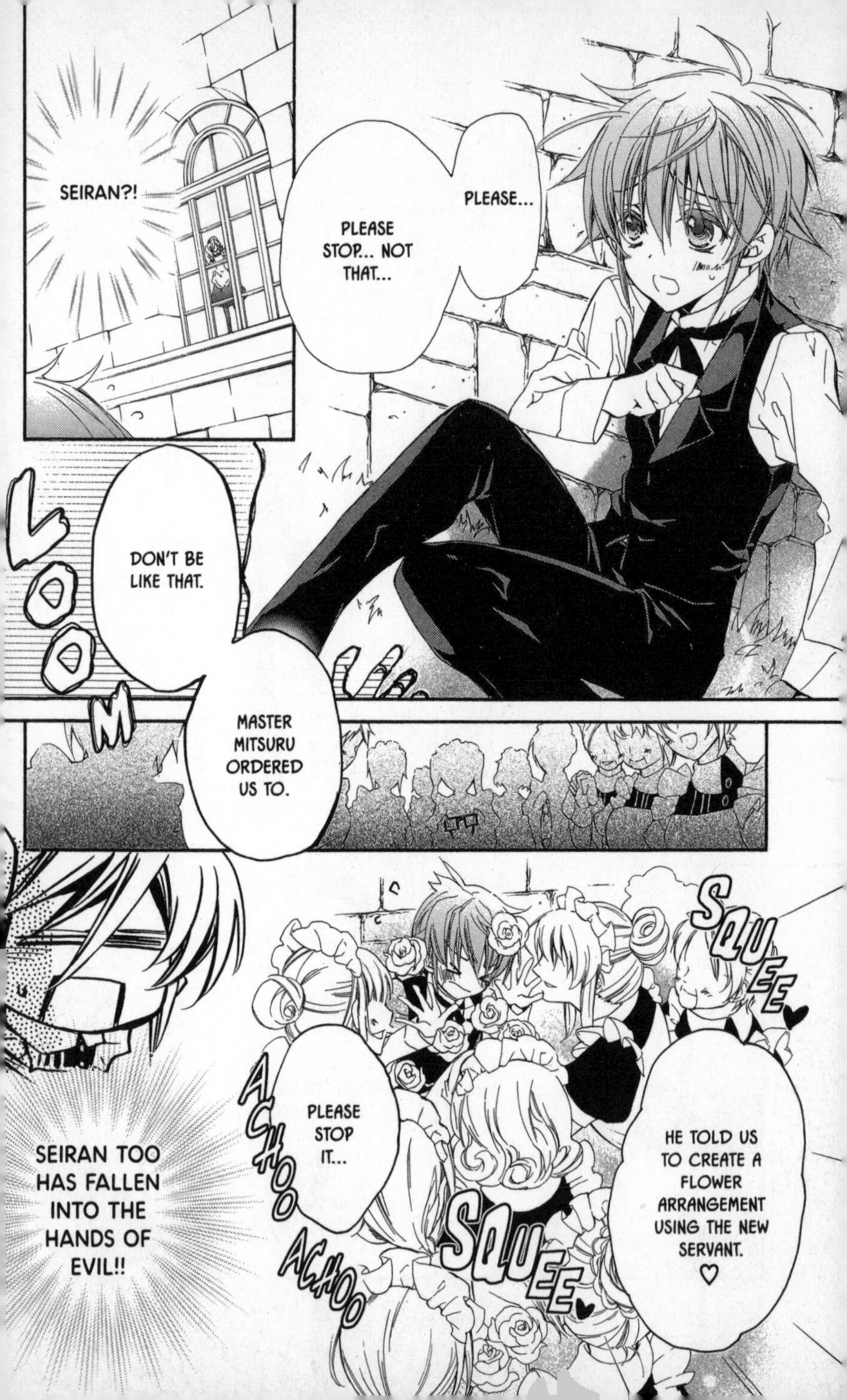
PLEASE...
PLEASE STOP... NOT THAT...
SEIRAN?!
LOOM
DON'T BE LIKE THAT.
MASTER MITSURU ORDERED US TO.
SQUEE♥
HE TOLD US TO CREATE A FLOWER ARRANGEMENT USING THE NEW SERVANT. ♡
PLEASE STOP IT...
ACHOO ACHOO
SQUEE♥
SEIRAN TOO HAS FALLEN INTO THE HANDS OF EVIL!!

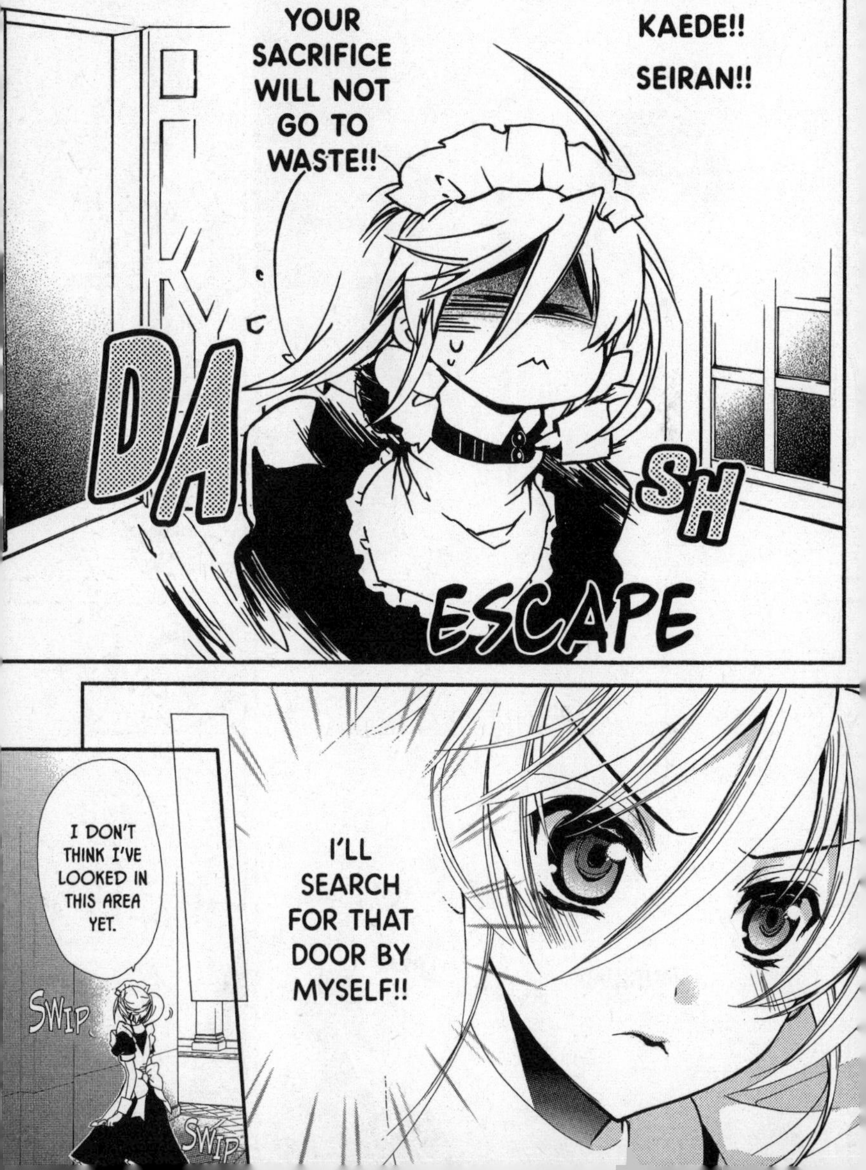
KAEDE!!
SEIRAN!!
YOUR SACRIFICE WILL NOT GO TO WASTE!!
DASH
ESCAPE
I'LL SEARCH FOR THAT DOOR BY MYSELF!!
I DON'T THINK I'VE LOOKED IN THIS AREA YET.
SWIP
SWIP

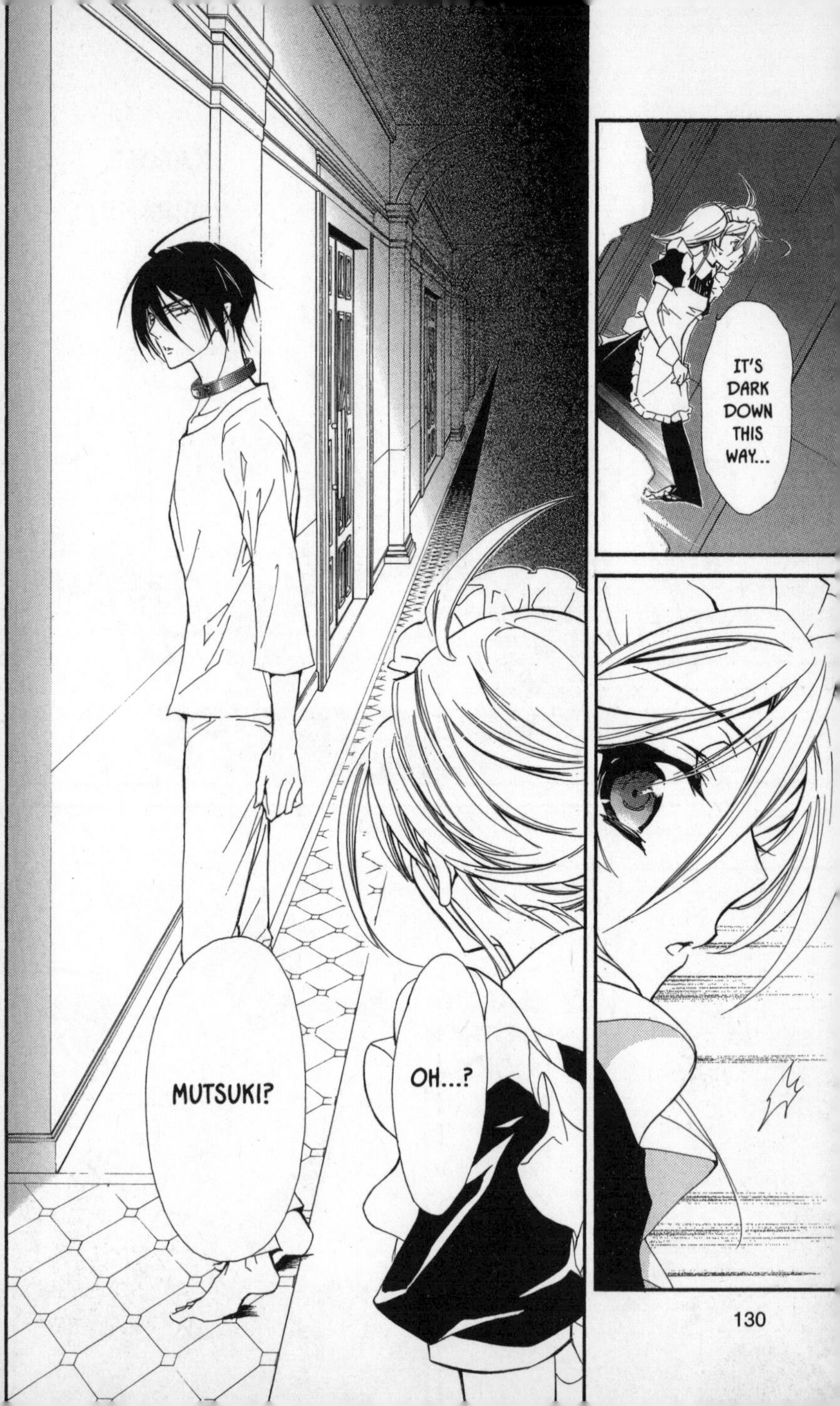
IT'S DARK DOWN THIS WAY...
OH...?
MUTSUKI?

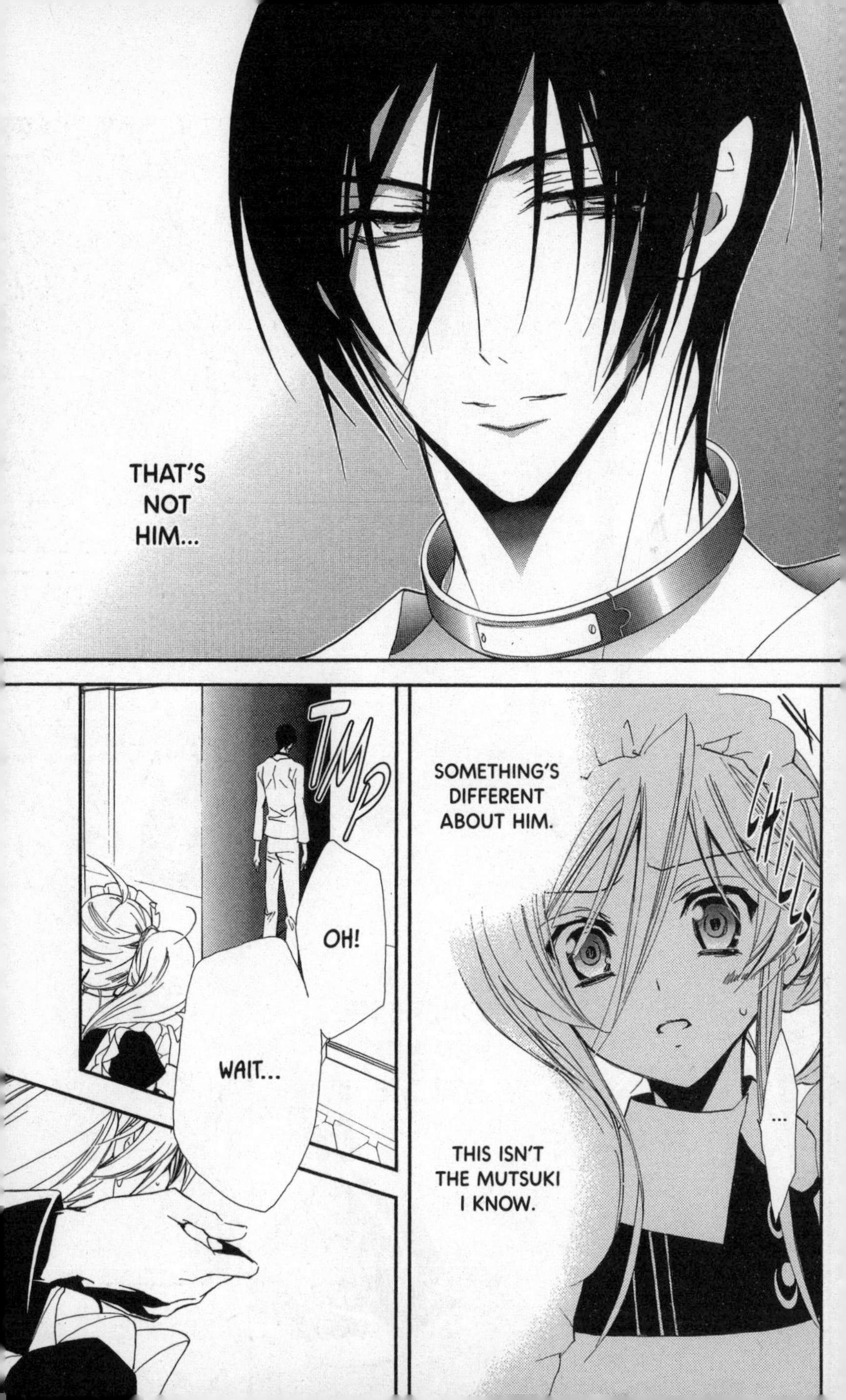
THAT'S NOT HIM...
SOMETHING'S DIFFERENT ABOUT HIM.
CHILLS
...
THIS ISN'T THE MUTSUKI I KNOW.
TMP
OH!
WAIT...

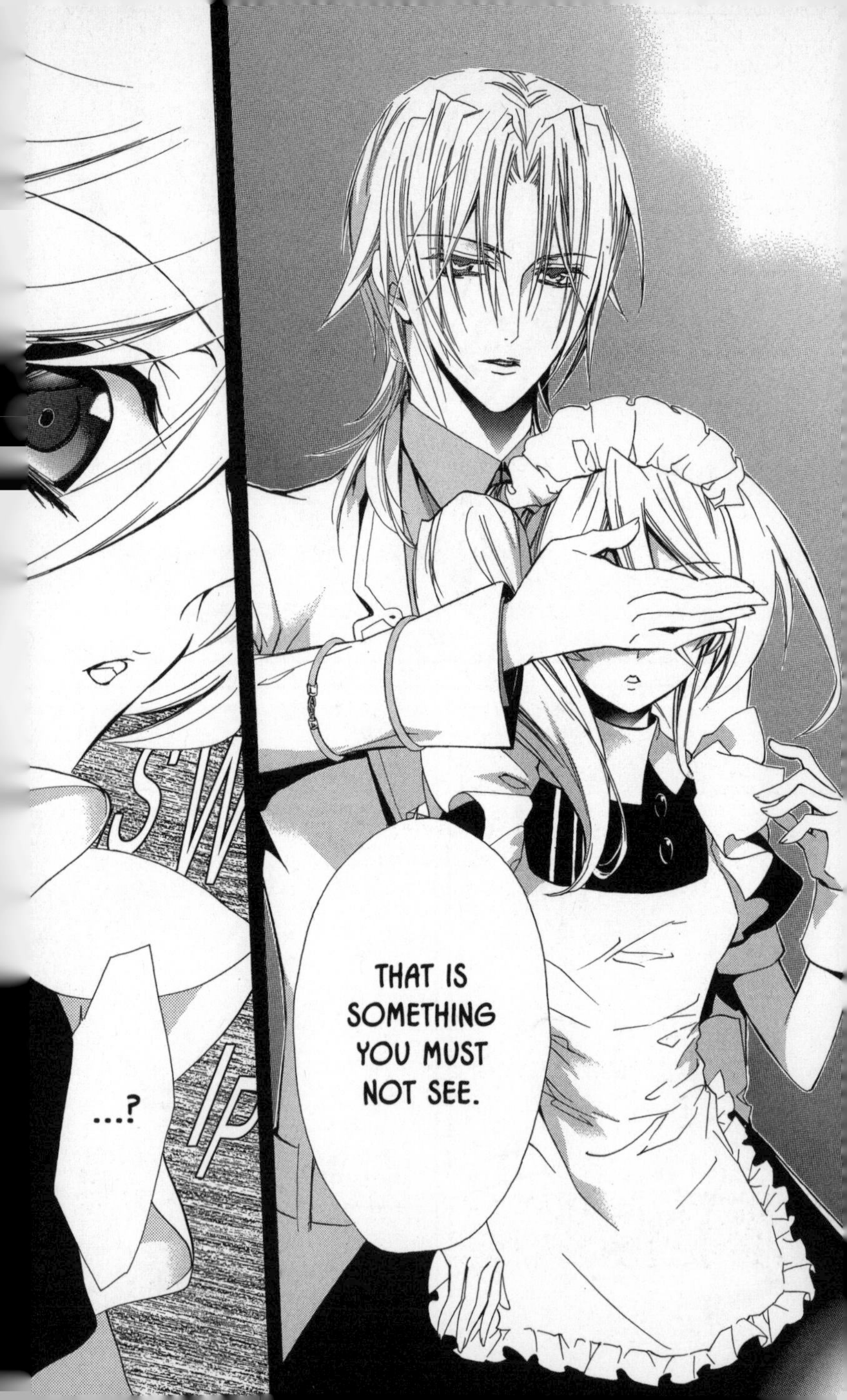
THAT IS SOMETHING YOU MUST NOT SEE.
SWIP
...?

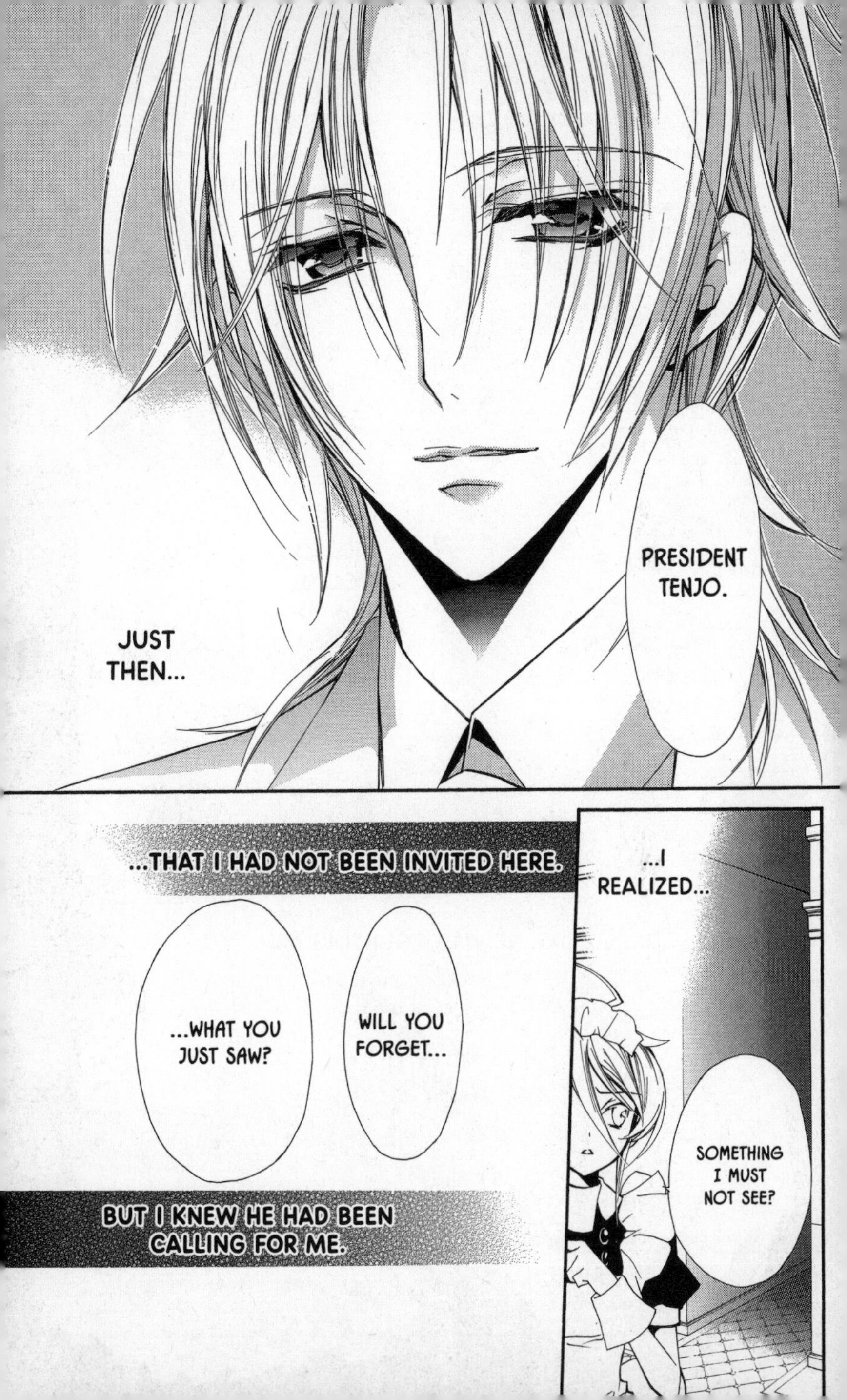
PRESIDENT TENJO.
JUST THEN...
...I REALIZED...
SOMETHING I MUST NOT SEE?
...THAT I HAD NOT BEEN INVITED HERE.
WILL YOU FORGET...
...WHAT YOU JUST SAW?
BUT I KNEW HE HAD BEEN CALLING FOR ME.

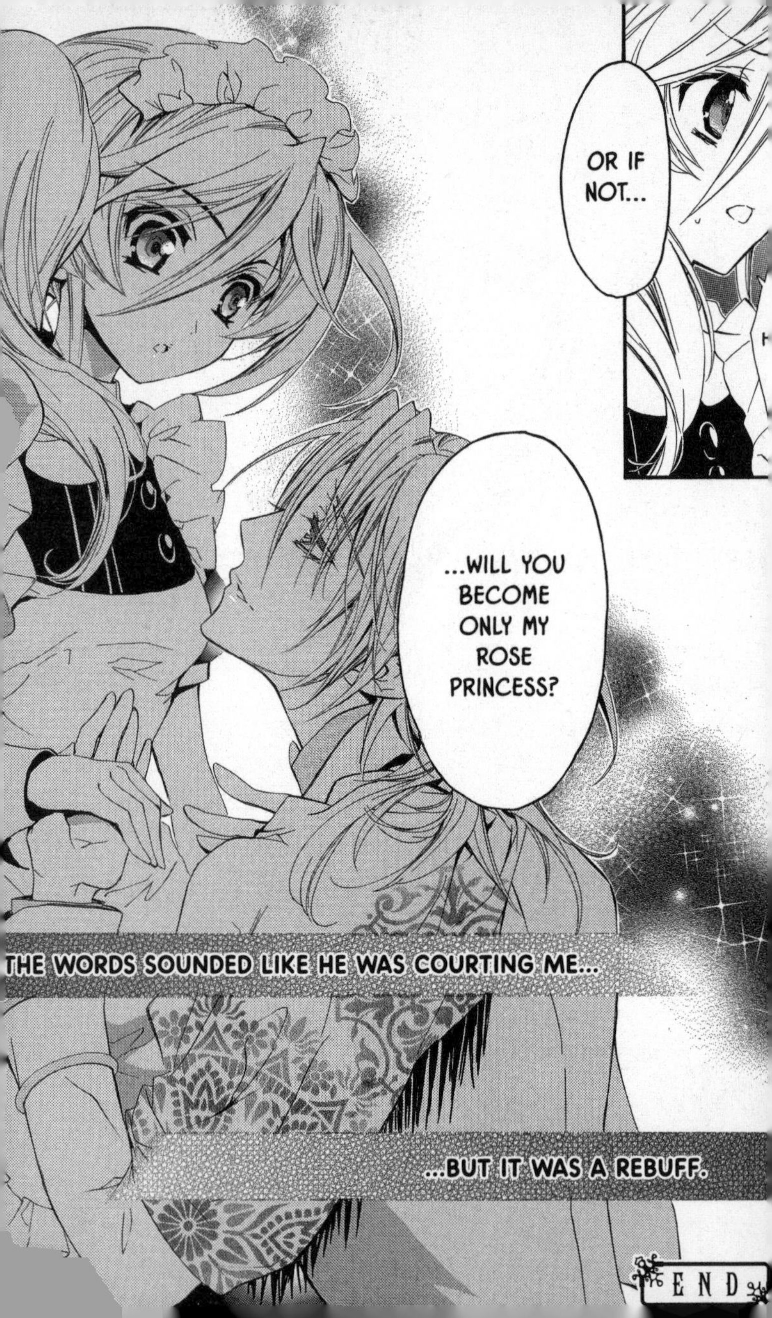
OR IF NOT...
...WILL YOU BECOME ONLY MY ROSE PRINCESS?
THE WORDS SOUNDED LIKE HE WAS COURTING ME...
...BUT IT WAS A REBUFF.
END

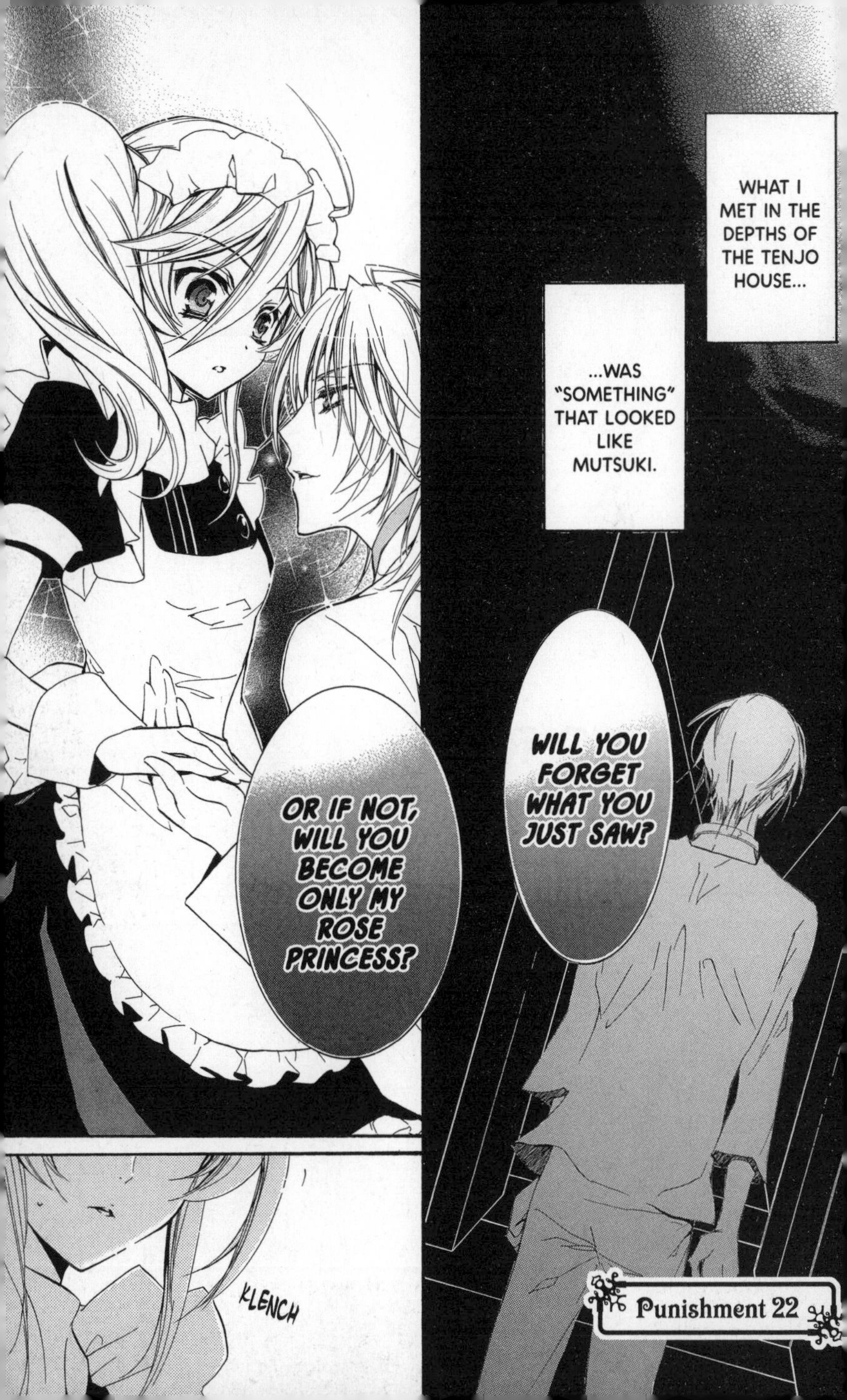
WHAT I MET IN THE DEPTHS OF THE TENJO HOUSE...
...WAS "SOMETHING" THAT LOOKED LIKE MUTSUKI.
WILL YOU FORGET WHAT YOU JUST SAW?
Punishment 22
OR IF NOT, WILL YOU BECOME ONLY MY ROSE PRINCESS?
KLENCH

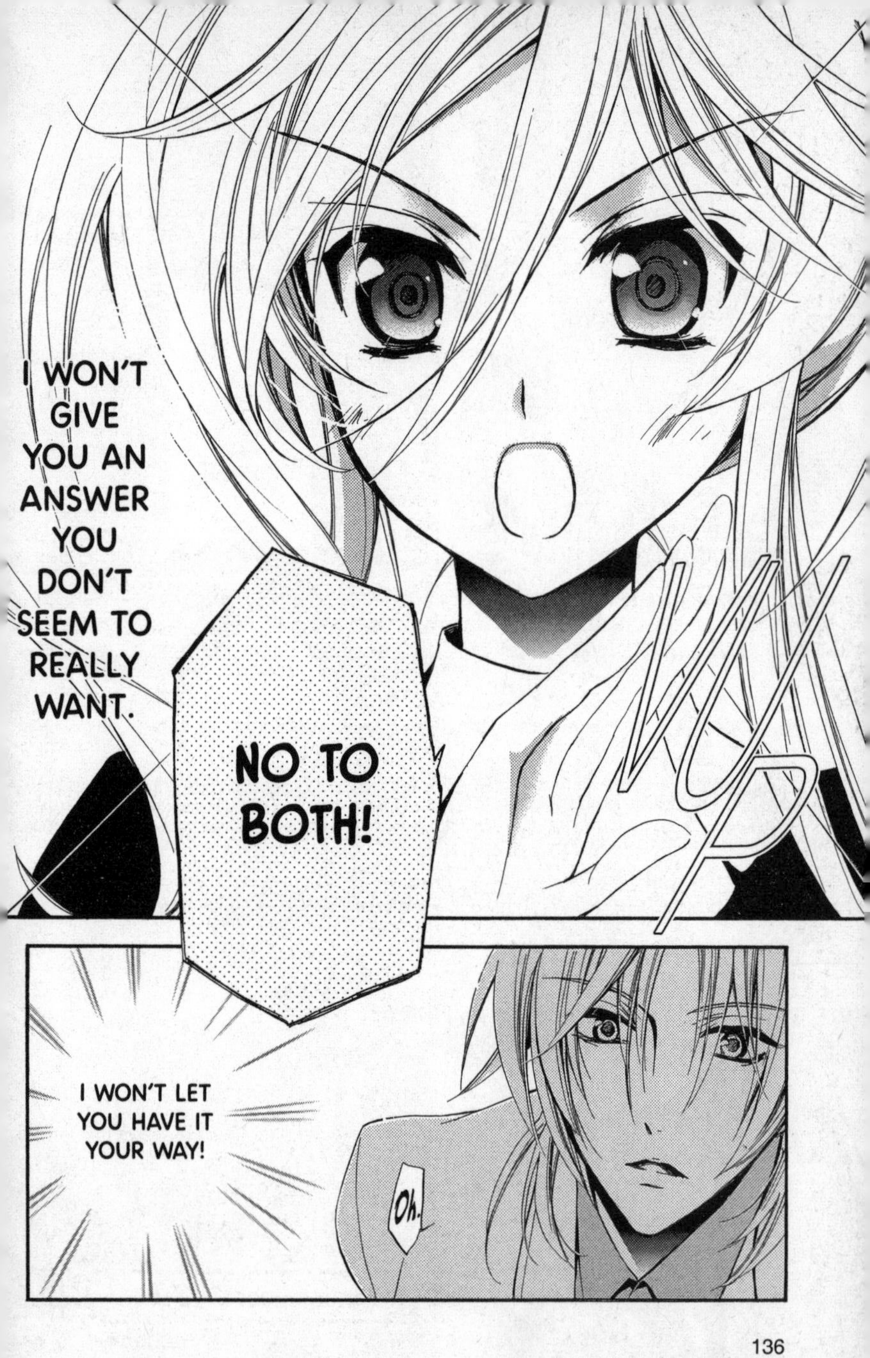
NO TO BOTH!
I WON'T GIVE YOU AN ANSWER YOU DON'T SEEM TO REALLY WANT.
Oh.
I WON'T LET YOU HAVE IT YOUR WAY!

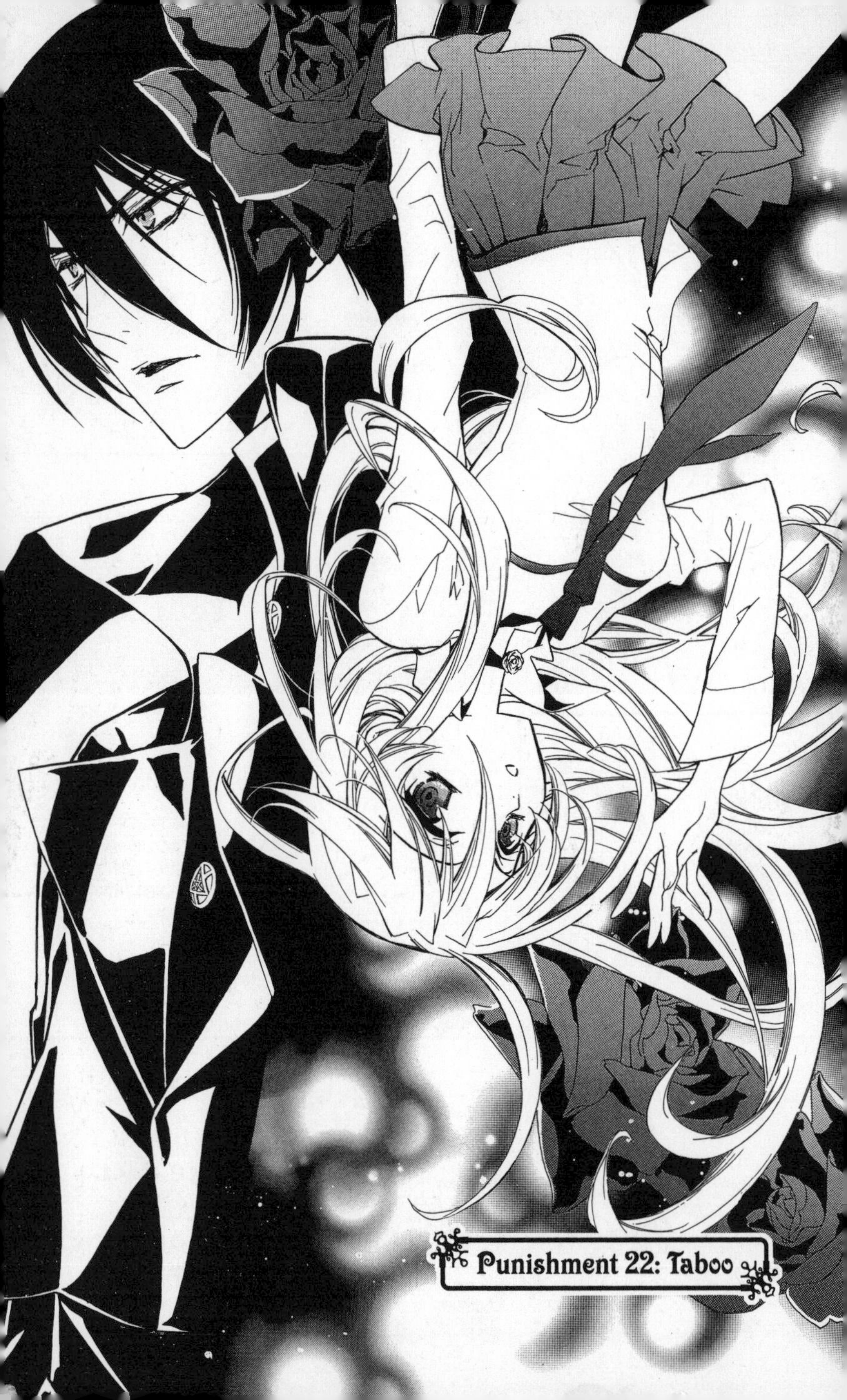
Punishment 22: Taboo

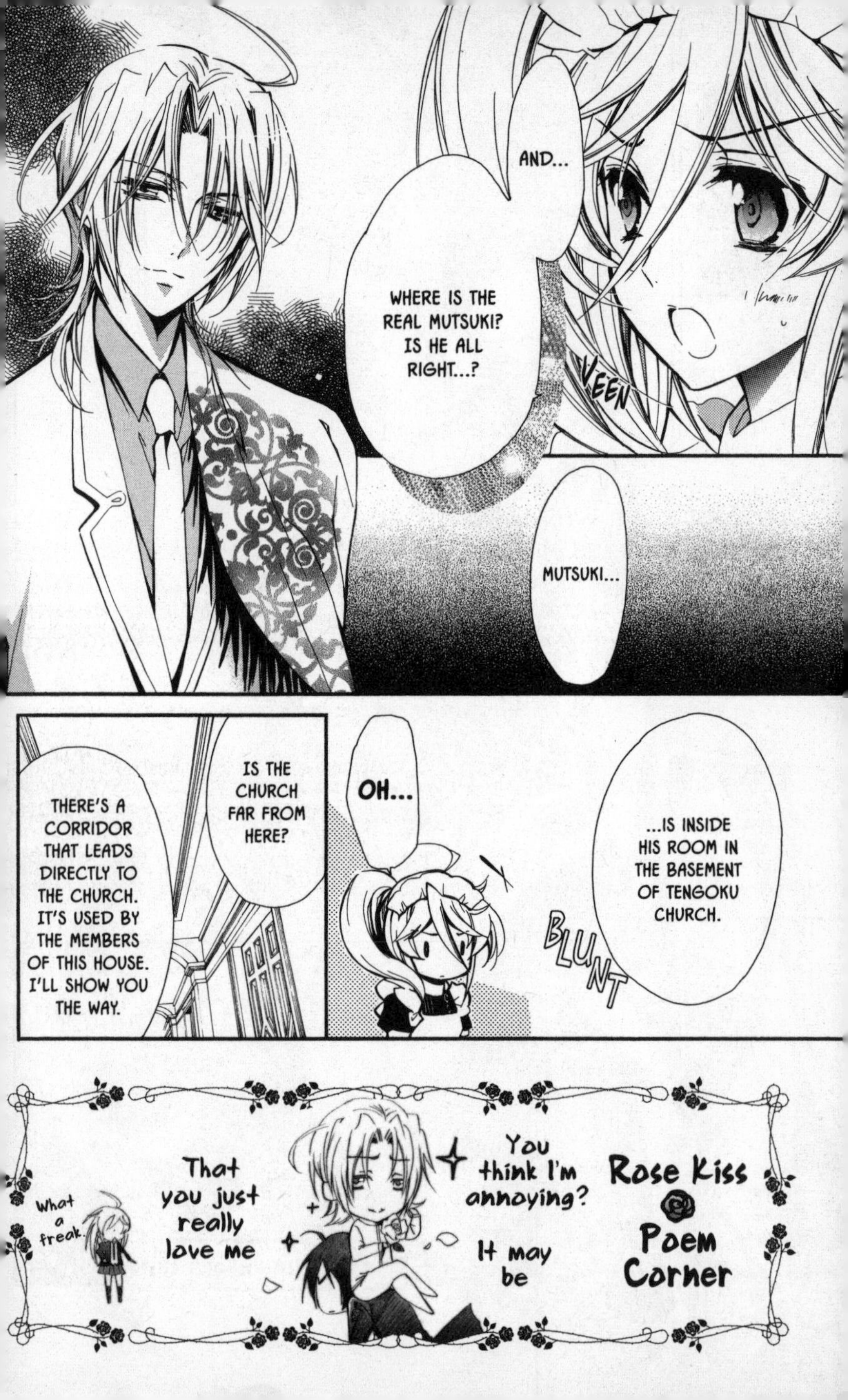
AND...
WHERE IS THE REAL MUTSUKI? IS HE ALL RIGHT...?
VEEN
MUTSUKI...
...IS INSIDE HIS ROOM IN THE BASEMENT OF TENGOKU CHURCH.
BLUNT
OH...
IS THE CHURCH FAR FROM HERE?
THERE'S A CORRIDOR THAT LEADS DIRECTLY TO THE CHURCH. IT'S USED BY THE MEMBERS OF THIS HOUSE. I'LL SHOW YOU THE WAY.
Rose Kiss Poem Corner
You think I'm annoying?
It may be
That you just really love me
What a freak.

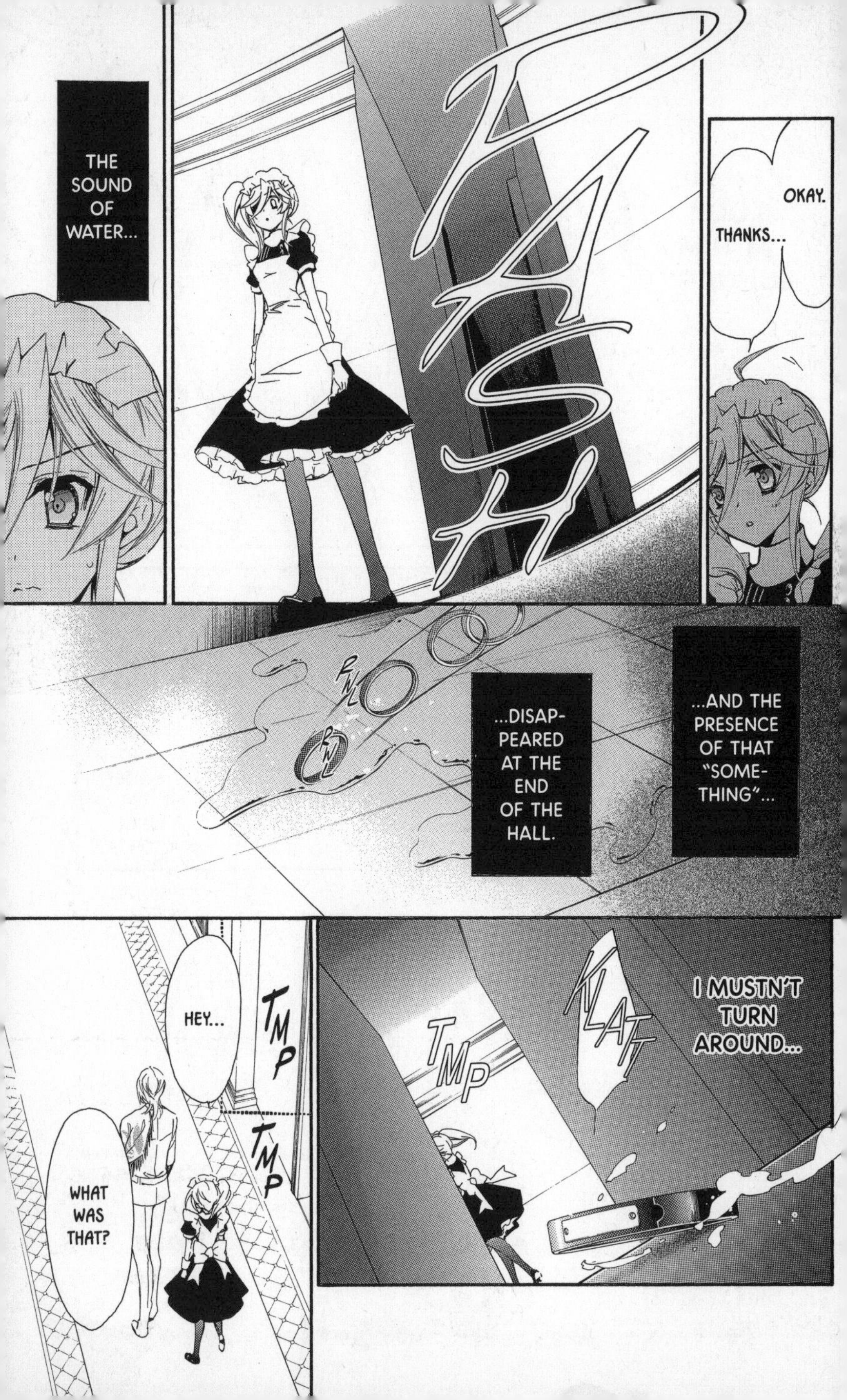
OKAY.
THANKS...
FASH
THE SOUND OF WATER...
...AND THE PRESENCE OF THAT "SOME-THING"...
...DISAP-PEARED AT THE END OF THE HALL.
I MUSTN'T TURN AROUND...
KLATT
TMP
TMP
TMP
HEY...
WHAT WAS THAT?

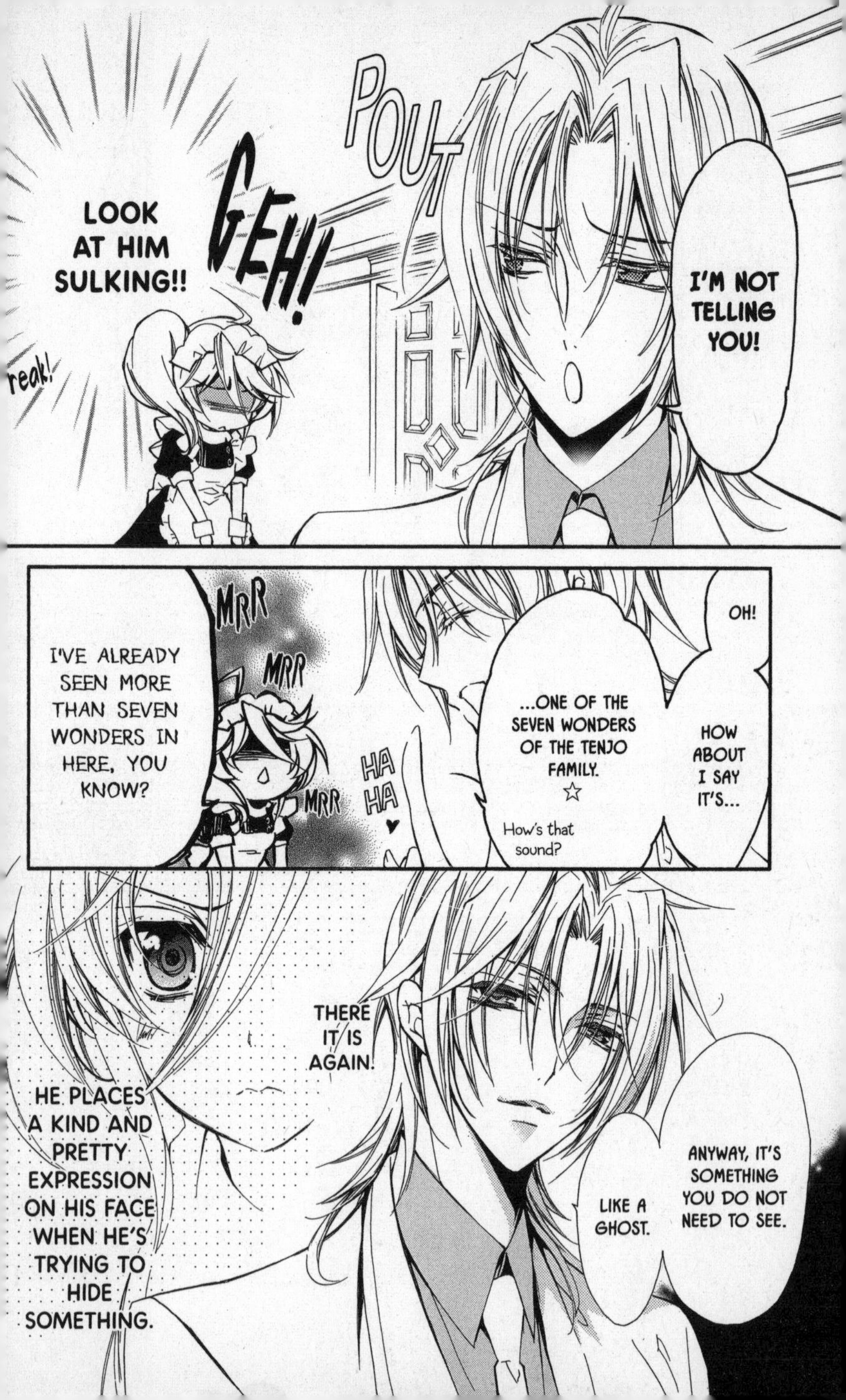
POUT
I'M NOT TELLING YOU!
GEH!
LOOK AT HIM SULKING!!
reak!
OH!
HOW ABOUT I SAY IT'S...
...ONE OF THE SEVEN WONDERS OF THE TENJO FAMILY. ☆
How's that sound?
HA HA ♥
MRR
MRR
MRR
I'VE ALREADY SEEN MORE THAN SEVEN WONDERS IN HERE, YOU KNOW?
ANYWAY, IT'S SOMETHING YOU DO NOT NEED TO SEE.
LIKE A GHOST.
THERE IT IS AGAIN.
HE PLACES A KIND AND PRETTY EXPRESSION ON HIS FACE WHEN HE'S TRYING TO HIDE SOMETHING.

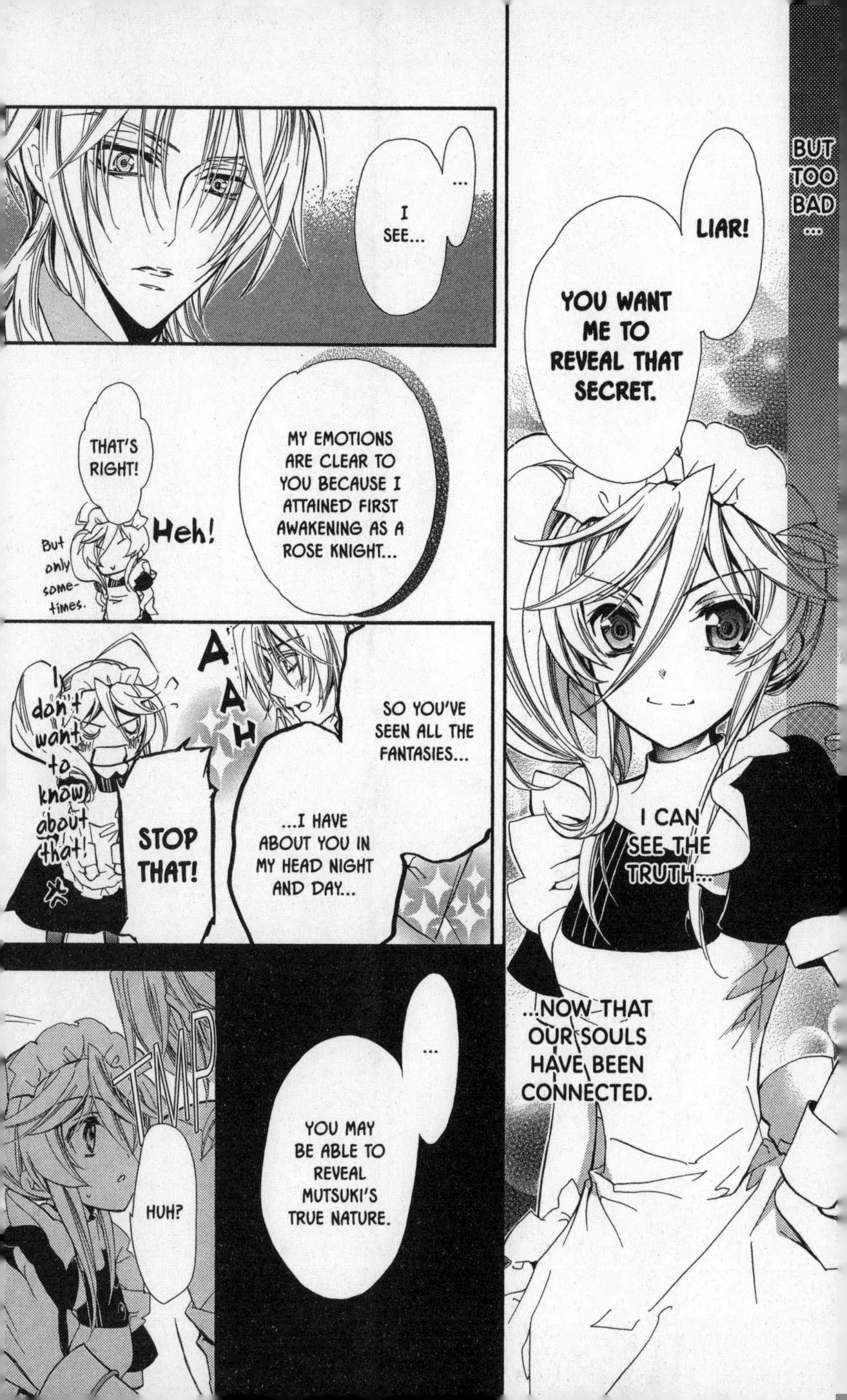
BUT TOO BAD...
LIAR!
YOU WANT ME TO REVEAL THAT SECRET.
I CAN SEE THE TRUTH...
...NOW THAT OUR SOULS HAVE BEEN CONNECTED.
...
I SEE...
MY EMOTIONS ARE CLEAR TO YOU BECAUSE I ATTAINED FIRST AWAKENING AS A ROSE KNIGHT...
THAT'S RIGHT!
Heh!
But only some-times.
SO YOU'VE SEEN ALL THE FANTASIES...
...I HAVE ABOUT YOU IN MY HEAD NIGHT AND DAY...
AAH
STOP THAT!
I don't want to know about that!
...
YOU MAY BE ABLE TO REVEAL MUTSUKI'S TRUE NATURE.
TMP
HUH?

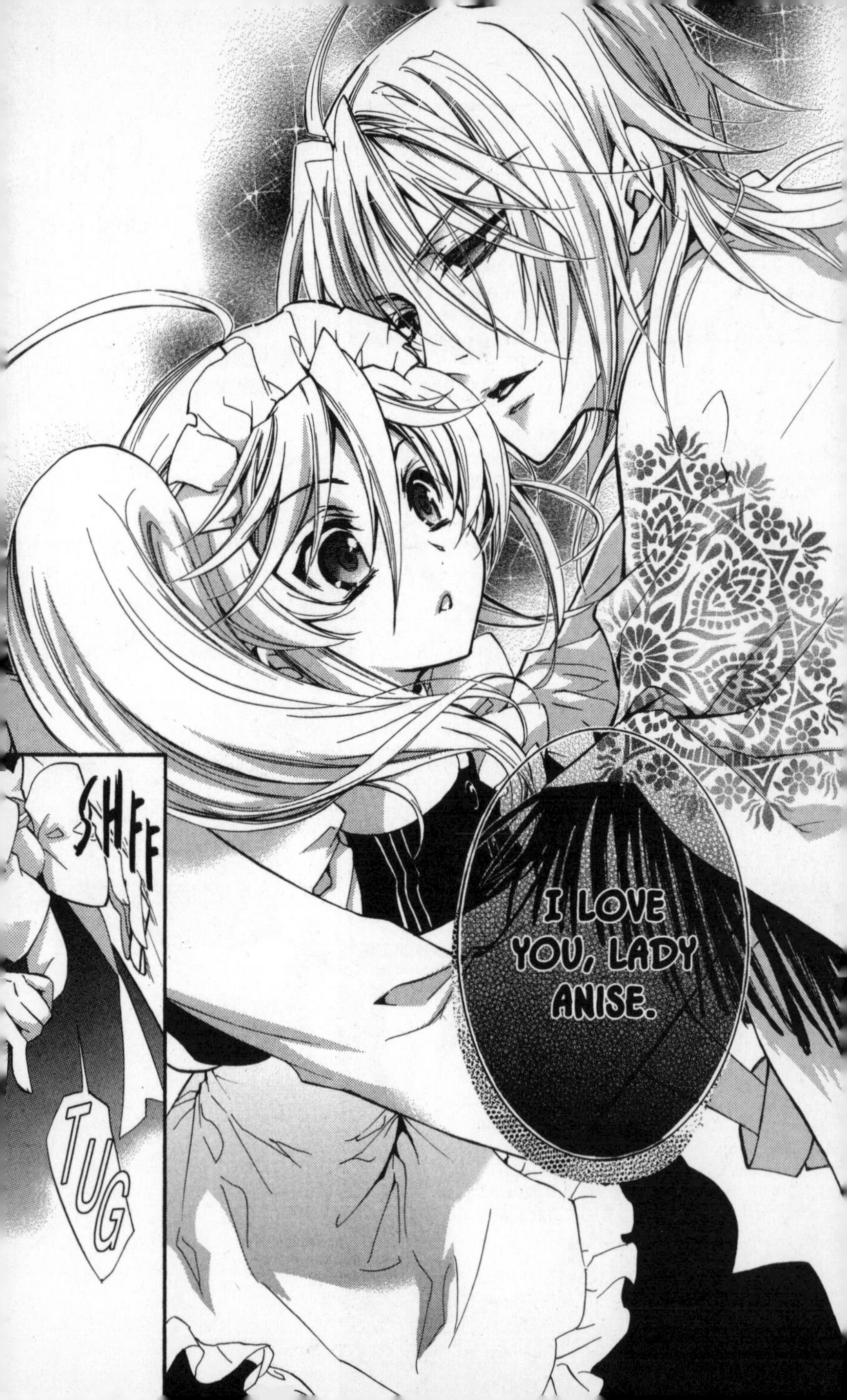
I LOVE YOU, LADY ANISE.
SHFF
TUG

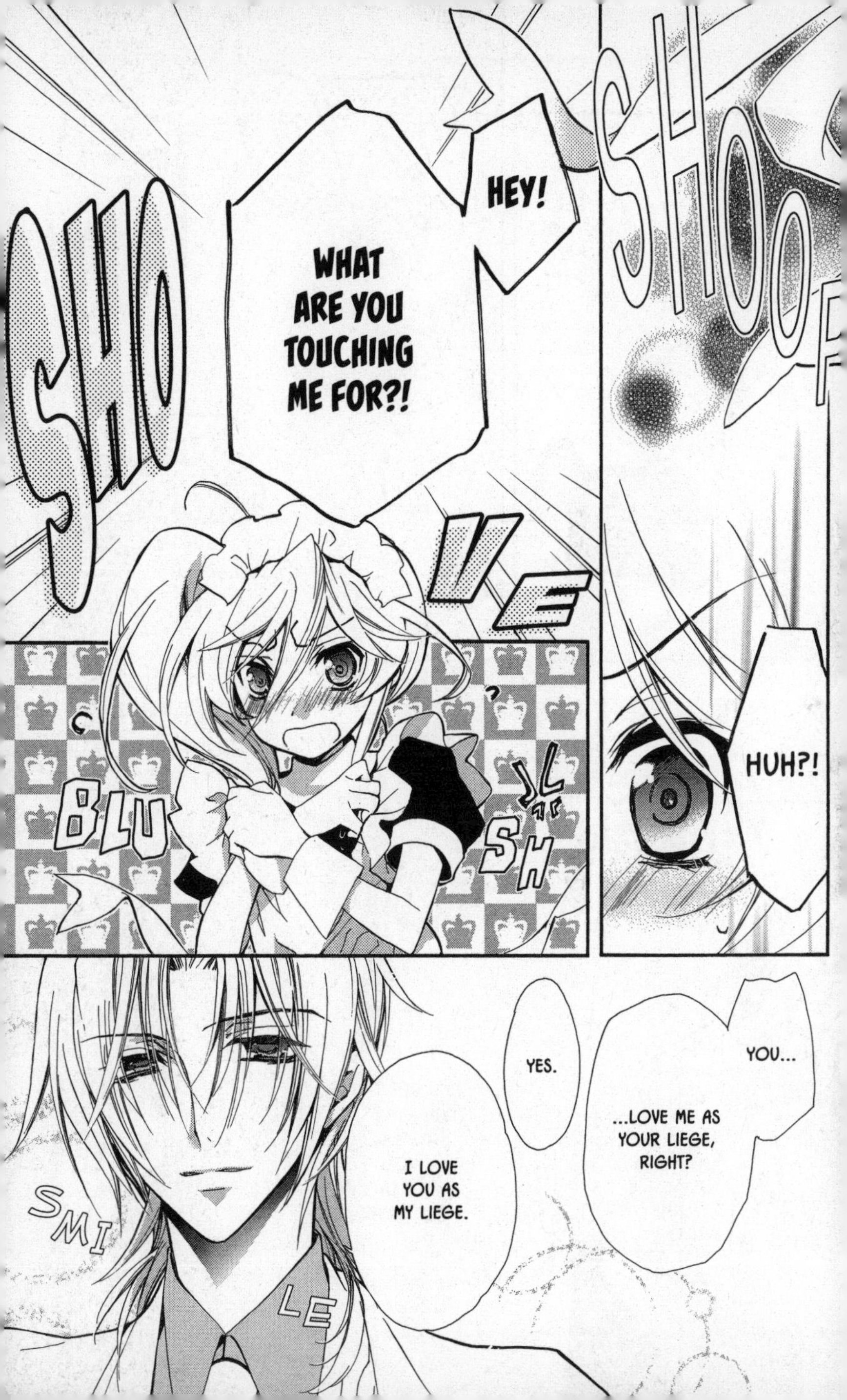
SHOOF
HUH?!
HEY!
WHAT ARE YOU TOUCHING ME FOR?!
SHO
VE
BLU
SH
YOU...
...LOVE ME AS YOUR LIEGE, RIGHT?
YES.
I LOVE YOU AS MY LIEGE.
SMI
LE

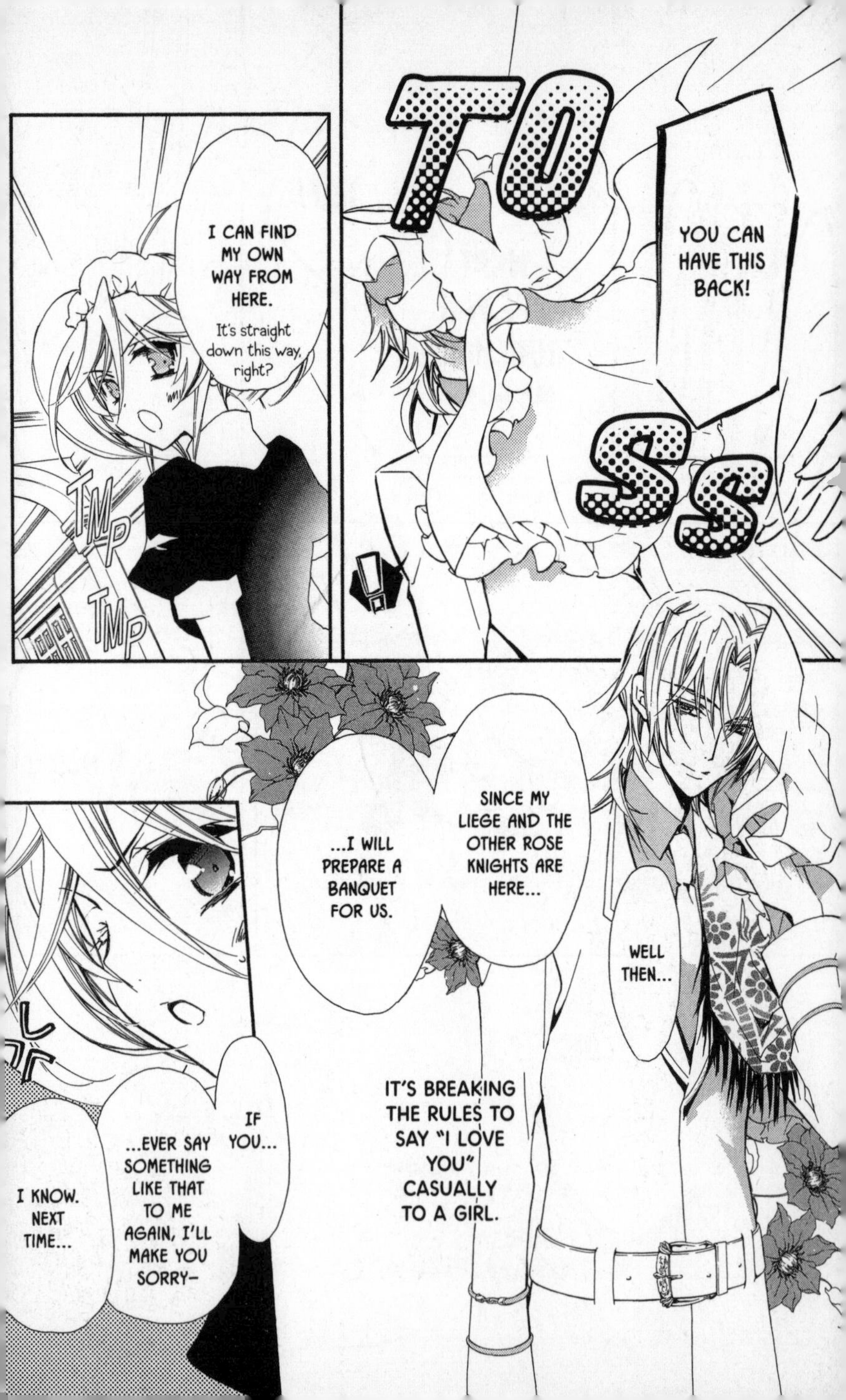
TOSS
YOU CAN HAVE THIS BACK!
!
I CAN FIND MY OWN WAY FROM HERE.
It's straight down this way, right?
TMP TMP
WELL THEN...
SINCE MY LIEGE AND THE OTHER ROSE KNIGHTS ARE HERE...
...I WILL PREPARE A BANQUET FOR US.
IT'S BREAKING THE RULES TO SAY "I LOVE YOU" CASUALLY TO A GIRL.
IF YOU...
...EVER SAY SOMETHING LIKE THAT TO ME AGAIN, I'LL MAKE YOU SORRY–
I KNOW. NEXT TIME...

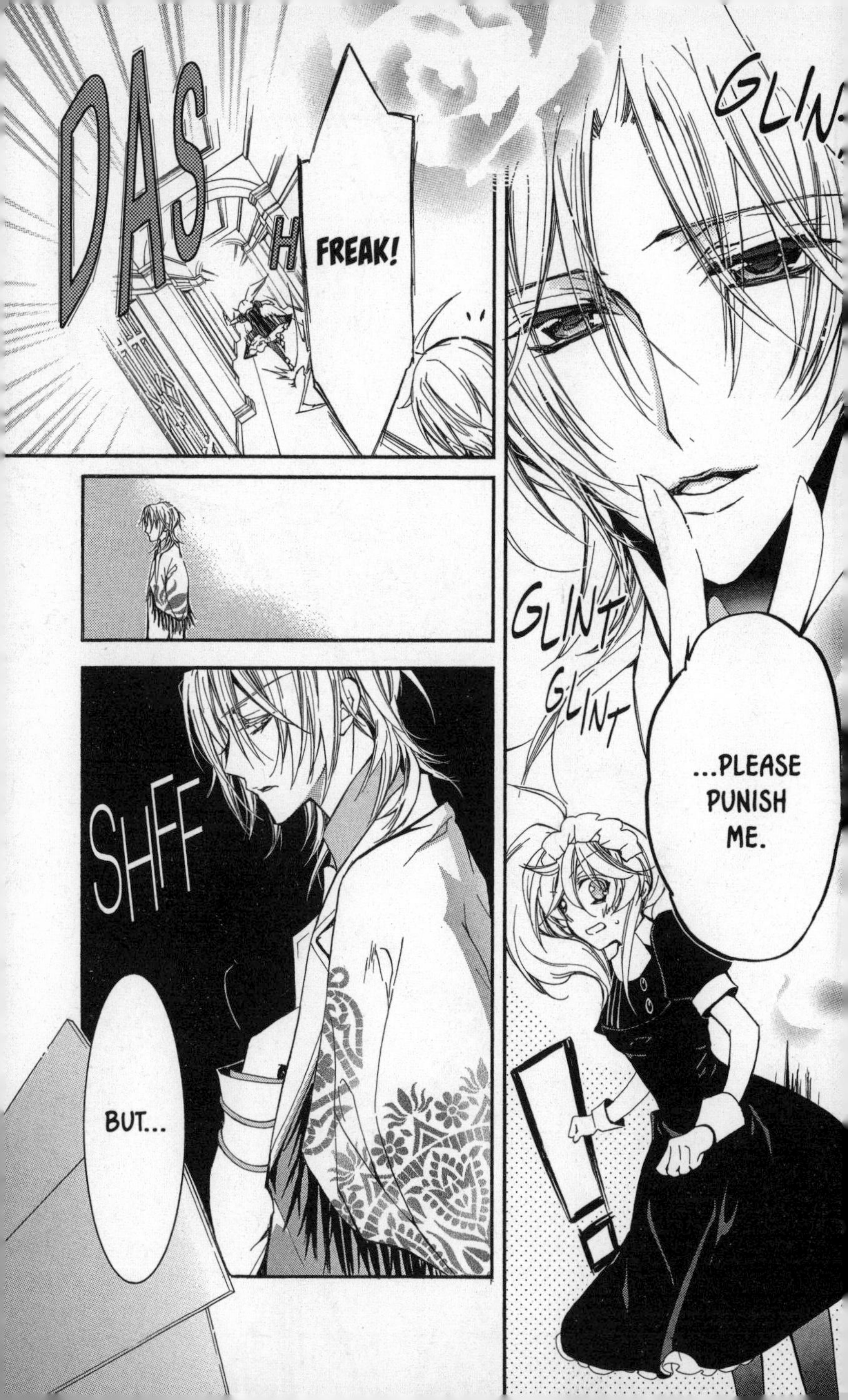
GLIN
GLINT
GLINT
...PLEASE PUNISH ME.
DASH
FREAK!
SHFF
BUT...

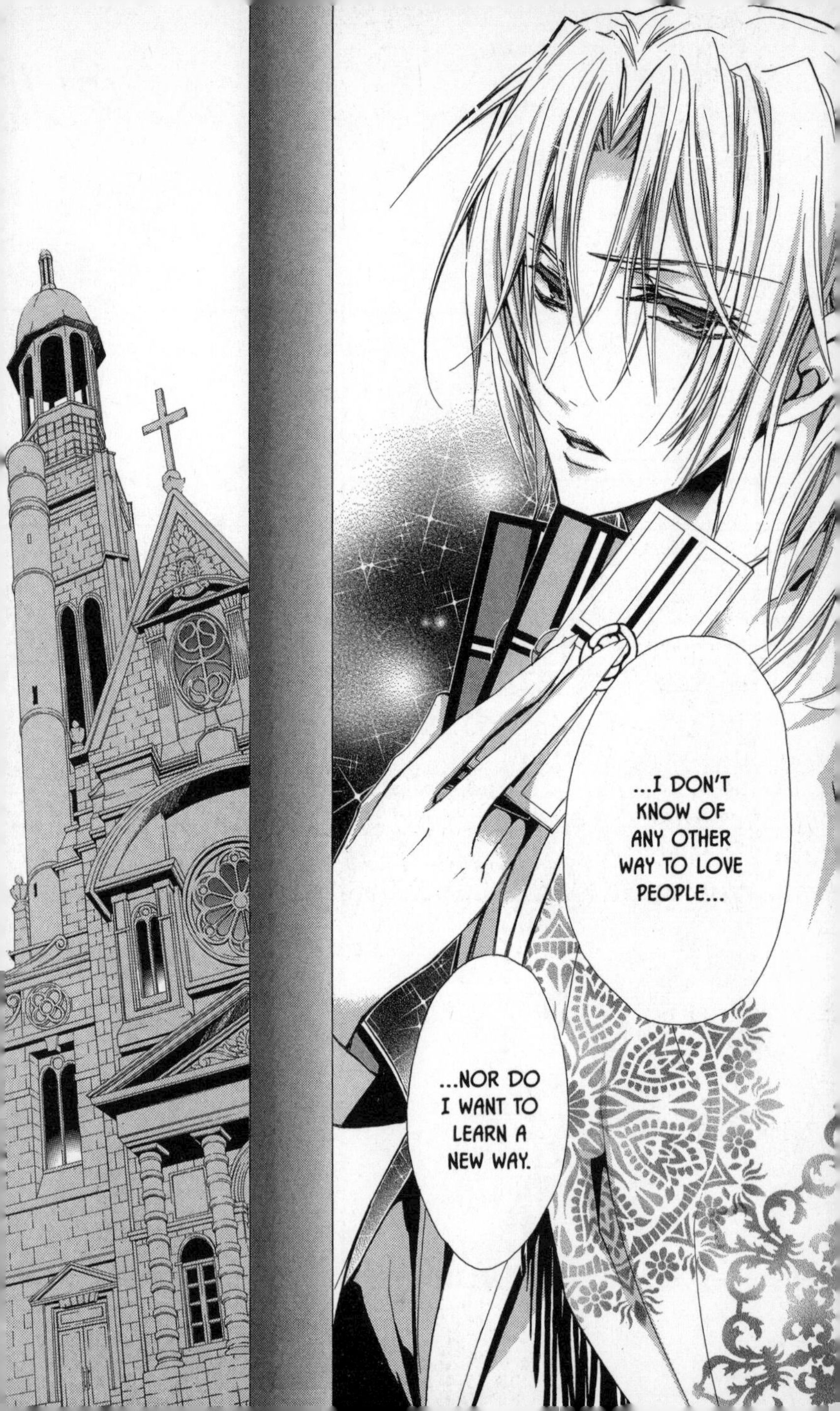
...I DON'T KNOW OF ANY OTHER WAY TO LOVE PEOPLE...
...NOR DO I WANT TO LEARN A NEW WAY.

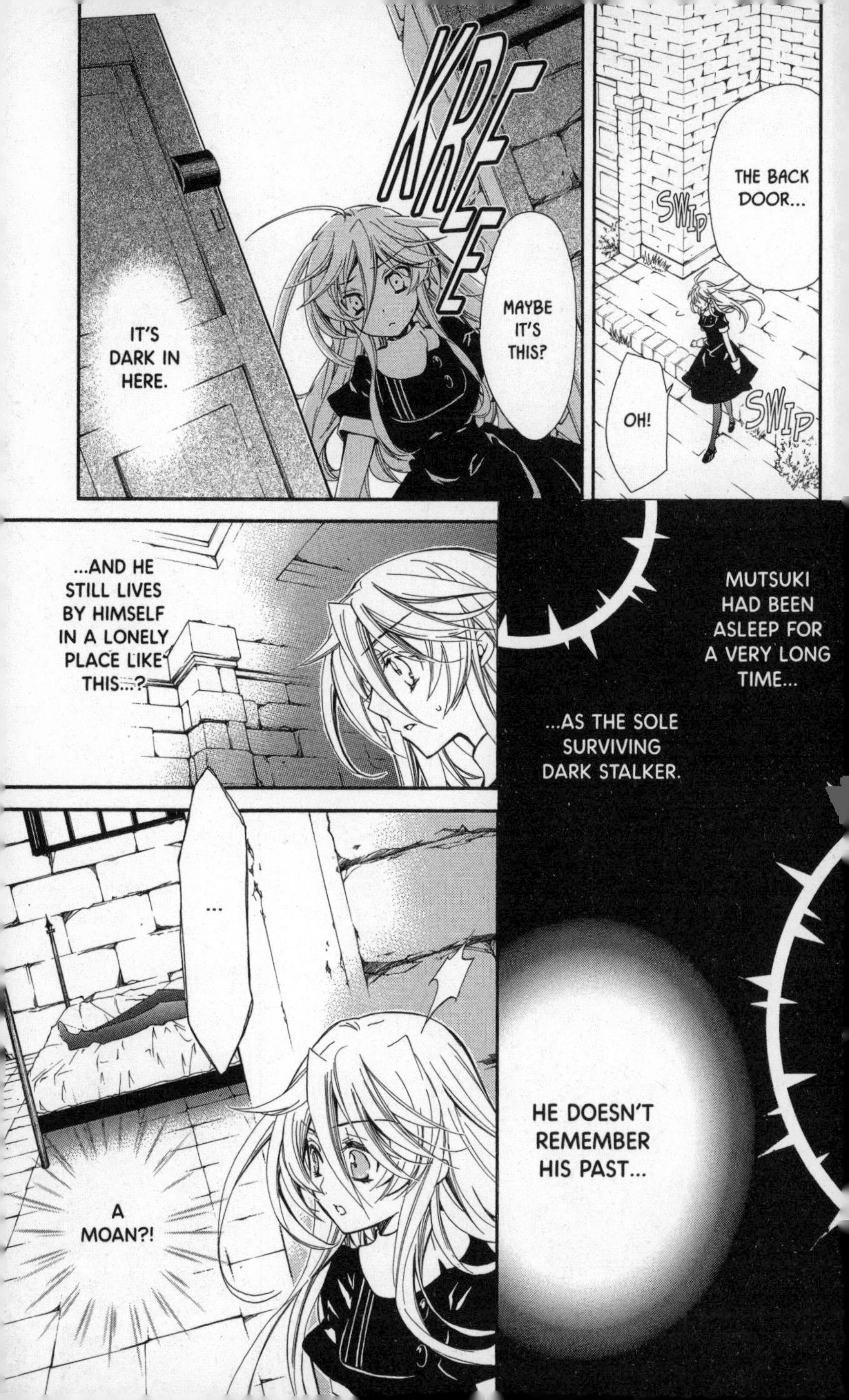
THE BACK DOOR...
SWIP
SWIP
OH!
KREEE
MAYBE IT'S THIS?
IT'S DARK IN HERE.
MUTSUKI HAD BEEN ASLEEP FOR A VERY LONG TIME...
...AS THE SOLE SURVIVING DARK STALKER.
HE DOESN'T REMEMBER HIS PAST...
...AND HE STILL LIVES BY HIMSELF IN A LONELY PLACE LIKE THIS...?
...
A MOAN?!

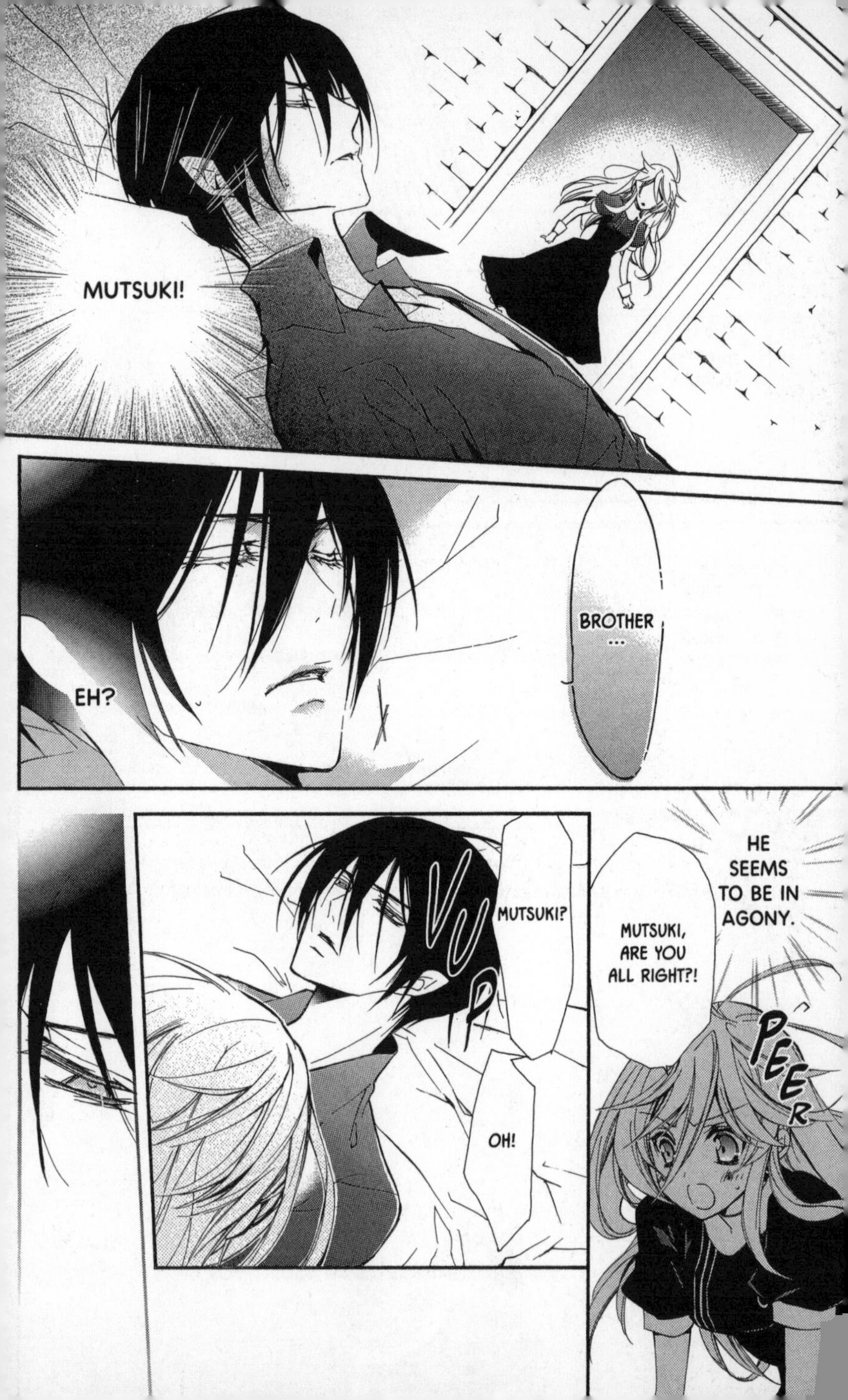
MUTSUKI!
BROTHER ...
EH?
HE SEEMS TO BE IN AGONY.
MUTSUKI, ARE YOU ALL RIGHT?!
PEER
MUTSUKI?
OH!

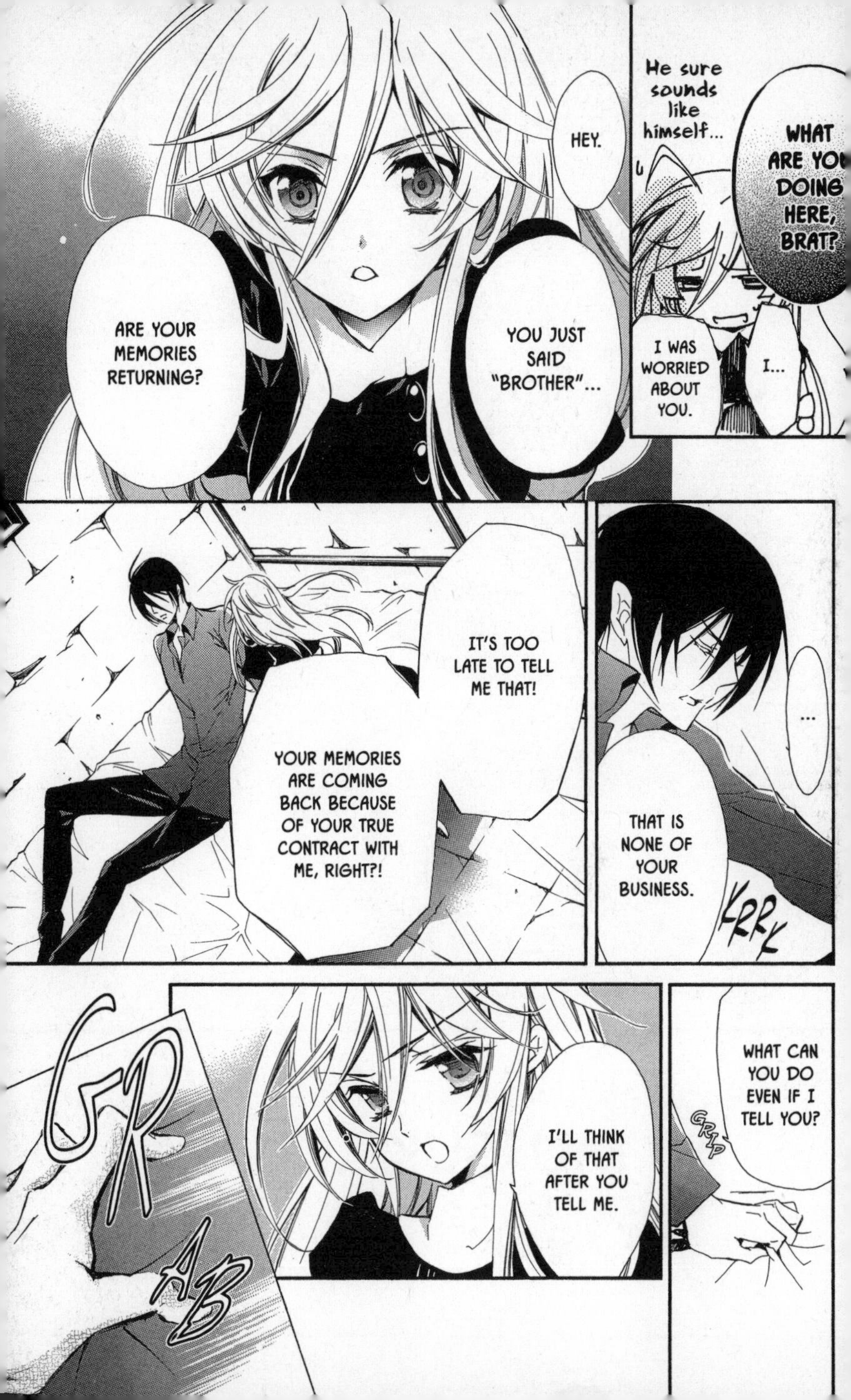
WHAT ARE YOU DOING HERE, BRAT?
He sure sounds like himself...
I...
I WAS WORRIED ABOUT YOU.
HEY.
YOU JUST SAID "BROTHER"...
ARE YOUR MEMORIES RETURNING?
...
THAT IS NONE OF YOUR BUSINESS.
KRRK
IT'S TOO LATE TO TELL ME THAT!
YOUR MEMORIES ARE COMING BACK BECAUSE OF YOUR TRUE CONTRACT WITH ME, RIGHT?!
WHAT CAN YOU DO EVEN IF I TELL YOU?
GRIP
I'LL THINK OF THAT AFTER YOU TELL ME.
GRAB

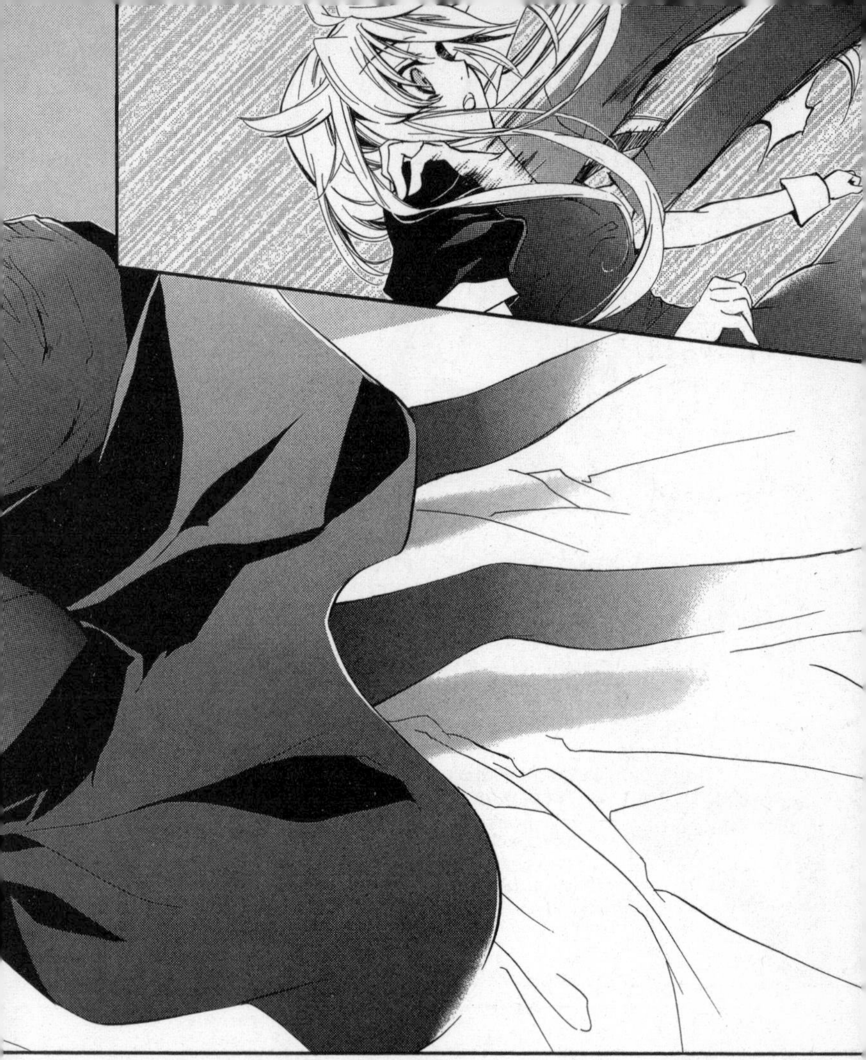

MUTSUKI...?!

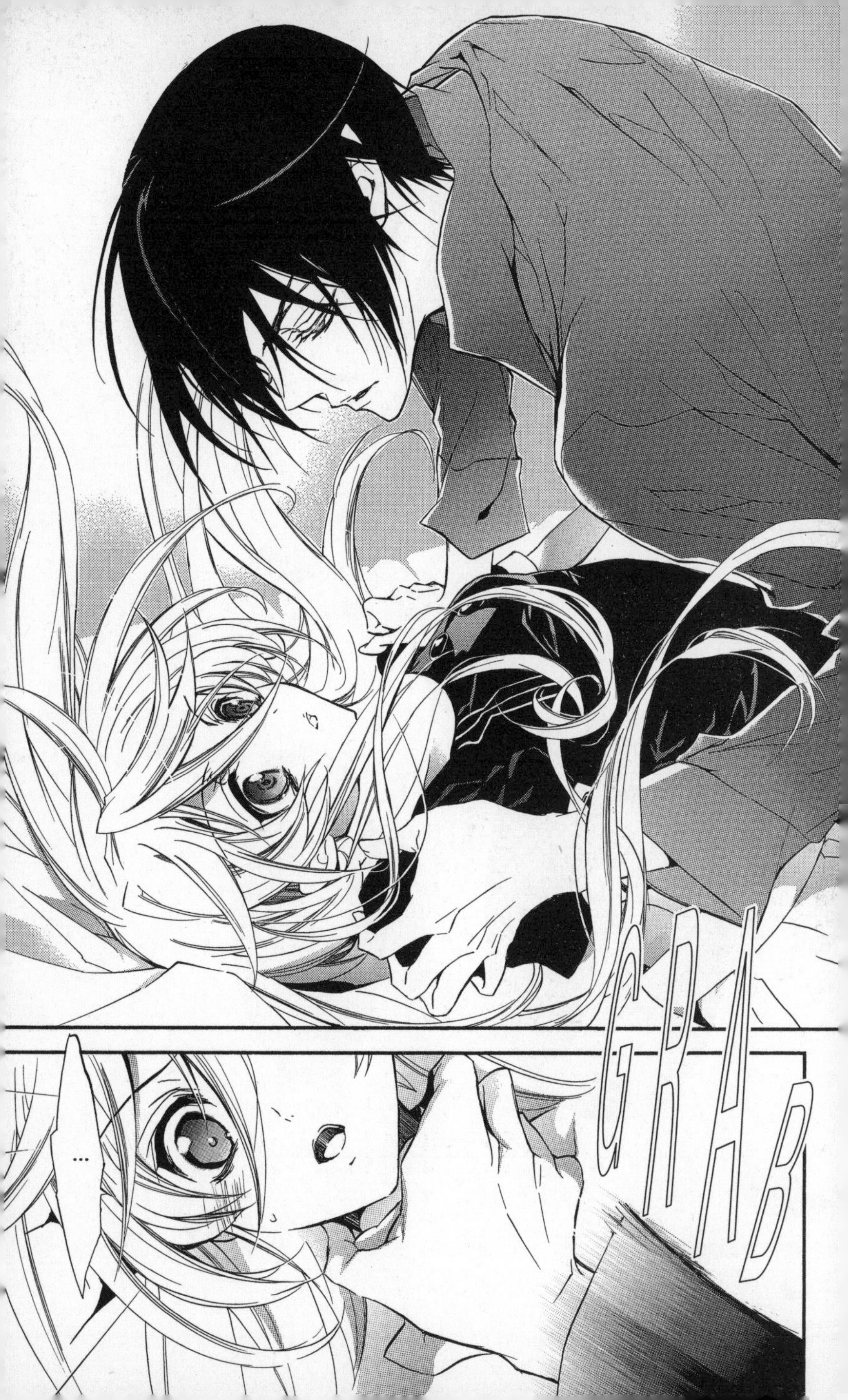
GRAB
...

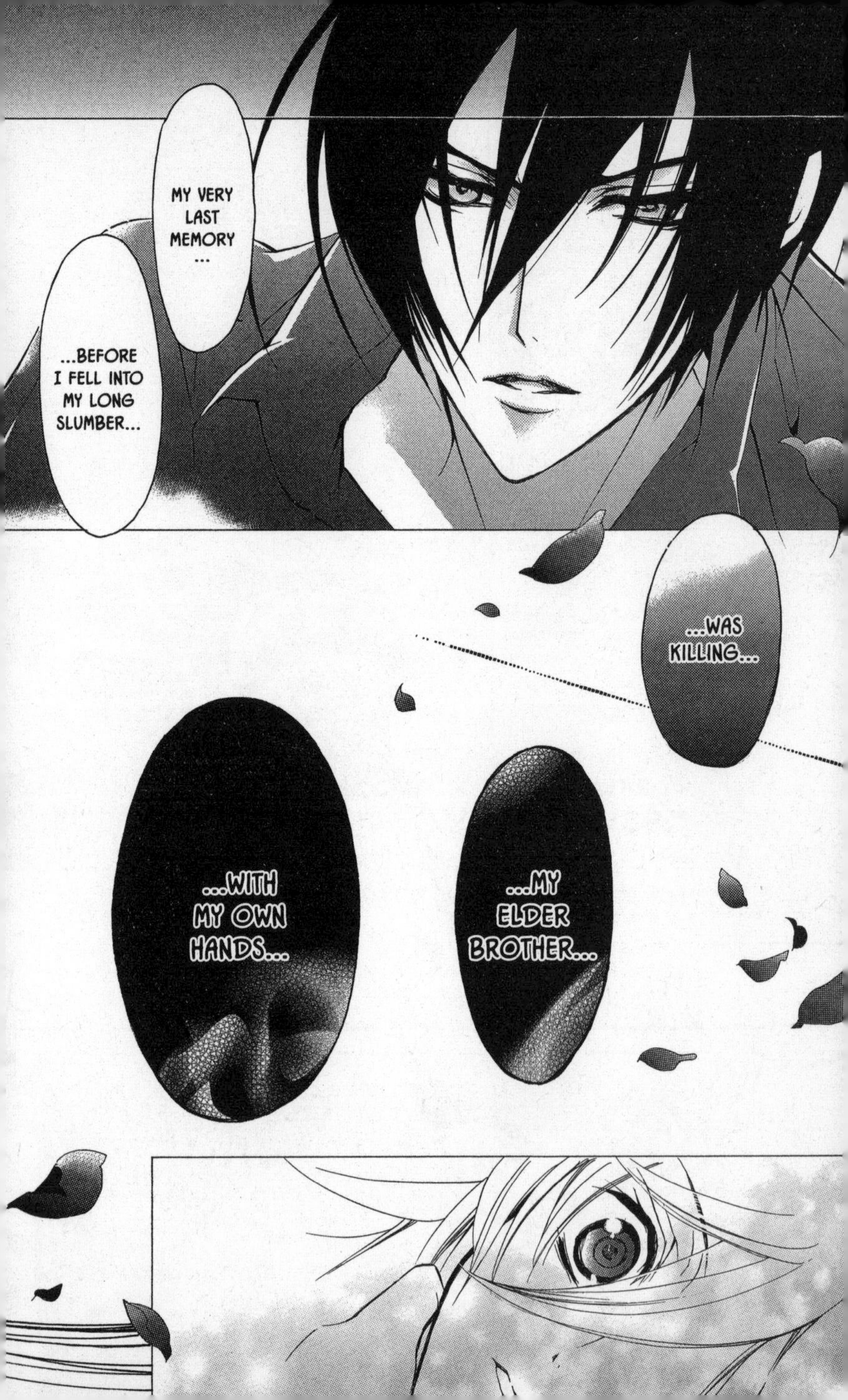
MY VERY LAST MEMORY...
...BEFORE I FELL INTO MY LONG SLUMBER...
...WAS KILLING...
...MY ELDER BROTHER...
...WITH MY OWN HANDS...

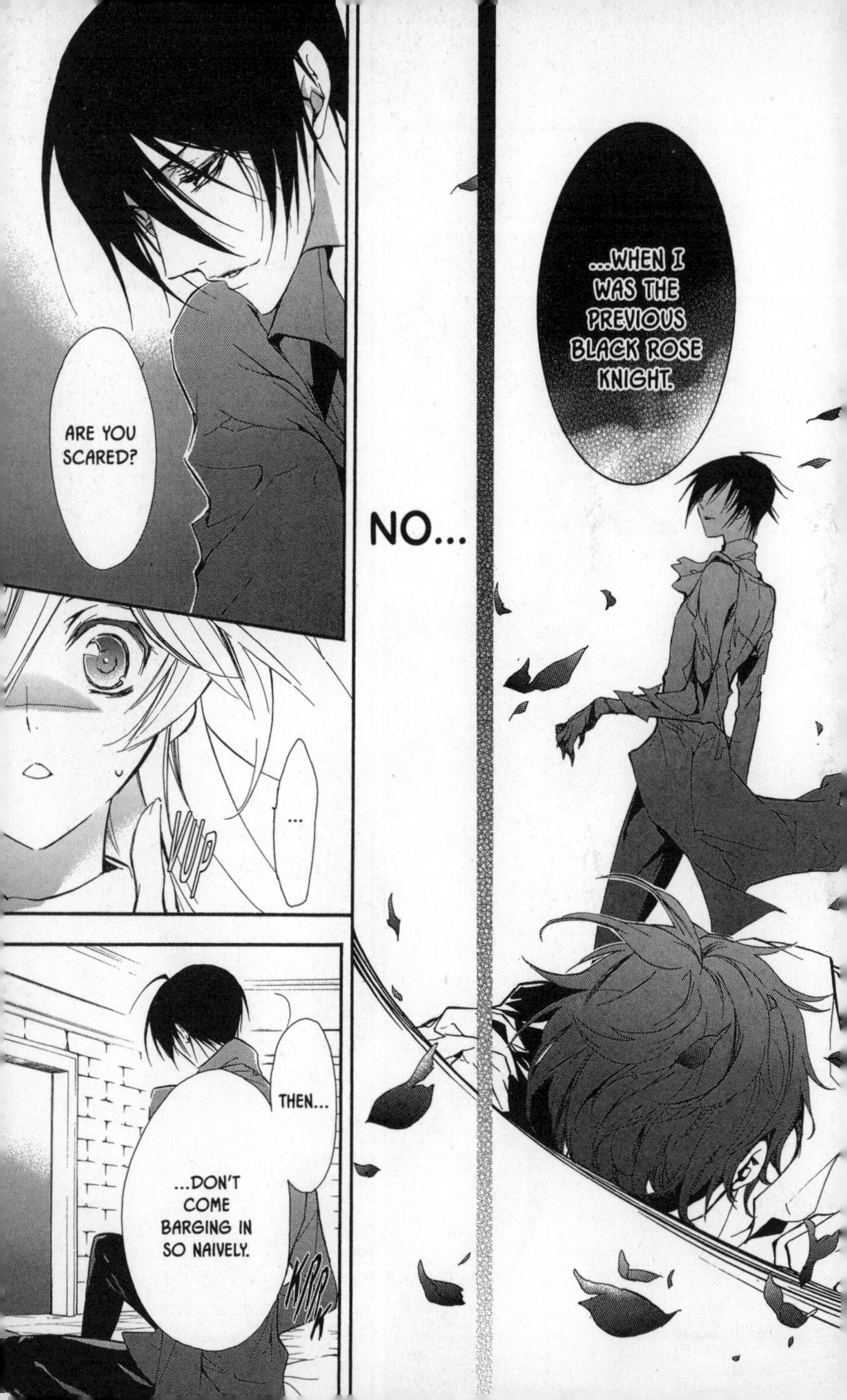
...WHEN I WAS THE PREVIOUS BLACK ROSE KNIGHT.
NO...
ARE YOU SCARED?
...
THEN...
...DON'T COME BARGING IN SO NAIVELY.

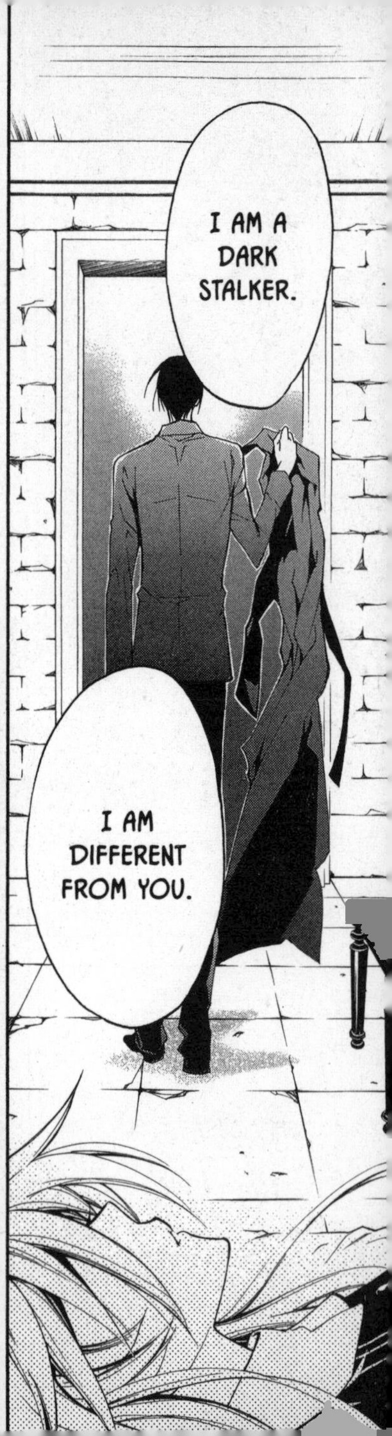
I AM A DARK STALKER.
I AM DIFFERENT FROM YOU.

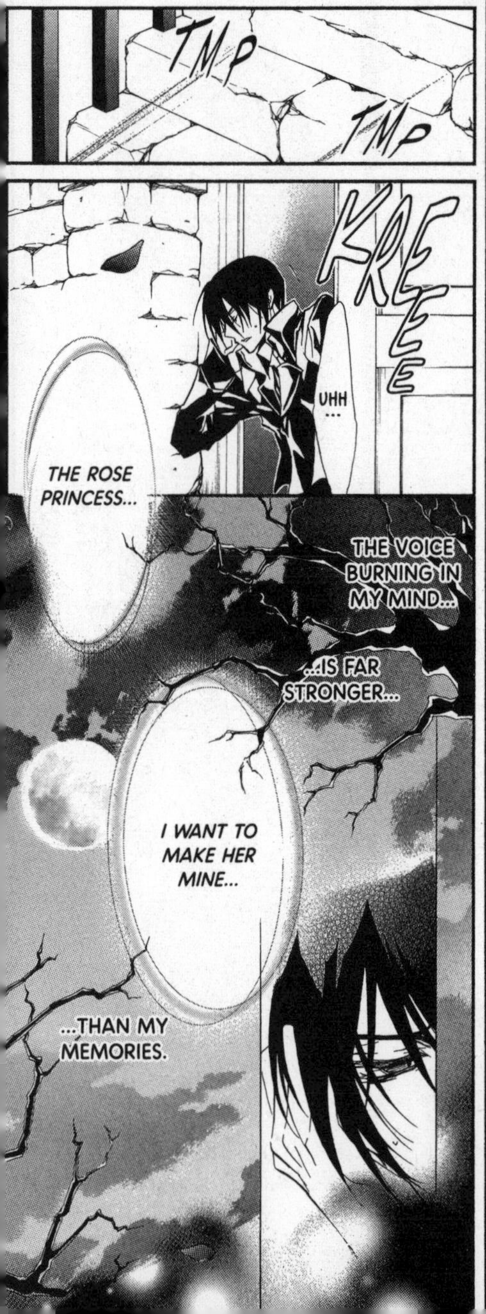
TMP
TMP
KREEEE
UHH...
THE ROSE PRINCESS...
THE VOICE BURNING IN MY MIND...
...IS FAR STRONGER...
I WANT TO MAKE HER MINE...
...THAN MY MEMORIES.

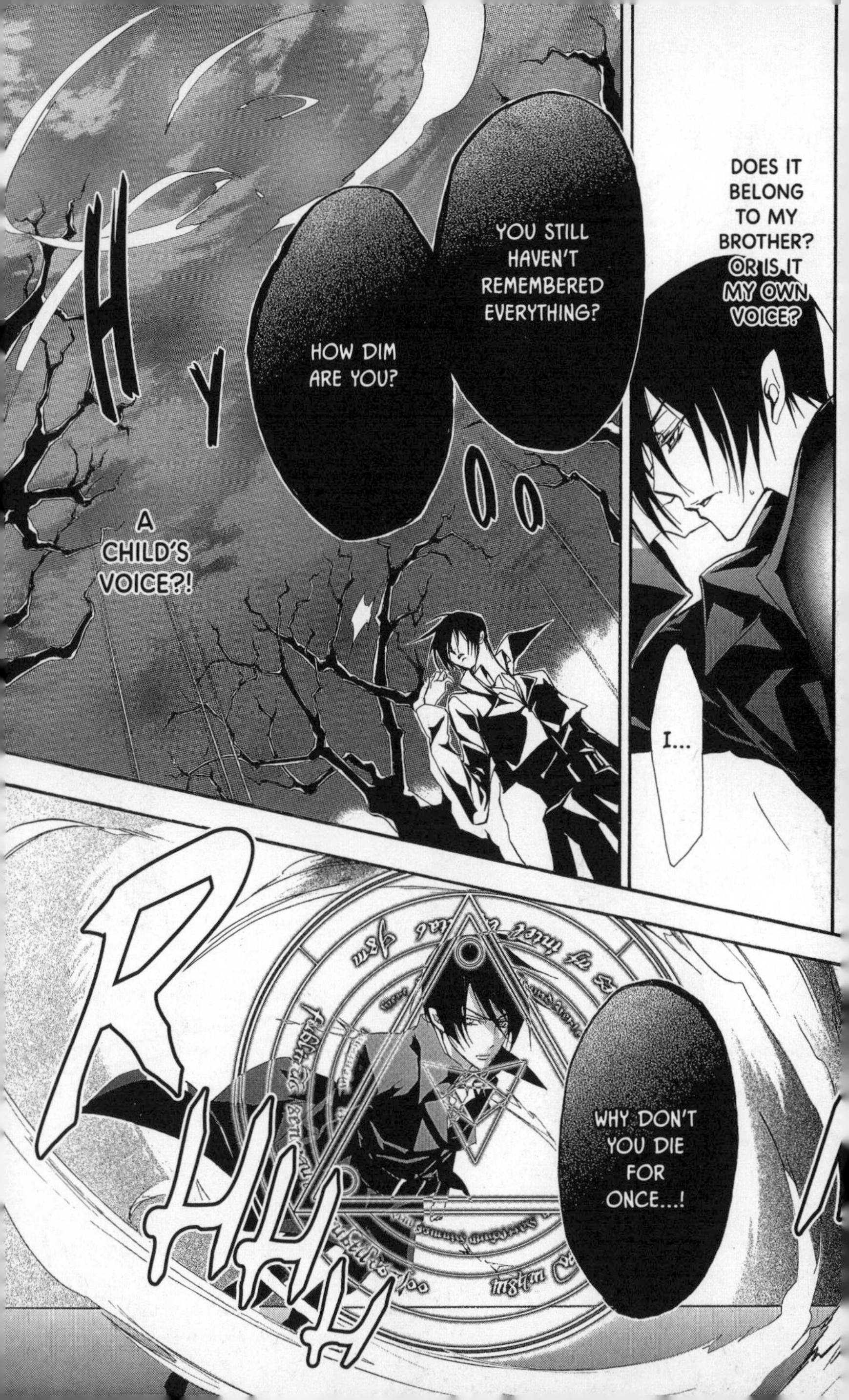
DOES IT BELONG TO MY BROTHER? OR IS IT MY OWN VOICE?
I...
HYOO
YOU STILL HAVEN'T REMEMBERED EVERYTHING?
HOW DIM ARE YOU?
A CHILD'S VOICE?!
WHY DON'T YOU DIE FOR ONCE...!
RHHHH

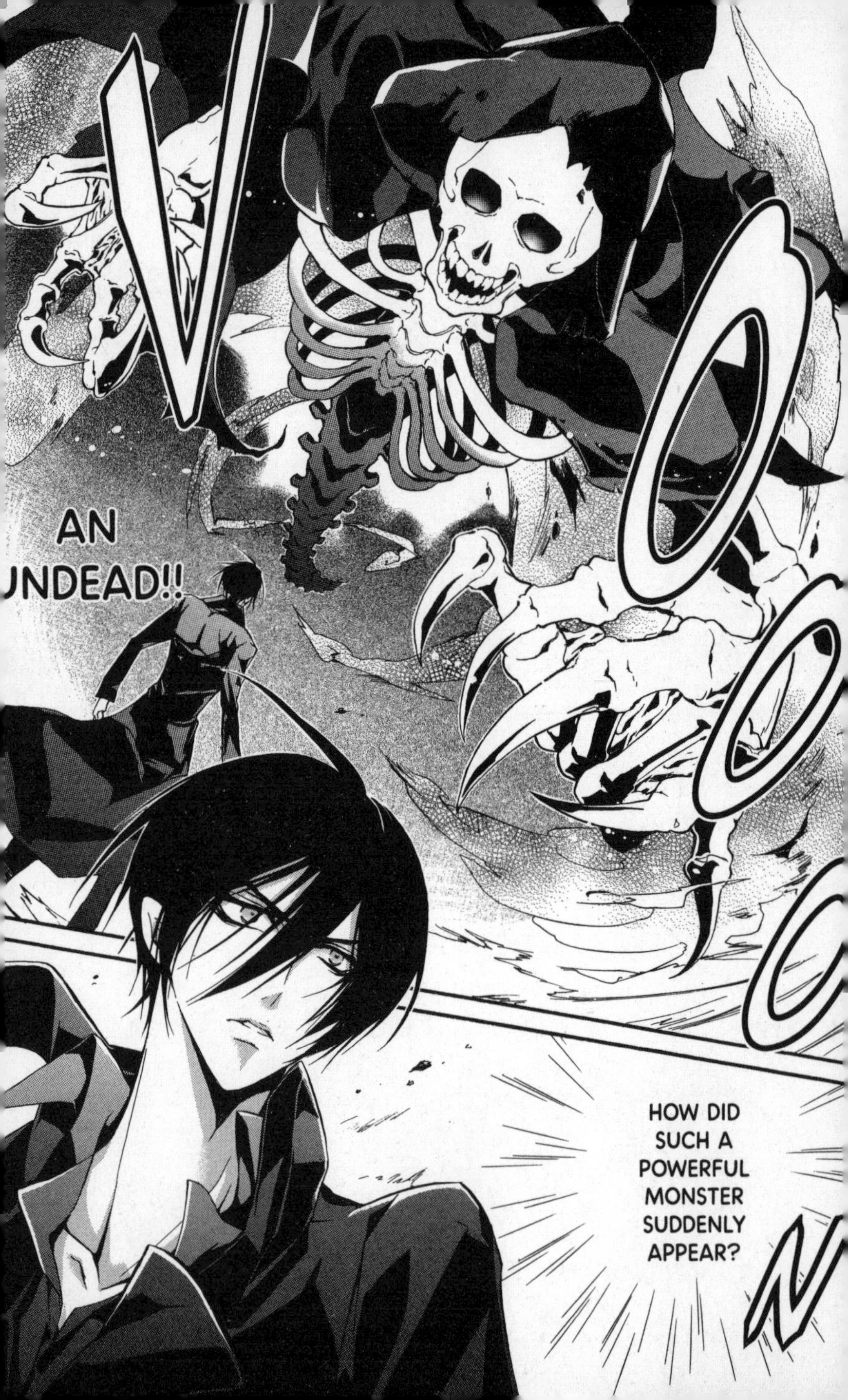
VOOOON
AN UNDEAD!!
HOW DID SUCH A POWERFUL MONSTER SUDDENLY APPEAR?

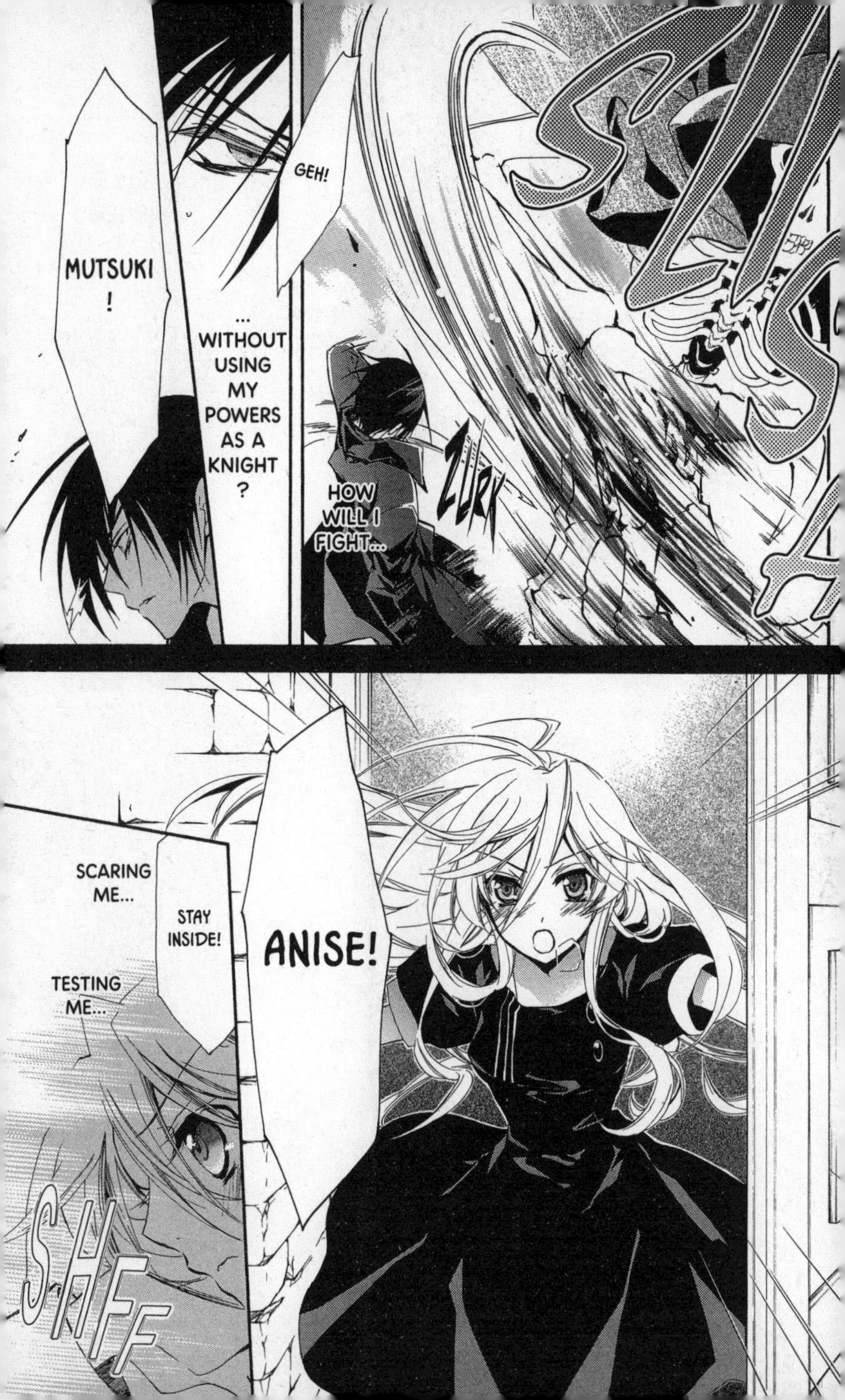
GEH!
ZURK
HOW WILL I FIGHT...
...WITHOUT USING MY POWERS AS A KNIGHT?
MUTSUKI!
ANISE!
STAY INSIDE!
SCARING ME...
TESTING ME...
SHFF

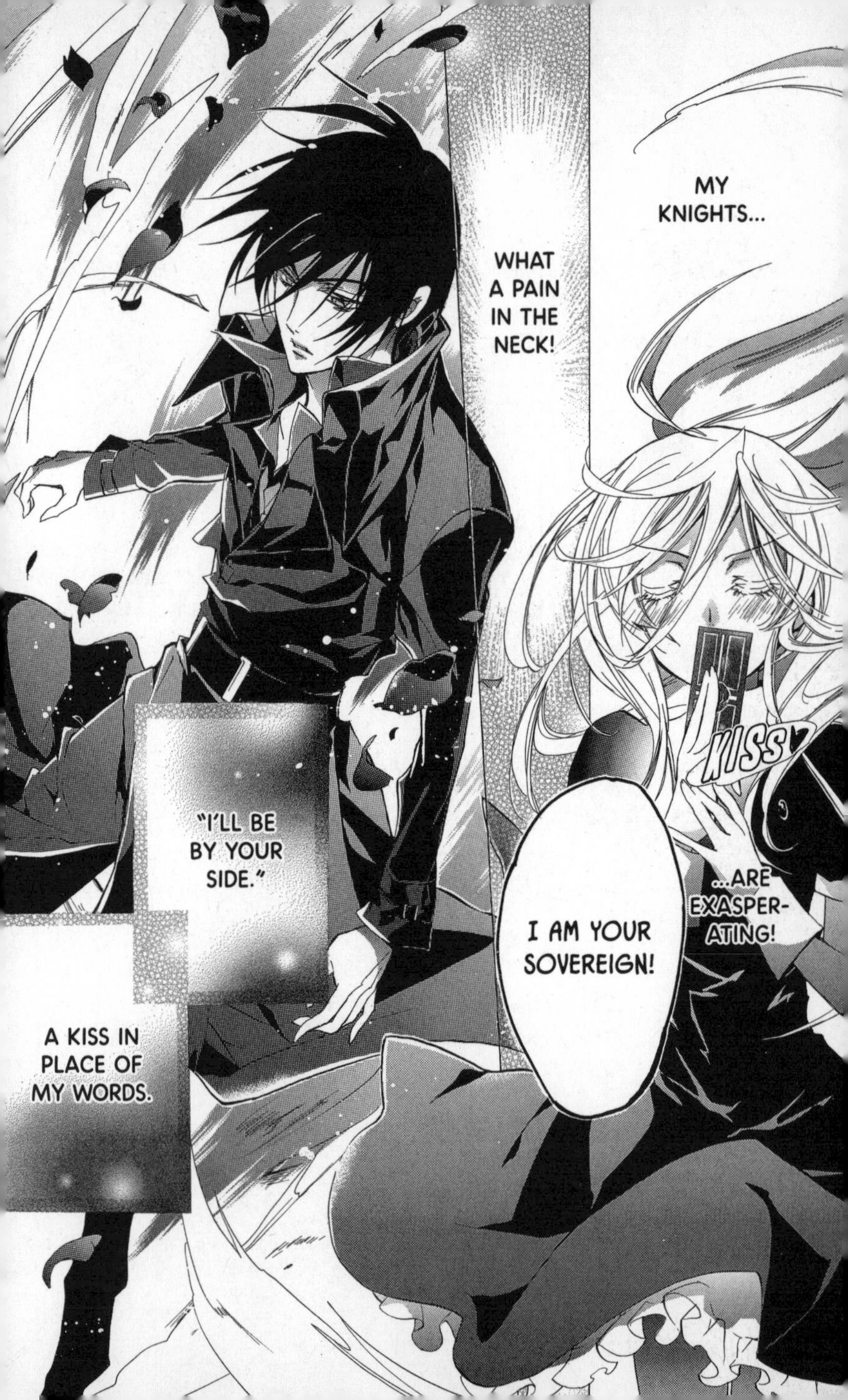
MY KNIGHTS...
KISS
...ARE EXASPER-ATING!
I AM YOUR SOVEREIGN!
WHAT A PAIN IN THE NECK!
"I'LL BE BY YOUR SIDE."
A KISS IN PLACE OF MY WORDS.

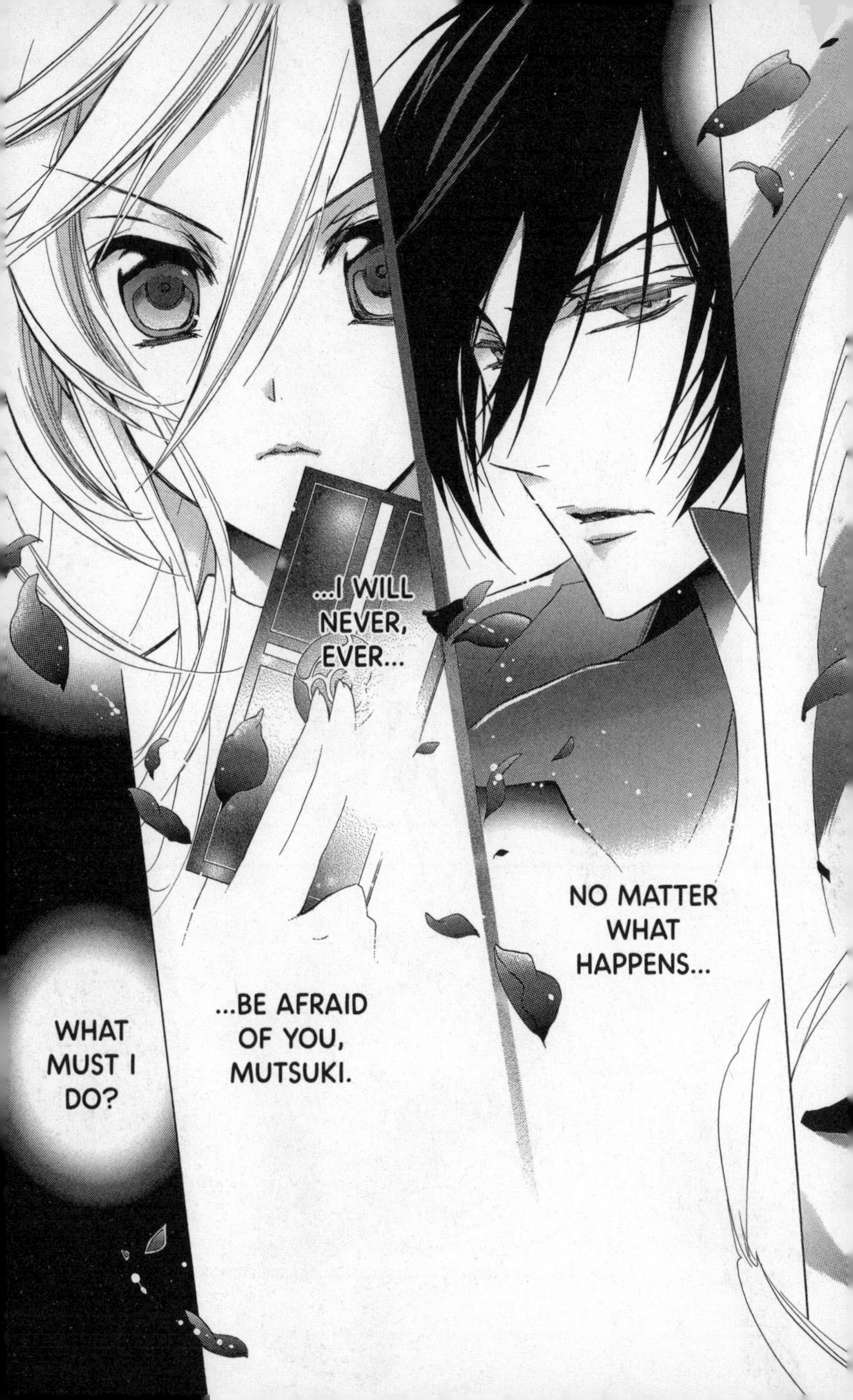
NO MATTER WHAT HAPPENS...
...I WILL NEVER, EVER...
...BE AFRAID OF YOU, MUTSUKI.
WHAT MUST I DO?

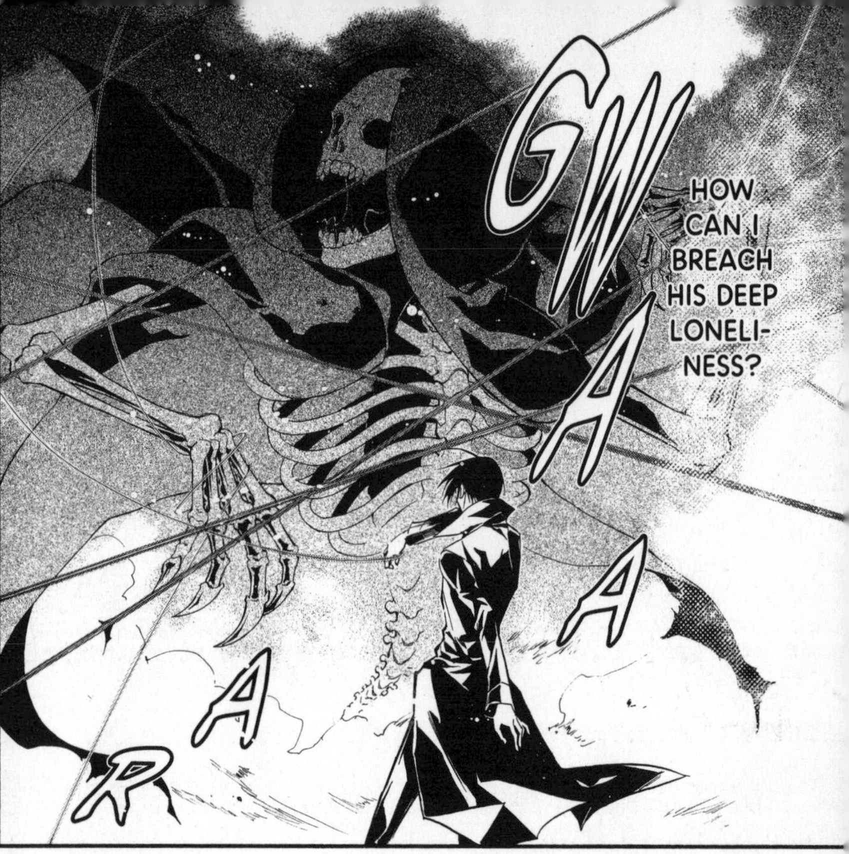
GWAAAR
HOW CAN I BREACH HIS DEEP LONELI-NESS?

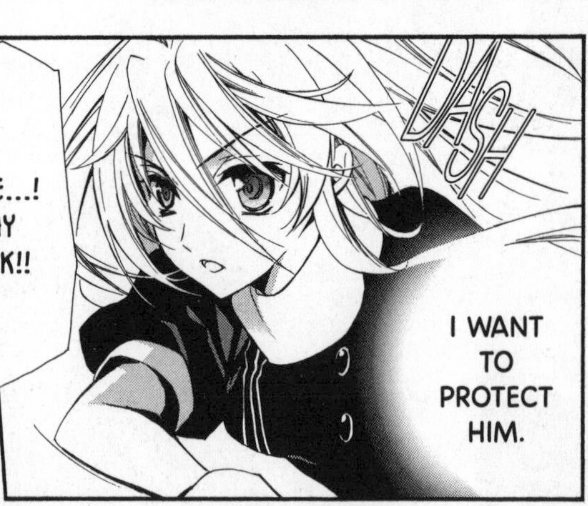
DASH
I WANT TO PROTECT HIM.

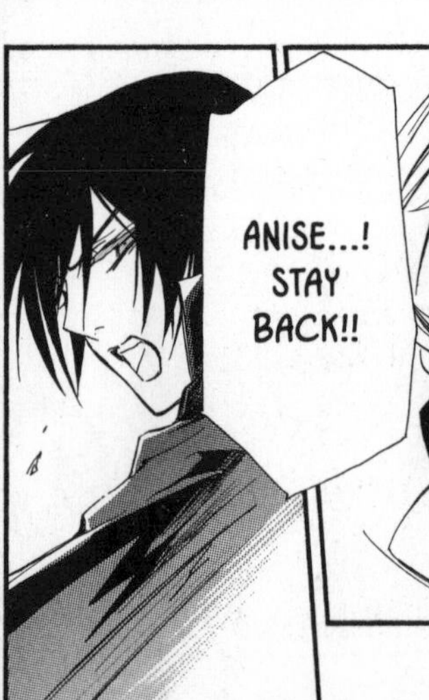
ANISE...! STAY BACK!!

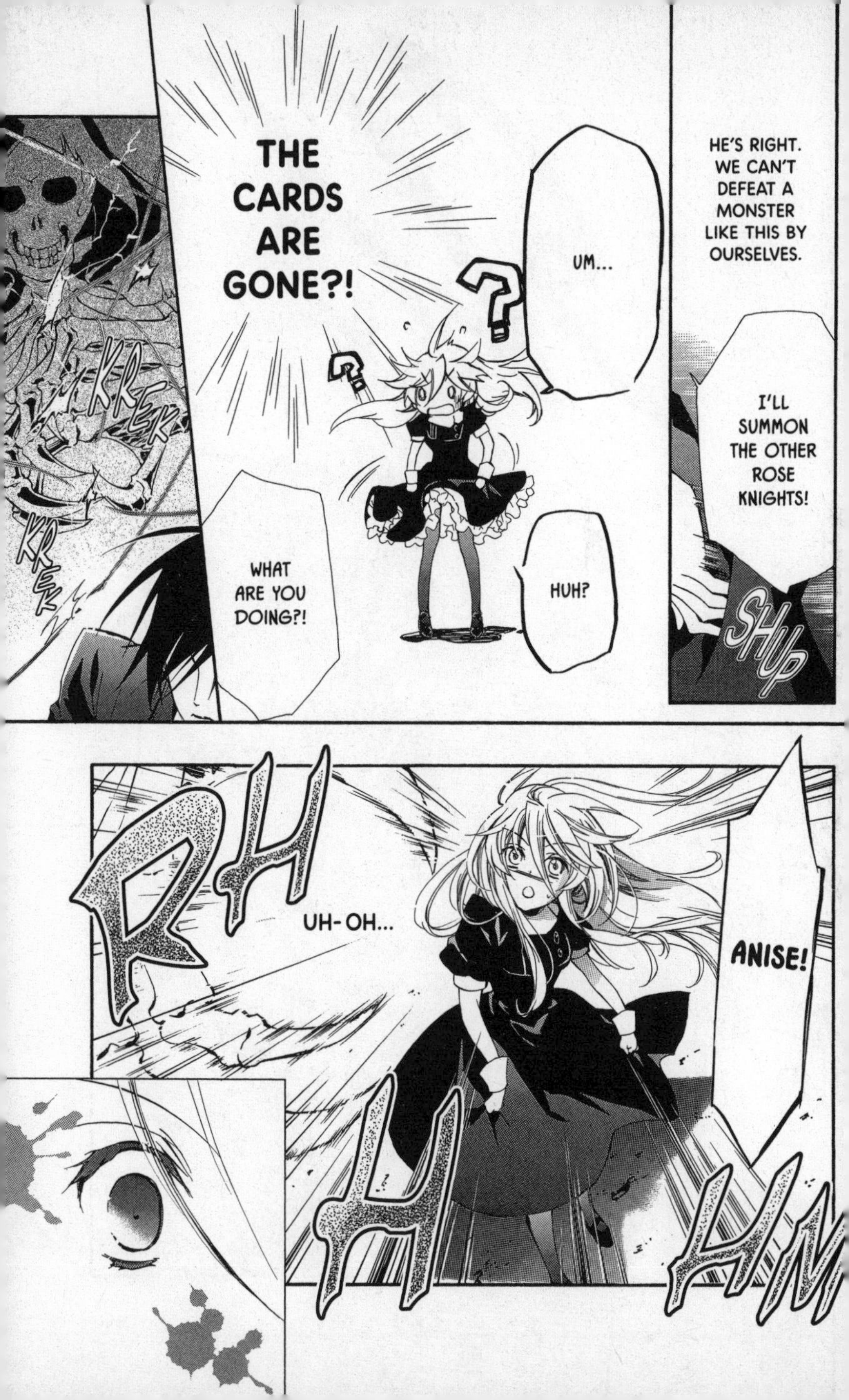
HE'S RIGHT. WE CAN'T DEFEAT A MONSTER LIKE THIS BY OURSELVES.
I'LL SUMMON THE OTHER ROSE KNIGHTS!
SHUP
UM...
THE CARDS ARE GONE?!
HUH?
WHAT ARE YOU DOING?!
KREK
KREK
ANISE!
UH-OH...

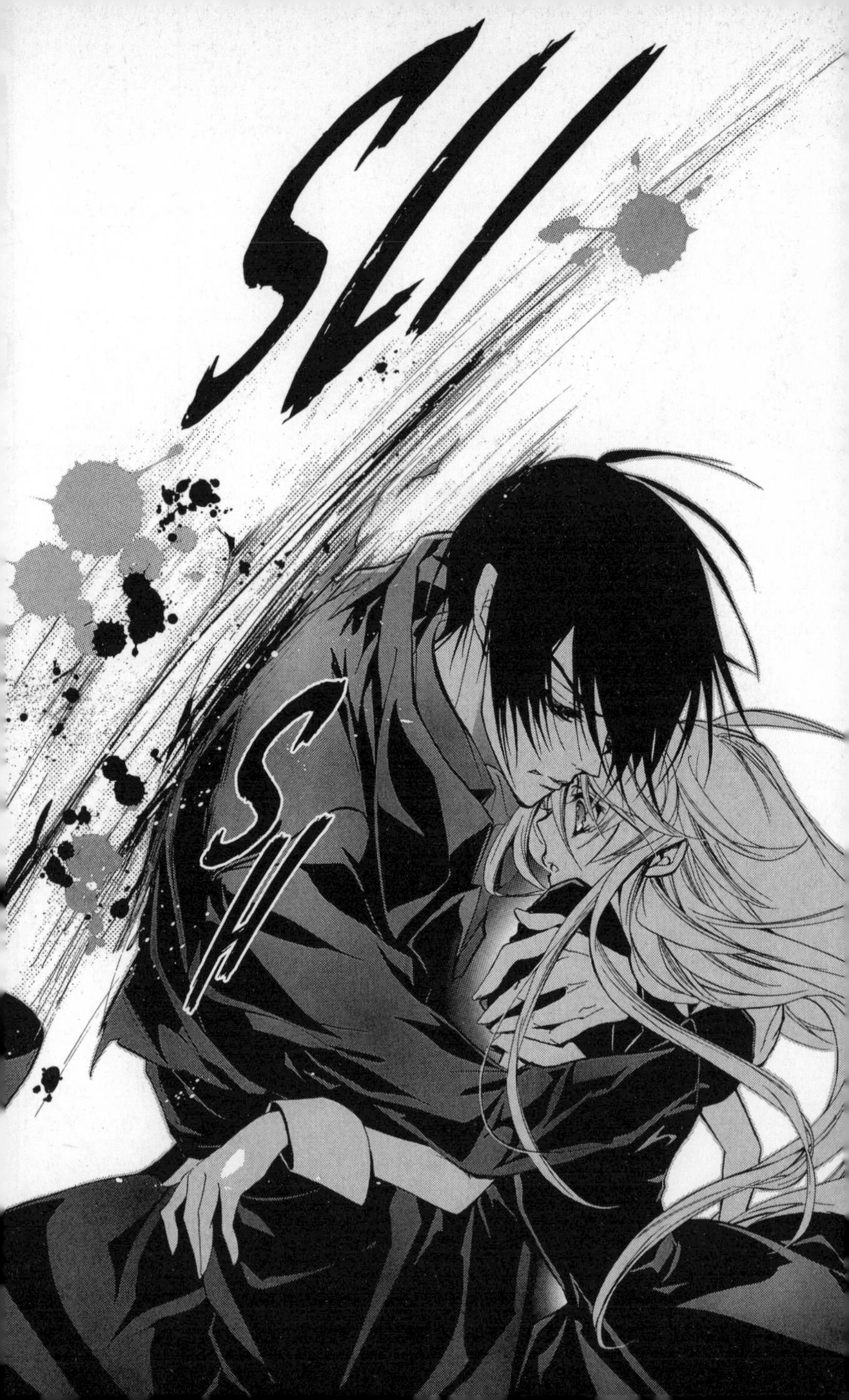

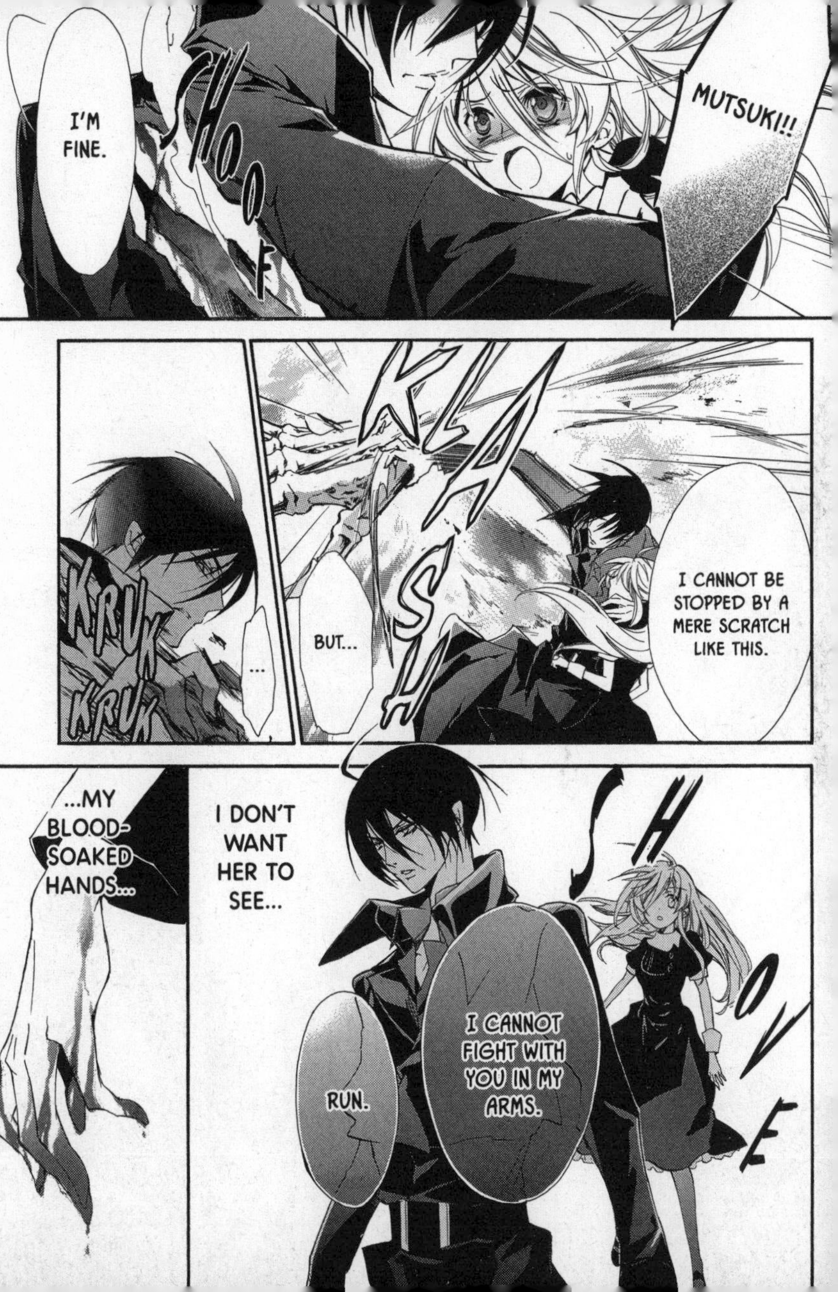
MUTSUKI!!!
SHOOF
I'M FINE.
I CANNOT BE STOPPED BY A MERE SCRATCH LIKE THIS.
KLASH
BUT...
...
KRUK KRUK
SHOVE
I CANNOT FIGHT WITH YOU IN MY ARMS.
RUN.
I DON'T WANT HER TO SEE...
...MY BLOOD-SOAKED HANDS...

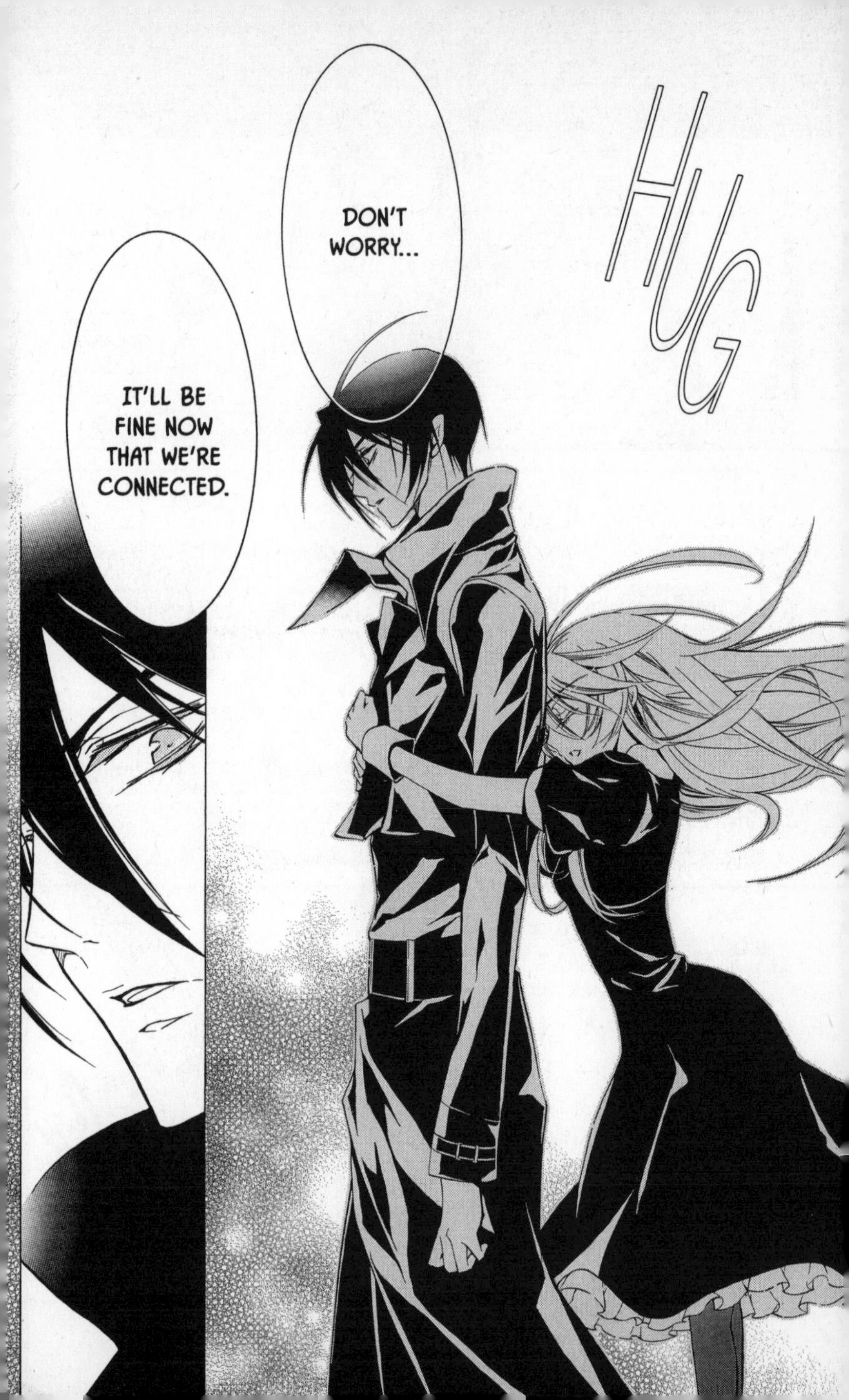
HUG
DON'T WORRY...
IT'LL BE FINE NOW THAT WE'RE CONNECTED.

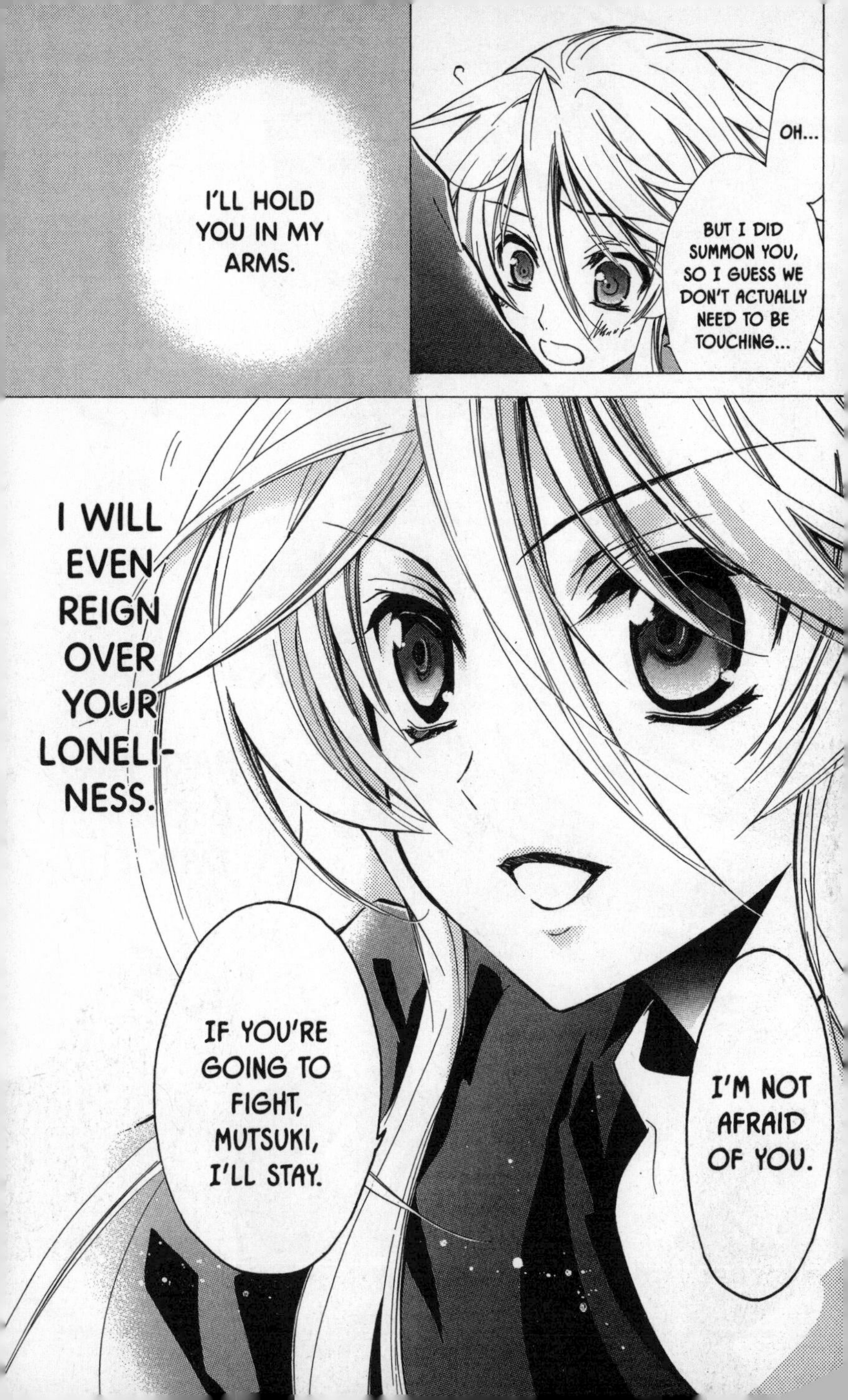
OH...
BUT I DID SUMMON YOU, SO I GUESS WE DON'T ACTUALLY NEED TO BE TOUCHING...
I'LL HOLD YOU IN MY ARMS.
I WILL EVEN REIGN OVER YOUR LONELI-NESS.
I'M NOT AFRAID OF YOU.
IF YOU'RE GOING TO FIGHT, MUTSUKI, I'LL STAY.

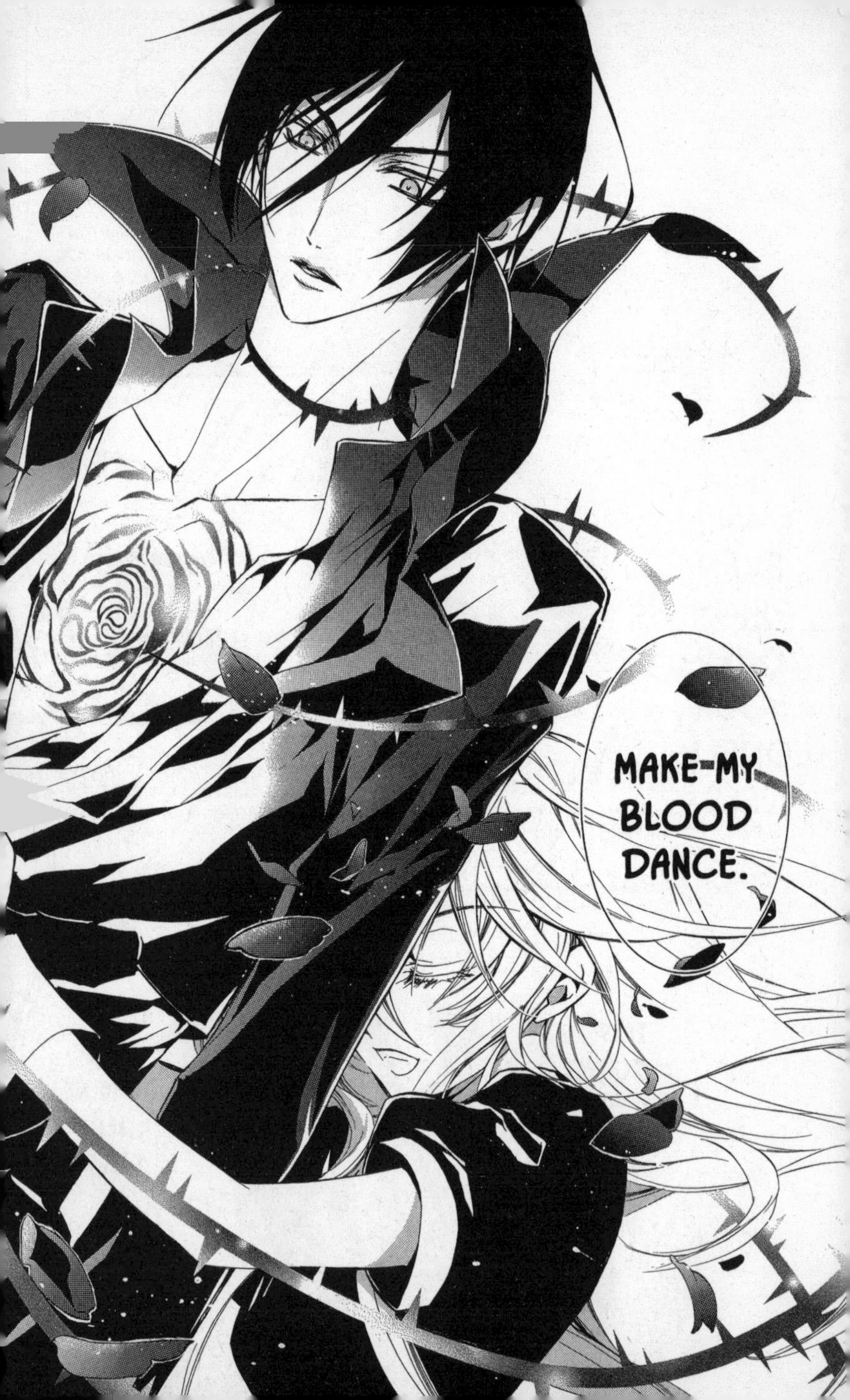
MAKE MY BLOOD DANCE.

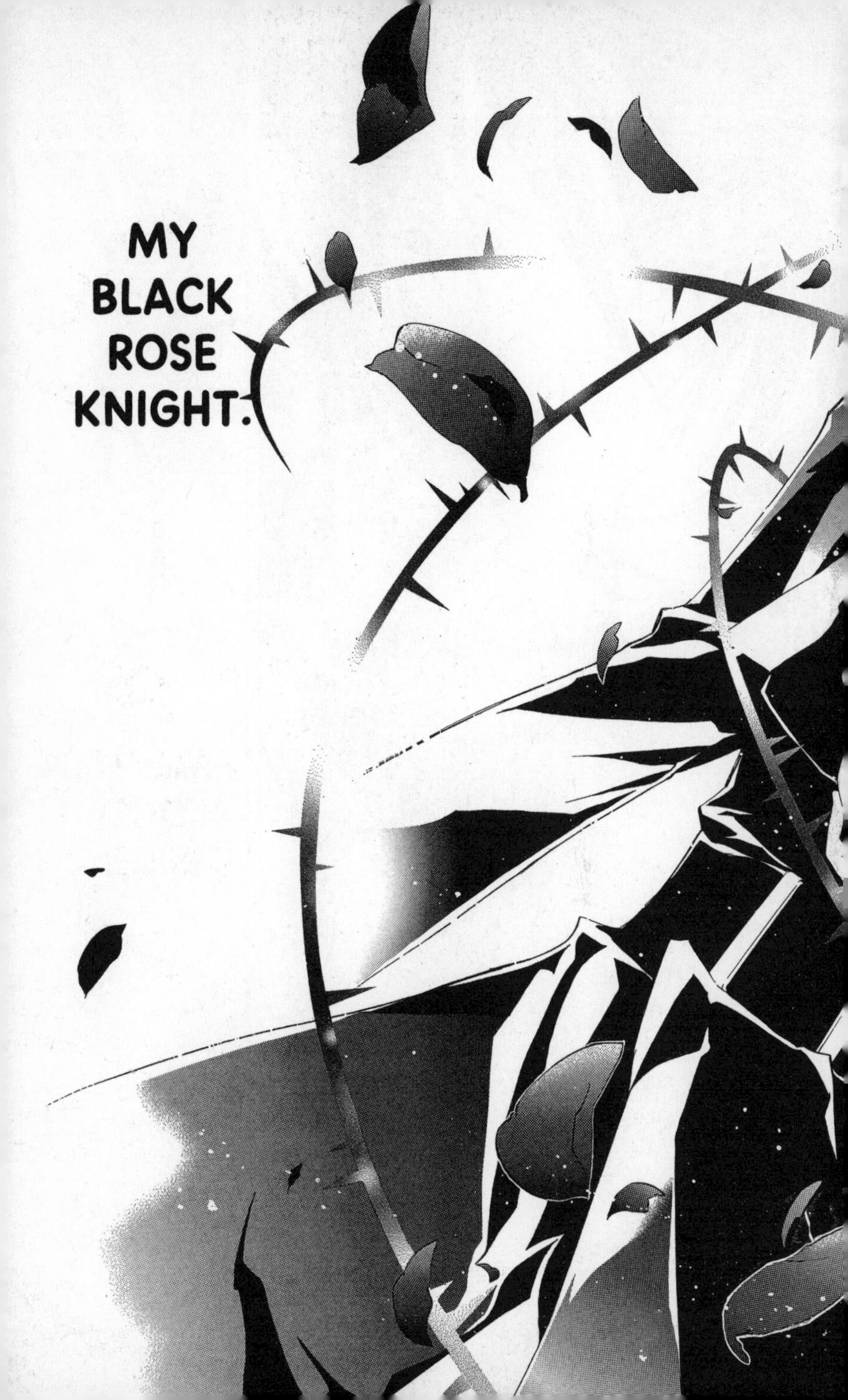
MY BLACK ROSE KNIGHT.

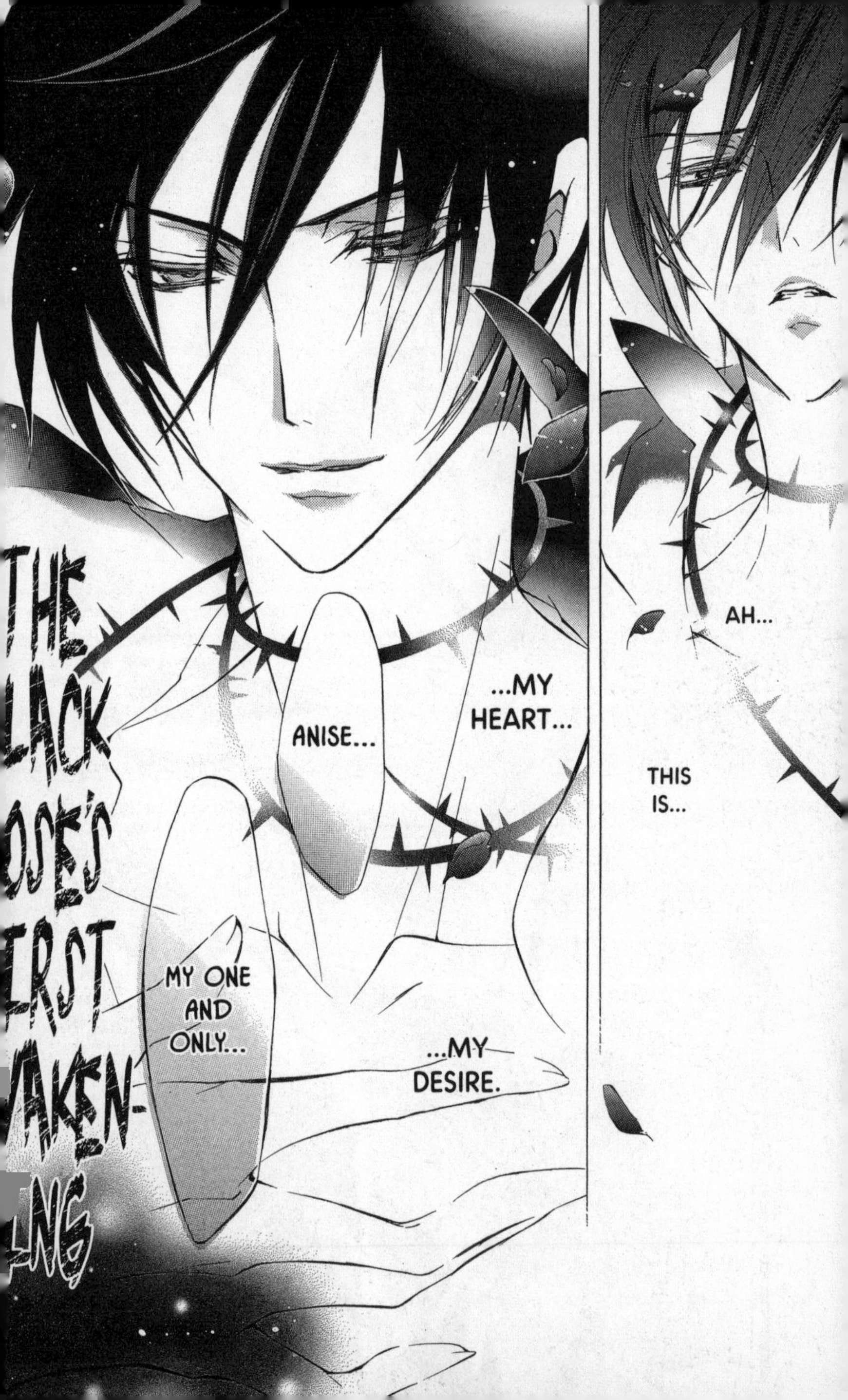
AH...
THIS IS...
ANISE...
...MY HEART...
MY ONE AND ONLY...
...MY DESIRE.
THE LACK OSE'S IRST VAKEN- ING

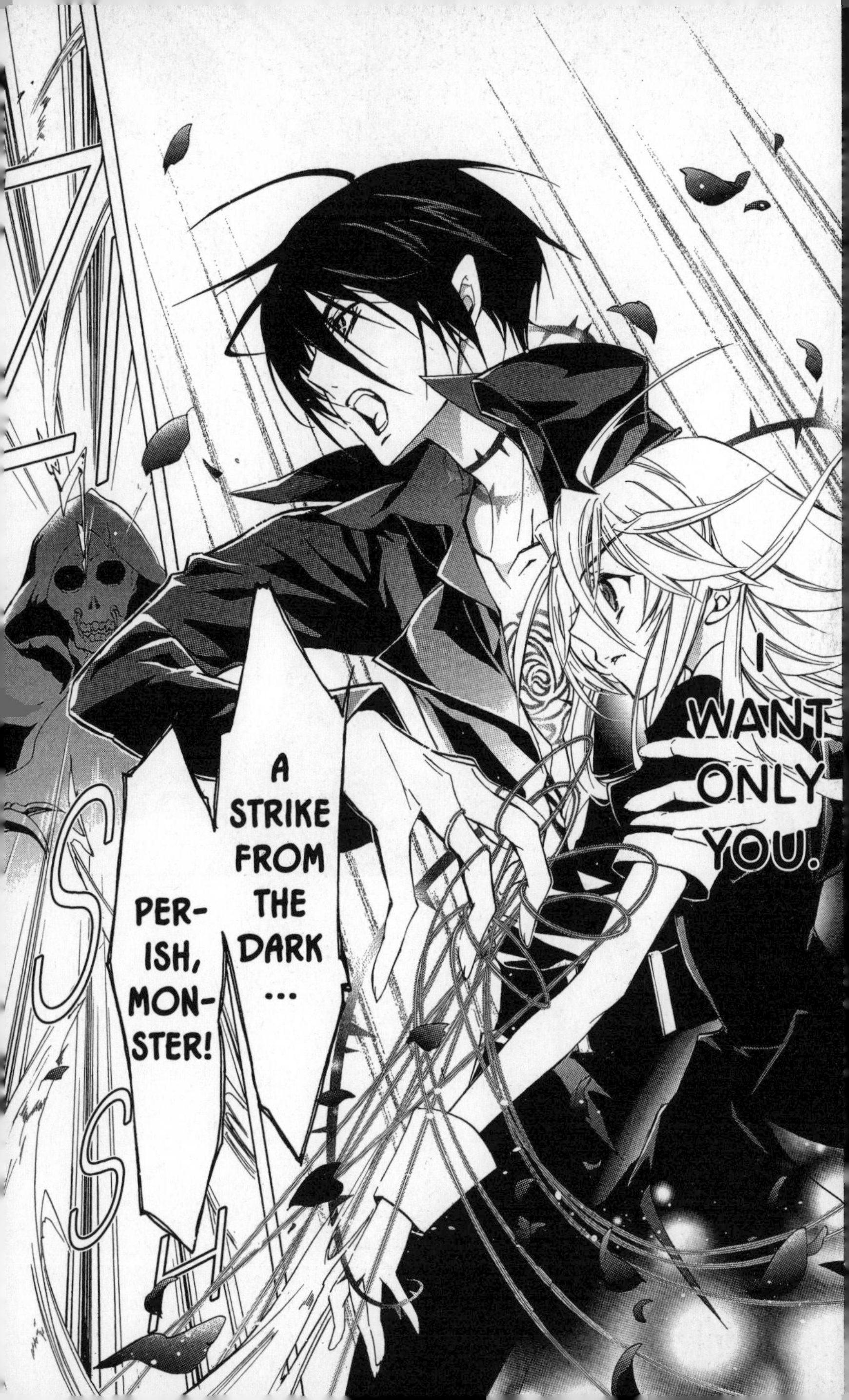
I WANT ONLY YOU.
A STRIKE FROM THE DARK...
PERISH, MONSTER!
SSH

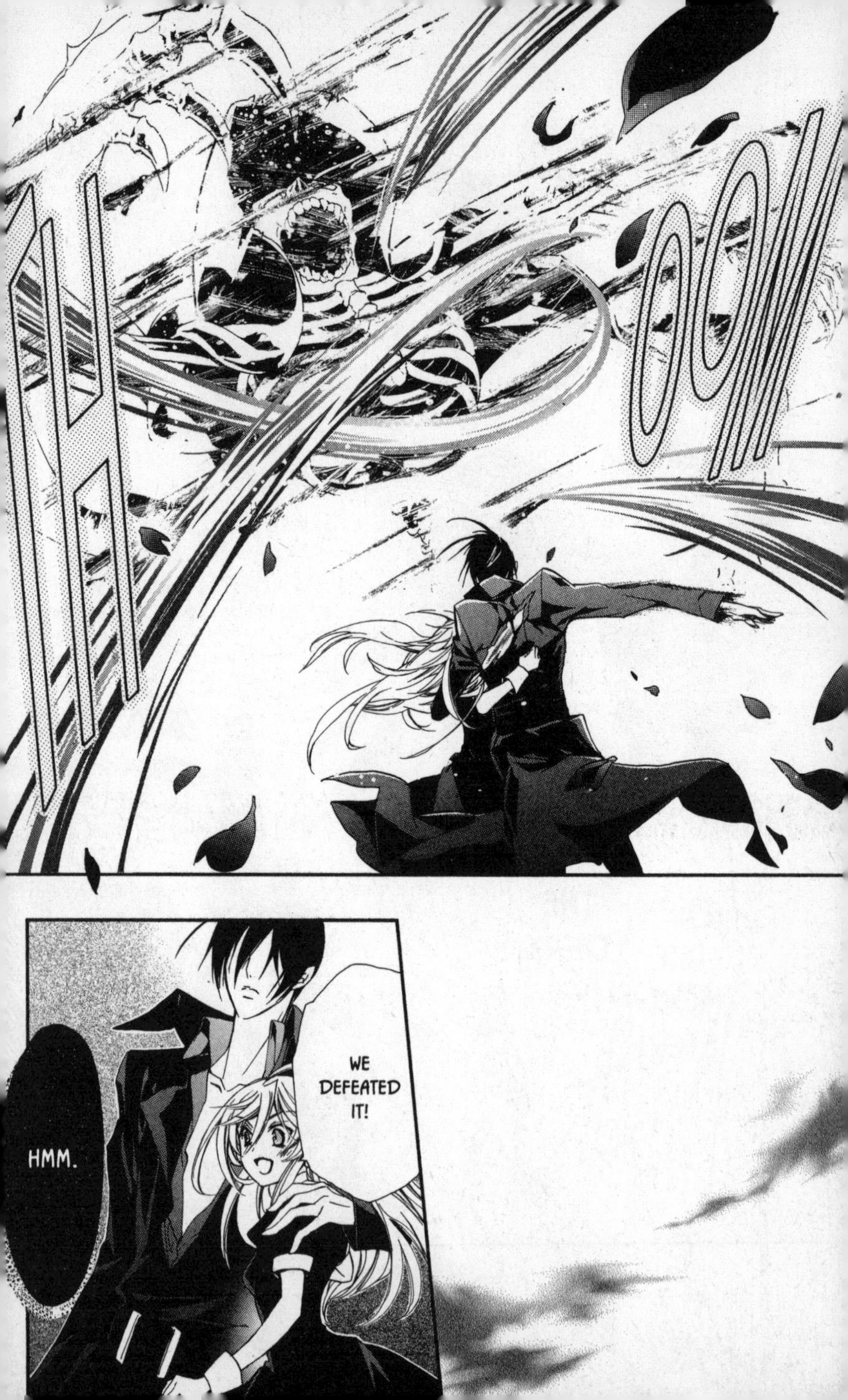
WE DEFEATED IT!
HMM.

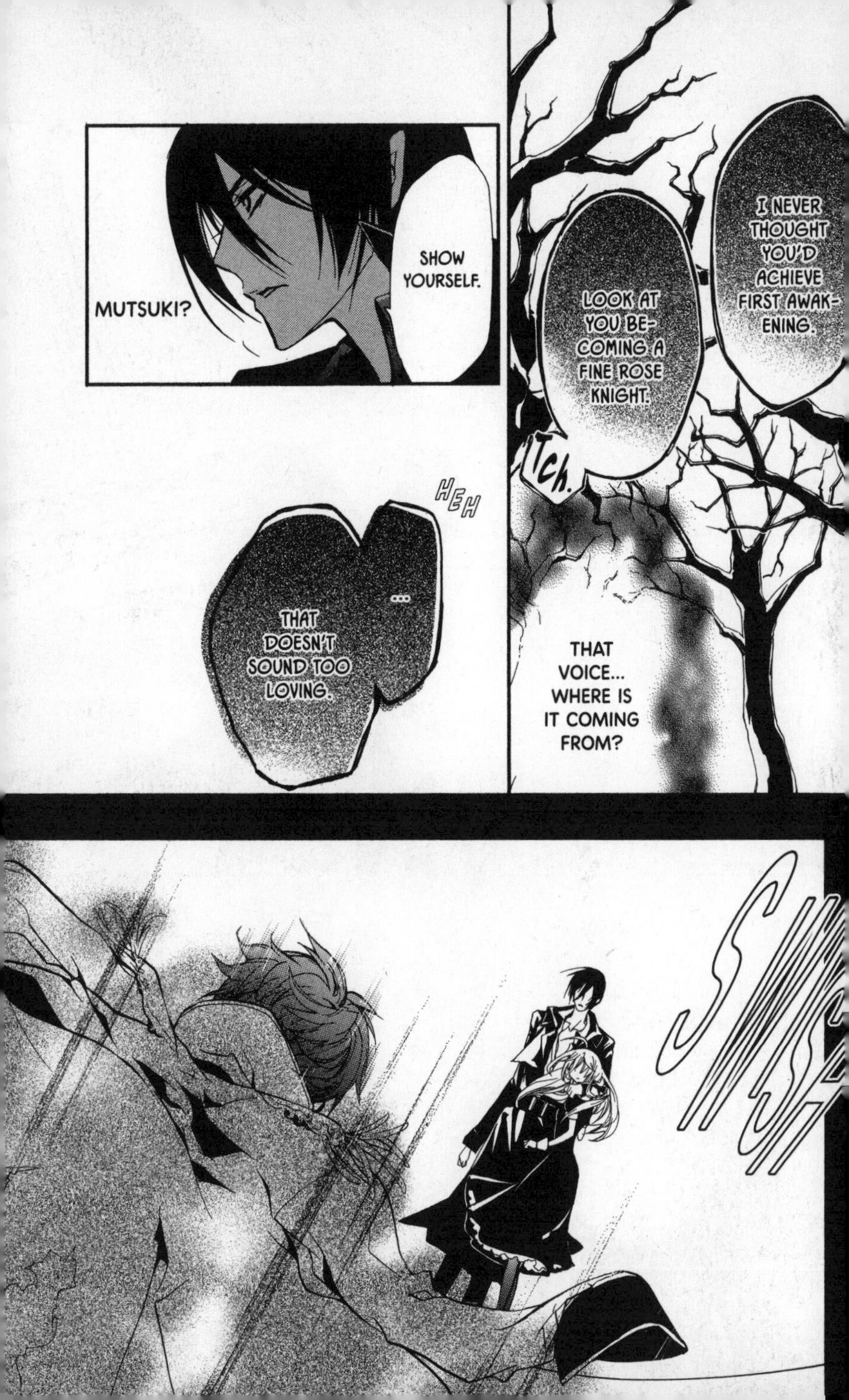
I NEVER THOUGHT YOU'D ACHIEVE FIRST AWAK-ENING.
LOOK AT YOU BE-COMING A FINE ROSE KNIGHT.
Tch.
THAT VOICE... WHERE IS IT COMING FROM?
SHOW YOURSELF.
MUTSUKI?
HEH
...
THAT DOESN'T SOUND TOO LOVING.

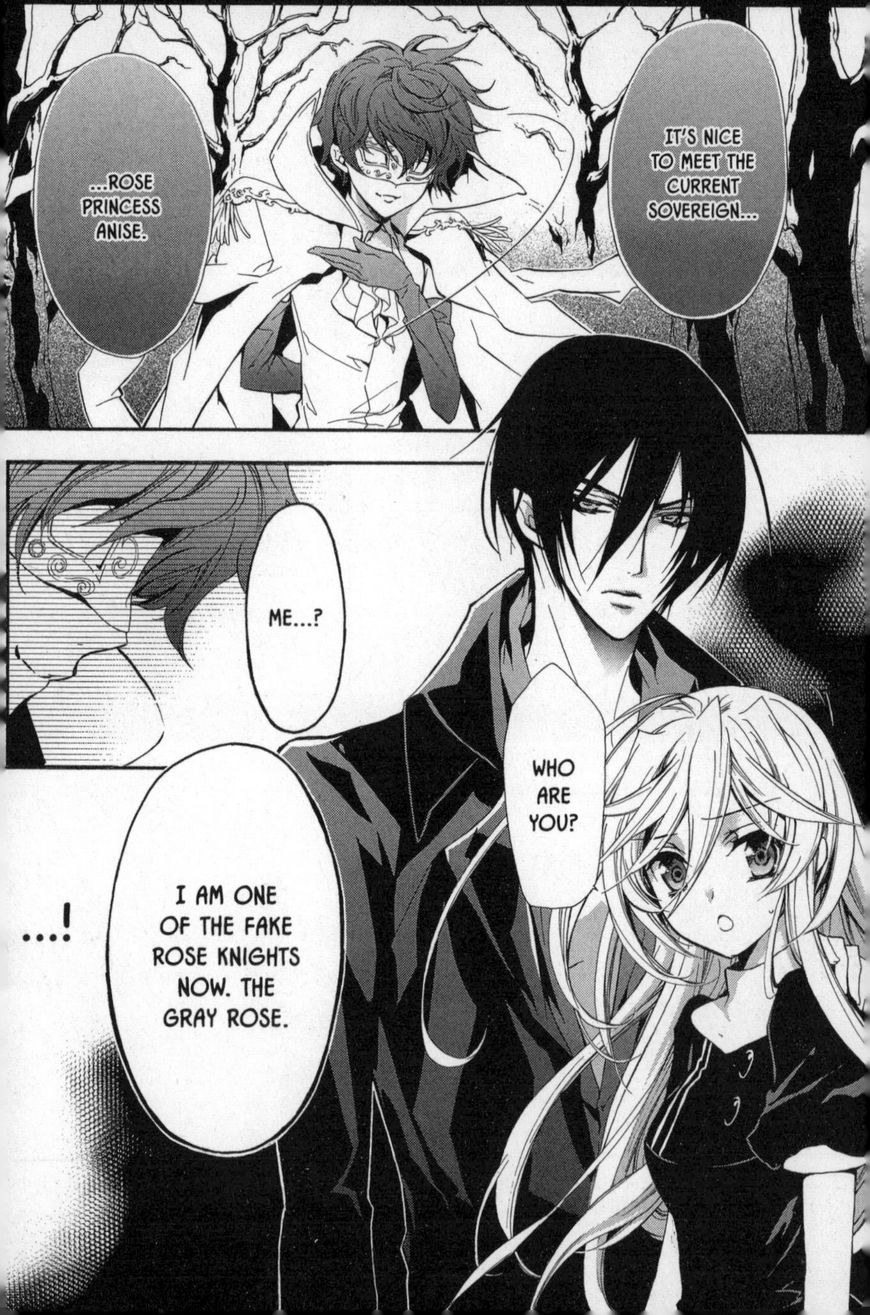
IT'S NICE TO MEET THE CURRENT SOVEREIGN...
...ROSE PRINCESS ANISE.
WHO ARE YOU?
ME...?
I AM ONE OF THE FAKE ROSE KNIGHTS NOW. THE GRAY ROSE.
...!

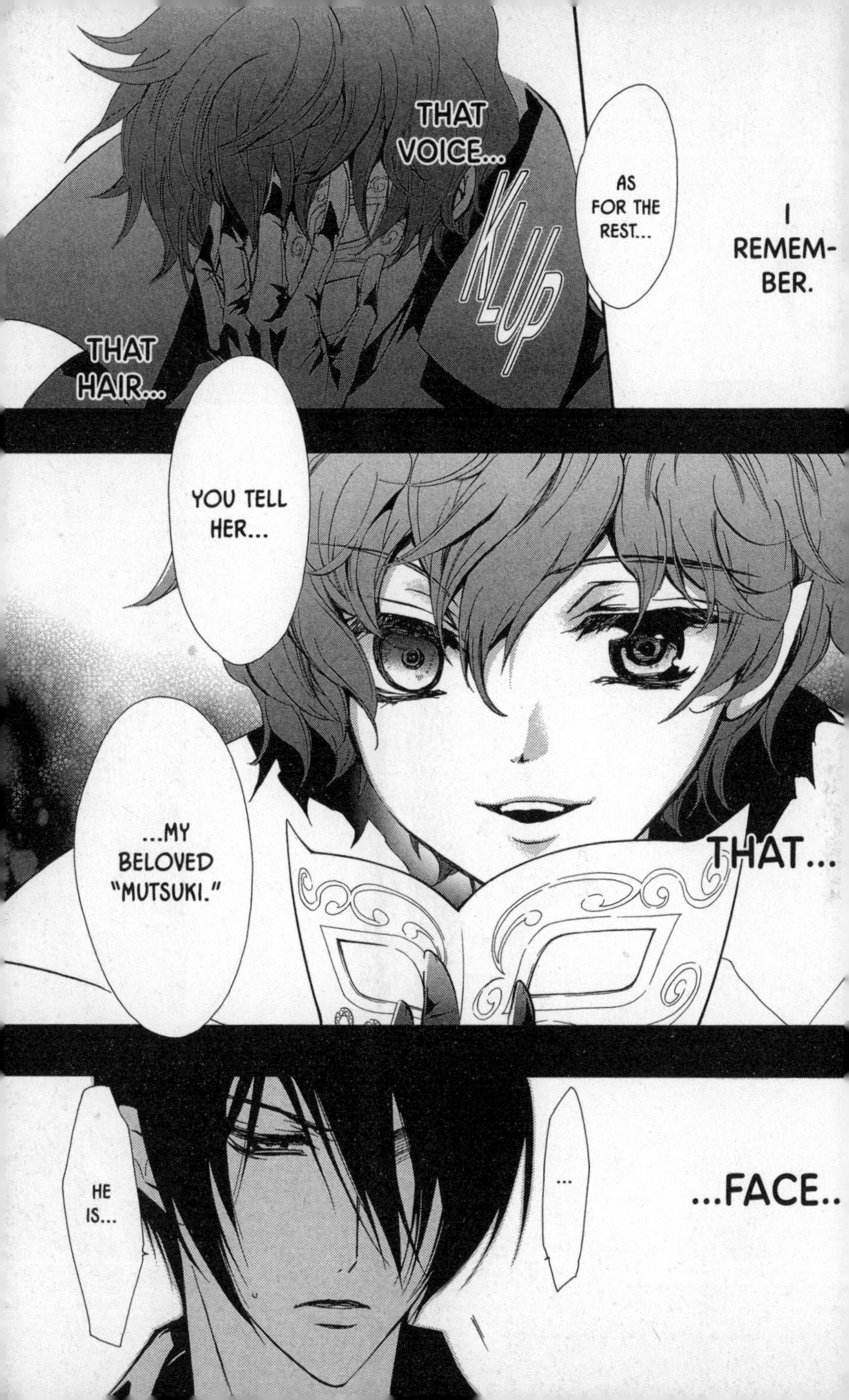
I REMEM-BER.
AS FOR THE REST...
THAT VOICE...
KLUP
THAT HAIR...
YOU TELL HER...
...MY BELOVED "MUTSUKI."
THAT...
...FACE..
...
HE IS...

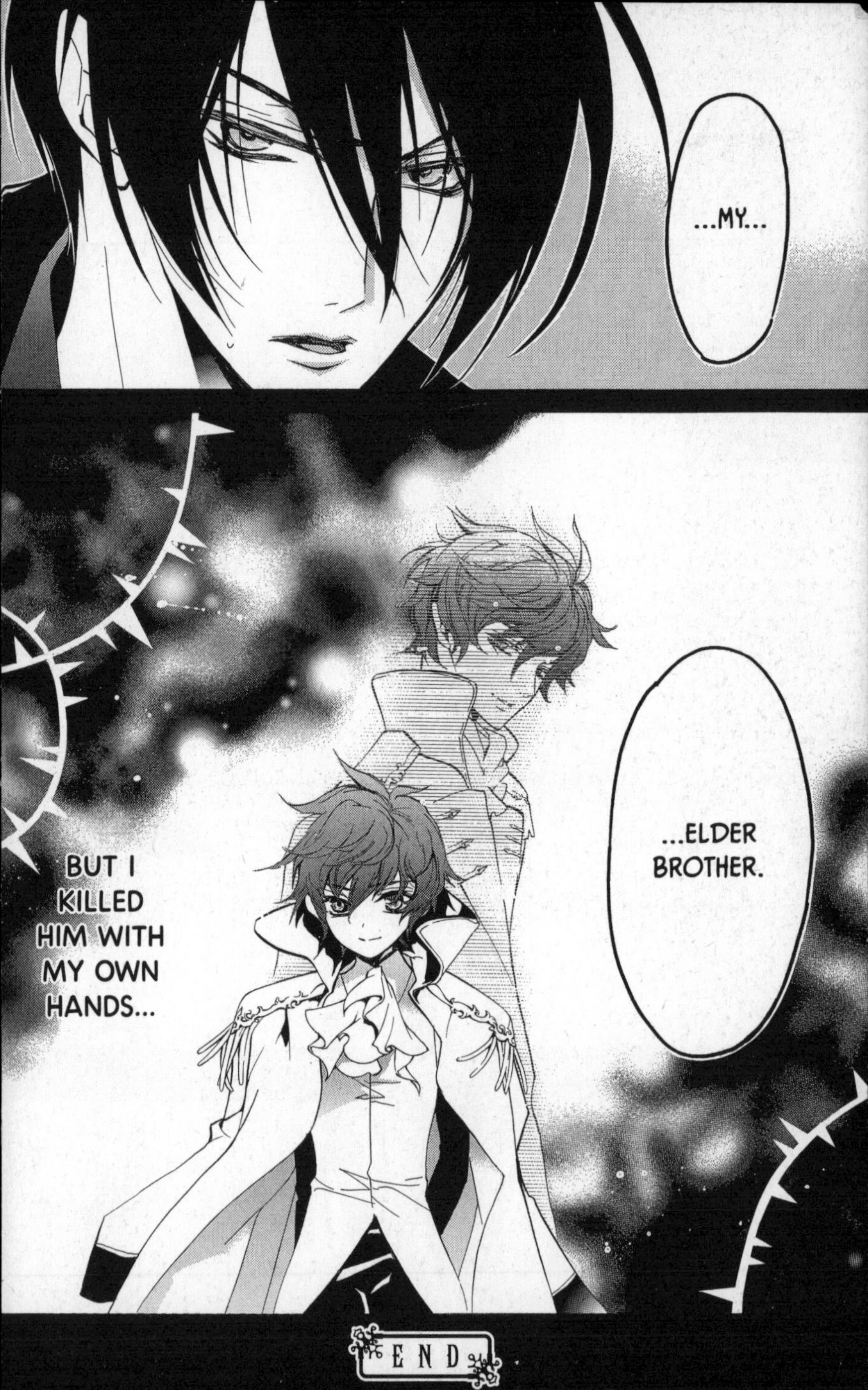
...MY...
...ELDER BROTHER.
BUT I KILLED HIM WITH MY OWN HANDS...
END

Kiss of the Rose
Princess

Kiss of the Rose Princess

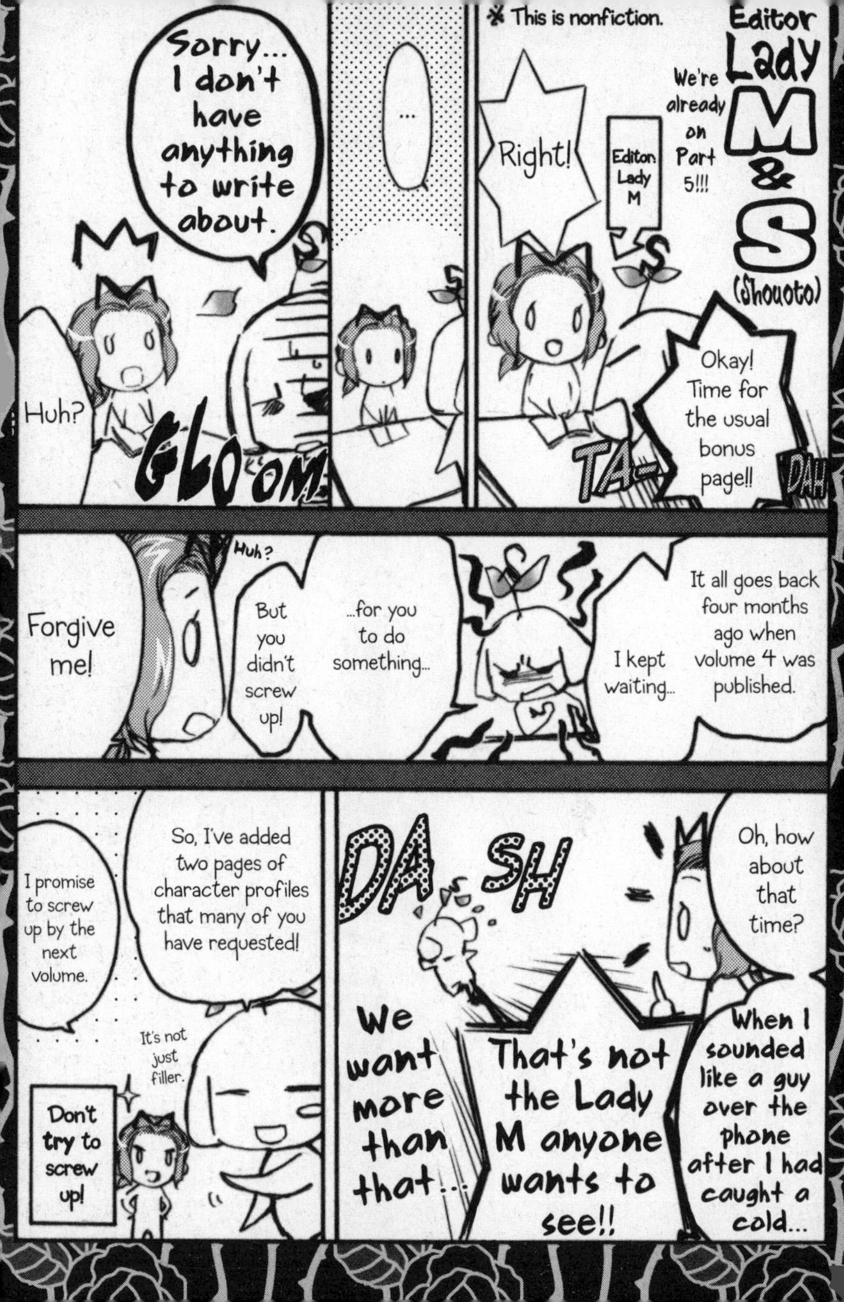
Editor Lady M & S (Shouoto)
※ This is nonfiction.
We're already on Part 5!!!
Editor Lady M
S
Okay! Time for the usual bonus page!!
TA-DAH
Right!
...
Sorry... I don't have anything to write about.
Huh?
GLOOM
It all goes back four months ago when volume 4 was published.
I kept waiting...
...for you to do something...
But you didn't screw up!
Huh?
Forgive me!
Oh, how about that time?
When I sounded like a guy over the phone after I had caught a cold...
That's not the Lady M anyone wants to see!!
We want more than that...
DASH
So, I've added two pages of character profiles that many of you have requested!
I promise to screw up by the next volume.
It's not just filler.
Don't try to screw up!

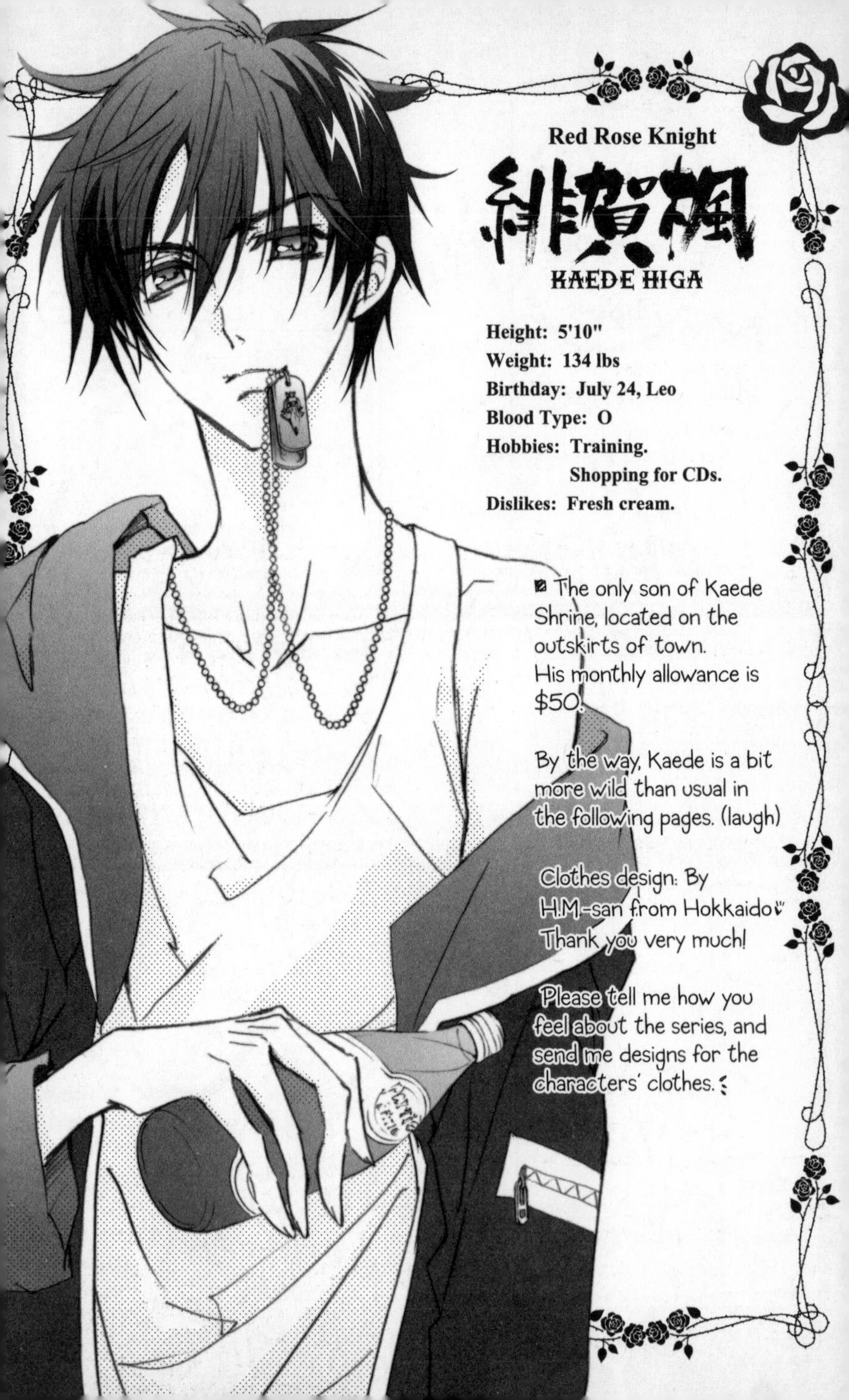

Red Rose Knight

緋賀楓

KAEDE HIGA

Height: 5'10"
Weight: 134 lbs
Birthday: July 24, Leo
Blood Type: O
Hobbies: Training.
Shopping for CDs.
Dislikes: Fresh cream.

▨ The only son of Kaede Shrine, located on the outskirts of town.
His monthly allowance is $50.

By the way, Kaede is a bit more wild than usual in the following pages. (laugh)

Clothes design: By H.M-san from Hokkaido
Thank you very much!

Please tell me how you feel about the series, and send me designs for the characters' clothes.

Blue Rose Knight

浅木晴嵐

SEIRAN ASAGI

Height: **5'5"**
Weight: **114 lbs**
Birthday: **January 26, Aquarius**
Blood Type: **B**
Hobbies: **Experiments (includes cooking). Research. Keeping a diary of his observations.**
Dislikes: **Sieves.**

■ Lives alone in a western-style house behind Kaede Shrine. He sometimes invites Mr. Itsushi, Ninufa, and Kaede to his house for a mysterious foods tasting party.

The next volume will have the White Rose and the Black Rose!! See you again in Volume 6!

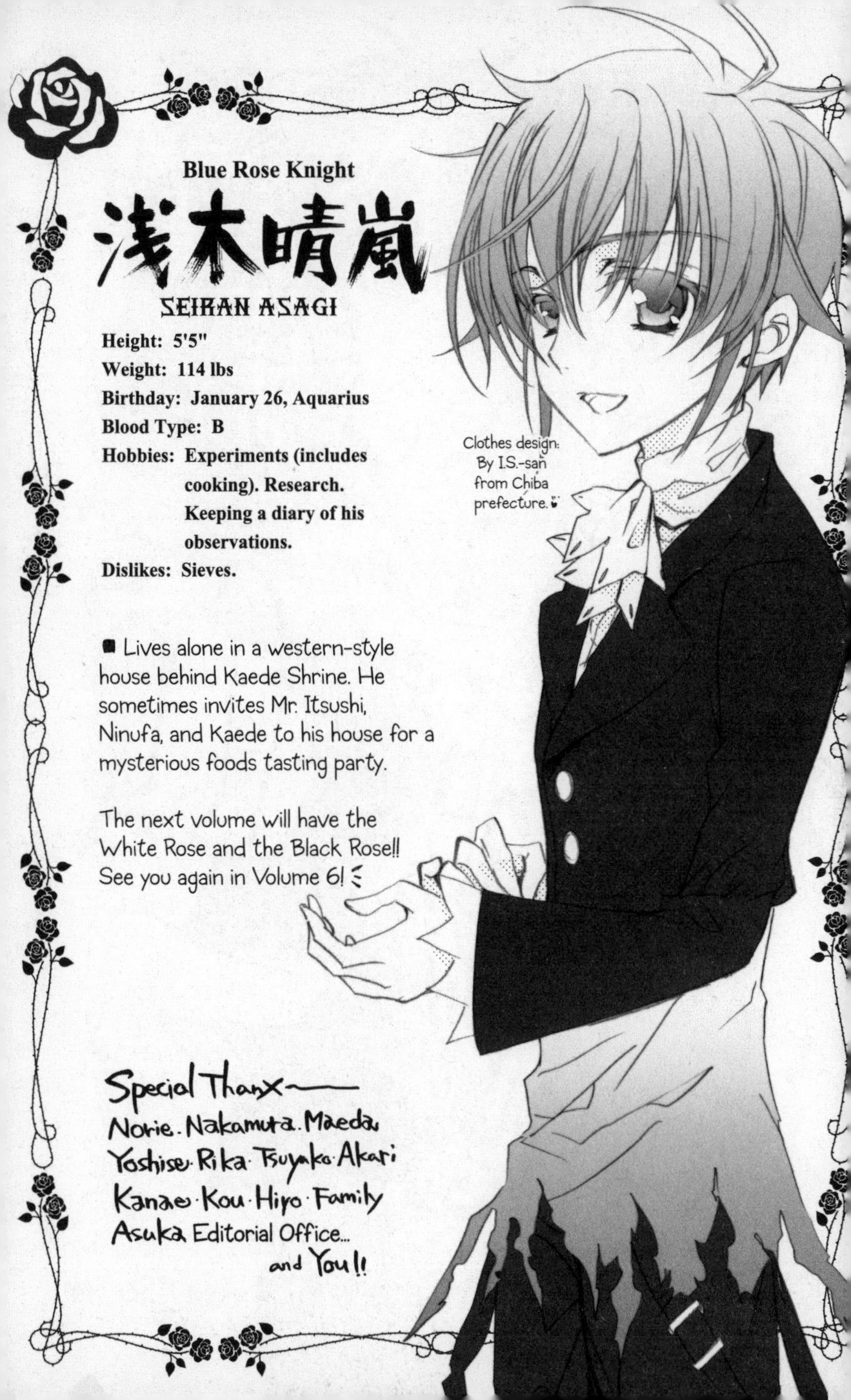
Clothes design: By I.S.-san from Chiba prefecture.

Special Thanx—
Norie. Nakamura. Maeda
Yoshise. Rika. Tsuyako. Akari
Kanae. Kou. Hiro. Family
Asuka Editorial Office...
and You!!

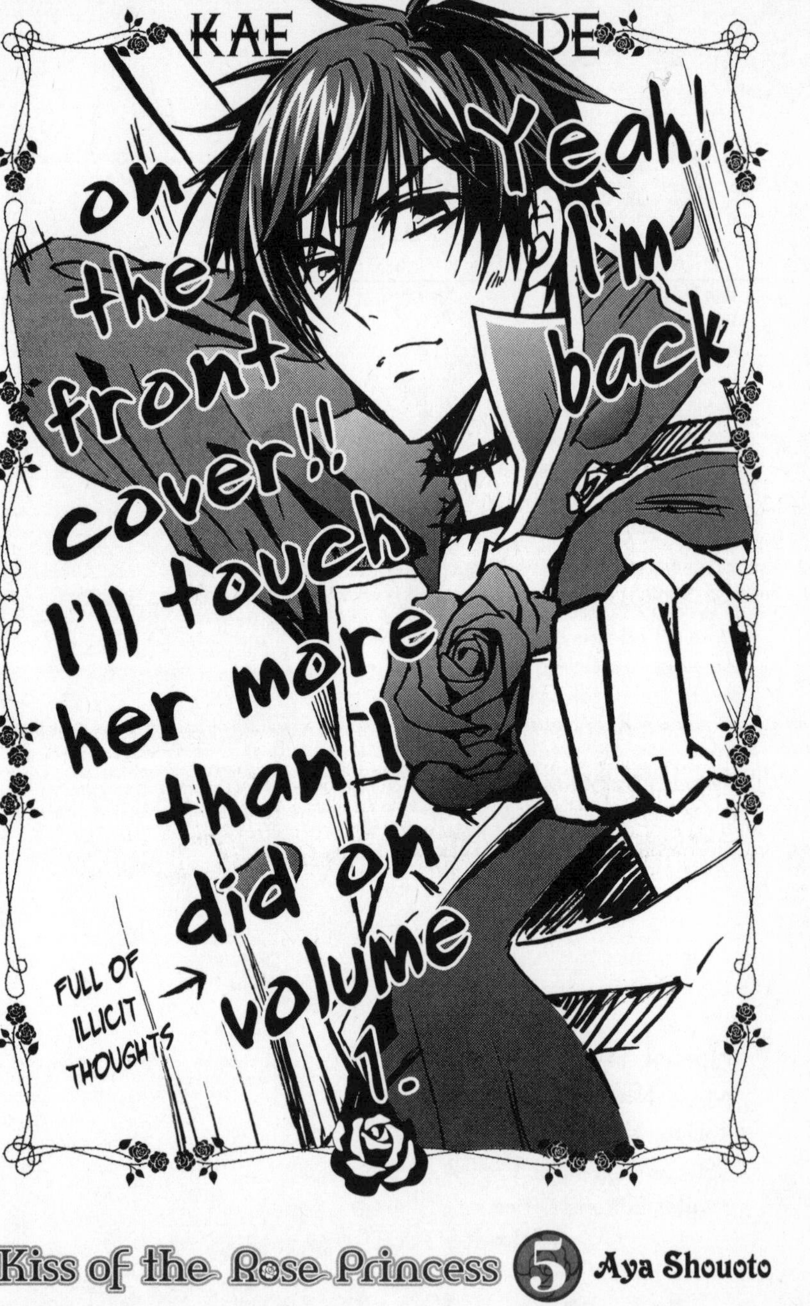
KAEDE
Yeah! I'm back
on the front cover!!
I'll touch her more than I did on volume 1.
FULL OF ILLICIT THOUGHTS

Kiss of the Rose Princess 5 Aya Shouoto

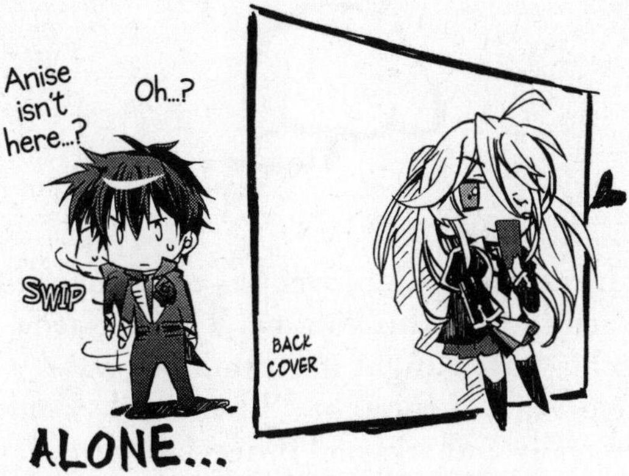
Anise isn't here...?
Oh...?
SWIP
BACK COVER
ALONE...

THE ABSENCE OF THE ROSE PRINCESS

AYA SHOUOTO

*There's Japanese wordplay on the word *rusu* (absent) and *kisu* (kiss).

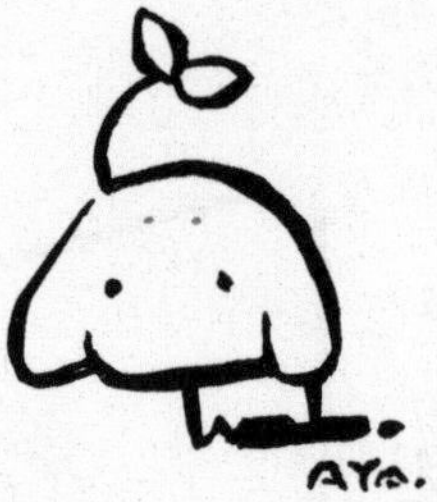
AYA.

The design of the cover has been changed starting with this volume. This is Kaede in his Rose Knight uniform. As I was coloring it, I thought, "I bet Kaede would be really embarrassed if his classmates saw him in this."

-Aya Shouoto

Aya Shouoto was born on December 25. Her hobbies include traveling, staying at hotels, sewing and daydreaming. She currently lives in Tokyo and enjoys listening to J-pop anime theme songs while she works.

Kiss of the Rose Princess

Volume 5
Shojo Beat Edition

STORY AND ART BY
AYA SHOUOTO

Translation/Tetsuichiro Miyaki
Touch-up Art & Lettering/Inori Fukuda Trant
Design/Yukiko Whitley
Editor/Nancy Thistlethwaite

KISS OF ROSE PRINCESS Volume 5
© Aya SHOUOTO 2010
Edited by KADOKAWA SHOTEN
First published in Japan in 2010 by KADOKAWA CORPORATION, Tokyo.
English translation rights arranged with KADOKAWA CORPORATION, Tokyo.

Printed in the U.S.A.

Published by VIZ Media, LLC
P.O. Box 77010
San Francisco, CA 94107

10 9 8 7 6 5 4 3 2 1
First printing, July 2015

www.viz.com

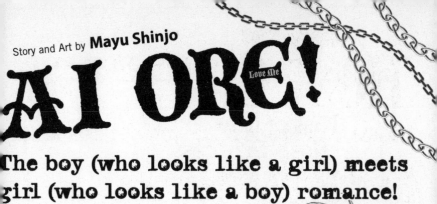

This is the last page.

In keeping with the original Japanese comic format, this book reads from right to left, so action, sound effects, and word balloons are completely reversed. This preserves the orientation of the original artwork. Check out the diagram below to get the hang of things, then turn to the other side of the book to get started!

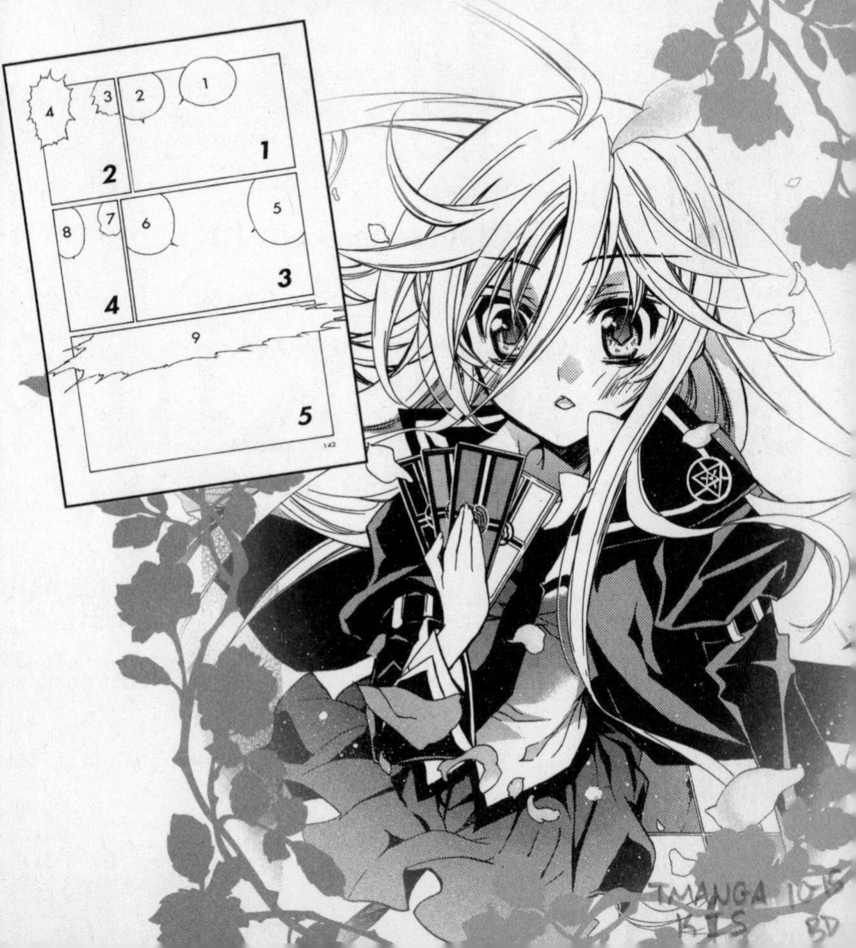
1
2
3
4
1
2
5
6
7
8
3
4
9
5
142